Racial Violence in Britain in the Nineteenth and Twentieth Centuries

Racial Violence in Britain in the Nineteenth and Twentieth Centuries

Revised Edition

Edited by Panikos Panayi

Leicester University Press
London and New York

LEICESTER UNIVERSITY PRESS
A Cassell Imprint
Wellington House, 125 Strand, London WC2R 0BB, England
215 Park Avenue South, New York, NY10003, USA
First edition 1993
This revised edition published in 1996

British Library Cataloguing-in-Publication Data
A catalogue record for this book is available from the British Library

ISBN 0–7185–1397–5 (Hardback)
      0–7185–2408–X (Paperback)

Library of Congress Cataloguing-in-Publication Data

Racial violence in Britain 1840–1950/edited by Panikos Panayi.
p. cm.
Includes bibliographical references and index.
ISBN 0–7185–1397–5
1. Great Britain—Race relations. 2. Great Britain—Ethnic relations. 3. Racism—Great Britain—History—19th century. 4. Racism—Great Britain—History—20th century. 5. Violence—Great Britain—History—19th century. 6. Violence—Great Britain—History—20th century.
7. Minorities—Great Britain—Crimes against—History. I. Panayi, Panikos.
DA125.AIR3355 1993
305.8'00941—dc20

                                        92–36259
                                        CIP

Typeset by York House Typographic Ltd, London
Printed and bound in Great Britain

Contents

Notes on contributors

Benjamin Bowling is Visiting Assistant Professor in the Department of Law, Police Science and Criminal Justice Administration at John Jay College of Criminal Justice in New York. He recently completed a London Ph.D. thesis, which looked at the emergence of violent racism in post-war Britain and responses towards it, and has published several articles derived from it.

Jacqueline Jenkinson is a Lecturer in Modern British History at the University of Stirling. She has recently written *Medical Societies in Scotland, 1731–1939* (Edinburgh University Press, 1993) and has co-authored *The Royal: Glasgow Royal Infirmary, 1794–1994* (Glasgow Royal Infirmary Trust, 1994). She has also written numerous articles and has contributed to several books on the 1919 riots. Her current ESRC funded research is into health policy in Scotland, 1919–48.

Tony Kushner is Marcus Sieff Lecturer in the Department of History at the University of Southampton. His major publications are *The Persistence of Prejudice: Antisemitism in British Society during the Second World War* (Manchester University Press, 1989) and *The Holocaust and the Liberal Imagination: A Social and Cultural History* (Basil Blackwell, 1994). He is also joint editor of the journal *Patterns of Prejudice*.

Donald MacRaild is a Lecturer in History at the University of Sunderland. He is currently revising for publication his 1993 University of Sheffield Ph.D. thesis, 'The Irish in North Lancashire and West Cumberland: Barrow, Whitehaven and Cleator Moor, *c*.1850–1906'.

Alan O'Day is Senior Lecturer in History at the University of North London and Professor (Honorary) of History at Concordia University, Montreal. He has recently been a visiting scholar at the Catholic University of America. His publications include *The English Face of Irish Nationalism* (Gill and Macmillan, 1977; reprinted 1994) and *Parnell and the First Home Rule Episode* (Gill and Macmillan, 1986). His *Irish Home Rule, 1867–1921* will be published shortly by Manchester University Press.

Panikos Panayi is Senior Lecturer in History at De Montfort University. His major publications include *The Enemy in Our Midst: Germans in Britain during the*

First World War (Berg, 1993) and *Immigration, Ethnicity and Racism in Britain, 1815–1945* (Manchester University Press, 1994).

Edward Pilkington is a staff writer for *The Guardian* and author of *Beyond the Mother Country: West Indians and the Notting Hill White Riots* (I.B. Tauris, London, 1988).

Lucio Sponza is Professor of Italian at the University of Westminster. He is the author of *Italian Immigrants in Nineteenth Century Britain: Realities and Images* (Leicester University Press, 1988). He has also written articles on, and continues to research, aspects of Italian settlement in twentieth century Britain.

Richard Thurlow is a Lecturer in the Department of History at the University of Sheffield. He is joint editor, with Kenneth Lunn, of *British Fascism* (Croom Helm, 1980) and author of *Fascism in Britain: A History, 1918–1985* (Oxford, Basil Blackwell, 1987) and *The Secret State: Internal Security in Twentieth Century Britain* (Basil Blackwell, 1994).

Preface

The essays in this collection represent the first attempt to bring together the history of racial violence in modern Britain. During the period from 1840 until 1950, as well as the years before and since then, no immigrant grouping in Britain has escaped attacks upon its persons and property. At the same time, some groups, notably the Irish, have acted as the perpetrators of racial violence, as a response to xenophobic hostility towards them. In the case of the Irish, like black youth in the 1980s, attacking the person and property of natives has represented a form of self-defence. The essays in this volume focus upon attacks upon pre-Commonwealth immigrants. They consist of a combination of empirical and more general studies.

My introductory essay 'Anti-immigrant violence in nineteenth- and twentieth-century Britain' outlines the history of attacks upon newcomers in British society since 1800, but it also traces a tradition of anti-immigrant violence from the medieval period, which became especially widespread during the eighteenth, nineteenth and twentieth centuries. The essay argues that no ethnic grouping in recent British history has escaped attack. The only way to understand this is by viewing anti-immigrant attacks as the most potent manifestation of a more widespread, ever present xenophobia in British society.

The second essay by Alan O'Day, 'Varieties of anti-Irish behaviour in Britain, 1846–1922', traces the history of hostility towards the Irish in Britain during the course of the nineteenth century, placing the riots against the Irish and the communal violence in which they participated against the background of more widespread animosity towards the immigrants. O'Day argues that anti-Irish riots never grew out of control, but outlines a decline in their frequency from the mid-nineteenth century.

Donald MacRaild, in 'William Murphy, the Orange Order and communal violence: the Irish in West Cumberland, 1871–84', based upon a thorough examination of local press reports, outlines the history of the communal violence connected with the anti-Catholic preacher William Murphy in an area so far ignored in the studies of riots connected with him, Cumberland. In this case, Irish immigrants represented both victims and perpetrators of attacks.

My essay 'Anti-German riots in Britain during the First World War' traces the most widespread anti-immigrant attacks in modern British history, which affected every part of Britain from Edinburgh to Exeter and Liverpool to

London. I place the disturbances within the Germanophobic atmosphere of the First World War, which meant that Germans suffered some of the most intense hostility ever experienced by any minority in modern British history.

Jacqueline Jenkinson, in 'The 1919 riots', provides an overview of the attacks directed against Britain's black communities in the period immediately after the end of the First World War. Jenkinson considers all factors which contributed to the events of 1919, economic, racial and political. In addition, she also deals with their policing as well as the reactions of the courts, government, public and press.

Richard Thurlow's essay, entitled 'Blaming the Blackshirts: the authorities and the anti-Jewish disturbances in the 1930s', deals with official reaction to the violence against Jews in the East End of London during the high point of the activities of the British Union of Fascists. Making particular use of Metropolitan Police and Home Office files in the Public Record Office, Thurlow offers new perspectives on the passage of the Public Order Act of 1936.

Lucio Sponza, making wide use of contemporary press sources, presents the first study of 'The anti-Italian riots, June 1940', which broke out as an immediate reaction to Mussolini's declaration of war on Britain during that month. The attacks occurred against Italian communities throughout Britain. Sponza deals with the pattern of the disturbances, as well as the reactions of both Italians and British. He further places the disturbances within the context of both long- and short-term British attitudes towards Italian immigrants, but views the disturbances as a minor shock for the British Italian community.

Tony Kushner, on 'Anti-Semitism and austerity: the August 1947 riots in Britain', offers the first account of the nationwide attacks which occurred against Britain's Jewish communities in at least thirteen locations, against the background of the anti-British campaign in Palestine. However, using a wide range of contemporary sources, Kushner argues that the explanation for the riots is far more complex than simply a reaction to events in Palestine.

I would like to thank the following institutions and individuals who provided assistance with the production of this book. First, the Alexander von Humboldt Foundation, as the editing took place when I held one of their Fellowships at the University of Osnabrück, during the 1991–2 academic year. I am grateful to De Montfort University, Leicester, for allowing me to take up the award. Among individuals, I would especially like to thank Colin Holmes who offered much early support with this project, and Alec McAuley, at Leicester University Press, who accepted it for publication. I am further grateful to Klaus J. Bade for accepting me as an Alexander von Humboldt Research Fellow at his Institut für Migrationsforschung und Interkulturelle Studien at the University of Osnabrück.

Panikos Panayi
Osnabrück

Preface to the Revised Edition

The present collection of essays was originally published in 1993 as *Racial Violence in Britain, 1840–1950*. The main change to this volume has been the addition of two new articles covering the period since 1950. The first of these new pieces, Edward Pilkington's on 'The West Indian community and the Notting Hill riots of 1958', covers the most serious anti-immigrant disturbances since the Second World War, focusing upon them especially in relation to the newly arrived Caribbean communities of west London. The second new essay, by Ben Bowling, entitled 'The emergence of violent racism as a public issue in Britain, 1945–81', contextualises the attacks upon immigrants since the Second World War within the growing British consciousness of post-war immigration, leading to a growth of a potent racism and, at the same time, an increasing political and media consciousness of the widespread nature of anti-immigrant violence. In addition to these two new essays, several of the original ones have been updated.

Panikos Panayi
Leicester
1995

1

Anti-immigrant violence in nineteenth- and twentieth-century Britain

Panikos Panayi

Writing in 1940, during a German air raid, and not long after having returned from the Spanish Civil War, in which he had taken part on the side of the Marxist POUM, George Orwell wrote a pamphlet entitled *The Lion and the Unicorn: Socialism and the English Genius*, whose opening section 'England Your England' lists what he views as the national characteristics of England. Before doing so he focuses upon other countries, stating that 'Spaniards are cruel to animals, Italians can do nothing without making a deafening noise, the Chinese are addicted to gambling'. Orwell describes English characteristics rather vaguely, which include lack of artistic ability and a 'love of flowers' (Orwell, 1986, pp. 38–9). He then moves on to the core of the chapter in which he asserts:

> The gentleness of the English civilisation is perhaps its most marked characteristic. You notice it the instant you set foot on English soil. It is a land where the bus conductors are good-tempered and the policemen carry no revolvers. In no country inhabited by white men is it easier to shove people off the pavement. And with this goes something that is always written off by European observers as 'decadence' or hypocrisy, the English hatred of war and militarism. It is rooted deep in history, and it is strong in the lower-middle class as well as the working class. Successive wars have shaken it but not destroyed it (Orwell, 1986, p. 41).

In an academic study of Britain during the First World War published forty-nine years later, John Bourne virtually repeats Orwell's words in his claim that during the First World War:

> The basic underlying values of British—and particularly English—society under-went no transformation. The British people were not 'militarized'. Wartime excesses of chauvinism, anger and hate became regarded with incredulous embarrassment and were then forgotten. Patience, tolerance and generosity returned (Bourne, 1989, p. 236).

Perhaps even more relevant to this essay on riots against immigrants in recent British history are Orwell's comments on attacks upon Italian shops in Soho following Mussolini's declaration of war on Britain, which he described as 'an interesting phenomenon, because English people, i.e. people of a kind who would be likely to loot shops, don't as a rule take a spontaneous interest in foreign politics'. Orwell explained, and almost justified, the attacks, by stating that 'The low-down, cold-blooded meanness of Mussolini's declaration of war at that moment must have made an impression even on people who as a rule barely read the newspapers' (Orwell and Angus, 1968, p. 394).

Nevertheless, this view of Britain as a peaceful society, devoid of violence, especially of a racial variety, is not the only one held by publicists and academics. In an article in *The Observer* of 13 October 1985, following the Tottenham riots when youths attacked policemen, Neal Ascherson wrote that 'Rioting is at least as English as thatched cottages and honey still for tea'. He continued: 'it is badly wrong to conclude that we are entering unknown territory, that a violent break has been made with some law-abiding, gentle past of plebian Britain.' One of the most forthright adherents of Britain as a society in which violence has always played a part is Geoffrey Pearson (1983), although the study of popular disturbances in British history became part of mainstream social history under the influence of, initially, E.P. Thompson (1971) and George Rude (1985) and, more recently, John Stevenson (1979).

But the history of racial attacks in Britain has not received thorough study. We can find no book which systematically covers this area of nineteenth- and twentieth-century Britain, although we can point to a small number of monographs on violence against specific minorities, notably the Irish in nineteenth-century Liverpool (Neal, 1988) and blacks in 1919 (Jenkinson, 1987). Nevertheless, a large number of articles have appeared on this subject, both referring to specific incidents and covering a particular time period. Examples of the former include the work of Jenkinson (1985; 1988), Swift (1984a, 1984b) and Panayi (1988, 1989, 1991b), while Holmes (1975, 1985) and Husbands (1989) provide instances of the latter. Nevertheless, the fact remains that racial violence in British history continues to be under-studied. How do we explain this?

In the first place we have to point to the fact that the history of minorities in Britain has only begun to move into mainstream history since the late 1970s, due particularly to the efforts of Colin Holmes, who has published four books in this area (Holmes, C., 1978, 1979, 1988, 1991) and who jointly edits the journal *Immigrants and Minorities*. But despite the work of Holmes and others, notably Kenneth Lunn (1980), the other editor of *Immigrants and Minorities*, and Tony Kushner (1989) who have also edited two important collections of essays together (1989, 1990), it is impossible to fill all the gaps in British immigration history in the space of less than two decades. Apart from the work still to be carried out on the history of racial violence, we can point to the fact that several significant minorities have received only incomplete attention, notably Germans and Italians, although even the Jewish community in Britain had until recently no continuous history stretching the course of the nineteenth and twentieth centuries. At the same time, scholars working in the history of immigration face indifference and even hostility from what might be described as the British historical establishment, as pointed out by Lunn and Kushner, who go so far as to claim that the lack of study of minorities in British history provides 'a measure of the scope and tenacity of British xenophobia' (Lunn and Kushner, 1990, 'Editors' Introduction'). The negative attitudes to the study of minorities in Britain reinforce the view of the country as 'tolerant', outlined in the opening paragraphs of this essay and held by wide sections of British society, as well as by the historical profession.

The reality of the experience of immigrants in Britain would suggest that the idea of Britain as a tolerant country needs modification. No newcomers who have entered Britain in the last two centuries have escaped hostility on a significant scale. The minorities which historians and sociologists have recognised as facing the most widespread animosity include the nineteenth-century Irish immigrants, the Jewish newcomers from eastern Europe in the late nineteenth century (Gainer, 1972) and the post-1945 immigrants from the British Empire and Commonwealth, particularly those originating in India, Pakistan and the West Indies (Holmes, 1988, pp. 255–70; Miles, 1984; Pilkington, 1988; Fryer, 1984, pp. 367–95; Panayi, 1991b). Nevertheless, we should not ignore the experience of smaller minorities such as the Italians in the nineteenth century (Sponza, 1988) or the German community which had developed through the course of centuries and faced virtual destruction as an ethnic group due to a combination of popular hostility and government measures during the First World War (Panayi, 1991a). Similarly, but not with such intensity, Cypriots faced hostility both in the 1930s and 1950s (Oakley, 1987; Fyvel, 1963, pp. 30, 100). Returning to mainstream racism, anti-Semitism has been ever present not just in nineteenth-and twentieth-century Britain but during the whole course of the country's history (Dobson, 1974; Hyams, 1974, pp. 277–83; Holmes, 1979; Kushner, 1989). We could make similar comments about anti-Irish prejudice, which became particularly potent as a result of the large-scale Irish immigration of the nineteenth century, but remained strong after 1900 (Curtis, 1968; Neal, 1988; Holmes, 1988, pp. 148–52, 251–3; Gallagher, 1987a, 1987b).

As mentioned above, the levels of hostility have varied for different groups but the manifestations of the intolerance have remained similar. The most primitive forms of hostility, which we might describe simply as refusal to enter into social or economic intercourse, are perhaps the most difficult to measure, but we could find the existence of such animosity towards post-1945 black immigrants, for instance, who faced colour bars in their attempts to find accommodation and to participate in English social life (Pilkington, 1988, pp. 41–52). Newspaper animosity has focused upon every minority which has made its way to Britain, as Sponza has shown particularly well with regard to Italian immigrants in the nineteenth century (Sponza, 1988, pp. 119–252). In some cases popular hostility towards newcomers has become so potent that it has led to the formation of political groupings opposing the newcomers and calling for their repatriation. We can find examples of such bodies at the start of the twentieth century in the form of, for instance, the British Brothers League, which opposed Russian and Polish Jewish settlers in East London (Gainer, 1972, p. 67). During the First World War numerous bodies became established with the aim of opposing German immigrants, most notably the British Empire Union (Panayi, 1990), while the post-1945 period has also resulted in the

growth of a large number of racist groups opposing Commonwealth
immigrants, from Oswald Mosley's Union Movement, founded in 1948, to the
National Front, established in 1967 and perhaps 'the most significant event on
the radical right and fascist fringe of British politics' (Thurlow, 1987, pp.
243–7, 275).

Together with these forms of unofficial hostility, we can also discover
government opposition to newcomers. While official racism has never taken the
forms that it has done in many other countries, such as, for instance, Russia in
the late nineteenth century, Germany under the Nazis, or the Ottoman Empire
under the Young Turk Movement, most immigrant groups have faced some
form of governmental opposition if only in the form of the introduction of
immigration controls to stop the entry of further members of the same
community. We might also see the introduction of laws to oppose further
immigration as the standard British governmental response to the entry of
newcomers, as such measures have almost invariably entered the statute book at
times of strong anti-alien hostility such as 1905, 1919 and 1962 (Gainer, 1972;
Holmes, 1988, pp. 112–13, 260–4). Nevertheless, at times of severe insecurity,
notably the two World Wars, when hostility towards immigrants reached
extreme peaks, the government introduced stronger measures, notably
internment (Panayi, 1991a, pp. 45–149; Seyfert, 1984; Lafitte, 1988).

In the light of such evidence, indicating the existence of a solid anti-
immigration thread running through modern British history, we should not be
surprised at the fact that every immigrant group which has entered Britain has
endured attacks. The scale of these attacks has varied, from isolated incidents
involving a few individuals, which we might see as ever present and not always
measurable, to nationwide riots on a large scale, involving thousands of people
attacking the property of a particular immigrant group. The latter has occurred
on two occasions in the twentieth century, against Germans in May 1915 and
blacks during the course of 1919.

The final part of this essay will attempt to reach conclusions about the
significance and patterns of racial violence in recent British history. However,
before doing so, it will chart the history of anti-immigrant violence during the
nineteenth and twentieth centuries. But before this can be done, some definitions are necessary. How exactly do we define a 'race riot' or 'racial attack'? By
race riot we do not simply mean violence involving members of minorities, but
incidents in which these minorities were targets. Thus the 'racial violence' in
Britain during the 1980s falls outside the scope of this essay because, although
black youth responded to milder forms of racism, they were not the victims of
racial attacks as blacks were in 1919 and 1958, when they responded to physical
violence (Peach, 1986; Joshua, Wallace and Booth, 1983). Race riot, or anti-
immigration riot, in this context means an attack by a large number, hundreds
or even thousands, of members of the dominant group upon members of a
minority who have been singled out for attack specifically because they belong
to that particular minority at a time when that racial group usually faces more
widespread animosity. In the course of this essay we shall trace the major 'race
riots' in modern British history.

However, not even a comprehensive history of racism in Britain, involving
several research assistants looking through hundreds of local newspapers over the

course of the past two centuries, could trace all 'racial attacks' which have taken place in Britain's recent past. A Commission for Racial Equality Report from 1987 included amongst its lists of racial attacks 'insulting behaviour', 'attempted damage to property', 'attempted theft', 'threats to damage or violence', 'physical assault', and 'damage to property'. Significantly, it pointed out that 'Many individuals and families do not report incidents of racial harassment', and that previous victims remained 'forgotten' (CRE, 1987, pp. 9, 11). We can only speculate about the regularity of everyday violence endured by minorities in the course of recent British history, in addition to the riots which now receive attention.

Before dealing with race riots in recent British history, we have to recognise that they do not represent a new phenomenon. They had previous traditions upon which to draw, just as, for instance, anti-Irish prejudice or anti–semitism did as both of these formed an integral part of the English world view for centuries. Throughout Britain's recorded past, large-scale racial violence has taken place and we can mention a few of the major incidents here.

Perhaps the worst race riot in any period of British history is the first about which we have substantial evidence, the 'massacre' of the Jews of York in 1190. Jews had begun to enter England following the Norman Conquest in 1066 and by the year 1200 the Jewish population of the country totalled approximately 5,000, mostly settled in the eastern half of the country, as far north as Newcastle. Money-lending became their main economic activity. Hostility towards the community had a religious basis and the most extreme stereotype viewed Jews as followers of the Devil and enemies of Christ. In the middle of the twelfth century, from 1144, hostility towards Jews had begun to rise within England, focusing upon the idea of the murder of a gentile child at Passover as part of the ritual of that festival. Such accusations became more widespread during the 1170s and 1180s (Hyams, 1974, pp. 270–3, 277–81; Dobson, 1974, pp. 15–16, 19–20).

The most authoritative account of the events of 1190 traces various developments which led to their occurrence. Probably the most significant of these was the death of the 'protector' of the Jews, King Henry II, in July 1189, and his succession by Richard I, whose coronation resulted in attacks upon Jews attending the ceremony. At the same time 'a crisis of authority' existed in York because the main religious and governmental authorities were abroad. During the years 1189–90 the Third Crusade took place, a time when Jews had previously faced extreme violence in other parts of Europe, during the First Crusade of 1096, and in which, on this occasion, Richard I participated. We can make a connection with the twentieth century here because both World Wars led to outbreaks of widespread violence. But not on the scale of 1190. Following disturbances in East Anglia in February of that year, which had taken the form of arson and murder, the violence spread to York in March, with extraordinary destructiveness in comparison with modern events in Britain, resulting in 150 deaths. A wide range of social classes seem to have participated (Dobson, 1974, pp. 15, 24–37; Moore, 1987, pp. 117–18).

Attacks upon Jews in medieval England took place regularly until their expulsion in 1290, leading one scholar to comment that many gentiles had their first introduction to Jews during a riot (Hyams, 1974, p. 277). In the later

Middle Ages other minority groups became the victims of violence, including foreign merchants, an ever present community from many parts of Europe, including Italy, Holland and France, throughout the medieval period (Lloyd, 1982). The Hansa merchants, from north Germany, faced hostility for much of the sixteenth century, leading to their eventual expulsion by Queen Elizabeth in 1598 (Dollinger, 1970, pp. 315–16, 341–3). Earlier in the century, in 1517, a riot had broken out against businessmen from other nations, leading to the description of the day on which it took place as 'Evil May Day'. The violence occurred against the background of a traditional anti-alienism present during this period (Chitty, 1966, p. 131). A twentieth-century account of 'Evil May Day' explains it by pointing to 'an unfortunate coincidence of anti-alien tension on several levels at once', i.e. both amongst English merchants facing rivalry and amongst the populace which felt exploited by the newcomers, although popular speakers did much to whip up this resentment. Isolated attacks upon foreigners occurred on 28 April but the main outbreak of violence broke out on 1 May. A notable aspect of this disturbance is the severity with which the rioters were dealt, as they faced charges of high treason and consequent execution, although many people escaped the gallows due to the intercession of King Henry VIII (Holmes, M., 1965).

If we move to the eighteenth century we can find numerous examples of attacks against immigrants. Dorothy M. George wrote that 'All foreigners in London who had an outlandish look were liable to be roughly treated, or at least abused, by the mob.' German Jews faced particular hostility and 'Jew-baiting became a sport, like cock-throwing, or bull-baiting or pelting some poor wretch in the pillory' (George, 1966, p. 137). These developments took place against the background of more widespread anti-Semitism during the late eighteenth century and the regularity of the attacks suggested by George reminds us of the experience of Asians in contemporary east London. Apart from German Jews, German gentiles also became the victims of violence during the eighteenth century. We can point to the experience of the Palatines, from south-west Germany, who entered London in 1708–9 after encouragement from Queen Anne, but, because of their large numbers, which meant that they had difficulty finding accommodation, they faced intense hostility from both Parliamentary opinion and the populace, which manifested itself, in some cases, in physical attacks by men armed with axes (Knittle, 1970). In addition to the Palatines, the Brethrens, a religious group from Germany, also faced isolated physical attacks during the eighteenth century because of their distinctness and the fact they did not speak English (Wauer, 1901). The Irish also became the victims of attacks by the native population, most notably in 1736, a time when the Irish 'had been coming to London in larger numbers than usual and were competing with English workmen in a wide variety of trades' (Rude, 1971, pp. 187–90).

The work of several historians, including Rude, Thompson and Stevenson, has demonstrated that popular violence became commonplace in eighteenth-century England. Stevenson has even used the term 'The Age of Riots'. Causes for disturbances could include political developments, such as the accession of the Hanoverian Dynasty in 1714 and its aftermath, food shortages, industrial disputes, and disapproval of particular aspects of theatre productions (Rude, 1971, pp. 183–227; Stevenson, 1979, pp. 17–151; Thompson, 1971). If we examine some of the disturbances studied by Rude and Stevenson, we see that they often had a xenophobic element within them. Rude, for instance, points out that theatre riots might arise 'from disapproval of the actors, particularly when they were French' (Rude, 1971, p. 185). The disturbances following the accession of the House of Hanover had as one of their causes, though not the most important, the foreign origin of the monarchy (Rogers, 1978, p. 91).

The most serious disturbances of the eighteenth century, the Gordon Riots of 1780 in London, revolved around xenophobic anti-Catholicism. Rude has pointed out that the riots lay firmly within the tradition of British anti-Catholicism and that they broke out at a time of war against both France and Spain (Rude, 1971, p. 220). Stevenson, meanwhile, links them with the anti-Catholic and anti-Irish disturbances of the nineteenth century. The concept of the anti-foreign, anti-Catholic and anti-Irish character of the disturbances receives support if we examine their victims. These included, on the first day, 2 June, the Chapels of the Bavarian and Sardinian ambassadors. On 3 June the rioters targeted 'Mr Malo, a native of Cambray', who 'carried on an extensive trade as a silk merchant', as a victim, and also attempted to attack Irish residents in Moorfields, but troops prevented them from doing so. Nevertheless, Catholics suffered in other parts of the capital, and remained the major targets during the duration of the disturbances which finally died down, after strong intervention from troops, on 8 June. Rude has shown that the rioters selected the Catholics whom they attacked. Few private houses suffered, a pattern confirmed in many subsequent racial disturbances. As Rude writes, 'once the priest and the schoolmaster had been dealt with ... it was the gentleman, the manufacturer, the merchant, or the publican, rather than the independent craftsman or the wage-earner who was the main object of the rioters' attention.' The disturbances resulted in 210 deaths, 450 arrests and twenty-five executions (de Castro, 1926, pp. 42–3, 47, 50, 52, 139; Rude, 1956, p. 109; 1971, pp. 221–6; Stevenson, 1979, pp. 78–83).

Although no riots broke out on the same scale during the nineteenth century, popular disturbances remained a fundamental feature of British society after 1800, with similar causes to those of the century before, sparked off by political developments, deteriorating agricultural conditions and industrial disputes. With regard to 'political disturbances', these accompanied every stage of the extension of the franchise during the nineteenth century, with major disturbances breaking out in Manchester in 1819 (Peterloo), resulting in eleven deaths; in 1830–2, during the passage of the Great Reform Bill through Parliament; and in 1866 during the campaign for the Second Reform Act which reached the statute book in the following year. Disturbances in the countryside became particularly widespread in southern England in the form of the Captain Swing Riots between 1830 and 1832 and from 1839 to 1843 with the Rebecca Riots in Wales. A complex set of causes revolving around a worsening of agricultural living conditions led to the disturbances. Industrial disputes, meanwhile, took place throughout the nineteenth century, affecting at varying times many different parts of the country. A fundamental development took place in the control of rioting during this period in the form of the foundation and subsequent growth of county police forces, a process beginning with the passage of the Metropolitan Police Act of 1829 (Stevenson, 1979, pp. 205–300; Rude, 1985, pp. 149–63; Richter, 1981).

Together with the political, rural and industrial disturbances of the nineteenth century, we can also identify an equally solid strand of violence against immigrants, particularly those of Irish descent, as the depth of research on anti-Irish disturbances during the Victorian period indicates. Throughout the course of the nineteenth century the Irish made up the main immigrant group within Britain, so that by 1870 one-quarter of all Irishmen abroad lived in England, Scotland and Wales, focused in industrial areas such as Lancashire, London, Glasgow, Tyneside, Cardiff and Yorkshire. The figures for Irish-born residents totalled 419,526 in 1841, 806,000 in 1861, and 632,000 in 1901. Movement out of Ireland took place throughout the course of the nineteenth century against a background of agricultural change and crisis, which peaked in the famine of the late 1840s. In their new environments the immigrants lived in the worst districts of the cities in which they settled, and usually obtained unskilled and semi-skilled jobs, although some became skilled labourers (Ó Tuathaigh, 1981, pp. 149–56; Fitzpatrick, 1980, pp. 129–30; Neal, 1988, pp. 80–105).

Apart from the problems faced by the immigrants in employment and housing, they also had to endure continuous hostility from the native populations which manifested itself in a variety of ways including constant attacks throughout the country. Underlying the anti-Irish violence, we need to be aware of the image of the Irish in the Victorian world view which had several traditions upon which to draw. In the first place we can point to traditional anti-Catholicism, so potent in the eighteenth century and remaining so into the nineteenth. At the same time, we can identify a racial Anglo-Saxonism which viewed the Celtic 'race' as inferior to the Anglo-Saxon. A typical member of the former was seen as consisting of an unreliable 'feckless, devil-may-care, rollicking, hard-drinking, and hard-fighting peasant'. On a more fundamental level, we might identify socio-economic prejudice in areas where Irish immigrants settled, which tended to have already existing social problems, and resented the appearance of newcomers who competed for their resources, and at the same time resentment against the fact that Irish workers sometimes acted as strike-breakers (Curtis, 1968, pp. 4–5, 151–2; Gilley, 1978; Gallagher, 1985, p.120).

If we turn to riots involving the Irish, we see that on many occasions when this immigrant community became involved in violence they did not simply become victims as some other communities would do, including Germans in the First World War and Asians in post-1945 Britain, but often fought back in large numbers, so that many of the disturbances involving the Irish during this period actually resembled fights or, to use the phrases favoured by historians working in the area, communal or sectarian violence. The main explanation for the retaliation of Irish immigrants may simply lie in their large numbers in the areas where they lived, which meant that they could mobilize against any attacks or threatened attacks against them. At the same time we might also place the riots involving the Irish into the wider context of Irish violence or crime in nineteenth-century Britain. Roger Swift has demonstrated that the Irish were more likely to face prosecution than their English neighbours and that disturbances broke out between Irishmen from different parts of Ireland when in England. He also mentions the violence connected with 'Saturday night saturnalia', and 'the celebration of weddings, wakes, and St Patrick's Day' (Swift, 1989, pp. 164–9).

If we turn to the violence between Irish immigrants and the dominant community we can identify at least two strands linked with the sources of anti-Irish prejudice in Britain previously mentioned. First were the labour disputes, particularly those involving railway navvies during the 1840s, which became almost endemic, a part of the working ritual of men involved in this trade in northern England and Scotland. Many of these incidents became savage involving thousands of men using tools of the trade such as pickaxes, and the burning down of the huts of Irishmen. Underlying the violence lay the poor working and living conditions of the Irish, Scottish and English labourers. The worst violence took place in February 1846 in Penrith, near Cumberland, and Gorebridge, about ten miles from Edinburgh (Coleman, 1986, pp. 93–103).

The second major strand of violence involving the Irish revolved around religion, and there exist numerous examples of disturbances throughout the country during the course of the century in which Protestant-Catholic rivalry acted as a focal point of disorder, although Swift has pointed out the 'multicausal' nature of much Anglo-Irish violence, in which economic factors also played a role (Swift, 1989, p. 171). We can briefly mention some of the major examples of Protestant-Catholic disturbances.

In Liverpool, for instance, violence between the English and Irish became a regular occurrence during the late 1830s and early 1840s, sparked off by a growth of 'Orangeism' and a strong anti-Catholic campaign with the city (Neal, 1988, pp. 45–64). In June 1852, anti-Irish riots broke out in Stockport against the background of the 'last major upsurge of anti-Catholicism in England', given a boost by the 'sudden influx into urban centres of large numbers of poor Irish Catholics fleeing from the potato famine of 1845–9', although Pauline Millward has also pointed to a variety of other factors including the support of anti-Irish feeling by the local Conservative Party. The spark for the disturbances came in the form of a Catholic march on 27 June. By the night of 29 June, twenty-four Irish homes and two churches had suffered damage while fifty-one Irishmen had sustained injuries and one had died. Only two of the 113 people arrested were English (Millward, 1985).

Further riots involving the Irish broke out in September 1862 sparked off by English supporters of Garibaldi, the Italian Nationalist leader, who made anti-Papal speeches in Hyde Park on the 28 September. As a response Irishmen gathered in the Park and attacked the platform. Similar disturbances broke out in the same location on the following Sunday and, during the course of October, further violence developed in public houses in the west of London in the area of Hyde Park. In the same month disturbances broke out in Birkenhead, while more violence occurred in Chesterfield in December (Gilley, 1973; Neal, 1988, p. 197).

Similar violence to that which broke out in 1862, in the sense that anti-Catholic speeches acted as the spark, occurred in other parts of the country in the mid-nineteenth century, for instance, in Wolverhampton in 1858 and on a wider scale in the late 1860s in connection with the Protestant lecturer William Murphy. The fierce anti-Catholic preaching of Murphy and his followers sparked off disturbances in Wolverhampton and Birmingham in 1867, and Rochdale, Stalybridge, Bacup and Ashton-under-Lyne in 1868, as well as in Tynemouth in the following year, although action by central and local government prevented further disorder (Arnstein, 1975; Swift, 1984b, pp. 90–104). After the 1860s violence involving the Irish decreased, but did not disappear. For instance, in July 1882 serious anti-Irish attacks occurred in Tredegar in South Wales with damage to over 160 houses inhabited by Irishmen, forcing many Irish people to leave the town and make their way to Cardiff. The disturbances had broken out against the background of an economic downturn and the murder of the Chief Secretary for Ireland, Sir Frederick Cavendish, in Dublin in May which had led to a growth of anti-Irish feeling (Parry, 1983). In Liverpool communal violence continued on a significant scale until the outbreak of the First World War (Neal, 1988, pp. 176–250; Waller, 1981, 249–51).

If we move into the late nineteenth and early twentieth century before the outbreak of the First World War we also discover attacks upon other minorities, notably Germans, Russian Jews and Chinese. Violence involving the first of these groups, which had developed ethnic communities in a series of British cities during the course of the nineteenth century (Panayi, 1991a, pp. 11–27), remained minor before the First World War. We can identify a few sporadic incidents such as an attack on a German Club in 1892 (*West Ham Herald and South Essex Gazette*, 3 September 1892), and more serious outbreaks in May 1900 following the arrival of the news of the Relief of Mafeking, a turning point in the history of the Boer War, a conflict which heightened nationalism in Britain, which would return with more destructive consequences for immigrant groups during the First World War. The celebrations following Mafeking turned violent towards those who did not participate in them, including Henry Bish, a north London German hairdresser (Price, 1972, pp. 132–7).

During the late nineteenth and early twentieth centuries small-scale attacks occurred with some regularity against the Russian Jewish communities which had developed in major British cities, notably east London, Manchester and Leeds, and also in smaller towns. Rather like the Irish immigrants, the Jewish newcomers settled together in poorer districts, especially in the large cities. Any account of the violence which they endured must take into consideration the strong hostility which developed against the immigrants in the late nineteenth and early twentieth century, manifesting itself in government inquiries, press hostility, the development of anti-immigrant groupings and the passage of the Aliens Act of 1905, preceded by a lengthy campaign before its passage. Against this background, we should not be surprised to learn of regular weekend attacks of Russian Jews in the Leyland area of Leeds in the early twentieth century, or of an attack upon a Jewish family moving into a house located in east London in November 1901, recently vacated by an English family which had received notice to quit. In fact, Cornwall Street, where the disturbance broke out, 'was the scene of frequent disturbances' (Gainer, 1972, pp. 3, 4, 16, 58; Krausz, 1964, pp. 4, 14, 21; Husbands, 1982, pp. 7–12; Holmes, C., 1979; Williams, 1990).

However, the most serious riots against Russian Jews before the First World War did not take place in areas which they inhabited in large numbers, but in South Wales, where the Jewish communities 'were minute'. The violence broke out in Tredegar on 19 August 1911 and during the course of the following week spread to Ebbw Vale, Rhymney, Victoria, Cwm, Waunllwyd, Abertysswg, Brynmawr, Bargoed, Glamorgan, Gilfach and Senghenydd, resulting in £16,000 worth of damage. The two academic articles on the disturbances have pointed to a range of long- and short-term causes. The former include the tradition of popular disorder in South Wales and the possible development of hostile images of Jews, while the latter include resentment of the economic success of some Jews in the area and, perhaps more importantly, the fact that the disturbances took place against the background of 'intense social unrest throughout the British Isles' which in South Wales manifested itself in the violent Cambrian Combine Strike in the coal industry (Alderman, 1972; Holmes, C., 1982).

The last factor would also help us to explain another outbreak of anti-immigrant violence in the years leading up to the First World War, against the Chinese in Cardiff in 1911, during a seamen's strike in which the Chinese acted as strikebreakers. On the evening of 20 July every Chinese laundry in Cardiff had its window broken. We also need to view these disturbances against long-term and widespread racial hostility existing towards the Chinese which had begun to develop during the nineteenth century and had become potent just after 1900 in connection with the idea of the possible importation of Chinese labour which would accept lower wages than English workers (Waller, 1985; Daunton, 1978, pp. 193–5; May, 1973, pp. 58–9; 1978).

The two most widespread occurrences of racial violence in Britain broke out within a few years of each other, in 1915 against the German communities of Britain, and in 1919 when Britain's black population became the victims. During the course of the rest of the twentieth century no violence of any sort took place on such a widespread nationwide scale until the riots of 1981. Any possible attempt to find common causes between the outbreaks against Germans and blacks proves less than straightforward. The main factor which links the two is the First World War and the fact that this led to the development of extreme nationalism and xenophobia within Britain to a peak rarely reached at other times in its history.

This particularly helps to explain the attacks against the German community, whose scale, and particularly their widespread nature, remind us of a late nineteenth-century Russian-style pogrom. Isolated disturbances broke out in east London and Keighley in August 1914, the month when the Great War began, and further incidents took place in October of the same year, as a reaction to setbacks suffered by the British army. But the riots reached a peak in May 1915, sparked off by the sinking of the passenger liner *Lusitania* by a German submarine off the coast of Ireland with the loss of over 1,000 lives, although these attacks came after several months of intense anti-German propaganda. The widespread nature of the events of May 1915 really distinguishes them from other riots in modern British history. They affected every part of Britain, from north to south and east to west. The worst violence occurred in major cities including Manchester, Liverpool, Sheffield and, particularly, London, where 2,000 properties suffered damage at a cost of £200,000. But German shops had their windows smashed virtually everywhere including towns such as Castleford, Bury St Edmunds, Greenock, Goldthorpe, and Walton-on-Thames. Further minor outbreaks of violence occurred against any remaining German property in London in June 1916 and July 1917, the first in response to the death of Lord Kitchener, the War Secretary, blamed upon German saboteurs within Britain, and the second as a spontaneous reaction to a German air raid. In order to understand attacks upon Germans we need to consider not only the fact that Britain fought a war against their land of origin, which meant the production of government propaganda which dehumanised Germans, but also the fact that violence took place against intense popular Germanophobia and the introduction of a series of government measures involving extensive internment and repatriation of Germans, together with confiscation of their property (Panayi, 1991a).

Against the intolerant background of the First World War, other groups endured violence, including pacifists and members of other minorities, notably Russian Jews in Leeds in June 1917 and east London in September of the same year, sparked off in both cases by the unfounded perception of the native population that Russian Jews avoided military service (Holmes, 1979, pp. 128–37). The illiberalism of the Great War and its immediate aftermath, with the December 1918 general election resulting in the biggest right-wing land-slide in modern British history (Panayi, 1991a, p. 221), may also help to explain the 1919 riots against blacks, but most commentators who have written on them have focused upon other factors.

Before the First World War Britain's black population remained 'miniscule and fragmented' but the 1914–18 conflict resulted in an 'enormous increase' in its size due to a labour shortage and consequent recruitment of black sailors. However, when the conflict ended many of them found themselves unem-ployed and competing for jobs with natives (Walvin, 1973, pp. 202, 204). This competition represents a major explanation of the disturbances by the scholars who have studied them. But the most sophisticated and detailed study by Jacqueline Jenkinson has also pointed to other causes. She has quite rightly mentioned 'the increased aggression displayed by those who had seen war service' and the underlying image of blacks in British society, whereby 'black people were robbed of their individuality, and as such passed into the national consciousness as caricatures, the object of xenophobic distaste to the white masses' (Jenkinson, 1987, pp. 4, 11). Another article has put this image within the context of the existence of the British Empire which ruled much of the West Indies and Africa and therefore enforced the ideas of white superiority (May and Cohen, 1974, p. 112). We can also see the existence of official racism towards blacks within Britain as one governmental response to the disturbances involved the repatriation of black seamen (Holmes, 1988, p. 110). At the same time, returning to social causes, we need to place the disturbances of 1919, rather like those of 1911, within the context of more widespread popular disturbances during the economic dislocation caused by the transition from war to peace (Stevenson, 1984, pp. 97–101).

Although the 1919 riots did not become as widespread as those against the Germans in 1915, they became almost as serious in other ways. Nine major locations experienced racial disorder between January and August: Glasgow, South Shields, Salford, London, Hull, Liverpool, Cardiff, Newport and Barry. But, in comparison with 1915, attacks occurred to a larger extent against individuals so that at least three black people were murdered. One of the killings, that of Charles Wotten in Liverpool, resembles an American lynching, with regard to the consciousness with which his killers murdered him, chasing him into Queen's Dock and then shouting 'Let him drown!' as they stoned him in the water (Jenkinson, 1987, pp. 3, 8; Fryer, 1984, p. 300). Much of the violence of 1919 also resembled the 1919 riots in America and the anti-Irish riots in nineteenth-century Britain in the sense that blacks did not simply become victims but also fought back (Jenkinson, 1987).

Further violence against blacks and Asians broke out after 1919 against the background of inherent racism within Britain (Jenkinson, 1988; Byrne, 1977). At the same time, communal violence continued between Catholics and Protestants in Edinburgh (Gallagher, 1987a, pp. 4, 24–5, 49–51). But it is the Jews, who had settled in east London at the end of the nineteenth century and had not yet moved out of the area (Smith, 1989, p. 53), who from the inter-war years became the victims of the racial incidents which have received the most attention from historians. In fact, the disturbances involving the reaction of the local Jewish community, working with the Communist Party of Great Britain and the Independent Labour Party, to anti-Semitism, rather than anti-Semitic attacks themselves, have become the focus of attention because racial violence became a major political issue due to the threat to public order. Of attacks upon Jews in East London, where the major street violence took place, Thurlow has pointed to 'the number of increased unprovoked attacks on Jews and communists by young hooligans in the Stepney, Bethnal Green and Shoreditch areas during 1936', together with 'the breaking of shop windows, the desecration of Jewish cemeteries and synagogues and the massive spread of anti-semitic graffiti' (Thurlow, 1987, p. 110). These occurrences took place against the background of the rise of anti-Semitism and fascism in Europe, which also affected Britain, though in a smaller way as witnessed by the growth of a series of fascist groups during the inter-war years, most notably the British Union of Fascists (BUF), led by Oswald Mosley.

It is the responses of left-wing movements, the Jewish community in the East End, and the government to Mosley and his followers which have become a major area of research. On 7 June 1936 the BUF held an east London rally which attracted 500 fascists but 5,000 anti-fascists. Between August and October of the same year about 2,000 meetings occurred in the area, involving substantial police resources. Matters came to a head on 4 October when 100,000 anti-fascists prevented 1,900 members of the BUF from marching through Jewish areas in east London. However, two weeks later, fascist youths in Mile End 'smashed windows of Jewish shops and houses and assaulted all those designated as Jews that they could lay their hands on' (Thurlow, 1987, pp. 110–12; Benewick, 1969, pp. 221–31).

The government responded to these developments by passing the Public Order Act, which became operative from 1 January 1937. As its name suggests, its concern lay not just in controlling racial violence but in maintaining public order, as it aimed at controlling both the activities of fascist demonstrators and anti-fascist counter-demonstrators. While it may have had success in preventing further large-scale disorder, it could not stop 'anti-semitic incidents which were becoming a part of the daily routine in East End life'. These incidents included the breaking of Jewish shop windows and greeting Jews walking in the streets with offensive remarks (Thurlow, 1987, pp. 112-16; Benewick, 1969, pp. 239–41, 278; Stevenson, 1980; Holmes, C., 1979, pp. 191–202).

As in the First World War, during the conflict of 1939–45 the British government introduced a policy of internment and repatriation of enemy aliens in the spring of 1940. This primarily affected German Jewish refugees who had made their way from Nazi Germany and the Italian community of Britain (Gillman and Gillman, 1980). The latter also became the victims of physical attacks following Mussolini's declaration of war on Britain on 10 June 1940. The point at which these disturbances broke out resembles many of the anti-German riots of the First World War in the sense that they followed a bad point in the war for British forces. But the events of June 1940 remained small and less widespread than those of May 1915, although they did affect several parts of the country, notably London, Liverpool, the North East, South Wales and Scotland (*The Times*, 11, 12 June 1940; *Scotsman*, 11, 12 June 1940).

In the post-war period the bulk of British anti-immigrant hostility has focused upon immigrants from the Commonwealth and Empire. Nevertheless, other groups have not escaped attention, notably Jews, made up of the late nineteenth-century newcomers, who came under serious attack in August 1947, following the killing of British soldiers in Palestine, a spark similar to those which set off the disturbances during the two World Wars. Areas in Britain affected included Liverpool, where violence continued for three nights, during which rioters burnt down a wooden synagogue. Elsewhere, several areas of London experienced disorder including Bethnal Green, Hackney, Lambeth, and Catford, while Manchester and its surrounding areas also suffered. Thousands of people took part in these incidents across the country (*The Times*, 2, 4, 5, 6 August 1947; *Liverpool Daily Post* 4, 5 August 1947; Holmes, C., 1988, p. 245).

Although anti-Semitism remained present within British society in the post-war world, it did not result in further major outbreaks of violence after 1947. The reasons for this may lie in the fact that the bulk of hostility since the war has focused upon the most visible immigrants who moved to Britain from the West Indies, India and Pakistan. At the same time we should recognise that immigrants have entered the country from smaller British colonies such as Cyprus, Malta, Hong Kong, Malaysia and Singapore (Holmes, C., 1988, pp. 218–27). Perhaps no movement into Britain since that of the nineteenth-century Irish has had as profound an impact on Britain as the migration from the Indian sub-continent and the West Indies because of the numbers involved and, more particularly, because of the areas of settlement of the newcomers since they have transformed both traditional immigrant areas such as east London, Manchester and Leeds, and have also fundamentally affected locations with less of a history of immigration such as Haringey in north London and Leicester.

But hostility towards the post-war immigrants has accompanied their arrival. We might describe this animosity as universal, affecting all sections of British society and manifesting itself on numerous levels. On a basic level the newcomers faced animosity in their everyday lives in the search for housing, employment and attempts to socialise with British society. Experiences of hostility in such areas meant that immigrants accepted employment in occupations for which many of them were overqualified. At the same time animosity helped to push the newcomers more towards their own ethnic groups, towards whom they would have gravitated in any case. More sophisticated media racism has remained constant throughout the post-war period, reaching peaks on occasions when immigration or race has become a major political issue. Furthermore, as we have seen, numerous anti-immigrant fringe groups have developed throughout the post-war period, although their influence has remained small. At the same time, despite the introduction of Race Relations Acts, the passage by the state of numerous pieces of legislation to control the entry of non-white immigrants since 1962 provides just one indication of the existence of state racism (Husbands, 1982; pp. 14–19, Holmes, C., 1988, pp. 255–70; Fryer, 1984, pp. 374–6; Pilkington, 1988, pp. 22–52; Miles and Solomos, 1987, pp. 88–102).

We need to consider the regular attacks against immigrants in Britain against this background of more widespread racism. We can best do this by dealing with the period until 1962, and then concentrating on the years since then. The first phase witnessed both isolated attacks upon individuals and their businesses, together with full-scale riots. An example of an individual attack includes the experience of a Jamaican who, during his first weekend in London in 1954, 'was abused by "a big fellow with side-burns", who shouted "You blacks, you niggers, why don't you go back to the jungle?" then lunged at him with a knife' (Fryer, 1984, p. 375). We can also develop an impression of the regularity of attacks during the 1950s from the perspective of a perpetrator who, during an interview, stated:

> we'd try to fight Blacks. We used to shout at them in the street 'You Black bastards' to try to provoke them, like. Over Brixton way, we'd try to stop them getting off buses, to frighten them. We'd often go for the Blacks we don't like them round here, we hate them (Fyvel, 1963, p. 34).

At the same time the 1950s also resulted in attacks on Cypriot cafés by 'Teddy Boys'. In another interview, one attacker claimed: 'One time we used to go regularly to the Angel where there's a lot of cafés and we aimed to start trouble with the Greeks and Turks, start a punch-up. They're Cypriots, you know, grease monkeys we used to call them—our chaps all hated them.' T.R. Fyvel, who analysed youth violence in the 1950s, explained the causes of attacks upon immigrants by referring to racial prejudice combined with resentment, especially against Cypriots, at the fact that they had progressed up the social ladder (Fyvel, 1963, pp. 13, 34, 100–2). At the same time we can also refer, again in the case of Cypriots, to political hostility towards them caused by the struggle for independence which resulted in the killing of British soldiers on the island (*Leicester Evening Mail*, 26 October 1956).

As well as these isolated incidents, the late 1940s and early 1950s also resulted in more large-scale disturbances on several occasions. The first of these occurred in Liverpool in 1948 between 31 July and 2 August. Its origins resemble those of the 1919 disturbances, as the National Union of Seamen again wanted the exclusion of black sailors from British ships at the end of the war. The first night of the disturbances involved an attack on a West African accused of attacking two white men with a knife. On the following night about 2,000 people attacked a hostel for black seamen in Upper Stanhope Street. The third night's disturbance involved fighting between police and blacks in a club in Upper Parliament Street, following the dispersal of a white crowd outside the club. In all, sixty black men and ten white men faced arrest (Richmond, 1954, p. 102–3; Fryer, 1984, pp. 367–71).

Similar incidents to this one occurred in May 1948, when 250 whites attacked a house inhabited by Indians in Birmingham, and in Deptford Broadway in south London, in July 1949, 'when a crowd of 1,000 whites besieged a number of blacks who were staying in a local hostel, Carrington House' (Holmes, C., 1988, p. 256). In 1954 a petrol bomb attack occured on a house inhabited by a West Indian family in Camden Town (Fryer, 1984, p. 378; Holmes, C., 1988, p. 298).

But the major anti-immigrant riots in post-war Britain occurred in Notting-ham and Notting Hill in 1958, between 23 August and 2 September, although, in comparison with events in May 1915 or in 1919, they remain relatively small in scale. The first incident began outside a public house in Nottingham but then spread to other parts of the city and involved 1,000 whites fighting with a significantly smaller number of blacks in the street. Police managed to prevent potential disorder in the city on 30 August and 6 September when crowds of hundreds of whites gathered in the streets. Although isolated incidents had occurred in early August, the first major outbreak of violence in Notting Hill took place on 23 August, followed by further large-scale attacks upon both individuals and property on 30 and 31 August and 1 and 2 September, resulting in 177 arrests of mostly whites, although blacks had retaliated. As in Notting-ham, hundreds of people had participated.

An attempt to explain the causes of the riots would focus upon a variety of levels. Fundamentally, they reflect the underlying concern in British society with the influx of post-war non-white immigrants, which began to reach a new intensity in the late 1950s and early 1960s in the period just before the passage of the Commonwealth Immigrants Act of 1962. Why the disturbances should have broken out where they did seems more difficult to establish. Some commentators, both contemporary and subsequent, have pointed to the activities of fascist groups in Notting Hill which 'fomented and intensified racial hatred', and also to the pressure on local housing (Pilkington, 1988, pp. 53–124; Miles, 1984, pp. 252–75; Holmes, C., 1988, p. 259).

The 'general race conscious climate of the country' (*Pakistan Times*, 22 August 1961) remained at a high level until at least the early 1960s, when further large-scale racial violence broke out on at least two occasions. For instance, in Middlesbrough, a town which had experienced only a small influx of Commonwealth newcomers, several thousand natives attacked the few Asian businesses which existed during the course of four nights between 19 and 23 August 1961. Local factors here included the suspected stabbing of a white youth by an Arab immigrant and a dispute between the owner of an Indian restaurant and a local resident, James Mulraney (Panayi, 1991b). Almost exactly a year after the events in Middlesbrough, 'riots' broke out in Dudley in August 1962, when hundreds of whites attacked blacks. Local conditions here included the perception that the local West Indian population enjoyed better economic conditions (Joshua, Wallace and Booth, 1983, pp. 46–7). Similar events occurred in Accrington in 1964 (Pearson, 1976, p. 52) and Wolverhampton in 1965 (Reeves, 1989).

Since the mid-1960s we cannot detect any large-scale riots against immigrant groups in Britain. Instead, we can point to two important developments. First, a move towards violence upon a small scale, involving numerous attacks on individuals and their property of the type which began to develop in the 1950s and which also affected Jews during the late nineteenth century and 1930s. And, second, the most serious rioting of any sort within the country has involved black youth as perpetrators on a large-scale during the 1980s.

Husbands has explained the first development by asserting that 'communal riots' occur in 'the "immature phase" in the establishment of relations between mutually hostile white and black groups', when immigration 'is continuing' as happened in the United States and Britain. He asserts that small-scale racial attacks received more attention in the 1980s, a 'mature phase' of race relations in Britain because 'they have now become the predominant form of overt inter-racial hostility' (Husbands, 1989, p. 96). His explanation contains substantial truth and we might point to a similar situation in Germany after re-unification. Although racial violence occurred on a nationwide scale, the only riots which occurred involving hundreds or thousands of people took place in former East Germany which has less experience of large numbers of newcomers, in Hoyerswerda and Rostock. The more numerous attacks which took place in West Germany, which has had a longer post-war history of immigration, involved small numbers of people attacking refugee hostels (Panayi, 1994).

The explanation for the second development in racial violence in Britain since the 1960s, the large-scale participation of members of ethnic minorities, particularly Afro-Caribbeans, in violence against property or police, finds its origins in both their socio-economic status and in state and police racial attitudes towards them. Major outbreaks of violence occurred in Bristol in 1980, and on a nationwide scale in 1981, followed by the Tottenham riot in October 1985 (Peach, 1986; Joshua, Wallace and Booth, 1983).

The smaller-scale attacks by natives on, particularly, Asian immigrants and their descendants have become serious, despite the small numbers of attackers involved. Tompson claims that sixty-three 'racist murders' occurred between 1970 and 1985 (Tompson, 1988, p. 171) while the CRE report, *Living in Terror*, stated that in 1986 one in four black residents living in the London Borough of Newham 'had been victims of some form of racial harassment in the previous twelve months' (CRE, 1987, p. 9). Husbands has also pointed to the spread of attacks to suburban areas and points to the late 1960s as the period when isolated incidents began to attract attention. Although a large percentage of such events take place in London, they have also affected other parts of the country, as Geoff Pearson has shown with regard to Accrington in Lancashire, where he tries to explain attacks by placing them within the context of 'the crisis of cotton culture in North East Lancashire, the evaporation of its industrial base, and the disappearance of Accrington's football team' (Pearson, 1976, p. 80). By 1993 official statistics suggested that between 130,000 and 140,000 racial attacks took place every year, although the true figure could be at least twice as high (Kushner, 1994, p. 37).

Whatever the correct total, why has racial violence broken out constantly throughout British history? This article has devoted much attention to the existence of xenophobia within Britain throughout its history. However, we can only view this as one level of explanation for attacks, although we can see it as the underlying, ever present factor involved in all attacks upon immigrants and their property. We might say that in some cases, where xenophobia becomes so intense and widespread, developing into a national issue, riots against an immigrant group almost become inevitable. We might make this point with regard to the German community in Britain during the First World War, as no other minority has faced both official and unofficial hostility on such a scale. Nevertheless, even here, sparks set off the disturbances just as sparks set off similar 'political' racial violence in June 1940 and August 1947. Although this almost suggests an inevitability in the outbreak of attacks in some particular part of the country at these particular times, local factors would have to play a part, with the exception of May 1915, where the entire country experienced some disorder, therefore representing somewhat unique events in the history of racial violence in recent British history.

Can we detect occasions when xenophobia becomes so widespread that 'economic' racial violence becomes inevitable? Here our concern lies with what we might describe as competition in jobs and housing which led to strong anti-immigrant campaigns in the years from about the mid-1880s to 1905 and from the mid-1950s to 1962. In the case of the latter, several outbreaks of racial violence did occur, but in the case of the former they did not. In fact, the most serious anti-Jewish riots in the early twentieth century actually broke out in 1911, when concern about poor Jewish newcomers had died down. Perhaps more surprisingly, they did not occur in areas where large numbers of immigrants lived, but in South Wales, where they had settled in small numbers. Clearly, as we have seen, local factors proved fundamental here, as the disturbances took place against the background of a strike in the coal industry.

If we turn to the disturbances in 1958 and 1961, we might suggest that their timing lends weight to the idea that anti-immigrant riots develop when xenophobia reaches a peak. However, this does not explain their location. Why Notting Hill, Nottingham and, most surprisingly of all, Middlesbrough which had a tiny influx of immigrants? Here, the importance of numbers seems to disappear because we have examples of riots in areas where both small- and large-scale communities lived. Ceri Peach's claim, referring to the 1981 riots, that 'riots are caused more by particular events than by general factors', seems convincing (Peach, 1986, p. 408). Peaks of 'economic' anti-immigrant hostility may make riots against a particular community likely but local factors play a large part in where a disturbance breaks out.

These conclusions seem straightforward compared with more sophisticated theoretical explanations for racial and other violence put forward by American scholars, particularly during the 1950s and 1960s. Gordon Allport explained disturbances by developing a scale of intolerance which moved from 'Verbal Rejection' on to 'Discrimination' and 'Physical Attack', although his ideas prove inconclusive in explaining why riots break out in particular places at particular times (Allport, 1955, pp. 48–65).

Neil Smelser provided a more convincing explanation for the outbreak of racial violence in which he stated:

> a racial incident between a negro and a white may spark a race riot. But unless this incident occurs in the context of a structurally conducive atmosphere (i.e. an atmosphere in which people perceive violence to be a possible means of expression) and in an atmosphere of strain (i.e. an atmosphere in which people perceive the incident as a symbolic state of affairs), the incident will pass without becoming a determinant in a racial outburst. (Smelser, 1962, p. 259)

Although his work looks at what he describes as 'The Hostile Outburst', ranging from stock market crashes to revolutions, the above quotation can be applied to British racial disturbances because, as we have seen, all incidents take place against a racial background. Smelser is clearly laying must stress on local factors here in the form of both sparks and the build-up of hostility more generally. Little of the research on British disturbances has tackled riots within their local context over a long period of time.

Allen D. Grimshaw has carried out the most widespread research on the United States, producing numerous articles upon the subject which consider the role of a variety of factors, including the police and 'ecological considerations' (Grimshaw, 1960; 1963a). Significantly, in connection with the conclusions reached above, he recognises that 'the background factors of prejudice, discrimination, and social tension are present in all urban centres in the North [of the USA]' (Grimshaw, 1963a, p. 288), but that violence results 'from reactions by the dominant group to real or perceived assaults upon the *status quo*'. This could include threats to housing or employment (Grimshaw, 1962; 1963b, p. 76).

In short, to refine the assertions previously put forward, racial violence breaks out against the background of underlying hostility towards an outgroup, exacerbated by recent developments, and sparked off by a particular incident. If we took the example of Germans in Britain during the First World War, we would need to consider the long-term development of Germanophobia in Britain, the effects of First World War on the intensifying of this hostility, and the sparks, such as the sinking of the *Lusitania* in May 1915.

At this point we can move wider to consider one point which Grimshaw looks at and broaden it further. He lays particular stress on the role of the police and military authorities. In an article comparing race riots in the United States and Britain, he viewed 'police impartiality' as a restraint on '*major* violence' in the latter (Grimshaw, 1962, p. 18), in comparison with the United States where 'White policemen have refused to protect Negroes and in some cases have actually joined in attacks on Negroes' (Grimshaw, 1963a, p. 272). Similarly, if we look at anti-Jewish pogroms in late nineteenth-century Russia we can find examples of police and military inactivity or support for rioters (Aronson, 1990, pp. 131–7). We can also turn to the anti-Jewish *Kristallnacht* in Germany of 9 November 1938, when members of the SA, under instruction from the Nazi Party hierarchy, instigated the destructive pogroms which resulted in almost 100 deaths and widespread destruction of property (Dawidowicz, 1987, pp. 136–7).

Here we seem to have moved a long way from events such as Tredegar in 1911, or Middlesbrough in 1961. In the case of Nazi Germany or tsarist Russia, racism became state policy, which meant the rioters possessed 'the absolute conviction that it was perfectly safe to rob and beat Jews with complete impunity' (Schapiro, 1959–61, p. 220). We can say that during the nineteenth and twentieth centuries no British government has pursued a policy of extreme racism, aiming at expulsion or destruction of minorities. The only possible exceptions would be the First and Second World Wars, when large numbers of enemy aliens faced repatriation. But this still remains a long way from the experience of minorities in some other countries.

If we attempted to devise a scale of racial violence we could move, from mildest to strongest manifestations, from: isolated attacks upon houses and individuals; anti-minority riots involving hundreds or thousands of members of the dominant population attacking people or property form other communities; ritualised lynchings, in which large numbers of people kill one or more members of an outgroup; riots in which the police and/or state authorities play a major role by instigating or ignoring riots, which can therefore result in massive destruction to property and a large number of deaths, as happened in late nineteenth- and early twentieth-century Russia, Chicago in 1919, and Germany in November 1938; to, finally, genocide, where the state systematically aims to exterminate a particular minority and places manpower, financial and other resources into achieving this aim.

In nineteenth- and twentieth-century Britain we can only point to the first two levels. Systematic lynching has not taken place in the ritualised fashion of the southern states of the United States (Zangrando, 1980, pp. 3–12), and neither have the highest two levels developed, although we can find examples in which the impartiality of the police authorities remains open to question. This has certainly formed a fundamental line in explaining many of the individual attacks which have taken place since the 1960s, in which the existence of a racist police force is widely accepted (CRE, 1987, pp. 30–1; Tompson, 1988; Holmes, C., 1991, p. 89; Fryer, 1984, pp. 391–5). Similarly, Richmond questioned the impartiality of the police in the Liverpool disturbances of 1948 (Richmond, 1954, pp. 103–4), as Jenkinson has done in her examination of the 1919 events (see Chapter 5). Nevertheless, on other occasions the police have acted firmly in suppressing anti-immigrant riots and arresting attackers, as in 1915 or 1961.

But the fundamental argument of this chapter concerns the existence of a racist culture in Britain which has manifested itself in a variety of ways, outlined in the introduction, most potently in the form of racial violence. The fact that Britain has not experienced the sort of intolerant acts which have developed in Turkey (Hovanissian, 1987), Australia (Evans, Saunders and Cronin, 1988) and Germany, which have all experienced genocide, or the

United States or Russia, where highly destructive violence has broken out in which large-scale killings have taken place, points not to the absence of racism within Britain but to its position within the political culture of the country. We could say that, as a liberal democracy in which race has not played a fundamental role in the way that it has done in the above states, it has not become a virtual obsession. However, when the *status quo* with regard to dominant/ subgroup relationships has been shaken, whether due to large-scale immigration, competition for social resources, or war, and a local spark in an area of conflict appears, racial attacks have broken out, often on a large scale. Ultimately we have to reject Orwell's opening quote because of the experience, particularly short-term, of minorities which have entered Britain. While Britain may have a more tolerant culture than many of the countries previously listed, its natives have attacked outgroups on a regular basis so that we cannot reject Colin Holmes's assertion that 'most ethnic minorities in Britain at different times in a variety of places have found themselves targets of physical attack and assault' (Holmes, C., 1982, p. 225). In fact we can change 'most' to 'all'. We cannot accept standard contemporary interpretations of riots, particularly those of the post-war years, which view racial disturbances as acts of hooliganism by individuals outside mainstream society. Research has demonstrated that rioters belong to mainstream working-class or even petty bourgeois society (Miles, 1984, p. 257; Panayi, 1991b, pp. 145–51), and we have to see attacks upon immigrants as the most potent, or even most honest, manifestation of xenophobia in modern British history.

References

Alderman, Geoffrey, 1972, 'The Anti-Jewish Riots of August 1911 in South Wales', *Welsh History Review*, 6: 190–200.

Allport, Gordon W., 1955, *The Nature of Prejudice*, Cambridge, Mass., Wesley Publishing Co.

Arnstein, Walter L., 1975, 'The Murphy Riots: A Victorian Dilemma', *Victorian Studies*, 19: 51–71.

Aronson, I. Michael, 1990, *Troubled Waters: The Origins of the 1881 Anti-Jewish Pogroms in Russia*, Pittsburgh, University of Pittsburgh Press.

Benewick, Robert, 1969, *Political Violence and Public Order: A Study of British Fascism*, London, Allen Lane.

Bourne, John, 1989, *Britain and the Great War, 1914–18*, London, Edward Arnold.

Byrne, David, 1977, 'The 1930 "Arab Riot" in South Shields: A Race Riot That Never Was', *Race and Class*, 18: 261–76.

Castro, J. Paul de, 1926, *The Gordon Riots*, London, Oxford University Press.

Cesarani, David (ed.), 1990, *The Making of Modern Anglo-Jewry*, Oxford, Basil Blackwell.

Chitty, C.W., 1966, 'Aliens in England in the Sixteenth Century', *Race*, 8: 129–45.

Coleman, Terry, 1986, *The Railway Navvies*, Harmondsworth, Penguin.

C[ommission for] R[acial] E[quality], 1987, *Living in Terror: A Report on Racial Violence and Harassment in Housing*, London, CRE.

Curtis, L.P., 1968, *Anglo-Saxons and Celts*, New York, New York University Press.

Daunton, Martin, 1978, 'Jack Ashore: Seamen in Cardiff before 1914', *Welsh History Review*, 9: 176–93.

Dawidowicz, Lucy S., 1987 reprint, *The War against the Jews*, 1933–45, Harmondsworth, Penguin.

Dobson, R.B., 1974, *The Jews of Medieval York and the Massacre of March 1190*, York, St Anthony's Press.

Dollinger, Philipe, 1970, *The German Hansa*, London, Macmillan.

Evans, Raymond, Saunders, Kay and Cronin, Kathryn, 1988, *Race Relations in Colonial Queensland: A History of Exclusion, Exploitation and Extermination*, St Lucia, Queensland, Queensland University Press.

Fitzpatrick, David, 1980, 'Irish Emigration in the Later Nineteenth Century', *Irish Historical Studies*, 22: 126–43.

Fryer, Peter, 1984, *Staying Power: The History of Black People in Britain*, London, Pluto.

Fyvel, T.R., 1963, *The Insecure Offenders: Rebellious Youth in the Welfare State*, Harmondsworth, Penguin.

Gainer, Bernard, 1972, *The Alien Invasion: The Origins of the Aliens Act of 1905*, London, Heinemann.

Gallagher, Tom, 1985, 'A Tale of Two Cities: Communal Strife in Glasgow and Liverpool before 1914', in Swift and Gilley (eds): 106–29.

Gallagher, Tom, 1987a, *Edinburgh Divided: John Cormack and No Popery in the 1930s*, Edinburgh, Polygon.

Gallagher, Tom, 1987b, *Glasgow the Uneasy Peace: Religious Tension in Modern Scotland*, Manchester, Manchester University Press.

George, Dorothy M., 1966, *London Life in the Eighteenth Century*, Harmondsworth, Penguin.

Gilley, Sheridan, 1973, 'The Garibaldi Riots of 1862', *Historical Journal*, 16: 697–732.

Gilley, Sheridan, 1978, 'English Attitudes to the Irish in England, 1780–1900', in Holmes (ed.): 81–110.

Gillman, Peter and Leni, 1980, *'Collar the Lot': How Britain Interned and Expelled its Wartime Refugees*, London, Quartet.

Grimshaw, Allen D., 1960, 'Urban Racial Violence in the United States: Changing Ecological Considerations', *American Journal of Sociology*, 66: 109–19.

Grimshaw, Allen D., 1962, 'Factors Contributing to Colour Violence in the United States and Britain', *Race*, 3: 3–19.

Grimshaw, Allen D., 1963a, 'Actions of Police and the Military in American Race Riots', *Phylon*, 24: 271–89.

Grimshaw, Allen D., 1963b, 'Three Major Cases of Colour Violence in the United States', *Race*, 1:76–86.

Hirschfeld, Gerhard (ed.), 1984, *Exile in Great Britain: Refugees from Hitler's Germany*, Leamington Spa, Berg.

Holmes, Colin, 1975, 'Violence and Race Relations in Britain, 1953–68', *Phylon*, 36: 113–24.

Holmes, Colin (ed.), 1978, *Immigrants and Minorities in British Society*, London, Allen and Unwin.

Holmes, Colin, 1979, *Anti-Semitism in British Society, 1876–1939*, London, Edward Arnold.

Holmes, Colin, 1982, 'The Tredegar Riots of 1911: Anti-Jewish Disturbances in South Wales', *Welsh History Review*, 11: 214–25.

Holmes, Colin, 1985, 'The Myth of Fairness: Racial Violence in Britain, 1911–19', *History Today*, 35 (10): 41–5.

Holmes, Colin, 1988, *John Bull's Island: Immigration and British Society, 1871–1971*, London, Macmillan.

Holmes, Colin, 1991, *A Tolerant Country? Immigrants, Refugees and Minorities in Britain*, London, Faber.

Holmes, Martin, 1965, 'Evil May-Day 1517: The Story of a Riot', *History Today*, 15 (9): 642–5.

Hovanissian, Richard G (ed.), 1987, *The Armenian Genocide in Perspective*, New Brunswick, Transaction Books.

Husband, Charles, 1987, *Race in Britain: Continuity and Change*, London, Hutchinson.

Husbands, Chris, 1982, 'East End Racism 1900–1980: Continuities in Vigilante and Extreme Right Wing Political Behaviour', *London Journal*, 8: 3–26.

Husbands, Chris, 1989, 'Racial Attacks: The Persistence of Racial Harassment in British Cities', in Kushner and Lunn (eds): 91–115.

Hyams, Paul, 1974, 'The Jewish Minority in Medieval England, 1066–1290', *Journal of Jewish Studies*, 25: 270–93.

Jenkinson, Jacqueline, 1985, 'The Glasgow Race Disturbances of 1919', *Immigrants and Minorities*, 4: 43–67.

Jenkinson, Jacqueline, 1987, 'The 1919 Race Riots in Britain: Their Background and Consequences', unpublished Ph.D. thesis, University of Edinburgh.

Jenkinson, Jacqueline, 1988, 'The Black Community of Salford and Hull 1919–21', *Immigrants and Minorities*, 7: 166–83.

Joshua, Harris, Wallace, Tina and Booth, Heather, 1983, *To Ride the Storm: The 1980 Bristol 'Riot' and the State*, London, Heinemann.

Knittle, W.A., 1970, *Early Eighteenth Century Palatine Emigration*, Baltimore, Genealogical Publishing Co.

Krausz, Ernest, 1964, *Leeds Jewry: Its History and Social Structure*, Cambridge, W. Heffer.

Kushner, Tony, 1989, *The Persistence of Prejudice: Anti-semitism in British Society During the Second World War*, Manchester, Manchester University Press.

Kushner, Tony, 1994, 'The Fascist as "Other"? Racism and Neo-Nazism in Contemporary Britain', *Patterns of Prejudice*, 28: 27–45.

Kushner, Tony and Lunn, Kenneth (eds), 1989, *Traditions of Intolerance: Historical Perspectives on Facism and Race Discourse in Britain*, Manchester, Manchester University Press.

Kushner, Tony and Lunn, Kenneth (eds), 1990, *The Politics of Marginality: Race, the Radical Right and Minorities in Twentieth Century Britain*, London, Frank Cass.

Lafitte, François, 1988, *The Internment of Aliens*, London, Libris.

Lloyd, T.H., 1982, *Alien Merchants in England in the High Middle Ages*, Brighton Harvester.

Lunn, Kenneth (ed.), 1980, *Hosts, Immigrants and Minorities: Historical Responses to Newcomers in British Society 1870–1914*, Folkestone, Dawson.

Lunn, Kenneth and Thurlow, Richard, 1980, *British Fascism*, London, Croom Helm.

May, J.P., 1973, 'The British Working Class and the Chinese 1870–1911, With Particular Reference to the Seamen's Strike of 1911', unpublished Ph.D. thesis, University of Warwick.

May, J.P., 1978, 'The Chinese in Britain, 1860–1914', in Holmes (ed.): 111-24.

May, Robin and Cohen, Robin, 1974, 'The Interaction of Race and Colonialism: A Case Study of the Liverpool Race Riots of 1919', *Race*, 16: 111–26.

Miles, Robert, 1984, 'The Riots of 1958: Notes on the Ideological Construction of "Race Relations" as a Political Issue in Britain', *Immigrants and Minorities*, 3: 252–75.

Miles, Robert and Solomos, John, 1987, 'Migration and the State in Britain: A Historical Overview', in Husband (ed.): 75–110.

Millward, Pauline, 1985, 'The Stockport Riots of 1852: A Study of Anti-Catholic and Anti-Irish Sentiment', in Swift and Gilley (eds): 207–24.

Moore, R.I., 1987, *The Formation of a Persecuting Society: Power and Deviance in Western Europe, 950–1250*, Oxford, Basil Blackwell.

Mungham, Geoff and Pearson, Geoffrey (eds), 1976, *Working Class Youth Culture*, London, Routledge and Kegan Paul.

Neal, Frank, 1988, *Sectarian Violence: The Liverpool Experience, 1819–1914*, Manchester, Manchester University Press.

Oakley, Robin, 1987, 'The Control of Cypriot Migration to Britain between the Wars', *Immigrants and Minorities*, 6.

Orwell, George, 1986 (originally 1941), *The Lion and the Unicorn*, Harmondsworth, Penguin.

Orwell, S., and Angus, I. (eds), 1968, *The Collected Essays, Journalism and Letters of George Orwell*, London, Secker and Warburg.

Ó Tuathaigh, M.A.G., 1981, 'The Irish in Nineteenth Century Britain: Problems of Integration', *Transactions of the Royal Historical Society*, 31: 149–73.

Panayi, Panikos, 1988, 'The Lancashire Anti-German Riots of May 1915', *Manchester Region History Review*, 2: 3–11.

Panayi, Panikos, 1989, 'Anti-German Riots in London during the First World War', *German History*, 7: 184–203.

Panayi, Panikos, 1990, 'The British Empire Union in the First World War', in Kushner and Lunn (eds): 113–24.

Panayi, Panikos, 1991a, *The Enemy in Our Midst: Germans in Britain during the First World War*, Oxford, Berg.

Panayi, Panikos, 1991b, 'Middlesbrough 1961: A British Race Riot of the 1960s?', *Social History*, 16: 139–53.

Panayi, Panikos, 1994, 'Racial Violence in the New Germany, 1990–93', *Contemporary European History*, 3: 265–87.

Parry, Jon, 1983, 'The Tredegar Anti-Irish Riots of 1882', *Llafur*, 3: 20–3.

Peach, Ceri, 1986, 'A Geographical Perspective on the 1981 Urban Riots in England', *Ethnic and Racial Studies*, 9: 396–411.

Pearson, Geoffrey, 1976, ' "Paki-Bashing" in a North East Lancashire Cotton Town: A Case Study and Its History', in Mungham and Pearson (eds): 48–81.

Pearson, Geoffrey, 1983, *Hooligan: A History of Respectable Fears*, London, Macmillan.

Pilkington, Edward, 1988, *Beyond the Mother Country: West Indians and the Notting Hill White Riots*, London, I B Tauris.

Price, Richard, 1972, *An Imperial War and the British Working Classes: Working Class Attitudes and Reactions to the Boer War 1899–1902*, London, Routledge.

Reeves, F., 1989, *Race and Borough Politics*, Aldershot, Avebury.

Richmond, A.H., 1954, *Colour Prejudice in Britain: A Study of West Indian Workers in Liverpool, 1941–51*, London, Routledge and Kegan Paul.

Richter, Donald C., 1981, *Riotous Victorians*, London, Ohio University Press.

Rogers, N., 1978, 'Popular Protest in Early Hanoverian London', *Past and Present*, 79: 70–100.

Rude, George, 1956, 'The Gordon Riots: A Study of the Rioters and Their Victims', *Transactions of the Royal Historical Society*, 5th series, 1956: 93–114.

Rude, George, 1971, *Hanoverian London*, London, Secker and Warburg.

Rude, George, 1985 (originally 1964), *The Crowd in History: Study of Popular Disturbances in France and England*, London, Lawrence and Wishart.

Schapiro, Leonard, 1959–61, 'The Russian Background to the Anglo-American Jewish Immigration', *Transactions of the Jewish Historical Society of England*, 20: 215–31.

Seyfert, Michael, 1984, 'His Majesty's Most Loyal Internees', in Hirschfeld (ed.): 163–93.

Smelser, Neil J., 1962, *Theory of Collective Behaviour*, London.

Smith, Elaine R., 1989, 'Jewish Responses to Political Anti-semitism and Facism in the East End of London, 1920–1939', in Kushner and Lunn (eds): 53–71.

Sponza, Lucio, 1988, *Italian Immigrants in Nineteenth Century Britain: Realities and Images*, Leicester, Leicester University Press.

Stevenson, John, 1979, *Popular Disturbances in England 1700–1870*, London, Longman.

Stevenson, John, 1980, 'The BUF, the Metropolitan Police and Public Order', in Lunn and Thurlow (eds): 135–49.

Stevenson, John, 1984, *British Society, 1914–45*, Harmondsworth, Penguin.

Swift, Roger, 1984a, ' "Another Stafford Street Row": Law, Order and the Irish Presence in Mid-Victorian Wolverhampton', *Immigrants and Minorities*, 4: 5–29.

Swift, Roger, 1984b, 'Anti-Catholicism and Irish Disturbances: Public Disorder in Mid Victorian Wolverhampton', *Midland History*, 9: 87–108.

Swift, Roger, 1989, 'Crime and the Irish in Nineteenth-Century Britain', in Swift and Gilley (eds): 163–82.

Swift, Roger and Gilley, Sheridan (eds), 1985, *The Irish in the Victorian City*, London, Croom Helm.

Swift, Roger and Gilley, Sheridan (eds), 1989, *The Irish in Britain 1815–1939*, London, Pinter.

Thompson, E.P., 1971, 'The Moral Economy of the English Crowd in the Eighteenth Century', *Past and Present*, 50: 76–136.

Thurlow, Richard, 1987, *Fascism in Britain: A History, 1918–1985*, Oxford, Basil Blackwell.

Tompson, Keith, 1988, *Under Siege: Racial Violence in Britain Today*, Harmondsworth, Penguin.

Waller, P.J., 1981, *Democracy and Sectarianism: A Political and Social History of Liverpool*, Liverpool, Liverpool University Press.

Waller, P.J., 1985, 'The Chinese', *History Today*, 35 (10): 8–15.

Walvin, James, 1973, *Black and White: The Negro and English Society*, London, Allen Lane.

Wauer, G.A., 1901, *The Beginnings of the Brethren's Church ('Moravians') in England*, Baildon, Moravian House.

Williams, Bill, 1990, ' "East and West": Class and Community in Manchester Jewry, 1850–1914', in Cesarani (ed.): 15–33.

Zangrando, Robert L., 1980, *The NAACP Crusade against Lynching, 1909–1950*, Philadelphia, Temple University Press.

2

Varieties of anti-Irish behaviour in Britain, 1846–1922[1]

Alan O'Day

I

Nowhere in England can our countrymen consider themselves safe from English
mob violence . . .

(The Nation, 6 June 1868)

Hostility to the Irish has ancient roots in Britain. It predates the Act of Union,
the Cromwellian period or even the Reformation. Nor was it the case that
English animosity was directed exclusively at the Irish. Strangers of all sorts
experienced unpopularity in England (Holmes, 1988; 1991). As a recent writer
has noted the Irish were not the chief targets of English malevolence in the
eighteenth century—Scots were more universally detested (Boyce, 1991, p. 30).
During the middle of the nineteenth century popular feeling against the Irish
reached a crescendo. The growth of anti-Hibernian sentiment was a consequence of economic, social, political and religious currents of the era and
intimately linked to an enormous influx of refugees from the Emerald Isle
during the Famine. These aliens hold a special interest for any evaluation of
British attitudes towards immigrants for they were the pioneers of large-scale
settlement. The Irish retained their place as the single greatest foreign component of the mainland population until the 1960s. Not surprisingly, the
massive transfer of peoples from Ireland to Britain spurred a native reaction
against the newcomers. Contrary to the dismal view of the *Nation* cited above
the numbers of incidents against the Celtic invaders were comparative few and
heavily concentrated in certain towns, notably in Lancashire, during the years
between 1850 and 1870. Psychological terror, small-scale brawls, attacks on
individuals and a routine diet of discrimination rather than regularized mob
violence were the more usual weapons by which the natives vented their
aggressions on the Irish. This essay explores the dimensions of anti-Irish
behaviour in the years from the Famine to the beginning of the 1920s. A main
thrust of the piece is to account for the decline in overt threats to the Hibernian

community. It will be suggested that the Irish offered an evasive target for physical assaults because the community developed appropriate strategies for copying with particularly dangerous situations and also as a consequence of the aliens' rapid absorption into the host society.

II

Who were the 'Irish', what made them distinctive, and why were these immigrants vulnerable to native hostility? They may be simply categorised as a people who originated from Ireland. Even prior to the Famine the Celtic invasion was a visible reality on the mainland. In 1841 the decennial census enumerated the Irish-born residents of England and Wales at 289,404, with a further 126,321 domiciled in Scotland (Jackson, 1963, p. 1963). Ten years later in the aftermath of the Famine the totals leaped to 519, 959 for England and Wales and 207,367 in Scotland. The Irish Famine catastrophe of the 1840s turned a stream into a torrent of emigration out of Ireland. A majority of those fleeing Ireland decamped in the United States but Britain was the second favoured destination. Many of the very poorest and also the best-educated preferred to emigrate to the mainland. In England and Wales the pinnacle of the invasion was reached in 1861 when the census recorded a total of 601,634 Irish-born. Another 204,083 then resided in Scotland. By the next census in 1871 the Irish-born numbers in the southern kingdom had receded to 566,540 but increased to 207,770 north of the border. There the upward march of the invasion did not cease until after the census of 1881 which enumerated 218,745 people as being born in Ireland. From the 1860s in England and Wales and after 1881 in Scotland the Irish-born total fell in each successive census. While the Irish were very plentiful in Britain both before and following the Famine they never formed more than a small proportion of the population. Even in 1861 the Irish-born were only 3 per cent of the English and Welsh population and at the peak in Scotland in 1851, 7.16 per cent. Thus, though significant, the Irish never posed a danger of swamping the natives. Official statistics did not discriminate between Catholic and Protestant immigrants; both were simply recorded as Irish-born. Furthermore, the designation Irish-born omitted the numbers of Irish children born in Britain. It is by no means certain how these two variables should be treated. As anti-Irishness generally was directed at Catholics alone it is appropriate to deduct Irish-born Protestants from the size of the ethnic community. They may have accounted for approximately a quarter of the estimated Irish numbers. Irish Protestants were particularly evident in London, Scotland and Lancashire. In the last region they played a part in stirring up opinion against Catholics.

Similarly, there is a problem in computing the numbers of British-born children of Irish parents. A generation after the Famine it is probably satisfactory to double the total of Irish-born Catholics. By the 1870s and 1880s the maximum size of the ethnic community may have been somewhere in the order of one to one and a half million or around 6–8 per cent of the national population. This figure should be treated as a theoretical maximum for it includes many Irish who had been assimilated into the host society or at least felt little identity with the immigrant group.

If the newcomers were voluminous, though not so numerous as to threaten the native peoples, they were observable in nearly every part of the land. The majority, however, were concentrated in certain places, notably northern industrial towns, the west of Scotland and in London. Irish numbers were greater in the north west than in Yorkshire or the north east. In 1851 the Irish-born were 10 per cent of the Lancashire population and 5 per cent of Cheshire's. Rural communities attracted relatively few permanent settlers though the Irish were not wholly absent from these districts. Many came to the countryside as harvest labourers though this pattern was of declining importance from the late 1870s. London had the highest absolute number of immigrants but even in 1851 they only comprised 4.6 per cent of the population of the Metropolis. Merely three registrar general's districts—St Giles in the Fields, St Olave in Southwark, and Whitechapel—had an Irish-born total which exceeded 10 per cent (Lees, 1979, p. 58). Northern towns often had larger proportions. Liverpool, the most Irish city in England, in 1851 had 22.29 per cent of its people recorded as being born in the neighbour island, but this proportion fell to 18.91 per cent by 1861 and then to 15.56 per cent a decade later. An Anglican religious survey lends credence to the formula of doubling the Irish-born Catholic numbers to arrive at an estimate of the maximum total for the ethnic community in the later Victorian period (R.B. Walker, 1968). Glasgow's figures were only a little below Liverpool's. There the percentages for the corresponding years were 18.17, 15.70 and 14.32. Elsewhere the proportions were smaller. During the same set of years the Irish-born in Manchester achieved percentages of 13.08, 11.31 and 8.59. A few Lancashire towns like Wigan had higher percentages. In the vital port city, Bristol, though, the Irish-born in 1851 were less than 3.5 per cent of the population (Large, 1985, p. 38). While the precise proportions of Irish varied from place to place not a single British city or substantial district had an Irish majority. The newcomers can be characterised as a vast horde spread widely though unevenly across the land. No subsequent group arrived in similar numbers or fanned out so thoroughly but most replicated the Irish pattern.

Within areas of settlement the Irish, like other immigrants before and since, lived in residential clusters. Two patterns of concentration have been detected. In one, the less common, they lived in virtual seclusion forming a 'ghetto'. Many of the early accounts of the Irish experience stressed the existence of immigrant courts, streets and districts (Werley, 1973, pp. 345–58). Lately several observers have noted the complexity of Irish residential preferences (Davis, 1989, pp. 112–13; Kirk, 1985, pp. 313–14). In London the immigrants could be found nearly everywhere. Middle-class areas had considerable numbers of Irish, principally domestic servants. There, also, were substantial though scattered pockets of 'little Irelands'. These enclaves were situated at considerable distances from one another. By 1851 in Liverpool the immigrants had already dispersed into distinct 'little Irelands'. One of the three wards with more than 40 per cent Irish-born was in the southern sector of the city while the remaining two were in the north (Pooley, 1977, pp. 364–83; 1992, pp. 71–91). These three areas maintained largely separate existences. By 1871 there were seven registrar general's enumeration districts with an Irish-born population in excess of 50 per cent and only one with none at all. Within each area there was a tendency for people from the same village, county and province of Ireland to coalesce into miniature Corks or Mayos. Differences in Ireland were reproduced in Britain. Three principal emigrant routes from Ireland to Britain attracted people from different parts of the old country and then deposited them in separate areas of Britain (Ó Tuathaigh, 1981, p. 152; Fitzpatrick, 1984, pp. 32–7). The immigrants were not a cohesive group on arrival and circumstances tended to maintain differences of class, geography and culture at home in the new environment. Ethnic loyalty was apt to be eroded through intermarriage or the attainment of superior affluence. Then the exiles would tend 'to forget their nativety, and in all things conform to English thought and English habit' (O'Day, 1990, p. 127). The better-off in Liverpool, for instance, usually moved to the fringe of the residential concentration. Furthermore, Irish neighbourhoods were unstable because of high mobility or changes in employment. In Liverpool by 1871 the southern Irish enclave had begun to disintegrate. Even in 1851 in Bristol there was not 'a single well-defined Irish ghetto' (Large, 1985, p. 41).

The Irish were opportunistic migrants. They were attracted to places with appropriate employment prospects. Once in Britain, they were notable for high levels of transience (Herson, 1989, pp. 84–103; Davis, 1989, pp. 104–33). Regular movement rendered the immigrants even more visible but undermined communal stability. Low levels of cohesion left the exiles with weakened defences against native hostility. As newcomers eagerly seizing available jobs, the Irish were disliked by those host peoples who saw them as rivals. Being mainly unskilled, the immigrants were perceived as flooding the market for day labourers and forcing down wages in this highly competitive sector. Frederick Engels believed that occupations which required strength rather than skill were 'especially overcrowded with Irishmen; hand weavers, bricklayers, porters, jobbers and such workers count hordes of Irishmen among their number (Engels, 1969, p. 125). His observation has never been disputed and a recent analysis of Irish employments in Stockport in 1851 and Stalybridge in 1851 and 1861 confirms the traditional picture (Kirk, 1985, pp. 326–8). A huge Victorian appetite for domestic servants created a large demand for the services of Irish women. The considerable Irish presence in middle-class districts noted in the census returns can be accounted for by live-in domestics. Eighty-two per cent of the Irish-born in 1881 were categorised as day labourers while the census report for 1891, after an investigation of a sample of Liverpool occupations, concluded that the immigrants were largely 'engaged in the rougher kinds of unskilled labour, the proportions of artisans and dealers of all kinds and grades being very small' (Inglis, 1963, p. 193; Census Report, 1891, pp. 61–3). Many sources underscore the natives' resentment of the Irish impact on jobs and wages. Engels thought that 'the pressure of this race has done much to depress wages and lower the working class' (Engels, 1969, p. 125). An editorial in *The Times* in late 1868 complained, 'these Celtic invaders lessen the rate of wages and this is their principal fault'. (*The Times*, 28 November 1868). It was recalled by a pioneer in the miners' union 'that stout north-country pit men had been driven to America by the wage competition of those strangers' (Welbourne, 1923, p. 200). One modern commentator has sought to add substance to this view, arguing that the Irish lowered wages in industrial districts thereby slowing the natural flow of native labour from southern rural areas into the northern towns (Hunt, 1973, pp. 286–305).

Without doubt economic friction exacerbated the native reaction to the newcomers. However, the pertinent question is the degree to which this competition impinged on intra-communal relations. Individual cases certainly can be cited. On Tyneside in the 1850s there were assaults on Irish workers and in Cheshire in 1883 Hibernian harvesters experienced attacks (O'Day, 1977, p. 114). However, the total of such instances was not enormous even in the mid-Victorian decades (Lowe, 1989, pp. 172–3). It in fact may be that the Irish impact on wage rates was tiny though their entrance into certain jobs, like cotton industrial employment, was especially provocative (Williamsom, 1986, pp. 693–721; Kirk, 1985, p. 326). Irish–native competition had not been exceptionally troubling before the Famine (Thompson, 1968, p. 480). During the mid-Victorian years the invaders were not ordinarily involved in strike-breaking. It has been pointed out that Irish and English cotton operatives generally acted in unison during moments of industrial militancy such as 1853–54 and 1859–61 (Kirk, 1985, p. 330). Moreover, the years after the 1860s saw a decline in economic rivalry. In 1872 Hugh Heinrick observed of the area around Wigan:

> nearly half the pit-men in the neighbouring coal and iron works are now Irish, though till recently, the English miner refused to work beside the Irishman, and hatred and hostility marked nearly every relation of the men of the one nationality to those of the other. (O'Day, 1990, p. 99)

He also commented on the possibilities of upward occupational mobility for his compatriots. In Birmingham, Heinrick noted: 'there are various trades and callings in which the Irish people—and particularly the young—are trained to skilled and artistic labour' (O'Day, 1990, p. 46). He indicated that there 'the Irish people, in proportion to their numbers supply a fair quota to the ranks of the more skilled employees in the manufactures.' Twenty years later John Denvir emphasised the improved employment status of the invaders (Denvir, 1892, pp. 389–462). Progress, though, was uneven between locations and over time. In Liverpool particularly, anti-Irish habits were deeply entrenched and it remained difficult for young men of Celtic stock to obtain an apprenticeship as late as the early twentieth century. Nevertheless, the Irish experience and the pattern of economic contact with the host peoples cannot be encapsuled in a single concise description.

Other Irish characteristics made them conspicuous, feared and disliked. Their menace to public health received frequent comment in the nineteenth century. As late as 1893 in Cardiff they were still singled out in an official report for habits contributing to the outbreak of typhus (Hickey, 1967, pp. 202–3). Furthermore, the Irish were believed to be ever ready to appeal to the Poor Law Guardians for relief though, in reality, the regulations, notably those allowing a pauper to be returned to his parish of birth if he sought support, militated against them in the mid-Victorian period. What was readily observable at all points, though, was that the Irish were prone to anti-social behaviour such as drunkenness, petty theft, prostitution and brawling. Criminal statistics establish that the immigrants and their progeny were overrepresented among prison inmates (Fitzpatrick, 1989a, pp. 25–9; 1989b, p. 656; Neal, 1990). While the Irish proportions may look less unbalanced if measured against an 'at risk' population, that is, the poor, most contemporaries were struck by the enormity of the problem (Neal, 1990). There certainly is no interpretative dispute concerning the tendency towards debauchery from drink. Heinrick, for one, observed:

> their own improvidence—it is only fair to add—in some instances lead to their degradation and destruction. The drink demon is the fatal phantom that lures thousands to their doom. Drink—drink is the crime and the curse of Irishmen in this country. It is the stigma which of all others is the most fatal to their character, the cloud that hides the brilliant lustre of their many virtues. (O'Day, 1990, p. 27)

Small-scale brawls between the immigrants and natives induced by drink were two-a-penny but these only infrequently extended into general racial affrays. Moreover, Irish crime and disorder were most disgusting to the middle classes and respectable working classes—people unlikely to respond by rioting or assaults against the aliens. On two matters there is substantial concurrence: the Irish lived in close proximity to their hosts and they shared a similar life-style, sometimes referred to as a 'culture of poverty' (Davis, 1989, pp. 112–13; Hickey, 1967, p. 105). The two groups' patterns converged more as time progressed.

Many factors animated native distaste for the newcomers. None, however, played so clear a part in igniting intra-communal violence as religion. Nearly all physical assaults and bias were directed at Catholics alone. Except by accident, Irish protestants and renegades from Romanism were not singled out as victims. Anti-Catholicism was deeply ingrained in Britain and received an immense boost in the middle decades of the nineteenth century (Norman, 1968; Arnstein, 1982). Ireland's politics and Irish immigrants fed Protestant fears but the response also was geared to the growth of the pretensions of the Catholic Church at mid-century and its capacity to enrol well-born converts during the next few decades. The Irish were the visible and actual backbone of an advancing Catholicism. Before 1801 Britain was unquestionably a Protestant nation. Incorporation of Ireland then turned the United Kingdom into a genuine multi-confessional state. That reality, together with issues raised by this opened a new political era where the quest for the civil equality of Catholics exercised politicians and public alike. Roman ambitions seemed much nearer to hand when the massive influx of Irish brought the problem to the country's doorstep. The Catholic Church on the mainland without the Irish was doomed to insignificance but with them it quickly became a potent force. Cardinal Manning in the 1880s estimated that three-quarters of England's Catholics were of Irish origin (Howard, 1953, p. 341).

Certain general conclusions about who the Irish were and what they represented can be advanced. It is clear that in the immediate post-Famine years they were not ideally positioned in Britain. As long as they retained their affiliation with Catholicism the immigrants and their offspring were differentiated from the host peoples. At the same time the newcomers were much too numerous to be invisible, but not settled anywhere in sufficient concentrations to be insulated from the hostility of the natives. Moreover, because the invaders did not bring major economic assets or skills to the adopted land, they were, and remained, dependent on the host peoples for employment, poor relief and even for physical safety. The newcomers arrived without well-practised techniques for coping with popular antagonism. In most of Ireland Catholics had only slender contact with Protestants. Their experience was limited to dealings with landlords, agents, providers of specialist services in the towns, and occasionally the state bureaucracy but not (except in Ulster) with working-class adherents of another faith. To increase the level of difficulty for the arrivals, they came without class or ethnic cohesion at home and without strong institutions of their own. Immigrants lacked traditions of political organisation and action—in both the old and now in the adopted country few possessed the ballot. They brought only the Church with them and it was scarcely able to meet the demands for religious and social comfort required by the invaders. Not all the newcomers were inclined to resort to religious solace in any event (Connolly, 1985, pp. 225–54). Although the immigrants soon began to establish formal and unofficial institutions, progress was slow in the short term and was as likely to provoke native feeling as to afford an Irish defence against physical attacks.

III

Anti-Irish and anti-Catholic riots were not unknown prior to the Famine. Many of the problems of crime and turbulence within both the host and Irish communities were prevalent earlier as well. *The Report on the State of the Irish Poor in Great Britain* in 1836 devoted extensive and unflattering attention to the impact of the immigrants. Yet the Irish presence in Britain after the Famine evoked a different response. Thompson and Foster among others have emphasised the relative harmony of Irish–native working-class relations before the 1850s (Thompson, 1968, p. 480; Foster, 1974, p. 244). Neither the greater numbers of Irish nor their poverty can account fully for the changed mood towards them by the host peoples. The chief distinction between the earlier and later periods is the escalation of religious discord in Britain. During the seventy-five years after 1846 the usual flash-point for an outburst of anti-Irish violence was a religious dispute. Rising levels of anti-Irish behaviour in the host population was intimately related to increased hostility to Catholicism. Intracommunal friction emanated from other grievances such as political developments but the combined total of all other causes did not equal the number of riots originating in confessional strife. Affrays such as at Birmingham in 1867 and at Tredegar in 1882 began from political as well as religious tensions, though both swiftly became traditional denominational battles.

In the dozen years following the Famine notable anti-Irish outbreaks took place in Cardiff, Birkenhead, Stockport, Preston, Ashton-under-Lyne, Blackburn, Wigan, London and Cheltenham. Lancashire was then, as later, the area most apt to experience racial conflict. The bulk of these incidents fell in the first half of the 1850s when religious antagonism was rekindled by the restoration of the Catholic Hierarchy in England and Wales. That event spawned what John Denvir would term an 'anti-popery mania' (Denvir, 1972, pp. 58–60). Both the public and the government went through a phase of anti-Catholicism in response to 'papal aggression'. The infamous riot at Stockport in 1852 was typical in its origin. This riot began over a Catholic religious procession. A local newspaper noted that the episode was started 'in a great measure by the taunting, insulting course adopted by the Irish, particularly in taunting the English as cowards for not preventing the procession of the Irish scholars on the Sunday before the disturbances took place' (O'Connor, 1972, p. 35). In this instance, as in many of the subsequent riots, the immigrants either provoked the trouble or responded physically to the provocations of the native community.

Following a lull in anti-Irish attacks in the second half of the 1850s, the 1860s were marred by levels of racial violence unseen earlier or subsequently. Serious riots at Ashton-under-Lyne, Oldham and Hurst Brook in 1861 initiated a period of difficulty. Further vicious incidents occurred at Oldham, Chesterfield and Stalybridge the next year. Racial hostility was at fever pitch in many northern towns. Stalybridge was reported to be 'in a chronic state of excitement . . . There have been street rows on a large scale or riots on a small scale, to be chronicled every week . . .' (Kirk, 1985, pp. 322–3). Irishmen were not passive victims. In Oldham racial tensions erupted into open confrontation when the English threatened 'to drive the Irish out of town' and the Celts responded 'boasting that they would have all Oldham to themselves'. (Lowe, 1989, p. 167).

Friction between the newcomers and natives more frequently ended in violence in the 1860s because of special factors present then. Membership in Orange Lodges rose rapidly at that time (Gallagher, 1987, pp. 27–8), Even in 1855 Oldham already had eleven Lodges (Kirk, 1985, p. 337). The strident atmosphere of the Orange Order was sure to enflame the situation. Garibaldi's visit to England in 1862 showed how combustible the state of communal relations was (Gilley, 1973, pp. 697–732). Whether the riots which accompanied his visit should be categorised as religious or racial is a moot point. There was always an Irish aspect to confessional conflict. These disorders often began when Catholic crowds attempted to disrupt pro-Garibaldi demonstrations. The agitation of the anti-Catholic lecturer, William Murphy, was another element in the explosive mood of the time. He was born a Catholic in Ireland and minced no words in his denunciation of the popish evil. This figure with his Irish background was odious to the Hibernian community. His appearances to lecture in English towns were met by Irish counter-attacks. Murphy's visits frequently sparked disorder and on occasion serious riots. The popular cry among his supporters of 'Murphy, Garibaldi and the Queen' was symptomatic of the growing alienation between the Celts and British peoples.

Conditions in Ireland added fuel to the flames of racial hatred at this moment as well. Fenianism both there and in Britain brought a sense of fear of the Irish to the host population. Between 1865 and 1868 concern about Fenianism reached a peak. In early 1867 the Fenians staged an abortive armed rebellion in

Ireland. Many Irish in Britain showed themselves sympathetic to the aims of the revolt. It found an echo on the mainland in the farcical Fenian attempt to seize arms stored in Chester Castle. In the wake of these events the temperature of feelings against the Irish ran high. In June Murphy touched off a major riot in Birmingham. Then in September the Fenian threat was affirmed by the dramatic rescue of prisoners at Manchester. In the course of that action a prison van guard was unintentionally killed. This incident set off another wave of revulsion against the immigrants. The *Nation* observed: 'we are only concerned for the hundreds of thousands of our people, who, after years of toil in the service of England, are threatened with extermination because the Government is baffled in pursuit of two brave and daring conspirators' (*Nation*, 12 October 1867). Three members of the rescue party were tried and sentenced to hang for the accidental murder of the van guard. Their fate lay heavily over the exile enclaves. Against the mounting backdrop of racial antagonism the *Nation* called upon the natural leaders of the Irish in London to assert themselves. If they came forward 'men would have little reason to dread the furious excesses of the English rabble; for their solid integrity could command peace' (*Nation*, 26 October 1867). The newspaper suggested: 'the present panic will not be altogether regretted, if it convince our people of the stern necessity of closing their ranks in the face of the peril which menace them.' Execution of the three Fenians for the Manchester killing in November drove another wedge between the alien and native peoples. Then in December—while the protests over the executions were in progress—there was a second attempt to engineer an escape of Fenian prisoners. Dynamite was planted outside the wall of the Clerkenwell House of Correction in London. Unfortunately, the device was poorly positioned and the explosion destroyed several nearby houses while also killing six civilians and injuring many others (Quinlivan and Rose, 1982, pp. 76–94). This miscalculation was an additional increment in the deterioration of intra-communal relations.

Voices in Britain sympathetic to the Irish plight now adopted a less friendly tone. A radical newspaper, the *Beehive*, expressed 'deep abhorrence' of the Clerkenwell operation (*Beehive*, 4 January 1868). A general panic resulted from the incident. Important buildings in the metropolis such as the Tower of London, St Paul's Cathedral, the Bank of England and the gasworks were believed to be the objects of probable attacks (Vincent, 1979, p. 325). It was even alleged that thousands of Irish labourers were constructing a tunnel under London in which they were placing dynamite to destroy the capital (*Beehive*, 4 January 1868). Rumours of Irish skulduggery were rampant. For a time ordinary criminal acts were attributed to Fenianism (*The Times*, 16 December 1867). To meet the presumed emergency there was an appeal for men to volunteer as special constables. Over 166,000 answered the call (*The Times*, 13 January 1868).

While the panic soon subsided, the atmosphere in many towns remained tense. In May 1868 Murphy riots gripped first Ashton under Lyme and then Oldham. It was in reaction that the *Nation* in the statement at the head of the article expressed doubt about the safety of the immigrants on the mainland. This same editorial observed: 'we do not seem to be entering upon a period of tranquillity.' During 1868 anti-Irish riots struck Rochdale, Preston, Blackburn and Manchester as well. Murphy's activities with often violent repercussions were unwelcome to civil authorities. However, he posed a genuine dilemma for many responsible people. Though deploring his impact, they were reluctant to tamper with the right of assembly (Arnstein, 1982, p. 104). Still, at one moment, the Liberal *Daily News* protested: 'it is simply intolerable that the common right of public meetings and public speaking should be abused by a professional agitator, whose stock-in-trade is rioting and disorder' (Arnstein, 1982, p. 104). By the 1870s the worst of the Murphy disturbances had passed. Murphy's own involvement in the anti-papal crusade largely ceased when he suffered debilitating injuries in an assault at Whitehaven in April 1871. He died in March of the following year (Arnstein, 1982, pp. 195–6).

Incidents of anti-Irish rioting declined after the late 1860s. There were instances in the St Patrick district of Glasgow in 1875 and at Liverpool in 1877, 1878 and 1880. These were followed by the extended clash at Tredegar in July 1882. That riot owed something to the strong feelings against the Irish as a consequence of the murders of the Chief Secretary and Under Secretary for Ireland in Phoenix Park, Dublin the previous May. However, in most respects the trouble in south Wales was a reversion to earlier sectarian battles. The episode began when the Salvationists who were active in the area successfully proselytised two local Irishmen (*The Times*, 10, 11, 12 July 1882). For the Irish the work of the Salvationists constituted aggression and they confronted the missionary group. Celtic attacks on the Salvationists invited retaliation from Welsh Protestants. What started as a minor sectarian brawl spread into a notorious racial riot. The Home Office, according to *The Times*, watched the incident carefully. However, the worry of the *Nation* that 'the effect of this outbreak . . . will be that in the neighbouring towns other anti-Irish riots will take place shortly' was proved false when the disorder failed to spread (*Nation*, 15 July 1882). Tredegar's riot was typical—a local conflict remained confined to the place where it began. Most of the subsequent attacks on Irish communities followed a similar course. There were outbursts of violence in the west of Scotland in 1883 and at Liverpool in 1886 as a response to the home rule crisis. There, though, the rioting did not begin to approximate the troubles which then afflicted Belfast.

From the mid-1880s Liverpool was the leading centre of sectarian violence. Waller (1981), Gallagher (1984; 1987) and Neal (1987) have dissected this experience. While racial hatred was ingrained in the city's history, it received a more specific outlet through the Protestant–Tory political machine which dominated municipal politics and in the activities of Pastor George Wise. The latter gave a lead to militant Protestantism after his arrival in the city in 1888. Between 1903 and 1909 Liverpool was the scene of numerous sectarian-motivated attacks and riots. The largest of these occasions was in 1909 when the city was on the edge of conflict for several months. Trouble began in May when Catholics, after obtaining official consent, attempted to hold a procession to commemorate the diamond jubilee of Holy Cross Church (Waller, 1981, pp. 237–41). Protestant crowds sought to deny Catholics the use of the streets. The violent clash ended with numerous arrests. In November Wise was imprisoned for his part in the confrontation. As in early conflicts, Catholics had some responsibility for the outrages. The *Tablet* lamented: 'during the disturbances it must be admitted that in a certain number of cases Catholics, unmindful of the teaching of their religion, were guilty of acts of aggression upon inoffensive people' (*Tablet*, 11 September 1909). There has been much emphasis on the pattern of strife in Liverpool and to a lesser extent in Lancashire. Liverpool, though, was not typical of Britain as a whole nor was the degree of sectarianism which flavoured Lancashire life present to the same extent everywhere else. Certainly sectarian feelings existed widely but the violence which characterised confessional relations there were less common in other towns. All was not completely peaceful after 1909. There were some minor anti-Irish troubles in London in November 1920 following the assassinations of British army officers in Dublin (O'Connor, 1972, p. 66). Riots, though, were never characteristic of intra-communal contacts even in the mid-Victorian years and they played a lesser part still in these relations with the passage of time. In post-1801 British history the early 1850s and 1860s stick out as a glaring anomaly. While it must be borne in mind that the catalogue of incidents cited does not pretend to completeness, neglecting, for instance, the numerous street rows, this list does constitute the significant occasions. Certainly the absence of continuous rioting is not evidence that the Irish did not experience considerable difficulty in British society. Immigrants and their children were regularly the victims of psychological and sometimes physical abuse throughout the period. Discrimination in many forms rather than rioting was the prevalent expression of racial hatred. This paucity of anti-Irish rioting may be usefully contrasted with the diet of disturbances associated with the beginnings of the Salvation Army. Between 1879 and 1891 the missionary efforts of the Army caused riots in sixty towns (Bailey, 1977, p. 234).

IV

Why were the Irish the subject of riots in the middle of the nineteenth century and then only infrequently so afterwards? What conditions made rioting a more common occurrence in certain places but not in others? The present state of research necessarily leaves many aspects of anti-Irish behaviour a matter of speculation. The problem of violence against the Irish has received relatively little attention. Generally, it has been assumed that the sudden increase in violence was a consequence of the huge influx of immigrants during the Famine era and the accompanying mid-Victorian fears of Catholicism. With a decrease in immigration, newcomers and hosts gradually reached an accommodation, a condition abetted by a Catholic Church which became less of a threat and even a respected part of the religious fabric of the nation. This explanatory frame-work has obvious and compelling ingredients. It certainly fits the chronology of riots, reveals the hosts and newcomers as adaptable peoples, and provides an understandable rationale for the persistence of higher levels of racial violence in some areas.

The traditional perspective, though satisfactory in several ways, still requires amplification. Once unleashed, ethnic or religious violence has been notori-ously resilient. Regimes can employ force to suppress racial outrages but recent

experience in Northern Ireland and eastern Europe demonstrates that a relax-
ation of government force is likely to lead to a recrudescence of the virus. In any
case there is some doubt that numbers alone were decisive in animating racial
violence. Neville Kirk has placed emphasis on the economic, social and cultural
characteristics of the Irish rather than their quantity as the means of understanding the host peoples' reaction (Kirk, 1985, p. 325). Tom Gallagher has
contrasted the differing patterns of violence between Liverpool and Glasgow,
cities with nearly equivalent Irish proportions of their respective populations.
He has suggested that the conditions of the receiving community provide the
determinant factor in relations between natives and aliens (Gallagher, 1987, p.
33). Neither internal (Irish) nor external (British) explanations are mutually
exclusive; both help amplify the standard picture. The perspectives of Kirk and
Gallagher allow the question of anti-Irish violence to be examined in fresh
ways.

At first sight it is not apparent that either the Irish or the host communities
changed dramatically over time. The years around 1870 did not mark a
turning-point. As has been noted, the Irish presence in Britain was substantial
before 1846 and immigration remained a salient feature on the mainland after
1870. The Irish-born percentage of the whole population declined but was
augmented by subsequent generations born in Britain. Objections to the
invaders had always revolved around the supposition that 'they live in the midst
of our civilisation without partaking of its spirit . . . If they only blended
harmoniously with the population amongst whom they are located, no-one
would have any right to complain of their presence in England. But they will not
blend at all' (Kirk, 1985, p. 320). An impressive literature has drawn attention
to the separateness of the Irish into the 1920s and their difficulties with regard
to integration into the host society (Ó Tuathaigh, 1981, pp. 149–74; Daunton,
1977, p. 145; McLean, 1983, p. 185). It might have been anticipated that a
prolonged existence of ethnic enclaves and life-style would exacerbate rather,
than ease tensions. Evidence from other countries points towards that outcome.
As has been seen, the British-born Irish retained a foul reputation, being, for
example, overrepresented among prison inmates.

Anti-Catholicism retained its hold on the popular mind and it definitely did
not begin to fade round 1870. The Irish Church controversy in the late 1860s,
the Vatican Council in 1870, attempts to enforce inspection of the nunneries,
and Gladstone's writings on the papacy in the middle of the 1870s, all were
reminders that suspicion of Rome was as alive and well in Britain as it was in
Germany. Indeed, Catholicism's threat to Protestant values was never far from
the minds of Nonconformists. The denominational education issue, routinely
fought out in school board elections, showed that keen vigilance of Catholic
ambitions was vital. When the Education Act of 1902 provided rate support for
denominational schools, religious animosity received a fillip. This was one of
the main issues which induced the Liberal revival behind that potent
Nonconformist cry, 'Rome on the Rates'.

It does not seem that the economy offered much grounds for a softening of
racial conflict. The Famine Irish came to Britain at the beginning of an era of
industrial expansion. Gallagher has suggested that the reaction to them in
Glasgow was less hostile precisely because their impact on the economy there

was not so traumatic as in Liverpool (Gallagher, 1987, p. 33). However, the decline in anti-Irish rioting came during a long time-span when agricultural employment contracted and industrial expansion slowed. Underemployment and unemployment were chronic in the later Victorian years. Emigration from Britain rose and the continuing stream of Irish into the mainland might be viewed as an even greater threat to a native people who found themselves increasingly forced to go overseas.

Finally, but by no means least in importance, politics stirred up rather than moderated anti-Irish feeling. After 1867 Ireland's grievances were at the centre of political discussion until the close of 1921. Its demands were advocated by a militant nationalist movement. The years after 1912 were exceptionally trouble-some in Ireland. In 1868 the *Nation* had projected that the exiles would be in the front line of the struggle for national rights, that this must place them in extreme danger of British retaliation (*Nation*, 6 June 1868). Leaders of the nationalist cause routinely tried to enlist the aid of the exiles in their movement. The Irish question and the exiles' presence in Britain played a considerable part in Lancashire politics and influenced national party calculations as well (Waller, 1981; Kirk, 1985, pp. 337–41; McCaffrey, 1970, pp. 30–6). Ireland's politics contained a good measure of violence which might have been transported into the exiles communal contacts with the host society. As it happened, though, excepting the Fenian period, anti-Irish violence coincided with an interlude of lower levels of visible politics in Ireland. One observation merits attention. Kirk has pointed out that ethnic hostility in Lancashire was fostered by capital operating through the Tory Party as a means of dividing and controlling the working class (Kirk, 1985, pp. 137–41). This argument has obvious ideological imperatives but it does broadly conform to the realities of political alignment in Lancashire and most assuredly to Liverpool. It is worth enquiring whether the absence or weakening of Conservative racism elsewhere contributed to the lessening of ethnic violence.

In sum we are left with something of a puzzle. There were no clear reasons for the decline in violence and some conditions were present after 1870 which might have added fodder to ethnic hatred. As L.P. Curtis has shown, the works of cartoonists revealed the depths of anti-Hibernian sentiment (Curtis, 1968, 1971). Neither the central government, local authorities nor responsible politi-cians encouraged or countenanced disorder. However, they were not always in a position to thwart it in the initial phase as the case of the Salvation Army and the troubled history of Liverpool illustrate.

What seems the most probable explanation of low rates of violence is that the Irish did not present a steady target for racial vengeance on the ground that some exiles did provoke trouble but the vast majority of Irish sought to avoid brutal confrontations. When circumstances demanded, the ordinary immigrant was quick to assert his or her loyalty and to condemn atrocities. In 1868 more than 22,000 Irish in London sent an address to the Queen which condemned the Clerkenwell massacre and also affirmed their own loyalty to the Crown. Other meetings made similar declarations (O'Day, Hartigan and Quinault, 1986, p. 55). In the 1880s the exiles steered clear of the Irish–American bombing campaign which damaged several public buildings in London (Short, 1979). Then later during the troubled times of 1920–2 the Hibernian community distanced itself from the excesses taking place in Ireland (*Catholic Herald*, 8 April 1922). Sympathy for national aspirations usually was tempered by an absence of support for acts of violence.

Naturally the instincts of the ordinary immigrant were not a matter of chance. Lay and clerical spokesmen always urged them to eschew confrontation with the host community. When he visited Glasgow in 1871 to rally the immigrants behind the home rule movement, Isaac Butt was at pains to warn his audience there: 'You should aim at the well-being of Glasgow, which is the city of your adoption; and in respect of the allegiance you owe it, I implore you, to let no angry feelings on your part be excited towards your English brethren' (*Nation*, 18 November 1871). Co-operation with the wider community took many forms. Many Irish began to support and even join local political and social organisations. In 1876 an important figure in Glasgow stated: 'I often think I might serve the cause of Ireland as much in the ranks of the British reformers as in those of Home Rule and I would like to see a fraternisation of the English and Irish Democracy that would enable a man to belong to both organisations (*Nation*, 6 January 1877). By the next year the Executive of the Home Rule Confederation of Great Britain chided the Irish for not coming forward to aid the national movement. It complained: 'many of the Liberal workingmen clubs, &c., find their chief and more intelligent supporters amongst the Irish' (*Nation*, 14 September 1878). After Gladstone took up home rule in 1886 the Irish tended to become more involved in Liberal groups. The close contact was a subject of a debate within the nationalist organisation (Brady, 1983, p. 139). Irish participation in trade unions was a feature of the later years of Victoria's reign as well. In the early twentieth century there was much talk about the decline in Irish unity. One newspaper which had an unfriendly view of nationalist politics distinguished between the behaviour of those 'long settled' in Scotland who were in all important ways integrated into the community and the comparatively recent arrivals (*The Scotsman*, 6 January 1906).

Clerics, though alert to maintaining confessional isolation in religious affairs, worked to soften intra-communal relations. In 1868 many gave a lead to the condemnation of the Clerkenwell incident (Neal, 1990, p. 161). The Hierarchy consistently refused to allow the Church to become a vehicle of Irish nationalist politics or for those groups to hold meetings on ecclesiastical property. This attitude was in marked contrast to the role of the Church in Ireland. Most immigrants were labourers and supported the Liberal and later the Labour Party in national politics. From the 1870s, though, the clerical interest was usually aligned with the Conservatives on education. In the mid-1880s some prominent ecclesiastics flirted with the idea of using the Irish Party as the basis of a confessional parliamentary group. That idea attracted only limited support and the Catholic interest continued to press its case through all of the existing parties (Green, 1975, p. 22). In October 1885 the *Tablet* added its influence to those who wished to work within existing groups when it pointed out:

> even if the congregation be practically all of Irish nationality, we cannot altogether leave out of account his relations with the surrounding English population, or help asking whether it is well that he should build up another barrier of separateness between him and those whom he must hope to convert. (*Tablet*, 31 October 1885)

In 1888 another Catholic periodical argued against always throwing support to the Liberals and advocated acting in differing ways according to the situation. It held:

> our contention is that in Parliamentary elections; we should go for Home Rule and support Home Rulers; in School Board elections we should support the friends of our schools and of all voluntary schools; for Boards of Guardians we should vote for those who will do justice to our Catholic poor; and for Town Councils we should, if no vital issue is at stake, go for a Home Ruler; but if there is any Catholic interest to which our Home Ruler friend is opposed then we should oppose him. This tying ourselves to vote for Liberals on all occasions is sheer madness and folly. It would, if carried out, ruin every Catholic and Irish interest in the country. (*Catholic Herald*, 9 November 1888)

By declining to form a specifically confessional political party, and, working through all British parties when appropriate, the Church helped prevent a polarisation in British society which would foster the temptation to single out the Irish as targets.

Moreover, the tendency for the Irish to disappear into British society reduced their exposure to riots and other physical expressions of ethnic hate. Much of the literature has neglected the function of Irish integration and treated them as a static element. In fact, the most vibrant feature of the Irish presence in Britain is the regular act of self-destruction which so many chose to commit through voluntary integration and assimilation. The literature gives emphasis to those Irish who retained their ethnicity rather than to people who drifted away. Heinrick in 1872 noted that his compatriots were on the verge of ethnic extinction (O'Day, 1990, pp. 128–9). Because of a continuous wave of immigration, he overestimated the pace of the process but the pattern was already apparent a generation after the Famine. Limp ethnic political organisation after 1870 was, in part, a consequence of Irish refusal to involve themselves in narrowly nationalist organisations (O'Day, 1989, pp. 183–211).

All in all, the Irish arrived and settled on the mainland in a way poorly calculated to defend either their ethnic survival or to ward off attacks from the native peoples. However, the state imposed severe restraints on racial violence, though it allowed nearly unrestricted discrimination against the immigrants and their children. Very quickly the Irish developed an appropriate strategy for dealing with the threat which did exist. No doubt the Irish approach was more the product of chance than careful design but it was none the less effective for that. Lancashire proved something of an exception. Its history stands as a vivid illustration that the potential for racial violence was real. Elsewhere, and even at most times in Lancashire as well, discrimination was a far better means of venting native hostility on the newcomers.

Note

1. Initial research for this chapter was undertaken as part of the European Science Foundation project, 'Governments and Non-Dominant Ethnic Groups in Europe,

1850–1940'. I wish to thank colleagues in the project for helpful advice and the ESF for assistance. I am indebted especially to the efforts of Geneviève Schauinger and Christoph Mühlberg at Strasbourg and also to Roger Swift.

References

Newspapers and periodicals

The Beehive
The Catholic Herald
The Nation
The Scotsman
The Tablet
The Times

Official Reports

Secondary materials

Alexander, Y. and O'Day, A (eds), 1984, *Terrorism in Ireland*, London, Croom Helm.
Alexander, Y. and O'Day, A. (eds), 1986, *Ireland's Terrorist Dilema*, Dordrecht/Boston/Lancaster, Martinus Nijhoff Publishers.
Arnstein, W.L., 1982 *Protestant versus Catholic in Mid-Victorian England*, Columbia, Mo, University of Missouri Press.
Bailey, V., 1977, 'Salvation Army Riots, the "Skeleton Army" and Legal Authority in the Provincial Town', in A.P. Donagrodzki (ed.): 231–53.
Boyce, D.G., 1991, *Nineteenth-Century Ireland*, Dublin, Gill & Macmillan.
Brady, L.W., 1983, *T.P. O'Connor and the Liverpool Irish*, London, Royal Historical Society.
Connolly, G., 1985, 'Irish and Catholic: Myth or Reality? Another Sort of Irish and the Renewal of the Clerical Profession among Catholics in England, 1791–1918', in R. Swift and S. Gilley (eds): 225–54.
Curtis, L.P., Jr, 1968, *Anglo-Saxons and Celts*, Bridgeport, Conn.; Conference on British Studies.
Curtis, L.P.; Jr, 1971, *Apes and Angels*, Newton Abbott, David & Charles.
Daunton, M., 1977, *Coal Metropolis*, Leicester, Leicester University Press.
Davis, G., 1989, 'Little Irelands', in R. Swift and S. Gilley (eds): 104–33.
Denvir, J, 1892, *The Irish in Britain*, London, Trübner & Co.
Denvir, J, 1972, *The Life Story of an Old Rebel*, Shannon, Irish University Press.
Donagrodzki, A.P. (ed.), 1977, *Social Control in Nineteenth Century Britain*, London, Croom Helm.
Engels, F., 1969, *The Condition of the Working-Class in England*, London, Penguin.
Engman, M, Carter, F.W., Hepburn A.C. and Pooley, C.G, (eds), 1992, *Ethnic Identity in Urban Europe*, Aldershot, Dartmouth.
Fitzpatrick, D., 1984, *Irish Emigration, 1801–1921*, Dublin, Irish Economic and Social History Society.
Fitzpatrick, D., 1989a, 'A Curious Middle Place: The Irish in Britain, 1871–1921', in R. Swift and S. Gilley (eds): 10–59.
Fitzpatrick, D., 1989b, 'A Peculiar Tramping People: The Irish in Britain, 1801–70', in W.E. Vaughan (ed.), vol. V.

Foster, J., 1974, *Class Struggle and the Industrial Revolution*, London, Weidenfeld & Nicolson.

Gallagher, T., 1984, 'A Tale of Two Cities: Communal Strife in Glasgow and Liverpool Before 1914', in Y. Alexander and A. O'Day (eds).

Gallagher, T., 1987, *Glasgow: The Uneasy Peace*, Manchester, Manchester University Press.

Gilley, S., 1973, 'The Garibaldi Riots of 1862', *Historical Journal*, 16: 697–732.

Greene, T.R., 1975, 'The English Catholic Press and the Home Rule Bill, 1885–86', *Eire-Ireland*, X (Spring): 18–37.

Herson, J., 1989, 'Irish Migration and Settlement in Victorian England: A Small-Town Perspective', in R. Swift and S. Gilley (eds): 84–103.

Hickey, J., 1967, *Urban Catholics*, London, Chapman & Oates.

Holmes, C., 1988, *John Bull's Island*, London, Macmillan.

Holmes, C., 1991, *A Tolerant Country?* London, Faber & Faber.

Howard, C.M.D., 1953, 'Joseph Chamberlain, Parnell and the Irish "Control Board" Scheme 1884–5', *Irish Historial Studies*, 324–61.

Hunt, E.H., 1973, *Regional Wage Variations in Britain, 1850–1914*, Oxford, Oxford University Press.

Inglis, K.S., 1963, *Churches and the Working Classes in Victorian England*, London, Routledge & Kegan Paul.

Jackson, J.A., 1963, *The Irish in Britain*, London, Routledge & Kegan Paul.

Kirk, N., 1985, *The Growth of Working Class Reformism in Mid-Victorian England*, Urbana/Chicago, University of Illinois Press.

Large, D., 1985, 'The Irish in Bristol in 1851: A Census Enumeration', in R. Swift and S. Gilley (eds): 37–58.

Lees, L.H., 1979, *Exiles of Erin*, Manchester, Manchester University Press.

Lowe, W.J., 1989, *The Irish in Mid-Victorian Lancashire*, New York, Peter Lang.

McCaffrey, J.F., 1970, 'The Irish Vote in Glasgow in the Later Nineteenth Century', *Innes Review*, 21: 30–6.

McLean, I., 1983, *The Legend of Red Clydeside*, Edinburgh, John Donald.

Neal, F., 1987, *Sectarian Violence*, Manchester, Manchester University Press.

Neal, F., 1990, 'A Criminal Profile of the Liverpool Irish', *Transactions of the Historic Society of Lancashire and Cheshire*, 140: 161–99.

Norman, E.R., 1968, *Anti-Catholicism in Victorian England*, London, Allen & Unwin.

O'Connor, K., 1972, *The Irish in Britain*, London, Sidgwick & Jackson.

O'Day, A., 1977, *The English Face of Irish Nationalism*, Dublin, Gill & Macmillan.

O'Day, A., 1985, 'Irish Influence on Parliamentary Elections in London, 1885–1914: A Simple Test', in R. Swift and S. Gilley (eds): 98–105.

O'Day, A. with Hartigan, M. and Quinault, R., 1986, 'Irish Terrorism in Britain: A Comparison Between the Activities of the Fenians in the 1860s and those of Republican Groups since 1972', in Y. Alexander and A. O'Day (eds): 49–60.

O'Day, A., 1989, 'The Political Organization of the Irish in Britain, 1867–90', in R. Swift and S. Gilley (eds): 183–211.

O'Day, A. (ed.), 1990, *A Survey of the Irish in England, 1872*, London, The Hambledon Press.

Ó Tuathaigh, M.A.G., 1981, 'The Irish in Nineteenth-Century Britain: Problems of Integration', *Transactions of the Royal Historical Society*, 5th Series, 31: 149–74.

Pooley, C.G., 1992, 'The Irish in Liverpool circa 1850–1940', in M. Engman, F.W. Carter, A.C. Hepburn and C.E. Pooley (eds), pp. 71–97.

Pooley, C.G., 1977, 'The Residential Segregation of Migrant Communities in Mid-Victorian Liverpool', *Transactions of the Institute of British Geographers*, II, (3): 364–83.

Quinlivan, P. and Rose, P., 1982, *The Fenians in England 1865–1872*, London, John Calder.

Short, K.R.M., 1979, *The Dynamite War*, Dublin, Gill & Macmillan.

Swift, R. and Gilley, S. (eds), 1985, *The Irish in the Victorian City*, London, Croom Helm.

Swift, R., and Gilley, S. (eds), 1989, *The Irish in Britain 1815–1939*, London, Pinter Publishers.

Thompson, E.P., 1968, *The Making of the English Working Class*, Harmondsworth, Penguin.

Vaughan, W.E. (ed.), 1989, *A New History of Ireland*, Oxford, Clarendon Press.

Vincent, J.R. (ed.), 1979, *The Political Journals of Lord Stanley*, Sussex, Harvester Press.

Walker, R.B., 1968, 'Religious Changes in Liverpool in the Nineteenth Century', *Journal of Ecclesiastical History*, 19: 195–211.

Waller, P., 1981, *Democracy and Sectarianism*, Liverpool, University of Liverpool Press.

Welbourne, E., 1923, *The Miners' Union of Northumberland and Durham*, Cambridge, Cambridge University Press.

Werley, J.M., 1973, 'The Irish in Manchester, 1832–49', *Irish Historical Studies*, 18: 345–58.

Williamson, J.G., 1986, 'The Impact of the Irish on British Labour Markets during the Industrial Revolution', *Journal of Economic History*, 46 (September): 693–721.

3

William Murphy, the Orange Order and communal violence: the Irish in West Cumberland, 1871-84[1]

Donald M. MacRaild

William Murphy and anti-Catholicism

The repercussions on British society of massive Irish migration, particularly after the Great Famine, were far-reaching. However, the greatest factor in fostering negative attitudes towards the Irish among the indigenous population was religion, an issue with deep historical roots. As one author attests, 'Since the days of Elizabeth most English had considered it part of their patriotic obligation to guard against unrelenting "Papist" conspiracy' (Richter, 1981, p.19). The arrival of thousands of Irish, and the fresh impetus that they gave to Catholicism in Britain, served to exacerbate divisions, evoking anti-papist attitudes and actions. Such prejudice was never far below the surface in a country where institutions bore the impress of the Protestant Ascendancy and a dominant culture antagonistic towards Catholicism. 'Church and State Toryism' presented the Irish as alien and unpatriotic, ideas perpetuated and compounded by a vast body of anti-Catholic literature (Norman, 1968, p. 13). Negative views of Catholicism were held by most sections of Victorian society, but the most spectacular manifestations of anti-Irish and anti-Catholic activity in Victorian society were enacted by the working class in urban Britain, gathering momentum in the wake of the mass Irish immigration, 1846–52, and the restoration of the papal hierarchy in England and Wales in 1850. This violent anti-Catholic trend continued for over twenty years, during which time working–class life was punctuated with outbursts of aggression and destruction and, as a result, working-class Toryism, Orangeism and anti-Catholicism, set within the wider context of Irish immigration, have provided historians with fruitful topics for consideration (Kirk, 1985, pp. 310–49; Gallagher, 1987; Neal, 1988; 1990–1), which, in turn, served to increase our knowledge and understanding of communal relations in Victorian Britain.

In the generation after the Great Famine, a number of Protestant lecturers played upon working-class fears of the Irish and Fenianism as well as the innate

British dislike of Catholicism. The most famous of these was the Irishman William Murphy, described by one writer as 'a flaming fox sent . . . among the corn' (Hanham, 1978, p. 304). Murphy was born and baptised a Catholic, in Castletown-Conyers, Co. Limerick, in 1834 (Arnstein, 1975, p. 52). His father converted secretly to Protestantism and when this was discovered the family fled to Co. Mayo. Murphy's father became a Protestant lecturer, in this providing an example to his son. The elder Murphy, like his son after him, was a colourful figure who continually aroused animosity at his meetings. In later life Murphy maintained that his father was stoned to death by an angry mob at one of his lectures (Richter, 1981, p. 35). The young William became a scripture reader, married in 1859 and, in the wake of his father's death, sailed for Liverpool in 1862. From there he walked to London, on arrival offering his services as an evangelist. The first recorded incident of rioting breaking out after one of Murphy's sermons, however, occurred four years later at Plymouth in 1866 (Quinlivan and Rose, 1982, p. 34).

Obviously a man of deep religious commitment, Murphy began his no-Popery lecturing career with the Protestant Evangelical Mission and Electoral Union (PEMEU) which aimed to uphold Protestantism by a combination of lectures, sermons, public meetings and the publishing of various tracts and pamphlets. Sales of several million copies of the latter were claimed by 1869 (Arnstein, 1975 p. 53). Murphy epitomised this type of religious extremism and as his career progressed he probably outgrew the organisation that gave him his first platform. He did, however, carry to all his meetings copies of PEMEU literature, such as the infamous *Confessional Unmasked*, condemned by two English courts as obscene (Richter, 1981, p. 36). Also available at these assemblies was *Maria Monk*, the most infamous of all anti-Catholic publications.

Murphy's role in the history of Irish immigration was significant for the part he played in undermining social cohesion and in creating new tensions. His efforts to undermine Catholicism were more important than his promotion of Protestantism because his brand of politics and theology was unacceptable to the more moderate minds among his co-religionists. Murphy's lectures, by highlighting what he perceived as flaws in Catholic liturgy and doctrine— matters such as the confessional—helped to delineate the cultural and political boundaries of the towns which he visited.

Murphy offered his predominantly working-class audiences various lectures that included topics ranging from politics and religion to temperance and history. These provided his public, in an era before mass communication, with a heady mixture of rhetoric and provocation. To his Protestant admirers Murphy was a public hero, a messenger of truth, defender of the faith and an accomplished performer. For the Catholic population, especially the Irish, Murphy was a rabble-rouser, a liar and an apostate. Where Murphy spoke, these opposites met and, not surprisingly, trouble broke out.

Murphy owes his place in history not merely to content, nature and delivery of his lectures, nor to his entertainment value and deliberate courting of controversy. The late 1860s were an opportune time for a man like Murphy. Fenianism was a powerful force, both in fact and in popular demonology. It excited almost hysterical fear and near-pathological hatred of the Irish in

Britain, among whom, it was popularly believed, Fenian activists were given encouragement and succour. This political and religious climate enabled Murphyism to become a populist anti-Catholic movement. It encapsulated strains of thought already present in Britain's deeply anti-Catholic culture. As well as representing widespread working-class Protestant religious ideals, then, 'Murphyism reflected the reaction to Fenianism at the grass roots level' (Quinlivan and Rose, 1982, p. 33). Murphy did not need Fenianism to attract an audience, but he was certainly aided in his efforts to denounce Popery by the awakening fears of a whole stratum of society—working-class Protestants— angered by Irish terrorism. Murphy's controversial career made him a living legend, a man, in the words of the *Carlisle Journal* of 25 April 1871, 'well-known throughout the country as an opponent of the doctrines of the Roman Catholic Church',

The tours of Murphy and his followers highlighted and to some extent isolated Irish Catholics. The meetings, indeed, have been described as 'reminiscent of Mosley's marches through London's East End' (Quinlivan and Rose, 1982, p. 33). After one Murphy riot in Ashton-under-Lyne, T.M. Healy visited the ruins of many Irish houses, declaring later, in his memoirs, that 'On a small scale they resembled the devastated regions of France in 1918' (Healy, 1928, p. 23). Murphy's oratory, then, served to strengthen the prejudices of the English working class and, to a degree, of Protestants generally. Murphy's particular influence was to bring an impressive coherence to hitherto inarticulate anti-Irish working-class sentiment. He put Roman Catholicism under some pressure in the industrial heartlands of the Midlands (Swift, 1984, pp. 94–104) and Lancashire (Lowe, 1990, pp. 151–73), exciting audiences and inciting violence wherever he appeared. Extreme as Murphy's outpourings were, they did represent the embodiment of what many Englishmen had been brought up to believe of Catholicism. He lectured with confidence and aplomb, and his powerful demagogic oratory provided the almost tribal mentality of the anti-Irish working class with a unifying focus and figure-head.

Murphy's meetings gave form and shape to the popular Victorian stereotype of the aggressive 'Paddy'. He so incensed groups of Irish immigrants that some did react violently. In 1866, for example, Murphy was attacked by 150 Plymouth Irish, some armed with shillelaghs and from whom he was only saved by a band of marines (Quinlivan and Rose, 1982, p. 37). Murphy believed, fundamentally, that Roman Catholicism was evil, but the Irish were outraged by what they regarded as his blasphemy. The Murphy Riots that followed in his wake caused extensive harm to property, people and to communal relations in the various towns that his entourage visited. His tours of the Midlands and south-east Lancashire, between 1868 and 1871, sparked off the most serious religious disorder of the whole Victorian period and 'a whirlwind of destruction was left in his wake' (Gallagher, 1987, p. 26). It is significant that the authorities usually blamed Murphy for the trouble that surrounded him, and he was regarded as a menace to society by local police and magistrates. That Murphy was, nevertheless, so seldom prevented from speaking does 'serve as a reminder of the intense Victorian commitment both to freedom of speech and the demands of public order' (Richter, 1981, p. 24). He certainly highlighted the particular difficulty of protecting these two principles.

Murphy's behaviour leaves no doubt that he believed passionately in what he preached, for he thought nothing of risking life and limb to get his message across. His language captivated the Orange-orientated mass of his supporters. He appealed to the Home Office on occasion, and to local authorities regularly, for personal protection but when such assistance was not forthcoming he continued his provocative rounds of Britain's industrial heartlands regardless.

The purpose of this essay, then, is to examine William Murphy's fatal visit to Whitehaven in 1871 and his impact upon communal relations in that area. It seeks also to consider the wider influence of Murphyism upon Protestant opinion and the rebirth of the local Orange Order. The discussion that follows is intended to add to the understanding of working-class anti-Catholicism in Victorian Britain. It also considers the relationship between the English host population and Irish migrant communities, and the violence that was habitual between the English and Irish.

The 'Flaming Fox' comes to Whitehaven.[2]

During the nineteenth century Whitehaven was an old and declining colonial port which had long-established connections with the Irish trade. As a consequence, Irish had settled there for several centuries before the period of mass immigration. During the 1850s, with the development of a local railway network, iron-ore mining colonies like Cleator Moor, which had been growing fitfully since the turn of the century, developed more rapidly (Marshall, 1978, 163–75). The Irish were attracted to this rapidly expanding town and, though its population never rose much above 10,000, a large minority of up to 36 per cent (1871) were Irish, and most were Catholic. It was the development of haematite iron-ore mining in West Cumberland and shipping links with Whitehaven that encouraged the Irish influx, as well as the proximity of the area to, and its connections with, the North East and Scotland. Consequently, Whitehaven harboured a sizeable Ulster Protestant population in addition to numerous Irish Catholics. Furthermore, as a result of these economic and cultural factors, the town witnessed moderate sectarian division throughout the nineteenth century which was similar to, but in no way as extreme as that which habitually spilled out in the Lanarkshire mining districts of Scotland (Campbell, 1979, pp. 178–204). Nor was there the same longevity, depth and resolve to Orange and Green rivalry as there was in Liverpool where, in addition to a massive Irish population, there existed sectarian competition for jobs, fostered by weak unionisation, and which polarised politics in the city (Swift, 1989, p. 169).

The predominance of Irish on Cleator Moor, and the drunken rowdiness that went on there, served to encourage the animosity of the already hostile English population in Whitehaven, and seemed to confirm stereotyped opinions of Irish Catholics. Cleator Moor Irishmen were regularly summoned before the Whitehaven magistrates, on various charges of drunkenness and disorder. In fact, their drunkenness is only one aspect of their lives which suggests they were cast in the mould of a navvying tradition (Coleman, 1986: Sullivan, 1983). The

Cleator Irish were loyal to themselves, not to a place, and their unity and kinship, whilst outwardly defiant, was nevertheless impressive. The press, however, held a more simplistic and negative view of the Cleator iron-ore colony and its reports, as was common in the Victorian period, echoed local prejudices and often derided the Irish inhabitants of Cleator. What is more, it was not only the Tory press that attacked the Irish; even liberal papers like the *Preston Guardian* regularly carried Irish jokes (Lowe, 1990, p. 148). Despite local concerns about the primitive nature of life on the Moor, negligible efforts were made by local employers to raise communal facilities above the most basic. Moreover, the town had only one policeman in 1870 (Barber, 1976, p. 13). It is a measure of employer apathy, need for self-help and Irish communality that the Cleator Moor Co-operative movement thrived. The town's first public library was, nevertheless, not erected until 1906 (Marshall, 1978, p. 171). Life on the Moor was hard, conditions were basic, and the Irish Catholic community isolated in what was in any case a remote area. Whitehaven was bigger and was better provided with basic amenities, but the populace dwelt in old and overcrowded accommodation. It was to this area that William Murphy came in 1871.

Murphy's first lecture in Whitehaven was planned for 19 April. Posters and placards announced a series of sessions to discuss '. . . the Sacraments of Rome, the Confessional and similar topics' (*Carlisle Journal*, 25 April 1871). The Whitehaven authorities claimed to have done all they could to prevent the visit. They requested Murphy himself to cancel his sojourn and asked the officials of the Oddfellows' Hall not to allow its use (ibid.). The Oddfellows, however, refused to comply and Murphy duly came. His first meeting proved to be a standard evening's work for the lecturer. He received a typically boisterous reception as the audience prepared to hear his views on the Seven Sacraments of Rome. Murphy began his speech by trying to placate the Catholics in the audience, asserting that 'it isn't against the person . . . that I am going to speak; it is against the system, because I believe it to be dishonouring God, and ruinous to the souls of men' (*Cumberland Paquet*, 25 April 1871). Murphy then challenged any Catholic to join him on the stage and argue the papist case 'not by brickbats and bludgeons' but by 'fair argument'. A militiaman answered this call and leapt up on to the stage at which point proceedings began to degener-ate. Murphy was reported by the *Cumberland Paquet* (25 April 1871) as at one juncture saying that 'unless all Roman Catholic priests, monks, popes and cardinals got married, they could never be saved', which was not as strong as the language he was known to have employed at previous gatherings.[3] Nevertheless, the Murphyite Orange section of the crowd cheered his remarks tumultuously and the militiaman retorted, 'I shall polish him off for that' (*Cumberland Paquet*, 25 April 1871). The militiaman, however, left the stage to cries of 'Put him out!'; the crowd hissed and jeered, and one of their number shouted 'Go on, Murphy lad, open yer mouth!' Murphy, though, managed only a cry of 'Englishmen' before 'he was forced to stop by the hooting of a body of Irish miners; and feeling that bodily harm might be done him, his supporters escorted him out of the hall' (*Nation*, 29 April 1871). The fears entertained by Murphy's coterie were well founded: during his retreat he was mobbed. At this, his supporters, hearing cries of 'they're killing Murphy!', rallied and a general, though short-lived, disturbance ensued, while Murphy and his bodyguard took refuge in the hall-keeper's house. The *Carlisle Journal*, 25 April 1871, maintained that it was several hours before the streets of Whitehaven were quiet again.

Undaunted by Wednesday's events, Murphy went ahead with plans for a second performance on the following evening, Thursday, 20 April 1871. This time he was met with an organised and altogether more sinister attack, which illustrated the strength of the local Irish populace, as well as their fierce independence and their unwillingness to tolerate Murphy's agitation. A body of Irish miners, who had arrived by train from Cleator Moor, marched with military precision to the Oddfellows' Hall in search of Murphy. Press estimates vary considerably, but it seems that their number was somewhere between two and four hundred.[4] The mob happened upon Murphy in an ante-room, preparing for the evening's proceedings. There ensued a rush, in which he was swamped. At Whitehaven Petty Sessions, some time later, he gave a brief account of the beating he took:

> I was knocked down and trampled on, and in consequence of several parties also being knocked down I was fortunately able to get into the street [from the hall]. When I got there, some of the men who came out of the hall set upon me again. I managed to get into the building adjoining the hall, and was again knocked down, and became insensible. I made two attempts to get into the building, but was set upon most savagely each time.[5]

While in the hall the mob had tried to throw him over the banister, but having failed in this task they threw him down the stairs. The attack was brief but vicious and Murphy incurred serious injury before the policeman in charge, Insp. Little, and his men could mount a rescue. According to the *Carlisle Journal*, 25 April 1871, projectiles and weapons were later found at the scene, including 'six large stones, a poker, and a thick stick which had been broken over the unfortunate man'. The police, heavily outnumbered, made no effort to thwart the departure of Murphy's assailants and the *Whitehaven Herald* (25 April 1871) reported:

> Having done their ill work . . . the Cleator Moor band lingered not, but at once marched up Lowther-street homewards, followed as far as the castle gate by a crowd of Whitehaven, but molested by none. They went by Corkickle, Harrington and Inkermann Terraces, &c., coolly smoking their pipes, and indulging occasionally in a triumphant hurrah and waving their hats.

The members of the mob were treated to an approving reception when they arrived back in Cleator but, the *Carlisle Journal* (25 April 1871) asserted, 'in order to escape the consequences of their conduct', many eschewed the celebrations, preferring to pack their belongings and flee the town.

For weeks after the assault feelings in the two towns continued to run high and, in an effort to deter further trouble, a detachment of militiamen was deployed in Whitehaven. Even the presence of the troops and a strong body of police, however, could not prevent all incidents which flowed from Murphy's visit. In the weeks which followed, at least two of the town's tradesmen suffered 'threatening demonstrations' at the hands of 'the more violent of the Roman Catholic element' from Cleator Moor. The Irish Catholics believed that these tradesmen shared some responsibility for bringing Murphy to the town. In an attempt to refute this, the *Whitehaven Herald* (29 April 1871) said, one of the men concerned, Henry Fitzpatrick, offered a £20 reward to anyone who could prove that he 'had or has any connection with Mr Murphy whatever'.

Not surprisingly, the police displayed particular caution in their attempts to apprehend the culprits. The authorities probably wished to return the town to normal conditions as quickly as possible, and had every reason for a cautious approach, since the slightest miscalculation could have caused an already simmering cauldron to boil over. In addition, Insp. Little had to wait for advice and instruction from the police chief in Carlisle.[6] Within a week of Murphy's visit, however, dozens of people had already been questioned and four arrested. The press was scathing about two iron-ore miners among those detained, the brothers Patrick and Dennis Doyle, 'with whom' it was said 'the police are well acquainted'.[7] Dennis Doyle had been arrested on 26 April 1871 at the local races, and was found to be carrying a revolver. Less than a week later a further seven men were taken into custody. There was a danger that Murphy's followers would seek to exact revenge upon these men. In Whitehaven a large crowd gathered to catch a glimpse of the detainees as they were brought to the local police station but, claimed the *Carlisle Journal* (28 April 1871), a strong police and militia presence kept the crowd in check.

The assault upon Murphy had left him gravely ill. He was confined to his bed and constantly watched over by a doctor, his wife and the police while, according to the *Carlisle Journal* (12 May 1871), his supporters maintained a vigil outside his lodgings, occasionally singing hymns. After a short period of recuperation, however, Murphy was able to attend the magistrates for the hearings against his assailants. Even in court Murphy, his head bandaged, could not pass up the opportunity to espouse his religious beliefs. An objection by the defence was overruled, and the anti-papist lecturer discoursed at length about the illegality of 'nunneries and convents'. In between this outburst, and divulging that his favourite subject for lecture was 'The Confessional Unmasked', Murphy identified Patrick Doyle as the man who first struck him. Doyle, his brother Dennis, and five other men were committed to the Cumberland Assizes at Carlisle;[8] the other four were released. The committed men were taken to Carlisle by train, each handcuffed and wearing foot irons. According to one report, which appeared in the *Whitehaven Herald* (13 May 1871), the crowd that congregated at the station contained a number of friends of the accused. The proceedings passed off without incident, although 'Great numbers of a low class of Irish followed [the omnibuses] and threatening epithets were freely used, but no serious attempt was made to rescue the prisoners' (*Barrow Times*, 10 May 1871). Within two weeks the men were granted bail, and on Friday 19 May they returned to Cleator Moor. In a report, entitled 'The Disturbed State of Cleator Moor', the *Whitehaven Herald* (27 May 1871) described their return:

> The reception they met with was of an uproarious character, and the 'demonstration', which had been 'got up for the occasion', was of the wildest description. Drinking

was freely indulged in, and, amongst a great many, the week end was devoted to celebrating the interim liberation of the accused.

The weekend of their return was certainly ribald, and there were a number of arrests. The police believed that disturbances were being deliberately provoked by hostile Irish Catholic residents still clearly angry about the events surrounding Murphy. The celebrations of the two Doyles and the other accused, however, proved to be short-lived; they had been bailed, but still faced the Assizes. Murphy, whose health remained frail, suffered a physical set-back and ill health prevented him from attending Carlisle Assizes when the cases were heard (*Barrow Times*, 18 July 1871). At the hearing, three of the men stood charged with 'feloniously wounding William Murphy with intent to disable', whilst all were charged with assaulting and beating him. Two barristers for the defence claimed that Murphy could not be too ill to attend, as placards had been posted saying that he would appear at an Orange demonstration in the town. In the end five of the men received sentences of twelve months' hard labour and two got three months.[9] The imprisonment of Murphy's assailants, however, in no way signalled the end of the affair. Sporadic outbreaks of violence and assaults on the police continued and at one point, the *Barrow Times* (5 May 1871) stated, the Wesleyan Chapel was stoned by a gang of Irish lads.

In the autumn, as the locality was settling back into a relatively tranquil state, fears were aroused afresh by the news that the Orangemen of Whitehaven had invited Murphy back. It was heard that Murphy intended to return to give a series of four lectures, between 5 and 8 December 1871. Insp. Little told magistrates that he was worried about the consequences of Murphy's return to the area (CRO, Carlisle, CQ/PW/8). The magistrates appealed to the Home Office, expressing their concern at being visited once more by the notorious Murphy and pointed out that they had insufficient police to deal with any protracted unrest. Despite the worries of the authorities, Murphy's visit went ahead. The magistrates immediately ordered him to find sureties of £100 to keep the peace and in addition two of his assistants were each ordered to find £50.[10] The Orangemen were delighted that Murphy was to visit them and a meeting held in the Oddfellows' Hall on 3 December 1871 moved a resolution 'to express its thankfulness to Almighty God for his favour to William Murphy in so far restoring him to health as to enable him to come once more to Whitehaven to preach the Gospel' (CRO, Carlisle, CQ/PW/8). Murphy delivered his four lectures, each reported to be only five minutes long and there appears this time to have been no significant outbreak of violence initiated by either the Orangemen or the Catholics.

The return of Murphy does not, however, mark the end the story. Nearly twelve months later he was in the news again; this time, though, the publicity surrounded his death. In March 1872, news filtered out from his adoptive home in Birmingham that Murphy had died, despite his previous good health.[11] Birmingham surgeons carried out a post-mortem and claimed that the causes of death were directly attributable to the events of 20 April of the previous year in Whitehaven. The news was met with solemnity by the local Orange Order and prompted a press attack on those Irish miners who were allegedly responsible. One editor claimed that if they had not been told the place of the assault, 'our readers might have imagined that the outrage had been committed by Kaffirs or Maoris, or some other savage tribe.'[12] The visit of Murphy had highlighted inter-communal hostilities, and helped to ensure that they remained in sharp focus for at least another fifteen years, whilst his death stimulated a sharp reversal in the previously waning fortunes of the local Orange Order, which now became the perfect vehicle for collective expression by Protestants and an organisational rallying-point for counterattack.

The legacy of William Murphy

The Orange fraternity drew inspiration from what it viewed as the martyrdom of William Murphy. The Orangemen were not, however, beginning from scratch: the Order had existed in the Whitehaven area long before Murphy's visit, but had never previously enjoyed the strength it attained during the 1870s. In these years the local Orangemen continued as before to confront the issues that they traditionally regarded as important, such as ritualism in the Church of England, the pervasive nature of Catholicism and 'Church and State Toryism'. Murphy's death, however, gave the Order a unifying theme and provided the exponents of Protestant values with a wider audience and an expanded scope of activity. Within four months of their hero's death, the West Cumberland Orangemen took to the streets for the first time in a radical change in the conventions of their organisation. Marching parades had became the norm, reflecting a change in attitude among local Orangemen and an increase in numbers, as well as a broadening of the scope of their activities.

This was not, however, the first boost that Orangeism in West Cumberland gained from the legacy of Murphy; already in July 1871, the 'Glorious Twelfth' celebration of Whitehaven's sole Orange Lodge (no. 66) drew a much increased crowd of 500 people, gathered, according to the *Whitehaven News* (15 July 1871), from the ranks of the county brethren. This was a much larger turnout than in previous years, and indicates that the allure of Orangeism was not confined to Whitehaven and that the upward trend in membership had begun to spread rapidly throughout the region. The *Whitehaven Herald* (13 July 1872) attested the waxing fortunes of the Orangemen, claiming that 'new life seems to have been introduced to the Order in this part of the country'. As will be seen, the source of this revival was Murphy's death. Furthermore, the Orangemen, their ranks swollen by new Irish Protestants members, were now finding new ways of expressing their attitudes. The *Whitehaven Herald* (13 July 1872, again) commented: 'for the first time we remember the Orange Anniversary was celebrated in Whitehaven by an imposing procession, the brethren parading the streets, in the well-known regalia of orange and purple, and headed by the recently purchased banner.' This trend towards marching and outdoor rallies illustrates the change in the emphasis, fortune and member-ship of the Order following Murphy's death. The Orange Order was never a mass movement, but in West Cumberland it enjoyed considerable popular support. Furthermore, the basic Protestant values of Orangeism were widely held, a fact highlighted by the local impact of Murphyism, renewing, as it did, old antipathies and creating fresh wounds. As a result of all this, the Order underwent a change in composition towards greater working-class participation, especially among Irish Protestants, whose support was vital if public shows of strength were indeed to be strong. In order to maintain this fresh impetus, numerous fife and drum bands appeared and the marchers donned their colourful regalia, adding to the spectacle of the occasions whilst providing a seductive appeal to potential converts. The tunes that the bands played, moreover—like 'Boyne Water', 'Croppies Lie Down' and 'To Hell With the Pope'—served to encourage the Orange sympathisers and, simultaneously, to revile the Catholic fraternity. By 1876 the Orangemen were well established. Their movement had succeeded in extending its appeal to groups beyond the Irish Protestants who had hitherto dominated. The Revd E. Jump, addressing the annual July meeting in that year, spoke proudly of Orangeism and its influence, and the *Whitehaven Herald* (15 July 1876) reported his words. 'Orangeism was growing mightily in West Cumberland,' he said, 'not only among those [Irish] from across the sea, but Cumbrians were also beginning to see its principles, and were joining its ranks.' The press in the area missed no opportunity to publicise the splendour of the annual Orange demonstrations and the size of the crowds that gathered. From the 500 brethren who assembled in 1871 the numbers steadily grew. According to the *Whitehaven News* (16 July 1874), the demonstration of that year attracted 1,500. By 1877, the meeting of the North Lancashire and West Cumberland lodgemen saw five to six thousand loyal supporters gather from far and wide in the town of Askam.

By the mid-1870s, the provincial Orange Order boasted members from all over West Cumberland. Towns from Carlisle to Workington and Whitehaven had numerous lodges, the latter alone hosting five. In addition, nearly all of the smaller towns, places such as Cleator and Egremont, had at least one lodge and so too did a number of smaller hamlets. So great was their collective strength that the *Whitehaven News* (16 July 1874) asserted:

> It is worthy of remark that while Orangeism was almost unheard of in this locality until within the recent period it has emerged into new life and developed so rapidly that the Whitehaven district is now . . . as regards financial contributions to the Grand Lodge—and that, we take, as implying the greatest number of members, the largest district lodge in the world.

The *Whitehaven Herald* (18 July 1874) was equally complimentary about the exertions of the Orange Order, additionally demonstrating a clear bias in favour of the Orangemen. The article tied the Orange renaissance directly to Murphy's demise: 'Of late the Orange institution, which the ill-advised attack upon the late William Murphy brought into sudden life and activity in this neighbourhood, has been making members at a rapid rate, every town and village in the district boasting at least one, and in some cases two lodges.'

The geographical widening of the Orange Order carried the influence of Murphyism well beyond Whitehaven and Cleator, the towns where feelings had heretofore run deepest. Furthermore, developments to the south, in the Furness area of Lancashire, served to raise further the regional profile of Orangeism. The growing shipbuilding town of Barrow was beginning, during the 1870s, to attract a growing number of Protestant Irish tradesmen; whereas work opportunities in the nearby iron-ore mining towns of Askam and Dalton had, for some years, been attracting Irish immigrants: Protestants and Catholics. The combined Orange Order in these two regions began to take on a very powerful role. Within the communities where it was gaining influence, the Orange Order provided a social and political network which transcended all others. It epitomised the religion of its members. The men involved spoke a common political language and often brought their families into the move-ment's activities. By the mid-1870s the lodgemen of West Cumberland could boast a number of juvenile and female lodges. Furthermore, Orangeism, offered the prospect of greater job security, especially as foremen and employers too were often members. It was these men, along with the Protestant clerics, who provided the principal ideological leadership who without doubt proved the greatest propagandists in the recruitment of new blood.

Although familial and peer-group pressure were an important determinant of many individual actions, including membership of the Order, it is important not to underplay the importance of clerical leadership. When they spoke, men like the Revd Wickes of Whitehaven and the Revd Armes, vicar of Cleator Moor, used scaremongering language, threatening religious doom at the hands of Jesuits and papist doctrines. The membership readily believed such language and the continual threats and fears about the safety of Protestantism, which these clergy commonly articulated, must have kept up the numbers of many of their flock. These men, then, gave the movement a certain *gravitas*, and served to voice the inchoate anti-papist, anti-ritualist and pro-Protestant religious and political views which the lodgemen held. At the demonstration of 12 July 1875, for example, the Revd Cole, a Baptist minister from Whitehaven, eloquently summed up the philosophical stance of the local Orangemen. His words — reported by the *Whitehaven Herald* (17 July 1875) — in linking the reborn Order with Murphy's demise, add clarity to the reasons why the Order had enjoyed such good fortunes during the early 1870s. 'The demonstration they had seen that day,' he told the Orange brethren, 'represented a principle, a party and a protest. It represented the principle of civil and religious liberty, the Protestant party, and a protest at the murder of William Murphy.'

A protest against the death of Murphy it was. The Protestantism of the Orange Order is also undeniable, but the principle of 'civil and religious liberty' begs further consideration. Simply put, Orangeism meant religious vilification of the local Catholic population. Its increasingly public profile throughout the 1870s served to exacerbate existing tensions. The denunciation of Catholicism caused dismay among the followers of that faith whilst brash displays, marches and anti-papal tunes incensed the local Catholics, sometimes to the point of violence. Within the confines of their meetings the Orange Order was probably manageable — to both police and Catholics, but when it marched through the local streets and mixed with the 'enemy' in the public houses, trouble was inevitable. Furthermore, the working class of Victorian England, men and women, were no strangers to a pub culture and heavy alcohol consumption. Despite the fact that there was a temperance affiliation among certain of the lodgemen, the majority imbibed just as deeply their Catholic counterparts.

The public house remained the fulcrum of working-class community networks. Not surprisingly, then, the local Irish Catholics, whose reputation for drinking was well established, cannot be seen as blameless when violence erupted. Given the nature of the area, the hard work, the heavy drinking, the shortage of police and the pugnacity of the Orangemen, it was inevitable that fighting should occur. The Orange rebirth heightened tensions and further alienated the Irish Catholics. The fighting that broke out in Workington in July 1871, for example, was typical in all respects aside from the fact that the recent attack upon Murphy added to its seriousness. The *Barrow Times* (18 July 1871) described the incident with the following words:

> An Orangeman, leaving a shop, was asked by a catholic if he wanted his face making all right, having had it swollen in a pub fight the night before. When the Orangeman said yes, the Catholic struck him a severe blow . . . in the course of a few minutes, about a hundred Catholics and Orangemen assembled and a general fight ensued . . . After considerable difficulty, the police succeeded in quelling the riot. Great excitement still prevails in the neighbourhood, and another outbreak is feared.

This incident illustrates that Orangemen and Catholics needed little excuse for a fight. Nor did it take long for trifling incidents to escalate out of proportion. The Catholic and Orange fraternities could very rapidly gather sufficient forces to present a threat to order. The most common of these situations developed on or around the 'Glorious Twelfth' when the Catholics often congregated to jostle the marching Orangemen. This was particularly the case, as at Harrington in 1873, when the local Orangemen had split from the main demonstration and were making their way home. A similar incident was reported by the *Whitehaven Herald* (19 July 1876), involving between 1,500 and 1,600 hostile Catholics who met up with the Cleator Moor Orangemen as they returned from a regional gathering at Whitehaven. The crowd, predominantly 'women and lads', booed and jeered, but their best was saved for later, when the local fife and drum band returned after entertaining their brethren in nearby Frizington. As the band progressed into the town, playing 'Tommy Make Room for Your Uncle', 'they were pelted with stones most unmercifully by the rabble, and had it not been for the prompt action of Inspector Brown and his excellent staff of officers, the consequences might have been somewhat serious.'

During the years of the Orange revival, the pages of the local press were littered with incidents of fighting and unrest which varied in intensity. Most Catholics, it seems, would have supported the sentiments of Mary Jane Kehoe. The *Whitehaven News* (27 July 1882) alleged that Kehoe, after an altercation with an Orange shopkeeper and his family, threatened to 'pull the Orange heart out of the daughter'. By a similar measure, few Orangemen were willing to stand by and take abuse; it might be said they were more likely to be responsible for it. In the eyes of a biased press, however, the Catholics were a mere rabble, whilst the Orangemen were perceived as determined, organised and provoked. The events of 12 July 1884, however, rather changed this image.

Cleator Moor, 1884: the climax of West Cumberland Orangeism

The habitual outbreaks of violence that occurred between the Orange and Green fraternities of West Cumberland reflect to some extent the basic divisions that existed between Catholics and Protestants. However, none of their clashes compared in magnitude to the outbreak that occurred on 12 July 1884 at Cleator Moor when the regional Orangemen decided to hold their annual meeting in that town. The intensity of the violence on this occasion outstripped even the attack made upon William Murphy thirteen years earlier and the height to which feelings ran equalled that achieved in both camps over Murphy. The reporter for the *Whitehaven News* (17 July 1884), covering the events in Cleator Moor, explained the change of plans on the part of the North Lancashire brethren: 'Members from Barrow had been invited and had said they could have sent about 2,000 people to the demonstration, but could not attend through want of work.' This figure was no doubt an exaggeration, although the turn-out in Barrow had been strong since 1877. The unfavourable climate may well have exacerbated tensions between the Irish Catholics and Orangemen in West Cumberland; indeed, such has been said before of similar conflicts in Lancashire (Lowe, 1990, p. 161). Had the Barrow and Askam contingent arrived, however, regardless of their number, their presence would unquestionably have served only to aggravate an already tense situation. Cleator Moor would seem a poor choice of venue for the celebration of Orangeism but the intent was, according to some members of the press, quite deliberate. 'Cleator Moor,' wrote the *Carlisle Express and Examiner* (19 July 1884), '[is] the stronghold of Roman Catholicism in West Cumberland', and: 'As if to court disturbance the Orangemen in circuit no. 8, Western Province, representing 1800 members including Maryport, Workington, Harrington, Parton, Whitehaven, and other districts, decided they would this year hold their annual demonstration in the stronghold of the enemy.' Why the Orange lodges of Cumberland should have been allowed to demonstrate within the county's Irish Catholic centre, that 'capital of the mining district',[13] is strange. The *Carlisle Express* (17 July 1884), however, did not condemn the Order as a whole over its choice of Cleator Moor as a venue. The editor argued: 'The rank and file . . . may not know, but the leaders certainly do that among the Catholic population of Cleator Moor the spirit of toleration is not much cultivated.'

In the early afternoon of Saturday 12 July, the marchers accompanied by eight bands arrived at the station and made their way, past the Catholic chapel, to Wathbrow where a public meeting was convened (*Barrow News*, 15 July 1884). At this meeting the Revd G. B. Armes said he was shocked to see so many police present. He asserted that 'Orangemen didn't need police' (*Carlisle Express*, 19 July 1884). Armes also said after the event that he did not know that Orangemen carried revolvers (*Carlisle Patriot*, 18 July 1884). In fact, the forty-five constables on duty arguably were too few, though on the Sunday following the event a detachment of ninety-one soldiers of the South Yorkshire Regiment was sent to Carlisle, for rapid dispatch to Cleator if needed (*Carlisle Express*, 19 July 1884).

Orange estimates put the size of the crowd at some 800,[14] whereas the *Carlisle Patriot* (18 July 1884) claimed there were 1,300–1,600 Orangemen present. The Cleator Moor lodge, wisely perhaps, did not muster many members. Overall, however, there were large crowds, men, women and children prompted by nice weather, as well as by the lure of Orangeism. Trouble began when the public meeting drew to a close and the paraders started to make their way back to the station. The atmosphere in the town centre was tense and many shop windows were boarded up for fear of what might ensue. As the procession moved forward the mood became more belligerent and a substantial crowd of local inhabitants began to assemble. The reporter for the *Whitehaven News* (17 July 1884) expected that the 'usual epithets' and the 'odd customary stone' might be exchanged, until 'I noticed that the young men held their coat pockets in a manner that raised the suspicion that the pockets were full of stones. The procession was now 200 yards behind us.' As the marchers closed in the first attack was launched, with the police also targeted. Superintendents Thornburrow and Taylor, of Whitehaven and Cockermouth respectively, were singled out 'because of their grander helmets', and 'While the police were diverted a rush was made on the procession.' This attack was maintained until after the Orangemen had reached the station and, in addition, the *Barrow Herald* (15 July 1884) reported: 'an attempt was made to destroy the banners and drums [of the bands, and] . . . in this the rioters were partially successful.'

In his report to the Home Secretary the Chief Constable of Cumberland, J. Dunne, said that the riot had begun after some Catholics had heard that an Orangeman had struck one of the crowd a blow to the face (*Whitehaven News*, 17 July 1884). Whether this is correct or not we shall never know, but it is clear that the Orangemen were not blameless. Later revelations show that they came well prepared for trouble. As the affray gathered momentum, many of the marchers added to the seriousness of the situation by drawing revolvers and firing on the crowd. One particular lodge, the Sons of Israel, was specifically blamed for carrying these weapons.[15] The press generally agreed that the majority of the shots fired must have been blanks, otherwise the death toll would have been fearfully high. Mr Ainsworth, a local employer, succeeded in getting the Irish portion of the crowd away from the fracas, but only temporarily. They soon charged again and 'volley after volley of stones was showered upon the crowd.' Unfortunately for Henry Tumelty, at least one of the shots was not a blank, and he died that afternoon with a bullet-hole through the head. The use of the guns infuriated the mob and 'they redoubled their ferocious attacks, and several hand to hand encounters ensued' (*Barrow Herald*, 15 July 1884; *Whitehaven News*, 17 July 1884; *Carlisle Express*, 19 July 1884). The Orange fraternity also came armed with other less startling, though potentially lethal, items of weaponry. Among these were swords, sabres and pikes, the latter wielded like quarterstaffs. There were numerous injuries, although, surprisingly, only one fatality from the afternoon's violence.

The rioting ended when the trains pulled out of Cleator Moor with the battle-weary Orange troops on board. The contingent of policemen led by Dunne, nevertheless, stayed on duty until early on Sunday morning. These men guarded the Moor on the Saturday night to keep the peace as there were threats circulating to 'do for' the prominent Orangemen in the town and many of the latter sought sanctuary in the local school. A rumour circulated after the violence which maintained that some of the Irish ringleaders, had been involved in 'the riot some years ago in Whitehaven, when Murphy, the Orange lecturer, was so seriously injured.'[16]

This shows something of the nature of prejudice and the rancour that lived in the minds of people in this isolated mining community. Similarly, that the Orange Order should remember and exhume the spirit of Murphy and anti-Murphyism illustrates the longevity of memories on both sides. The mood of all the press reports is one of slight sympathy with the Irish community and of exasperation with the Orangemen. Father Burchall, the Roman Catholic priest at Cleator, when asked by the press for his comments on the events, stated: 'A more scandalous and outrageous affair never took place.' His sentiments were echoed by Father Wray, whose feelings were contained within the pages of the *Whitehaven News* (17 July 1884): 'Imagine them playing such tunes as 'Croppies Lie Down', 'Come Out if You Dare', and 'To Hell with the Pope'. Armed with swords and pistols, they were simply frantic and it was utterly impossible to restrain the people.'

The priest complained further at the activities of the Orange Order, defending his people who, under such duress, he believed had been forced to act. It was evidently the bands as much as anything that had annoyed them. Father Wray was full of woe about the implications of these events for the future, claiming: 'It has thrown us back at least twenty years as far as feeling is concerned at Cleator Moor.'

Following these events, the police tried rapidly to mop up resistance. The list of those arrested illustrates something of the social composition of the Orange Order, which elsewhere in the country has been described as working class (Neal, 1988, pp. 40, 71–2, 170–1). In this case, there was little variance with what Frank Neal has said. In fact, the two groups, Catholics and Orangemen, were clearly from the same class but different occupational groups. Outwardly nothing divided them; culturally, they were separated by a fissure which on occasions yawned into a huge chasm. Principal among the sixteen arrested was John Bawden, aged 53, who was head of the Cleator Moor Orangemen and a foreman iron-ore miner. Doubtless he was instrumental in recruiting to the ranks men mindful of their job security. He was apprehended for having fired shots and for wielding a sword. All sixteen of those apprehended, eight Orangemen and eight Catholics, were refused bail. The Orangemen varied in occupation and came from various towns around the Workington and Whitehaven area; among their number were labourers, furnacemen and a pit worker. In contrast, the Catholics came from Cleator and all were miners but for one beerhouse-keeper. Early in August, the press reported that four further Cleator iron-ore miners were arrested but, in the end, eleven were set free and the remaining men were sent for trial at the assizes, each being offered bail of £30.[17] It is not clear what the majority were charged with, though Bawden, widely accepted as the ringleader, was accused of killing Tumelty. At the Cumberland and Westmorland Assizes, in November 1884, Mr Justice Day Moore directed the jury to return a verdict of not guilty against Bawden, because the evidence was conflicting. All the others pleaded guilty (*Carlisle Express*, 1 November 1884). The judge regarded the whole episode as a 'disastrous riot' and commented that it was the first such case that an English judge had dealt with. In warning the guilty parties and in discharging them, he ordered: 'Be well conducted men and you will hear no more of the offences of which you have pleaded guilty. Go away and take care to keep the peace in the future' (ibid.). On their return to Whitehaven, the Orangemen were met at the station by a fife and drum band. A large crowd of between 800 and 900 gathered and marched through the principal streets of the town, as the band played familiar tunes and, according to the *Carlisle Express* (1 November 1884), there was no feeling in the town other than one of elation.

However, in Cleator Moor the prominent feelings were anger and fear for, in the wake of this communal unrest, the local miners were at greater risk than their more scattered enemies. So bad was feeling on the Moor that the local employers, fearing the miners, who had easy access to dynamite, might cause serious trouble, threatened to sack all those involved. Naturally, this threat did not apply to Orangemen, for those apprehended were not within the grasp of the Cleator employers. This news caused obvious anger, to add to that which was felt over certain evidence which the Whitehaven magistrates had heard in July 1884. Two women, giving evidence in the cases against the Orangemen, claimed they heard Dan Hamilton, a police officer present at the Cleator riot, encouraging the Orangemen gun-wielders: 'Fire, men, fire and shoot the b. . .s.'[18] The revelation about Hamilton no doubt confirmed the already common convictions that many, including men responsible for the upholding of law and order, regarded Irish Catholics as inferior and openly sided with the Orangemen. The Catholic fraternity was further incensed by the verdict which was returned by the inquest into the shooting of Henry Tumelty, namely, 'Death by a shot fired from a pistol or a revolver, by a person unknown.'[19]

Tumelty was exculpated by the press of any involvement in the riot, although this was scant consolation for his family and co-religionists. Tumelty, a post-man, had also been a member of the local Parnell-Davitt branch of the Irish National League, a fact which would not have endeared him to the Orange fraternity, nor have induced much remorse from among the more pugnacious followers of Orangeism. The wider public, moreover, may have held this association to imply guilt. At a meeting, held at the Crown Star Hotel, Cleator Moor, Tumelty's fellow Home Rulers moved a 'vote of condolence' with the family of their 'esteemed fellow-member'.[20] At the next meeting, John Kavanagh, the secretary of the local INL branch, urged all Irish Catholics in Cleator to join their ranks. Meanwhile, another INL member also became embroiled in the saga. This was a man by the name of Edward Ennis, a miner and a prominent figure in the local INL, who was arrested for an alleged assault upon Dan Hamilton, the policeman who was supposed to have ordered the Orangemen to open fire (*Nation*, 2 August 1884; *Carlisle Express*, 16 August 1884). Ennis claimed he had twenty witnesses who would swear that Hamilton was responsible. Fr Burchall was also of this opinion. Ennis was acquitted by magistrates, and the INL passed a resolution of congratulations welcoming him home.[21]

Bad feeling in the area did not subside with the conclusion of this unsavoury event. The Catholic population was without doubt disillusioned and angered at the fact that Tumelty's assailant went unpunished. The following year, when the Orangemen of the district met in Cockermouth, events seem to have been continuing in the same vein. Although the occasion passed off without riot, the

Whitehaven Advertiser (18 July 1885) reported that the 'Orangemen had again recourse to their revolvers' and one youth was injured. In order to attend the Cockermouth demonstration a special train had been enlisted to convey the Orangemen from Cleator Moor via Frizington to the venue. The train, it appears, was attacked at its point of departure by a large group of youths, aged between 15 and 19. They hurled bricks and stones at the vehicle, and the Orangemen repaid the assault with interest, firing pistol shots. One of the stone-throwers, a lad named McAnulty, was hit by a shot 'in the thick of the thigh'. On their return to Cleator, the paper reported that the Orangemen were 'further molested'. Despite such events, further study of the press up to the 1890s has revealed no further outbreaks of violence to match those which broke out in 1871 and 1884. In fact, the Order began to decline rapidly thereafter.

Conclusion

It is perhaps ironic but certainly apt that Murphy's memory should have been commemorated with such violence. His activities and the response in West Cumberland to his death indicate the depth and richness of the seam of anti-Catholicism which he tapped. Murphy himself was a firebrand demagogue, 'a master of incitement' (Norman, 1968, p. 17) and was undoubtedly 'one of the greatest showmen of his age' (Hanham, 1978, p. 305). He and his entourage, moreover, were everywhere accompanied by riot and violence, and it is clear that he was lucky to escape serious molestation on numerous occasions. In the isolated town of Whitehaven, Murphy was not guaranteed the same degree of protection as could be deployed in the larger urban centres of Lancashire or the Midlands. Nor did many places in Britain harbour an Irish Catholic population as hardy, determined and fiercely independent as that which resided in Cleator Moor. Because of Murphy's bellicosity, most historians have concluded that there was 'relief all round' at the news of his demise (Hanham, 1978, p. 306); and that once dead, 'the public tried to forget him as soon as possible' (Richter, 1981, p. 48). Such was not, however, the sentiment among the Irish Protestant population in West Cumberland; nor, it seems, of likeminded Cumbrians. They could not forget him because his blood was on their soil and they had failed to protect him. For them, Murphyism was a focal point: his martyrdom (for that was how they saw it) turned the unfocused anti-Catholicism of the public house and the workplace into a popular movement which with a common sentiment united men, women and children, the working class and their social superiors, clergy and the laity. In attacking Murphy, those Irish miners helped to revivify an organisation with whose prejudices they were already fully conversant, whose intolerance, indeed, Murphy symbolised and encapsulated. Murphy highlighted basic divisions between the two Irish communities of West Cumberland. As this essay has endeavoured to show, such dissonance remained an intrinsic part of Cumbrian life for fifteen years or more after the event. Even today, the locals remember the Murphy legend, and Cleator Moor is still dubbed 'Little Ireland'. The strength of local Orangeism lay in the breadth of its appeal. It was a family concern, surpassing all but the public house and the church as a basic network within Cumbrian society.

In one sense, the revival of local Orangeism in the area had an element of revenge about it. In which case, a strong continuity between the events of 1871 and 1884 must be assumed. Episodes like the attack upon Murphy exemplify the ethnic rivalry which was recurrent in Victorian Britain. Within the folklore and tradition of sectarian violence it must have seemed to all concerned that those Cleator Moor miners who attacked Murphy had succeeded in 'putting one over' on their rivals. Although this alone is insufficient to explain sustained Orange growth, there was an element of rivalry and bravado about communal strife. If revenge was the only motive, however, why did the Orangemen wait thirteen years to meet at Cleator? After all, it is likely that the public houses of West Cumberland saw regularly some Catholic victim pay for Murphy's pains with his own. In a broader sense, the nature of the area played perhaps the largest part in the power of local Orangeism. Murphy was the catalyst for regrowth but the ingredients were already present. Behind Murphyism lies an important point: the Irish and Catholicism were not necessarily synonymous; and Cumbrian communal conflict was as much about intra-Irish hatred as it was about inter-communal disaffection. Indeed, as one author has said, 'both Connaught men and the Orangemen from Ulster were despised by their fellow countrymen' (Davis, 1989. p. 114).

The events at Cleator Moor in 1884 were a turning point, signalling as they did the end of the boom period of Orange growth. Press reports in the years that followed suggest that the West Cumberland Order was in decline. In 1885, fourteen lodges turned out for the July demonstration at Cockermouth. In the following year there were twelve and by 1890 the lodgemen could muster only 140 hardy souls at the Workington meeting. Of the numbers of up to 6,000 that had gathered in the 1870s and early 1880s, this figure represented a woeful fraction. Given the post-Murphy boom, this decline was remarkably rapid. The fifteen years of growth, nevertheless, suggest that the Orange revival was no flash in the pan. There are, in fact, a number of arguments for decline, which point to wider cultural and economic influences as well as to the nature of the order itself.

Throughout these years, West Cumberland was an isolated area. Despite developments in transport, it remained on the fringe of industrial development. For a hundred years, the port of Whitehaven had been declining in the face of competition from Glasgow and Liverpool (Williams, 1955, pp. 403–4). Furthermore, the growth of ports at Workington and Maryport added competition, although these towns never rose to the position of prosperity which Whitehaven once held. As a consequence of these factors, and of the gradual exhaustion of local iron-ore supplies, out-migration became the area's chief demographic trait, a fact continually referred to by the press. North Lancashire continued to flourish but the Orangemen of Barrow, Askam and Dalton gradually severed links with their West Cumberland counterparts, preferring instead joint meetings with brethren from Lancashire.

For these increasingly isolated Cumbrian Orangemen, the events of 1884 in Cleator Moor represented a climax. Until then, they had enjoyed effective leadership which masked rather than tempered the violent excesses of their ranks. The orderly nature of their meetings had usually meant that violence between Orangemen and Catholics had been limited to pub fights and street riots which did not involve the bulk of the demonstrators. This factor, combined with overt press bias, meant that Irish Catholics were always blamed for any disturbance. In terms of violence, there was usually little to separate working-class Orangemen or Catholics: neither eschewed the fist as a tool of argument. The Irish Catholics, however, never employed pistols and they never used intimidatory songs and chants. Nor, indeed, did they do these things on the public platform. Murphyism had popularised the Orange Order and his death had caused its members to take to the street, banging drums and thumping dummy bibles. July 1884 showed that the Orangemen still did all these things, but after this episode it seems that the clergy and their richer patrons abandoned the order, sickened by its excesses. As a consequence of what happened that day, the Order rapidly dwindled. It had been the public nature of the Order which had perpetuated the continuously violent response of the incensed Catholics at whom, ultimately, Orange verbosity and swagger were aimed. In the wake of the events at Cleator Moor in 1884, the *Carlisle Express* issued the following lament: 'There are very few people (outside the Orange ranks) who do not condemn these annual [Orange] demonstrations as good for nothing but promoting party strife among two sections of the community who, if left alone, would soon learn to live together in harmony.' This view is both simplistic and over-optimistic; but it is true in one sense for it pins down the very cause of anti-Orange excitement. Whether the two communities really could have lived in harmony is debatable: Orangeism merely publicised already existing cultural and religious differences and there were other spheres of conflict to which each group might turn. However, the events of 1871 and 1884 both served to illustrate the excesses of the two sides and to revile the silent majority. In the end, both events backfired on the perceived perpetrators of the initial violence: in 1871 the populace of Cleator Moor was castigated and had to watch in dismay as popular Orangeism reared up, whilst, after the incidents of 1884, the Orangemen were largely deserted by their once sympathetic press. Their movement—although still surviving in West Cumbria—became a shadow of that which had flourished after the death of William Murphy.

Notes

1. This work forms part of a doctoral study, 'The Irish in North Lancashire and West Cumberland: Barrow, Whitehaven and Cleator Moor, *c.*1850–1906', on which I am currently working. I wish to thank Colin Holmes, David E. Martin and Len Scales, who have offered advice and encouragement during the preparation of this chapter.
2. This description is from Hanham, 1978, p. 304.
3. For example, he was supposed to have told an audience in Chelmsford that 'Ireland could never be quiet till every Catholic priest was hanged', *Hansard*, CXCII (1868), 830, 820; Richter, 1981, p. 36.
4. *Ulverston Advertiser*, 27 April 1871. The *Weekly Register*, 29 April 1871, put the number at 300.
5. *Barrow Times*, 9 May 1871. General accounts of the assault are available in the

national, and much of the provincial press. *The Times* first printed a brief piece on the affair, evidently sent from Whitehaven by telegraph. *The Times*, 22 April 1871.

6. That this was the case caused some irritation in the locality, and press were quick to pick up on the point. See *Whitehaven Herald*, 29 April 1871.

7. *Whitehaven Herald*, 29 April 1871. The report claimed that both men had been ringleaders, each playing an active role in the assault upon Murphy. In addition, Dennis Doyle's character was sketched in for the benefit of readers unacquainted with his capabilities: 'Dennis is a pugilist of considerable local pretensions, and has acquired a degree of popularity in Cleator Moor in that capacity.'

8. The seven miners were James, Patrick and Hugh Magee; Thomas and Francis Morgan; James Bilton; and Jeremiah Bradyn. *Whitehaven Herald*, 5 May, 1871. Eventually, Bradyn and Morgan were freed.

9. All of the final seven, who were found guilty of assaulting Murphy, were sentenced to custodial terms with hard labour:

> James Belton, collier, aged 38 yrs: three months.
> Patrick Magee, collier, aged 26 yrs: three months.
> James Magee, collier, aged 27 yrs: twelve months.
> Hugh Magee, miner, aged 21 yrs: twelve months.
> Patrick Murray, aged 35 yrs: twelve months.
> Patrick Doyle, miner, aged 23 yrs: twelve months.
> Dennis Doyle, miner, aged 20 yrs: twelve months.

10. One of these assistants was Robert Steele, of the PEMEU. The 'Surety Recognisances', which laid out conditions and sums involved were dated 4 December 1871. CRO, Carlisle, CQ/PW/8.

11. *Barrow Times*, 14 March 1872 . There is some dispute over the timing and location of death; Hanham, 1978, p. 306, for example, states Workington and St Patrick's Day 1872, whereas Richter, 1981, p. 48, and Arnstein, 1975 'The Murphy Riots', both point to 12 March and Birmingham.

12. The editor of the *Belfast News* quoted in the *Whitehaven Herald*, 6 May 1871.

13. *Whitehaven News*, 17 July 1884. The capital of the mining district which, as has been seen in earlier chapters, was inhabited by a significant proportion of Irish Catholics.

14 *Whitehaven News*, 17 July 1884. This estimate is supported by the evidence of Henry Jefferson, JP. CRO Carlisle, CQ/PW/9.

15. *Whitehaven News*, 17 July 1884 . The 'Sons of Israel' came from Workington. *Carlisle Patriot*, 18 July 1884.

16. It is fairly obvious that contemporary commentators saw the link between Orangeism and Murphy. *Barrow News*, 15 July 1884.

17. *Carlisle Express*, 2 August 1884. The Secretary of State, the press reported, ordered that the cases against the men should be conducted as a public prosecution. The reason for this was 'The public interest, and for the maintenance of peace and good order and the protection of life and property.' This news was reported in the *Carlisle Express*, 16 August 1884.

18. Evidence of Eliza Woolaghan, corroborated by Mary Murry. *Carlisle Express*, 26 July 1884.

19. *Carlisle Express*, 26 July 1884. It is clear that no one could know exactly who fired the bullet or shot. However, the Catholics quite naturally wanted revenge and were unlikely to see the complexities of charging one of the eight Orangemen with murder.

20. Laurence Byrne moved the motion and William Cromwell seconded. *Nation*, 19 July 1884.

21. Fr Burchall claims that the 'men were ready to swear that a certain police constable

told the men to fire', *Carlisle Patriot*, 18 July 1884. The celebration of Ennis's home-coming was reported in the *Nation*, 23 August 1884.

References

Arnstein, W.L., 1975, 'The Murphy Riots: A Victorian Dilemma', *Victorian Studies*, 19 (1): 51–71.

Barber, R., 1976, *Iron Ore and After: Boom Time, Depression and Survival in a West Cumbrian Town: Cleator Moor 1840–1960*, York, York University.

Campbell, A.B., 1979, *The Lanarkshire Miners: A social History of Their Trade Unions, 1775–1974*, Edinburgh, John Donald Publishers, Ltd.

Coleman, T., 1986, *The Railway Navvies*, 2nd edn, London, Penguin.

Davis, G., 1989, 'Little Irelands', in R. Swift and S. Gilley (eds).

Gallagher, T., 1987, *Glasgow, the Uneasy Peace: Religious Tension in Modern Scotland*, Manchester, Manchester University Press.

Hanham, H.J., 1978, *Elections and Party management: Politics in the Age of Gladstone and Disraeli*, Sussex, Harvester Press.

Healy, T.M., 1928, *Letters and Leaders of My Day*, vol. I, London, Thornton Butterworth Ltd.

Kirk, N., 1985, *The Growth of Working Class Reformism in Mid-Victorian England*, Beckenham, Croom Helm.

Lowe, W.J., 1990, *The Irish in Mid-Victorian Lancashire: The Shaping of a Working Class Community*, New York, Peter Lang.

Marshall, J.D., 1978, 'Cleator and Cleator Moor: Some Aspects of Their Social and Urban Development' *Transactions of the Cumberland and Westmorland Archeological and Antiquarian Society*, 78: 163–75.

Neal, F., 1988, *Sectarian Violence: The Liverpool Experience, 1819–1914*, Manchester, Manchester University Press.

Neal, F., 1990–1, 'Manchester Origins of the English Orange Order', *Manchester Region History Review*, 4 (2): 12–3.

Norman, F.R., 1968, *Anti-Catholicism in Victorian England*, London, Allen & Unwin.

Quinlivan, P. and Rose, P., 1982, *The Fenians in England, 1865–1872: A Sense of Insecurity*, London, John Calder.

Richter, D.C., 1981, *Riotous Victorians*, London, Ohio, Ohio University Press.

Sullivan, D., 1983, *Navvyman*, London, Coracle Books.

Swift, R., 1984, 'Anti-Catholicism and Irish Disturbances: Public Order in Mid-Victorian Wolverhampton', *Midland History*, 9: 87–108.

Swift, R., 1989, 'Crime and the Irish', in R. Swift and S. Gilley (eds).

Swift, R. and Gilley, S. (eds), 1989, *The Irish in Britain, 1815–1939*, London, Pinter Publishers.

Williams, J.E., 1955, 'Whitehaven in the Eighteen Century', *Economic History Review*, 2nd series, 8: 393–404.

4

Anti-German riots in Britain during the First World War

Panikos Panayi

During the course of the nineteenth century, the mass migration of tens of millions of people out of Europe represented one of the most fundamental developments in the continent's history. Germany became one of the countries to suffer a great loss, with 4.8 million people leaving the country from 1815 to 1930 (Baines, 1991, pp. 8–9). Although most German emigrants went to North America, a small community developed in Great Britain, which had reached a total of 53,324 in 1911, a peak for a community which had developed over hundreds of years.

Within Britain a series of cities counted major German communities during the nineteenth century, notably London, which held about half the German population throughout the Victorian and Edwardian period, but also Liverpool, Manchester and Bradford. In addition, in cities all over the country there were small numbers of Germans, including Belfast, Dundee and Nottingham. Among the occupations in which Germans became particularly important we can include teaching. In the late nineteenth century Germans became significant as waiters and also established themselves as retailers in the form of butchers, bakers and barbers. In addition, we can also identify major businessmen or financiers, including Sir Jacob Behrens and Sir Ernest Cassel, amongst many others. German communities throughout the country maintained their ethnicity, revolving around religion, politics and clubs of a wide range.

Hostility against Germans in Britain, while it may have existed on an underlying level throughout the course of the nineteenth century and which came to the surface during diplomatic crises such as the Boer War and the Franco-Prussian War, became stronger as the First World War approached. While some of this hostility had its basis in connection with the general xenophobia against immigrants which led to the passage of the Aliens Act of 1905, the bulk of hostility to Germans resulted from the worsening of Anglo-German economic and political relations from about 1890. This manifested itself in the form of hostility to particular trades such as clerks. At the same time wealthy German Jews received attention from a series of radical right-wing publicists such as Leo Maxse and his *National Review*. The Edwardian years also resulted in the development of 'spy fever', a widespread belief put forward by large sections of the press that Germans acted in Britain in the service of their government in preparation for an approaching war. But pre-war anti-German sentiment did not result in any great hardship for Germans within Britain (Panayi, 1991, pp. 11–41). We can detect physical attacks, but the only significant one recorded took place in 1900 after the relief of Mafeking during the Boer War (Price, 1972, pp. 132–7).

The situation changes dramatically following the outbreak of the First World War in 1914 as British society became saturated with Germanophobia. 'Spy fever' became rife and eventually developed into a conspiracy theory of a 'Hidden Hand' of German influence which controlled Britain and hindered the war effort. Germans in all trades lost their employment and public figures with any connection with the enemy faced constant vilification in the press. Organisations aimed at eradicating German influence came into existence.

At the same time, the government introduced a series of measures to control the German community in Britain. In the first place the passage of the Aliens Restrictions Act on 5 August, the day after the declaration of war, meant that the government could introduce subsequent Orders in Council to control virtually any aspect of the life of enemy aliens, including movement and social life, as German newspapers and clubs faced closure. The Trading with the Enemy Acts, meanwhile, meant the confiscation of virtually all businesses owned by Germans in Britain. German males of military age also faced internment, affecting over 30,000 people, while repatriation at the end of the war secured the destruction of the German communities in Britain, as their number declined from 57,500 in 1914 to 22,254 in 1919 (Panayi, 1991, pp. 45–149, 153–222).

Any consideration of the anti-German riots which broke out during the First World War needs to take account of this background of widespread official and unofficial Germanophobia as the fundamental underlying factor against which the disturbances developed. The rest of this essay describes the riots which broke out and considers their short-term causes and the reactions of the judiciary. The disturbances broke out on five main occasions: August 1914, October 1914, May 1915, June 1916 and July 1917. The riots in this sequence resulted in the most widespread disturbances in twentieth-century British history as areas from Glasgow to Winchester and Liverpool to London experienced violence. During the events of May 1915 thousands of people faced arrest for public order and looting offences while thousands of properties suffered damage at a cost of hundreds of thousands of pounds.

During the opening month of the war a series of isolated attacks upon German properties occurred in various parts of the East End of London. For instance, on 6 August, 'a crowd of hooligans raided a bread shop in Old-Ford road.' In Poplar, meanwhile, disorder occurred at the beginning as well as the very end of August. The first outbreaks centred around Sabbaston Street and both the local press and the police believed that those who came under attack provoked the disturbances. In one case a German baker had allegedly hoisted an enemy flag while another attack 'was the result of a provocative remark made to a drunken man by the occupier's wife, a German, at a time when feeling against the Germans was very strong.' On 31 August, meanwhile, 'two German bakers in Upper North Street invited trouble by making insulting remarks regarding the British people and troops with the result that the windows of their shops were smashed.' The Mayor of Poplar believed that drink had played a large part in these riots and therefore called a public meeting 'to discuss the advisability of closing the public houses of the borough earlier' (*East London Advertiser*, 15 August, 5 September 1914; PRO HO45 10944/257142/4).

The most serious disturbance of August 1914 broke out at Keighley, in Yorkshire, against the background of a moulders' and engineers' strike which had developed in the town over several months. This may well have influenced the disturbances. More immediately, feeling against the German community began to develop after several of its members faced arrest. The first shopkeeper to face attack reputedly displayed contempt for the British army while his wife was believed to have danced in the streets upon the announcement of 2,000 British casualties.

At 9 p.m. on 29 August an Irishman named Kelly entered the premises of Andrassy, a pork butcher's, in order to make a purchase. An argument developed when Kelly asked for a pie without poison in it. Andrassy ordered him out of the shop and, according to Kelly, hit him in the face. He returned with many more people, mostly Irishmen as this was an Irish neighbourhood, and from about 11.30 until 2.30 the shop was bombarded with stones and bottles. Because the aim was not very good the adjoining property also suffered. Andrassy and his family were taken to the local police station for protection while mounted police, with the help of the fire brigade and a Catholic priest, brought the situation under control.

On 30 August seventy extra policemen were brought in from surrounding areas, making a total in the town of 148, eight of whom were mounted; there were also twenty-five held in reserve by the Chief Constable of Bradford and others at Shipley. After 10 p.m. that night the disturbances started again. Dense crowds numbering a thousand 'thronged the streets and the windows of three other pork shops occupied by Germans in different parts of the town were smashed, the premises raided and their quantities of stock taken away.' Andrassy's shop was set alight but the fire brigade managed to put it out. After this the crowd made a move towards the residence of a large employer who had held out against the moulders and engineers. However, the police managed to prevent the rioters from getting near the house and eventually succeeded in dispersing them. But before this happened, the windows of the police station were also broken by stone throwing and a few policemen suffered injuries, although none serious.

On 31 August a crowd gathered outside the Police Court but no violence broke out. At the Borough Court the Mayor said that those guilty of riotous behaviour:

> were no doubt suffering from indignation at the way in which some Germans were behaving on the Continent—an indignation shared by the whole civilised world. But this was no excuse why the people should attack in a cowardly and un-English way the homes of unfortunate Germans who found themselves in England. (PRO HO45 10944/257142/2a; *Manchester Guardian*, 31 August 1914)

As we mentioned previously, it proves difficult to establish precise causes for the early disturbances. From those we have discussed, we can blame the effects of the first excitement of war, a provocative act by those who came under attack, and, in the case of Keighley, the local economic situation. If we turn to the first major riots in London, which broke out in Deptford and surrounding areas in October 1914, we can establish precise causes. In the first place these disturbances took place against the background of the first peak of anti-German hostility consequent upon the rapid advance of the German armies through Belgium and the atrocity stories which surrounded their movement. As we have seen, this resulted in milder manifestations of hostility towards the Germans in Britain such as the sacking of waiters following a campaign against them in the Northcliffe press. The anti-German riots occurred when this animosity reached a peak. However, local factors also played a part. For instance, from the start of the war 'hostility of a very determined character' had been shown towards the shopkeepers of German nationality in Deptford High Street. 'Early in the crisis a fracas arose consequent upon disrespect being shown to a body of territorials as they marched through the street, and a butcher's shop, kept by a German, was threatened in such a manner that he was compelled to close.' What finally set off the disturbance was the arrival of 800 Belgian refugees in the area who were taken to Carrington House. One journalist wrote that 'the sight of these people and the remembrance of the terrible sufferings which they had undergone at the hands of the Germans provided the spark which set on fire the ugly portion of the crowd.'

The violence began on Saturday 17 October at about 10 p.m. when a shop in Deptford High Street owned by F. Reigler had a brick thrown at it by a member of a crowd which had been standing outside and preventing customers from entering. All sorts of missiles were then hurled and the premises were set alight. A crowd of 5,000 had soon gathered and turned its attention to two other German shops. At one of them, a butcher's belonging to F. Arold, the family had to use the roof to escape to the house of a neighbour. Police reinforcements arrived and surrounded the three shops mentioned to prevent members of the crowd from entering. 'Women as well as men took part in the rioting, while children kept running to and from buildings in the course of demolition bringing supplies of bricks.' The rioters then moved to a confectioner's shop in another part of the High Street owned by J. Goebel. After smashing every window about fifty men and youths, 'many of them in various stages of intoxication', entered the premises and destroyed everything they could on the ground floor. They subsequently went upstairs and threw items of furniture out of the windows. An attempt was made to get out a piano but this failed. The police then moved in and eighteen people trapped in the house by the piano were arrested. Various other shops in Deptford were also attacked. At about midnight, when the riot was at its height, the police decided to call in the army and about 350 men stationed nearby arrived. Armed with rifles they surrounded the shops and kept the crowds back. By about 3 a.m. the streets had been cleared by mounted police.

On the following day Deptford High Street became full of people who began rioting at 11 p.m. despite the presence of policemen in the area. The attack centred on a public house owned by R.G. Ingledew whom the crowd believed to be an Austrian. For over an hour an estimated five to six thousand people pelted the premises with missiles of every description. 'Numerous other shops were visited, but there the damage was inconsiderable, the crowd perhaps having consideration for the fact that the tenants were not alien enemies.' Order did not return until 2 a.m. People crowded the High Street again on Monday but a police presence of more than 400 managed to maintain control.

Meanwhile, similar events had taken place in other parts of south London on a smaller scale. On Saturday a crowd of several thousand surrounded the shop of a butcher called Eberlen in Old Kent Road and smashed the windows with the help of glasses obtained from a nearby public house. Furthermore, the shop of another butcher in Albany Road, George Melsheimer, also came under attack. This was despite the fact that he had a notice up declaring that he had become naturalised in 1909. In Atlantic Road, Brixton, a shop belonging to a baker called Zoller was surrounded by a crowd of about 500 people who attempted to enter it. But the police intervened and the mob dispersed.

On Monday night between 8 and 10 o'clock a huge crowd assembled at Lee Green, 'it having been freely rumoured that an attack was to be made on the Old Tiger's Head.' Although the landlord was a German, his loyalties unquestionably lay with England as the building acted as headquarters of the local rifle club. In fact, the decision to attack the pub had more to do with its licensing hours than the nationality of the publican. In the end about fifteen policemen surrounding the premises succeeded in controlling the situation. On the same night another large crowd gathered on Rushey Green in Catford with the intention of attacking the shop of a German who had resided in England for thirty or forty years. However, the police also managed to prevent violence from breaking out here.

Between fifty and sixty people were arrested as a result of the weekend disturbances. Thirty appeared at the Greenwich Police Court on Monday. Their ages varied from 15 to 49 and all lived locally. They included a soldier who had taken items of jewellery. The Magistrate remanded all the prisoners with the exception of one woman with six children. When the defendants appeared at the London Sessions on 3 November, the Chairman declared: 'Nothing could be more dangerous . . . than to permit a general mob to take the administration of justice into their own hands.' He therefore imposed some severe sentences of up to 12 months' hard labour, although in most cases he bound people over (*Kentish Mercury*, 23 October 1914; *South London Press*, 23 October 1914; *Daily News*, 19 October 1914).

The south London riots received widespread coverage and condemnation in the national press. Two of the major Liberal journals, the *Westminster Gazette*, on 20 October, and the *Daily News*, on 19 October, complained of 'the injury inflicted on the honour and fair name of England in the eyes of the world'. Both blamed the Unionist newspapers for the violence. The *Daily News*, for instance, in an editorial entitled 'The Pogrom Mongers', talked of 'that portion of the Press which for days past has been assiduously inciting against unfortunate aliens in this country every passion which insane suspicion can arouse and mean vindictiveness cherish into flame.' The *Evening News* and *Daily Mail* of 19 October, however, rejected all responsibility and the latter blamed the 'apathy of officialdom in dealing with the German and Austrian subjects in our midst'.

A week after the Deptford riots came another serious outbreak of violence, this time in Crewe. No male alien enemies actually lived in the city as the last one had recently been arrested and taken to an internment camp. However, feeling ran high against pork butchers of German origin who had become naturalised. The riot took place on Saturday 24 October. It began at about 10 p.m., as the public houses closed, with a gathering of people who went to the shop of a butcher called Gronbach and proceeded to smash the windows and then make off with the contents. The proprietor managed to escape to the police station. The crowd which now numbered over 1,000 'many of them girls and women and mere spectators', then split in two. Each half went to a different butcher's shop, one of which was opposite the police station. Here, two soldiers who assisted the police were seriously assaulted and needed medical treatment. The police eventually dispersed the crowd. However, about fifty to sixty 'young men and boys' proceeded towards Nantwich, about four miles away, where Gronbach had another shop. Nevertheless, the Chief Constable of Cheshire, making his way to Crewe, persuaded them to return to the city. Extra police were drafted in but violence did not break out again (*Manchester Guardian*, 26 October 1914; PRO HO45 10944/257142/19).

In fact, no serious disturbances occurred in any part of the country until May 1915. The intervening period proved quite peaceful with regard to the incidence of anti-German hostility. However, May 1915 witnessed some of the most widespread riots during the twentieth century in Britain affecting practically every part of the country. They began in Liverpool then spread to Manchester and subsequently to the Midlands, Yorkshire, Derbyshire, the North East, South Wales and London. They resulted in vast damage. Before describing their development we need to establish their immediate causes.

Contemporaries offered three reasons which basically, though not exclusively, reflected their position on the political spectrum. In the first place the Unionists held responsible simply the act of the sinking of the passenger liner *Lusitania* as well as the government's aliens policy, which they viewed as weak. Liberals, meanwhile, blamed press reaction to the *Lusitania* incident. In addition, Sylvia Pankhurst, the socialist and feminist, regarded the disturbances as hunger riots. We can discuss each of these in turn.

The *Lusitania* was sunk by a German submarine on Friday 7 May with the loss of over 1,000 lives. The first act of violence occurred in Liverpool on the following day. *The Times*, the voice of Unionism, drew a direct connection between the two developments because the city 'regarded the magnificent ship as its own special possession, one of the glories of its great port.' More importantly, 'to add to the sense of personal loss, the captain and nearly every man of the crew came from Liverpool' (*The Times*, 8, 10 May 1915). A local Conservative journal, the *Liverpool Courier*, on 11 May, described the situation in more emotive language:

> The disaster to the Lusitania, in which helpless non-combatants were foully murdered, has affected Liverpool in particular. By one coward blow hundreds of homes in the city have been bereft. Can there be any wonder that among the less disciplined classes, who have had to freely sacrifice their menfolk on the battlefield, the feeling of bitter enmity against the Germans should he exacerbated beyond restraint?

These assertions receive support from Pat O'Mara who participated in the rioting and recalled 'the cries of the women whose husbands and sons had gone down in the "Lusy" ' and 'the bitter threats made against Germany and everything with a German name' (O' Mara, 1934, pp. 224–5).

Nevertheless, this explanation of the riots seems unconvincing. Firstly, it cannot apply to other parts of the country, unconnected with the *Lusitania*. Even in Liverpool, hardly any of the rioters appearing in court had relatives on the ship, according to reports of legal proceedings in the press. At the same time a number of important figures in Lancashire made some highly explosive statements which incited the local population. Lord Derby, for instance, declared: 'this country calls no longer for men to fight an honourable foe. It calls for men to hunt down and crush once and for all a race of cold-blooded murderers.' A Liverpool priest, meanwhile, wrote to the *Liverpool Courier* stating that if 'popular fury' resulted in the expulsion of Germans from Britain, 'it will be a blessing in disguise' (*The Times*, 10 May 1915; *Liverpool Courier*, 12 May 1915).

At this point we can turn to the liberal interpretation of the riots. The *Manchester Guardian* explained it in a leading article of 14 May 1915 which asserted that although:

the fury of the people is only too intelligible . . . it has taken forms which are unworthy of us, and some of the responsibility for the violence must fall on the men who, without the mob's excuse of ignorance, have written thinly-veiled incitements to violence, and in one case even to murder.

The *New Statesman*, meanwhile, published a powerful editorial on 22 May which asserted:

Last week's anti alien riots made it only too clear that there are journalists of a Prussian ferocity in this country who exercise on evil influence over the mob far beyond what is justified by anything but their shouting. They also made it clear that they have the power to injure the good name of this country in the eyes of the civilised world as no mere defeat by land or sea could do. They are an incitement to cruelty and violence.

In order to establish the truth of such assertions, we need to take a brief look at press comment from as early as April 1915 because the sinking of the *Lusitania* 'came towards the end of a month in which the tide of popular feeling in this country against Germany and German methods of war had been steadily rising to a height never before reached' (*Manchester Guardian History of the War*, 1915, vol. 2, p. 353). In the first place, stories had appeared in England about the treatment of prisoners of war in Germany and on 10 April the government published a white paper claiming that the Hague Convention had been violated. The press made the most of this information. On 20 April, for instance, the *Daily Mail* claimed that:

while the hapless British prisoners in Germany have been savagely misused, half starved, deprived of medical attention and clothing, and treated with a calculated ferocity, the German prisoners in this country have been 'coddled', to the disgust of all right-thinking women and men.

In May 1915 *The Navy*, the official journal of the Navy League, condemned the acts of Germany's 'naval highwaymen'. This referred to the fact that since February German submarines had attacked all types of vessels found in British waters, whether armed or not. Between 18 February and 28 May the German navy sank twenty-five merchant ships. On 3 May alone eight British trawlers were destroyed near North Sea fishing grounds. Meanwhile, on the same day the press carried news of the German poisoning of wells in South-West Africa.

However, 'among all the evidence of calculated cruelty on the part of the Germans probably none roused more widespread horror and indignation, when its nature and consequences were fully realised, than did the use of asphyxiating gas.' The German army first employed it on 22 April during the second battle of Ypres and 'for the next three weeks attacks begun and supported by this hideous weapon were an almost daily episode on this part of the French and British front.' Among national newspapers, both the *Daily Express* and *The Times* reacted particularly strongly. The former stated that 'we must expect the Germans to fight like savages who have acquired a knowledge of chemistry.' The latter, meanwhile, wrote: 'The wilful and systematic attempt to choke and poison our soldiers . . . will deepen our indignation and our resolution, and it will fill all races with a horror of the German name' (Haste, 1977, pp. 98–100; *Manchester Guardian History of the War*, 1915, vol. 2, pp. 355–7; Ponsonby, 1928, p. 146).

It was in this atmosphere that news of the sinking of the *Lusitania* reached the British press which immediately conveyed its impressions of the act to the British public. Both national and provincial newspapers used powerful and provocative language. On the day after the event a leading article in *The Times* declared that 'the whole world is ringing with the stories of this crowning crime'. It asserted that 'the Germans and their pliant tools' would 'wreck the fabric of civilisation' unless 'every civilised power' joined in 'branding with eternal infamy the renegade among the nations'. On the same day, 8 May, Manchester's *Evening Chronicle* carried the following headline: 'LOSS OF 1,457 LIVES IN THE LUSITANIA. GERMANS GLOAT OVER THE MURDER OF WOMEN AND CHILDREN'.

On this day, Saturday, the first disturbances broke out in Liverpool. They did not spread to Manchester until Monday afternoon. In the meantime, a series of highly inflammatory articles appeared in many newspapers. The *Weekly Dispatch* published one of these by Robert Blatchford, with the headline, 'THE BRANDED RACE. WHY ARE ANY GERMANS LEFT OUTSIDE GAOLS IN BRITAIN? LESSON OF LUSITANIA MURDERS'. The author claimed:

The Germans who sank the *Lusitania* are the same scoundrels as the Germans who poisoned the wells, who shelled Scarborough, who dropped bombs in Paris, who used poison gas at Ypres. They belong to the same people who are frantic with desire to drop bombs on the crowded area of London: the same people who, women as well as men, would go mad with joy if their uniformed savages could get loose in an orgy of atrocity in some quiet English village . . .

How many Germans are living in this country—and not in Gaol? What are they doing here? Why do we allow them to mix with decent people? What are we going to do about Germany after the war? Are we going to treat Germany as we treat civilised and moral nations?

Significantly, Blatchford made no distinction between the German army, the German nation, and the German people wherever they might be: Germans in Britain were certainly no exception.

The most inflammatory press article of all appeared on Saturday 15 May in *John Bull*. This must be quoted at length because, as the *New Statesman* commented a week later, it seems to be 'the most disgraceful passage we have ever read in an English paper'. It was written, like all the leading articles in *John Bull*, by its editor, Horatio Bottomley. However, on this occasion, Bottomley addressed his readers in the first person so 'that there may be no doubt as to its authorship, and no uncertainty about the identity of the individual to be arrested and prosecuted if, in the view of a timorous and nerveless executive, I have transgressed the bounds of legitimate journalism.' Bottomley began: 'I call for a Vendetta—a vendetta against every German in Britain, whether "naturalised" or not. As I have said elsewhere, you cannot naturalise an unnatural beast—a human abortion—a hellish freak. But you *can* exterminate it. And now the time has come.' Bottomley continued to use language of such intensity for a further two pages. After pointing out that 'thousands upon thousands of German savages are in our midst' and suggesting that the crews of U-boats should be hung 'at the mast of a British ship', he explained to his readers the meaning of a vendetta. He then continued:

And now for *my* vendetta. I have used the words 'blood feud'—and I am not afraid of them. Personally, I am prepared to avenge every German outrage *in kind*. And I should welcome the formation of a National Council of Righteous Retribution—a national Vendetta, pledged to exterminate every German-born man (God forgive the term!) in Britain—and to deport every German-born woman and child. 'Red ruin and the breaking up of laws' have no terror for me, *in these times*. I would let loose the bloodhounds of vengeance. I would pay the Germans in their own coin. I would hang the pirates, or let them drown. Like Mr. A.G. Hales, I would put in the field an army of Zulus and Basutos and other native and half-civilised tribes—and let them run amok in the enemy's ranks. I would give them all the asphyxiating gas they wanted. I would allow no prisoners to be taken, on either land or sea; and I would do a lot of other things. But it would all be very 'wicked' and very 'cruel'—and there would be the danger of German 'reprisals', and all that sort of thing. At least, that is what you would be told; and it sounds so very plausible that you would probably believe it. As a matter of fact, it would end the war in a few weeks. But I will restrain myself and plead for a milder form of vendetta—and yet one which would be all-powerful for the peace of the world and the good of mankind.

Four proposals were put forward. Firstly, that the banner of the Kaiser should be removed from St George's Chapel. Secondly, that enemy alien property should be seized. Thirdly, that every German woman should be 'kept under lock and key, and every man put to work—either mine-sweeping, or on trawlers, merchant ships and passenger vessels sailing within the prohibited "zone". Then the Kaiser will know that each time he sinks a vessel he will be expediting a fellow countryman on his way to Hell.' As for naturalised Germans, they should be *'compelled to wear a distinctive badge*, prominently displayed', while none of their children 'should be allowed to attend any school, either public or private'. Bottomley's fourth proposal was that all interned German ships should be confiscated. He then went on to say: 'No German must be allowed to live in our land. No shop, no factory, no office, no trade, no profession must be open to him . . . In short, the moral leprosy of the tribe to which he belongs must be emphasised by a boycott in every relation of life.'

The *New Statesman*, on 22 May believed that Bottomley 'has given utterance to what can only be interpreted as a gospel of murder and atrocity on a level with the most fiendish crimes the Germans have committed in Belgium.' On the same day that Bottomley's article appeared, serious riots broke out throughout the country. Bearing in mind the contention of *John Bull*, that it had the 'largest circulation of any weekly journal in the United Kingdom', his comments may well have had some effect. Nevertheless, we do need some caution on the whole subject of press responsibility for the riots. In the first place it proves impossible to find a direct link between a newspaper article and the actions of any individual rioter. No records of court proceedings would support this, for instance. At the same time, the relationship between the press and the public is two-way: newspapers print what they believe will be popular and bring in revenue. Therefore, we can argue that press reaction to the sinking of the *Lusitania* simply put into writing the views of much of the populace, which *may* have rioted in any case. However, we can also argue that the press brings to the surface the subconscious thoughts of its readers and urges them into action. Riots would probably not have occurred if people had not read the strength of language quoted above which, explicitly or implicitly, called for violence against enemy aliens. At the same time, we should also remember that on other occasions when serious anti-German disturbances broke out, October 1914 and June 1916, feelings against Germany again reached a peak of intensity and the press drew clear links between enemy aliens in Britain and their countrymen in Germany.

Nevertheless, we also need to look at the more radical explanation of the riots advanced by Sylvia Pankhurst. She wrote that what took place in the East End 'was largely a hunger riot; the women and children who snatched bread and meat from the aliens snatched it not from hatred of Germany, but because they were hungry.' With specific reference to Salford, meanwhile, another source stated: 'There would be many a breakfast table set better this morning than it has ever been' (Pankhurst, 1932, p. 171; Roberts, 1971, p. 155). However, we can dismiss the idea of hunger riots for at least five reasons.

First, the disturbances did not remain confined to 'working-class' areas, as the description of their course below will show. While Liverpool and east London may have suffered in particular, we should remember that districts with no tradition of 'racial violence' also suffered. Any examination of the 'culture and social history' of the areas which suffered would only offer a very partial explanation of the violence. While we can admit that Liverpool had a powerful tradition of sectarian violence which formed the background for the anti-

German disturbances, not even the East End of London had a strong tradition of large-scale racial violence upon which the rioters could draw. We can obviously direct similar comments towards disturbances in towns such as Hull, Walton-on-Thames and Ipswich.

Second, the Great War meant an alleviation in the conditions of the 'working classes'. Arthur Marwick has written that 'constant employment, longer hours, and war bonuses meant an upward movement in earnings, clearly noticeable from February and March 1915.' In most cases this offset the rise in food prices and the deterioration in housing conditions. A more thoroughly researched study by J.M. Winter has substantiated these views (Marwick, 1986, pp. 124–8; Winter, 1986, pp. 213–15).

A look at court proceedings also helps to dismiss the idea of hunger riots. For instance, the occupational and social status and the gender and age of the rioters varied. Of those people who appeared in the Marylebone Police Court, in connection with disturbances in Kentish Town and Camden Town in London, we can basically place most of the rioters within the 'working classes'. Nevertheless, within this stratum those concerned ranged from cabinet-makers and locomotive firemen to 'paper-hangers' and labourers. Ages also show no uniformity. For instance, of those reported by the *Saint Pancras Guardian* to have appeared at the Marylebone Police Court on 13 May, four were under 20, two between 20 and 30, three between 30 and 40, and one over 40. Similarly, no pattern emerges with regard to the sex of the rioters. These comments apply equally to those prosecuted in Manchester and Liverpool (Panayi, 1988, p. 9).

More revealing is an analysis of the premises attacked. In the East End of London, for instance, Russian Jews and Englishmen suffered in addition to Germans (*Daily Sketch*, 13 May 1915). However, as one contemporary wrote: 'In the opinion of the British in the East End, it is better that a Scotsman with a German-looking name, or an Irishman with a German-sounding accent, should suffer (both being colourable imitations of Germans) than a genuine German should escape' (MacDonagh, 1935, p. 64). There remains little doubt that the vast majority of premises attacked throughout the country belonged to Germans, naturalised Germans, or people assumed to be Germans. For instance, a list of fourteen shops which suffered damage in St Pancras shows that all had German names (*St Pancras Chronicle*, 14 May 1915). Within London, of the bakers' premises attacked (over 150), few did not belong to Germans. The fact that such a large number of bakers did suffer damage, resulting in a temporary bread shortage, might suggest hunger riots. However, we have to bear two things in mind. First, the fact that so many Germans owned bread shops throughout London. And, second, bakers represented only a fraction of the 2,000, properties which suffered in the capital (*Bakers Record*, 14 May 1915).

An examination of the nature of the charges faced by those who appeared in court reveals no clear figures with regard to the incidence of theft and looting compared with public order offences. For the first sixty-seven people who appeared at the Dale Street Police Court in Liverpool, the offences included stealing, looting, doing wilful damage to property, and assaulting a policeman. On the following day, 11 May, a further forty-five prisoners faced a similar variety of charges. However, the majority of the 300 people appearing at the same court on Monday 17 May were charged with looting or receiving stolen goods. A similar pattern emerges in proceedings in courts in Birkenhead, Salford, Thames and Marylebone, i.e. early defendants faced public order charges while later ones faced theft and looting charges. This evidence cannot persuade us that the events of May 1915 were hunger riots. Although many people did take food from butchers and bakers, the majority of people appearing in court throughout the country on charges of theft had stolen not edible products but clothing, furniture, carpets, crockery, jewellery, machine fittings and, in one case, even a crucifix (Panayi, 1988, pp. 9–10; *St Pancras Guardian*, 14, 21 May 1915; *East London Observer*, 15, 22 May 1915). The safest conclusion we can reach about the disturbances is that they were sparked off and fuelled by press reaction to the sinking of the *Lusitania*, but resulted in large-scale looting of a wide variety of goods. They remain anti-German because the majority of premises attacked belonged to enemy aliens or people of enemy alien origin, as a description of their course will now demonstrate.

As already mentioned, the initial outbreaks of violence occurred in Liverpool on Saturday 8 May. The first affected district of the city was the North East, where a Mr Fischer's premises in Walton Lane had windows smashed, and foodstuffs thrown into the streets. Dimler's in County Road, suffered similarly. The police eventually arrived to clear the crowd away but simply succeeded in forcing it into Spellow Station where three more shops suffered damage. About sixty police officers now attempted to disperse the rioters but by this time they had doubled in number. They pulled down the shutters of Deeg's shop, in Fountains Road, flinging them into the street, and destroyed the front of the premises. Meanwhile, nineteen people were arrested during an attack on a pork butcher's shop in Robson Street. This appears the extent of the rioting on Saturday night.

It increased in intensity on the following day, when Dimler's again came under attack, and spread to other parts of Liverpool with shops attacked in Heyworth Street, Fox Street, Richmond Row, Juvenal Street and Mile End. One of the worst incidents took place in Scotland Road where a pork shop was 'absolutely and entirely looted'. During the course of the weekend the police had made about sixty-seven arrests. The bulk of the rioting had taken place in the North End.

The most serious disturbances in Liverpool broke out on Monday when men, women and children wrecked shops throughout the day in many parts of the city. By this time the rioters destroyed the shops of all pork butchers, whether or not they were of German origin, as well as German shops of every description. The day's rioting began early in the morning when a crowd of about 2,000 armed with a variety of weapons marched into the Mill Street neighbourhood. Despite the posting of policemen outside shops kept by those believed to have German connections, much damage occurred. Butchers' shops were wrecked in Mill Street, Warwick Street, Upper Hill Street, Northumberland Street, Windsor Street, North Hill Street, St James Street, Lodge Lane and Crown Street. Further disturbances broke out in the North End where Deeg's shop lost its remaining windows and contents. Rioting also occurred in Paddington while in Great George Street the property of a butcher named Yaag was demolished.

During Monday afternoon and evening the rioting spread to Bootle, Birkenhead and Seacombe and became just as serious as earlier events. One of the worst incidents involved an attack on a fountain pen factory in Seacombe which had 'been carried on by a supposed German' for the preceding two years. A large force of police and special constables eventually restored order during the evening. In fact, special constables were quite widely used and transported in cars. But during Monday the Chief Constable of Liverpool had contacted the Home Office about the possibility of receiving military aid. The latter agreed but in the end troops made no appearance.

Less violence occurred on Tuesday but the rioters who had left few German shops unscathed now attacked German houses. In Wallasey a crowd of 2,000 attempted a march on the suburbs but a police cordon across Wexford Road turned it back. It is not clear whether the rioters wanted to attack richer German properties in this area or whether, by this time, they had become intent on looting any houses, irrespective of the nationality of the owner.

It does seem certain, however, that by now, also as a result of the destruction of all the German shops, the disturbances had developed into anti-alien, and not simply anti-German riots. Scandinavians, Italians and Russians all suffered. But most evidence survives about the Chinese who first came under attack on Monday. On Tuesday morning the Chinese legation in London received a letter 'from an English friend in Liverpool' which asserted that, 'owing to the sinking of the "Lusitania" by the Germans the crowds of the Liverpool roughs have completely wrecked many Chinese residences in this city.' On the following day the legation received a petition with thirty-nine signatures requesting protection from the 'British Authorities. The Chinese 'Minister' therefore informed the Foreign Office which, in turn, contacted the Home Office. However, nothing happened because the violence had run its course by 12 May (*Liverpool Daily Post*, 10, 11, 12, 13 May 1915; *Liverpool Weekly Post*, 15 May 1915; *Liverpool Courier*, 12 May 1915; PRO HO45 10944/257142/36).

The Times estimated that during four days of rioting Liverpool had suffered £40,000 worth of damage and that 200 'establishments' had been 'gutted'. In fact, the latter figure underestimates the situation because over the following weeks the City Council received 563 claims for compensation. This indicates local violence on a vast scale (*The Times*, 13 May 1915; Liverpool Record Office, 352 POL1/37). It finally ceased because of a combination of factors including the decision of the local police to intern enemy aliens and the appearance of rain. Furthermore, by this time a substantial percentage of properties belonging to foreigners had been destroyed. But perhaps most important was simply the fact that the courts had begun to sentence large numbers of rioters.

The first sixty-seven prisoners, arrested as a result of the weekend disturbances, appeared at the Dale Street Police Court on Monday. Most of those found guilty were remanded for seven days. The Stipendiary declared that although he could understand that the first news of the *Lusitania* affected everybody, he rejected it as a justification for the riots and pledged that future rioters would not receive such lenient treatment. On the following day a further forty-five people appeared before the Stipendiary. The prisoners included young men of military age and the Magistrate suggested that they should 'be fighting the Germans at the front'. He carried out his threat of the preceding day by imposing many sentences of 21 or 28 days' imprisonment. Various other courts in Liverpool dealt with rioters on this day and in most cases the Magistrates remanded prisoners.

Most of those appearing at Dale Street on Wednesday belonged to 'the class of habitual offenders, a class prone to fly at drink at each opportunity and eager to join in any display of hooliganism.' The Magistrate dealt severely with people who had attacked friendly aliens, particularly Russians. For instance, he sentenced one woman to 28 days for being drunk and disorderly and to 52 days for wilfully breaking two glass windows. On this day the Stipendiary kept to a consistent policy of sending to prison those who had previous convictions and fining those who had not. In fact, Magistrates throughout Liverpool adhered to this policy during the trials of other rioters over the next week (*Liverpool Daily Post*, 11, 13, 14, 17, 18 May 1915; *Liverpool Courier*, 12 May 1915; *Manchester Guardian*, 13 May 1915).

Although the disturbances in Manchester may not have become as serious as those in Liverpool, they remain the worst anti-alien riots in the city's recent history, casting serious doubt over ideas about Manchester's 'tradition of tolerance towards strangers and foreigners consistent with' the city's 'great liberal tradition in trade and politics' (Crawford, 1962, p. 110). Although during the weekend of 8 and 9 May a few minor incidents had developed, the first major outbreak of violence occurred on Monday 10 May. On this day three areas experienced disorder: Gorton, Openshaw and Salford. In the first of these, a pork butcher's came under attack in the morning but a police presence managed to keep the situation under control. Many of those involved in this incident subsequently made up some of the estimated 10,000 crowd which attacked two pork shops belonging to Leonard Lambert in Openshaw. One lay in Ashton Old Road and the other in Abbey Hey Lane.

The first signs of a disturbance in Salford came at about 7 p.m. when a small crowd threatened the premises of a pork butcher in Regent Street. However, no damage resulted. Shortly afterwards, a large crowd of people destroyed and looted a pork shop in Eccles New Road belonging to a naturalised British subject of German origin. Meanwhile, crowds attacked a pork butcher's and a fruiterer's in Cross Lane. However, a substantial police presence managed to limit the damage. At about the same time people collected outside a pork butcher's shop in Tatton Street which had formerly belonged to a German but had recently been taken over by an Englishman. After the rioters broke the windows, a patrol van with a dozen police arrived and moved them on, but they only went as far as a naturalised German jeweller's shop in Regent Road where they failed to inflict any great damage. The crowd then passed into Trafford Road and broke some windows at the Trafford Hotel. The police finally restored order at about 2 a.m.

Manchester experienced its worst riots on Tuesday 11 May, which the *Manchester Courier* described as 'without parallel in the history of the city. The windows of scores of shops were damaged and the occupants in many cases had to be smuggled away secretly by the police' to prevent personal violence. The disorder affected many areas of Salford and Manchester. In the former, crowds, of mainly women, had gathered outside the shop of a pork butcher named Hoffer in Greengate from 7 a.m. During the course of the afternoon shops and houses came under attack in West Union Street, Oldfield Road, Cromwell Road and numerous other streets throughout Salford.

After dark, Ellor Street became a 'principal storm centre'. The crowds wrecked five shops here, none of which belonged to Germans. Subsequently, over one thousand people attacked the Royal Hotel at the corner of Tatton Street and Phoebe Street where the licensee was Mrs Georgiana Pressler. Other shops attacked in Salford during the evening included a pork butcher's shop and an eating house in Regent Road, the Trafford Park Hotel in Trafford Road, and a jeweller's in Chapel Street. Thousands of people also wrecked a series of properties in Lower Broughton Road where the available police, including two on horseback, remained powerless. The Salford Hospital treated 'several persons' for injuries received during the rioting. At the same time, 'about a score of Germans called at the Town Hall and outlying police stations to seek police protection.'

Violence spilled into Eccles and Patricroft. In the former, three premises came under attack in Church Street. At Patricroft a crowd threw stones at a second-hand clothes shop owned by an Englishwoman married to a German. Other areas which experienced violence on Tuesday included Ancoats, Bradford and Clayton, Ardwick, Gorton and Openshaw. In Ancoats, mill girls attacked and looted several pork shops during the afternoon. In the evening rioting spread to Ardwick where a crowd, estimated at 5,000, wrecked houses and business premises belonging to Germans. Mounted police eventually restored order. In Hyde Road, West Gorton, meanwhile, a house belonging to an English widow of a German suffered serious damage, as did that of her daughter, living next door. Extremely violent scenes occurred in Chancery Lane, Ashton Old Road, and Abbey Hey Lane (*Manchester Evening Chronicle*, 10 May 1915; *Manchester Guardian*, 11, 12 May 1915; *Manchester Courier*, 12 May 1915; *Reporter for the County Borough of Salford*, 15 May, 5 June 1915; *Eccles and Patricroft Journal*, 14 May 1915).

These proved the most serious incidents on the worst day of the Manchester disturbances. Although people took to the streets on Wednesday, only a few minor incidents developed. It is difficult to estimate the exact amount of damage caused during the three days of rioting. In Salford thirty properties had come under attack and subsequent claims for compensation amounted to over £2,000. Manchester City Council, meanwhile, received 107 claims totalling £2,375. Although a large proportion of those whose property suffered damage were naturalised British subjects, the local police still decided to round up unnaturalised male alien enemies for internment. The *Manchester Guardian* held this action partially responsible for the fact that the rioting ceased on this day because it gave 'the public a sense that justice had been done' (Manchester Reference Library Archives, Manchester Watch Committee Minutes, vol. 47; *Manchester Guardian*, 13 May, 8 June 1915).

This newspaper also mentioned the 'sobering effect' of the arrests of the previous day. Twenty-one people appeared in the Manchester City Police Court on 12 May when the Magistrate handed out generally lenient sentences. However, he warned that although he could 'quite realise the provocation people have had in this country . . . this sort of conduct does no good, and must not be continued.' Therefore, on the following day, as well as imposing fines, he also jailed three men (*Manchester Evening News*, 12 May 1915; *Manchester Guardian*, 13, 14 May 1915; *Manchester Evening Chronicle*, 13 May 1915).

When we turn to events in London it becomes clear that we are dealing with extremely serious violence. Out of the twenty-one Metropolitan Police districts, only two remained free from disorder (Reay, 1920, p. 159). Violence did not badly affect London until Tuesday 11 May. At this point it is important to bear in mind that the disturbances took place against a background of a boycott of Germans by all the major trade establishments, including the Stock Exchange and many other London institutions and provincial exchanges (Panayi, 1991, pp. 199–200). This boycott spread to Smithfield market where hundreds of Germans, who had used the market for years were to experience hardship (*Manchester Guardian*, 12 May 1915).

Kentish Town became one of the first areas to experience violence. Feeling started to run high on Sunday night when one of the bakers to suffer gave a party above his shop which 'was taken by some of the people in the vicinity as a token that rejoicing was taking place over the hideous tragedy perpetrated by the Germans on Friday.' On Tuesday evening a recruiting meeting was held at which the speakers called for the government to intern all alien enemies. In addition, a resolution was passed 'pledging those present not to deal with alien shopkeepers'. Some of those at the meeting must have misinterpreted this because from 9 o'clock, bakers in Kentish Town came under fierce attack. The few police at hand were initially quite powerless and did not restore order until they received support from a combination of mounted police, special constables and territorials (*Saint Pancras Chronicle*, 14 May 1915; *Saint Pancras Guardian*, 14 May 1915; *The Times*, 12 May 1915; PRO HO45 10944/257142/40a).

The most serious rioting of Tuesday occurred in East London. Germans came under attack in Poplar, Limehouse, Bow, Canning Town, Plaistow and North Woolwich. About 200 police and sixty special constables dealt with the disorder 'and were assisted by any military who were about and off duty'. Fifteen constables sustained injuries and thirty-six people were arrested. Sixty-five shops suffered damage, including more than twelve in Poplar where some of the worst disturbances occurred. The violence here began when a pork butcher's shop had stones thrown at it by a group of boys. Within a few minutes a large crowd had assembled and only the presence of many troops and police prevented serious damage. In St Leonard's Road a crowd of five or six thousand people 'were still marching up and down' at 11 o'clock (*East London Observer*, 15 May 1915; PRO HO45 10944/257142/40a).

Other London districts affected on Tuesday included Walthamstow, where crowds smashed the windows of bakers in the High Street; Kensal Town, where damage was done to four or five premises 'by catapults used from windows', and Epsom. The Commissioner of Police believed that all the shops attacked belonged to Germans. Superintendents anticipated further trouble, but surely not on the scale on which it arrived, for on the following day London became 'one vast riot area' (*Hackney and Kingsland Gazette*, 14 May 1915; *Daily Sketch*, 12 May 1915; *Daily Mail*, 13 May 1915; PRO HO45 10944/257142/40a).

Some of the most violent scenes occurred in Smithfield Market, where most of the German butchers turned up to buy meat despite the boycott announced on the previous day. They were at once attacked by 'troops of porters'. One German was chased by 300 people across Farringdon Street and into Holborn. He eventually escaped by jumping into a bus. A different individual was ducked in a horse trough while being taunted with the cry, 'You drown the women and children and now we'll drown you.' Many Germans who arrived at the market with carts saw their horse's harness cut. It is clear that some people were badly beaten up, 'their clothes in some instances being torn from their backs.'

Outside Smithfield, Germans and Austrians throughout London, 'whether naturalised or not, were hunted by men, women, and children, attacked in the street, and in their shops, and in many cases severely handled.' The *Daily Mail* claimed: 'Stranger scenes have never been witnessed in London than occurred yesterday when the attacks made overnight on the premises and persons of German shopkeepers in the East End broke out afresh and spread like wildfire in many widely spread quarters of the town.' As this quote makes clear, the East End once again suffered most seriously. But, within this district, 'It was not one particular area alone that was affected. From Aldgate to Canning Town, and from the River to Bethnal Green and Old Ford, there was serious rioting and destruction' (*Daily Sketch*, 13 May 1915; *Daily Mail*, 13 May 1915; *Daily Graphic*, 13 May 1915; *Manchester Guardian*, 13 May 1915; *East London Observer*, 15 May 1915).

The Times of 13 May described the situation as follows:

> There was very little work done in the East-end throughout the day. Shopkeepers of unequivocal British birth in the areas where rioting was most violent thought it wise to close their doors for the day, and in some of the streets which run off the Commercial-road there was scarcely a shop which was not shuttered.
>
> The damage done by the rioters was very great. Not content with smashing doors and windows and looting the whole of the furniture and the contents of the shops, the interiors of the houses were in numerous instances greatly damaged. Staircases were hacked to pieces and ceilings were knocked down. Shops were completely wrecked before the police had time to arrive on the scene. At Poplar, for instance in an area of a quarter of a mile half a dozen houses were attacked simultaneously by different crowds in the early afternoon. Before the constables were able to attempt to disperse the mob, horse-drawn carts, handcarts, and perambulators—besides the unaided arms of men, women, and children—had taken everything away from the wrecked houses. One saw pianos, chests of drawers, dressers, and the heaviest type of household furniture being carted triumphantly through the streets. 'Here is wealth for the taking', said one man who had possession of several spring mattresses, and was calmly driving his overloaded donkey-cart down C[h]risp-street.

Apart from Chrisp Street, other seriously affected thoroughfares included Salmon Lane, Roman Road, Poplar High Street, Upper North Street and East India Dock Road. At the junction of the last two, a shop belonging to W. Theis, described as 'one of the pillars of the Government party in Poplar', was 'completely emptied. It was said that "tons of flour" were thrown into the street, and the constables on duty, with their whitened clothes, bore testimony to this statement' (*East London Advertiser*, 15 May 1915; *Daily Mail*, 13 May 1915; *East London Observer*, 15 May 1915).

Apart from the East End, another area which witnessed violence during the day was Kentish Town and Camden Town. This was a continuation of Tuesday' s disturbances. Trouble started from as early as 8.30 in the morning on Wednesday when women and children were involved. But many men of military age were among the crowd which gathered outside the shop of Petzold in Camden High Street, which was not actually destroyed until after nightfall. By this time the trouble had spread from Camden Town and Kentish Town to affect the rest of the borough of Saint Pancras (*Saint Pancras Chronicle*, 14 May 1915; *Saint Pancras Guardian*, 14 May 1915).

In fact, it was during the evening that rioting really became widespread throughout London. In south London, for instance, Wandsworth Road and Elephant and Castle experienced serious disorder, and violence also broke out in Fulham, Blackfriars Road, Tooting, Pimlico and Vauxhall. To the west, Shepherd's Bush, Acton and Harlesden suffered, while in North London violence flared up at Tottenham, Highgate, Islington, Holloway and Wood Green. As one contemporary wrote, there was disorder 'in parts of London which would be offended if you described them as the abode of the *proletariat*.'

East London, outside the East End, which has already received attention, suffered some of the worst riots of Wednesday night. In Plaistow, for instance, along Barking Road, many English shops, after being denounced as German-owned, were destroyed by large crowds, while in Stratford approximately 3,000 people wrecked about twelve establishments. In Clapton, a mob of several thousands attacked a bakery belonging to Joseph Engel while he and his wife were in a back room. Adjoining shops were also damaged. Some of the attackers then moved from Median Road to Chatsworth Road where they broke the windows 'of all the bakers' and butchers' shops which were not ostensibly English'. Properties were also damaged in Stoke Newington and Dalston. In Hoxton Street, a very serious disturbance occurred outside the premises of a naturalised Russian Jew called Schneiderman. After smashing the windows, everything was looted and the owner and his family 'were in danger of their lives'. However, after Schneiderman produced his naturalisation certificate, the crowd dispersed. Meanwhile, violence also occurred in Leyton, Leytonstone and Walthamstow (Reay, 1920, p. 158; *Daily Graphic*, 13 May 1915; *The Times*, 13 May 1915; *Daily Sketch*, 13 May 1915; *Daily Mail*, 13 May 1915; *Manchester Guardian*, 13 May 1915; *Hackney and Kingland Gazette*, 14, 21 May 1915).

On Thursday, the rioting died down. In the East End, for instance, Bromley, Poplar, Limehouse, St George's, Mile End and the parliamentary division of Stepney were deserted because 'the rain kept people indoors'. But despite this claim of the *East London Observer*, the same paper mentioned that seven fires were caused on Thursday—four more than the previous day. At one of them, in Duckett Street, Stepney, three policemen were 'partially suffocated, and had to be conveyed to a local surgery for treatment.' Furthermore:

> All the evening, in spite of the rain, Roman-road was fairly full of people; but there was a large force of police, mounted and on foot, as well as special constables, on duty, and they kept the crowd moving, breaking up the gangs of youths which sought an opportunity for mischief.

Disturbances also broke out in Upton Park and Plaistow. In addition, 'Up to 10 o'clock . . . there had been over 100 cases of window breaking and shop wrecking in Hackney, Islington, and Tottenham.' Meanwhile, 'A large crowd destroyed a baker's shop in 'King's-road, Chelsea.' Not far from London, in Gravesend, there was a serious incident involving 1,500 people, including 500 dockers. Calm did not return until 'All the regiments quartered at Milton Barracks were called out and ordered to fix bayonets' (*East London Observer*, 15 May 1915; *East End News*, 18 May 1915; *Daily Mail*, 14 May 1915).

Friday remained relatively quiet, although violence broke out in Peckham and Tottenham. The worst disturbance occurred in Tottenham High Road where a crowd of 5,000 looted a jeweller's. On Saturday morning a German was beaten up in Covent Garden after insisting that the salesmen should serve him. Later on in the day a crowd in Bermondsey 'attacked a baker's shop in Jamaica-road, despite the fact that the owner displayed in his window a portrait of his two sons who are serving in the British Army. The windows were smashed, but the police prevented any looting.' The crowd then broke the windows of a German butcher's in Dockhead after which they moved to a French baker's in Tooley Street. However, a strong police presence here gradually dispersed the crowd (*Weekly Dispatch*, 16 May 1915; *Daily Mail*, 15 May 1915; *Manchester Guardian*, 17 May 1915; *Sunday Pictorial*, 16 May 1915).

Saturday proved the last day of the London riots. What were their effects? In terms of damage to property, extremely severe. By 21 May the Receiver of Police knew of 1,100 cases of 'damage and theft'. Of these, 250 were reported as 'looted', sixty 'wrecked' and seventy 'looted and wrecked'. Over 250 people had suffered injuries. By the end of June the number of claims had reached 1,200 and the amount claimed exceeded £100,000. In late October these figures had increased to 1,950 and £195,000 respectively (PRO HO45 10944/ 257142/84, 89, 151).

The riots also resulted in 866 arrests (*Hansard*, 5th series, vol. 71, col. 1970, 17 May 1915). Therefore, people appeared in the London Police Courts for a time during and after the disturbances charged with offences arising out of them. It is most instructive to look at events in two of the Police Courts: Thames and Marylebone. The former received its first set of prisoners on Wednesday 12 May. The Magistrate dealt lightly with offences such as stone-throwing but quite severely with assaults on police officers. For instance, he sentenced William Swainedon to 21 days' hard labour for striking a sergeant and knocking down a constable who tried to prevent him from pulling down the shutters of a shop in Upper North Street. Individuals found in unlawful possession of goods were given sentences varying from 10 to 20 shillings, and some were remanded. The magistrate remanded a further ten women on the following Monday for the same offence. On the next day he imposed fines of £5 each on three men who had taken five and a half sacks of flour. He also jailed three men for a month because they had stolen furniture from a house belonging to the daughter of a naturalised German (*East London Observer*, 15, 22 May 1915; *East London Advertiser*, 21 May 1915; *East End News*, 21 May 1915).

Seventy-two people appeared in the Marylebone Police Court on 13 May facing public order charges. *The Times* complained that the Magistrate on this day, Paul Taylor, 'had ideas of suitable punishment for disorder . . . somewhat stricter than those of his fellow magistrates.' For instance, he sentenced an artilleryman to one month's hard labour for wilfully breaking a plate glass window and told him that his uniform aggravated the offence. Taylor also imposed prison sentences on many people charged with obstructing the police. More defendants appeared at Marylebone the following week. Out of a group of ten, charged with stealing or receiving stolen goods from a baker's in Kentish Town, four were given prison sentences varying from 14 days to 3 months' hard labour, while the rest were fined, bound over or discharged (*Saint Pancras Guardian*, 14 May 1915; *The Times*, 14 May 1915).

As well as London, Liverpool and Manchester, South Yorkshire also experienced widespread anti-German riots in May 1915. Violence broke out in this district as early as Monday 10 May when a crowd attacked a pork butcher's shop in Mexborough High Street belonging to Councillor George Schonhut. The rioters smashed the windows and the police did not manage to restore order until 2 a.m. Minor disturbances also broke out at Denaby and Conisborough during the same evening. On the following day, another shop belonging to Schonhut, this one in Denaby, was completely wrecked during the morning by a crowd composed mainly of women and youths. Meanwhile, similar scenes occurred in Conisborough.

One of the most bizarre and bloodiest riots occurred in Goldthorpe on Wednesday night. During the day rumours had been circulating to the effect that various people were of enemy nationality. One of the victims was J.R. Bakewell, owner of the London Tea Stores, who was in fact a Derbyshire man. Fearing an attack, he began to build a barricade outside his premises. However, this had the consequence of attracting a crowd which started to throw sticks and stones. The twenty-five policemen present could do little. Someone then stated that Mr Bakewell and his sons were using revolvers. In the confusion that followed one rioter was shot and police reinforcements from Barnsley and Doncaster charged the crowd with batons and eventually restored order. Six people had suffered injury from bullets, two of them seriously. Bakewell and his sons consequently appeared in court facing charges of 'shooting to do grievous bodily harm'.

A few incidents occurred in Sheffield and Attercliffe on Thursday involving the smashing of shop windows, but none of them amounted to very much, partly due to the actions of the police. On the following day, however, the violence became more serious. During the morning, a crowd composed of mainly women and children looted two shops on Attercliffe Common. They then moved to Attercliffe Road where they dealt similarly with the shop of George Hanneman and Sons. After police had arrived on the scene in motor cars and restored order, the rioters moved to the shop of H. Leech, an Englishman, in Staniforth Road. They also ransacked these premises. Further incidents occurred in the afternoon and evening in Newhall Road, Worksop Road and Bright Street.

Meanwhile, there were also serious disturbances in Rotherham where the victims were Germans or naturalised Germans. The trouble started during the afternoon when a group of women and children gathered outside the branch shop of L. Fisher in Hatherley Road 'and demonstrated by shouting and making one or two ugly rushes, but the police were soon on the scene, and no serious damage was done.' The crowd, 'which gradually grew in dimensions', then moved to the premises of C. Hanneman in Frederick Street but the police once more managed to control the situation. 'The next point of attack was a shop of Mr F. Schonhut' where some stones were thrown. But the 'presence of police again prevented serious damage.' However, after this the situation became serious. Shops faced attack in Bridgegate and Bridge Street. When the crowd reached the shop of J. Schonhut in Main Street, it caused between £400 and £500 worth of damage. 'Later, at Mr. C. Keekners, Fernham Road, Masborough, very extensive damage was done and about half an hour afterwards there was a renewed "call" at the shop of Mr Schonhut, of Doncaster Gate, where a large amount of destruction was wrought.' In fact, it seems that a 12-year-old boy was killed outside these premises when he 'fell under the wheels of a heavy motor wagon'. The *Sheffield Daily Telegraph* stated: 'writing at midnight, our reporter described the day as one of the most exciting in the history of the borough. The damage done, it was roughly computed, amounts to over £5,000, many of the premises being completely wrecked.' The Borough Magistrates met hurriedly to consider the situation. Special constables were called to join the regular police, some of whom were mounted. Furthermore, the fire brigade had to deal with a fire at the shop of H. Carley in Wellgate.

On the following evening, Saturday 15 May, even more violent scenes occurred. A crowd gathered outside the Red Lion Hotel in College Street which was kept by F. Schonhut. The local police decided to act and six mounted men were called out along with 160 special constables. 'The throwing of missiles soon became much too frequent and dangerous, and the temper of the hostile mob was distinctly ugly.' The mounted men 'charged through College Square at a gallop when two tramcars were standing at the terminus and people were waiting to board them.' Meanwhile, the foot police 'had commenced to use their batons with effect, and broken heads in plenty were reported. Charge after charge were made, and this method of driving caused a regular stampede.' Sixteen people were treated in hospital although only one was detained overnight. In addition, five policemen were struck by missiles, including Chief Constable Weatherhogg. Only two arrests appear to have been made. On the following night Rotherham was fairly quiet (*Sheffield Daily Telegraph*, 11, 12, 14, 15, 17 May 1915; *Daily Mail*, 14 May 1915; *Manchester Guardian*, 17 May 1915).

As we have mentioned, not only South Yorkshire and the three major cities already mentioned experienced disorder: the violence took place on a truly national scale. In order to emphasise this point we can briefly look at details of events in other parts of the country. In Newcastle, for instance, shops came under attack between Monday 10 May and Thursday 13 May. On Friday violence broke out in Greenock and Bury St Edmunds. In the latter, a crowd attacked a hotel with a German landlord. 'Many troops were called out and they came with fixed bayonets. There was much disorder. Several policemen were knocked down and trampled upon.' Soldiers also made an appearance in Peterborough and violence further occurred in South Shields.

But it was on Saturday that the violence became most widespread. In Scotland, for instance, a crowd wrecked a pork butcher's shop in Annan

belonging to C. Feyerabend. At least four towns in the North East were
affected. At Crook, for example, both a German and an English butcher had
their premises destroyed by a crowd reported to have numbered 8,000. In
Hebburn, meanwhile, the disorder lasted for six hours and the police made
baton charges. In South Shields, seven shops had their windows broken and the
police made fourteen arrests (*The Times*, 11, 13 May 1915; *Weekly Dispatch*, 16
May 1915; *Daily Mail*, 15 May 1915; *Manchester Guardian*, 17 May 1915; *Daily
Sketch*, 17 May 1915.

Further down the coast, in Hull, three pork shops belonging to naturalised
Germans were attacked by a 'good-humoured' crowd (*Eastern Morning News*, 17
May 1915). The local pork butcher also had his shop smashed up in
Chesterfield and nearby Whittington Moor. In Castleford, meanwhile, there
was rioting of a fiercer nature. Again the German pork butchers' shops suffered
together with several English properties (*Sheffield Daily Telegraph*, 17 May
1915). More violent scenes occurred in Neath where the police made seven
truncheon charges in an attempt to clear the streets. Fifty civilians and six
policemen were injured, one very seriously. In Ipswich, meanwhile, the local
pork butcher had his windows smashed. In Tamworth it was a German jeweller
who suffered. Trouble also broke out in the, apparently, most respectable of
places such as Tunbridge Wells and Winchester. In the latter a shop belonging
to a local dairy was attacked 'owing to the belief that the manager was a
German' (*Manchester Guardian*, 17 May 1915).

In Walton-on-Thames the violence was of a more serious character. The
victim was Mr Hilbrand who had lived in the town for twenty-eight years and
whose jewellery shop was singled out by the local population. On Friday the
word 'German' had been chalked up on the premises and on Saturday
Hilbrand, expecting trouble, had closed early and covered the window with the
shutters. A crowd began to assemble outside from about 8.30 p.m. and at 10
o'clock the first stones were thrown. The crowd 'was too much for the ordinary
police on duty to deal with' and so the special constables were called. As they
too could not restore order, the fire brigade was sent for 'in order to "wash" the
crowd away'. But they could do nothing because their hose was cut almost
immediately. Two companies of the Honourable Artillery Company were
finally summoned. Their actions, combined with a threat by the local JP to read
the Riot Act, helped to restore order. More trouble was feared on Sunday and
Monday evening but it did not materialise (*Surrey Herald*, 21 May 1915).

Saturday 15 May proved the last day of the riots. Before coming to any
conclusions a few points will be made about the effectiveness of the police and
special constables. The official historian of the latter claimed that they 'did their
duty at all points, against both honest demonstrators and flagrant thieves, and
they accepted a good deal of knocking about in the effort.' These assertions
remain generally accurate. However, wide of the mark is the claim that 'The
riots were everywhere either suppressed or adequately circumscribed till they
burned themselves out' (Reay, 1920, p. 159). We can judge the inaccuracy of
this sentence by remembering that close to 2,000 properties came under attack
in London alone. During Wednesday 12 May, mobs in the East End, for
instance, destroyed German shops at will. The police presence was minimal
and did not increase until after dark. But perhaps one reason for this lies in the

fact that there just were not enough local policemen available to deal with crowds of up to five thousand or more, while a nearby garrison may not have existed from which troops could move into action. When the army did make an appearance, it proved very successful in containing the violence as in Gravesend and Walton-on-Thames.

Can we find any pattern to the riots? In some instances they were begun during the evening by a group representing all sexes and age groups, continued the following morning and afternoon by women and children, and completed the same night when the men returned from work. This happened in Salford and Kentish Town, for instance. However, in the East End many men seem to have stayed away from work on Wednesday 12 May in order to participate in the rioting and looting. In the minor incidents, the damage occurred during the courses of one or two evenings: Ipswich, Bury St Edmunds and Hull can all be cited. Nevertheless, each disturbance arose out of an individual set of circumstances and each took a unique course.

After the *Lusitania* riots no anti-German violence developed on a comparable scale. The most obvious reasons for this would appear to be the fact that so many German properties had suffered destruction, together with the government's policy of interning enemy aliens and closing down retail businesses owned by Germans. Nevertheless, violence did break out again on various occasions. For instance, June 1916, following the death of Kitchener, was another period when hostility towards Germany reached a peak. Once again the blame for the disorder lies at least partly with press reaction to Kitchener's death. He died on 5 June when the ship which carried him away from Scapa Flow struck a mine (Taylor, 1985, p. 92). On Wednesday 7 May, the *Daily Mail* carried a headline asking, 'WHO SPIED UPON LORD KITCHENER?' On the same day the front page of the *Evening News* declared 'INTERN THEM ALL!', and then carried details about Germans in Britain.

Three areas of London experienced violence: Acton, Islington and Tooting. At the first of these trouble broke out on Wednesday when a crowd gathered outside the shop of a naturalised German in Churchfield Road and broke one of the windows. The demonstrators returned on the following night and caused further damage. They did not disperse until a detachment of special constables arrived on the scene. More serious disturbances occurred in Islington where 'Organised bands swarmed through' Chapel Street, Essex Road and Exmouth Street. In the first of these they attacked several shops and broke plate glass windows. Mounted police managed to clear this thoroughfare but the crowds simply moved into Liverpool Road and Essex Road. Between 10.30 and 11 o'clock reinforcements of police and special constables arrived on the scene and cleared the streets. On Friday, meanwhile, between 500 and 1,000 people assembled outside a shop belonging to a naturalised German in Tooting High Street. The protesters smashed most of the windows in the building and did not disperse until 11 o'clock by which time fifty policemen, eighteen mounted police and a large number of special constables had arrived on the scene (*Acton and Chiswick Express*, 9, 16 June 1916; *Manchester Guardian*, 9 June 1916; *Islington Daily Gazette*, 9 June 1916; *Globe*, 9 June 1916; *South Western Star*, 16 June 1916).

The next outbreak of anti-German disorder in Britain, again in London, occurred in July 1917. On this occasion it proves difficult to blame the press, as the disturbances appear to be a spontaneous reaction to a German air raid. This had taken place on the morning of Saturday 7 July and resulted in fifty-seven deaths and 193 injuries, mostly in the north of the metropolis. The bombs had actually fallen at about 10 a.m. (Castle, 1982, pp. 195–7; *South London Press*, 13 July 1917) and the first disturbance occurred at 2.45 p.m. when a crowd of about 1,000 people assembled outside a butcher's shop in London Fields previously carried on by a naturalised German. In fact, the business had closed after suffering damage during the 1915 riots, although people still resided in the living quarters of the building. The members of the mob smashed the windows, destroyed the furniture and stole the safe. Some of the crowd moved to a baker's shop occupied by an alien enemy in Westgate Street, and proceeded to destroy it. They subsequently made their way to an establishment in Broadway and inflicted damage there. During the course of the afternoon the crowd had grown to between 2,000 and 3,000. Further trouble developed during the evening although the police managed to restore order by 11 p.m. However, not far from here youths paraded the vicinity of Hackney Road at about midnight and smashed the windows of three shops. Peace did not return until about 3.30 a.m. In Tottenham, mean-while, a crowd of about 1,500 surrounded a baker's shop, owned by an alien enemy, at about 10 p.m. and broke the windows. Violence also occurred in Highgate Hill where about 3,000 people attacked three shop's occupied by Germans.

Further disturbances developed on Sunday evening. At about 8 p.m., for instance, a crowd attacked a baker's shop in Pownall Road, Dalston. 'There was a lot of hooting and booing, followed by a fusillade of stones, which broke all the windows in the house.' People then entered the building and stole 200 loaves of bread. Another hostile mob, meanwhile, destroyed the windows of a shop in Murray Street, Hoxton. At the same time, violence again flared up in Tottenham and Highgate. During the course of the weekend thirty shops had come under attack, fourteen police had suffered injuries, and thirty-seven people had been arrested (*Hackney and Kingsland Gazette*, 11 July 1917; *East End News*, 10, 13 July 1917; *Evening News*, 10 July 1917; *The Times*, 9 July 1917; PRO HO45 10944/257142/187).

More widespread and serious disturbances broke out on Monday. In Church Street and Exmouth Street, for instance, mounted police were required to clear large crowds which had damaged shops 'alleged to be occupied by traders of German extraction'. Other areas in north London which experienced disturb-ances included Clerkenwell, Clapton and Hackney. In Green Street, Bethnal Green, about 500 people attacked a Dutch family which had moved there in order to escape another threatening crowd. In Holloway Road, meanwhile, about 5,000 people smashed the windows of a baker's shop belonging to a naturalised British subject of German origin. At the same time, the Metropolitan Police, Home Office and War Office became seriously concerned about the appearance of a crowd outside the internment camp in Islington. Therefore, troops at Chelsea barracks went into a state of readiness. However, they were ultimately not required because by 11 p.m. the police had managed to bring the situation under control (*Hackney and Kingsland Gazette*, 11 July 1917;

Islington Daily Gazette, 11 July 1917; *East End News*, 13 July 1917; PRO HO45 10944/257142/186; Reay, 1920, pp. 164–5).

During Monday evening disturbances also broke out in South London. These had resulted from hostility aroused by Saturday's air raid and by 'an impression which had gained currency that alien enemies were conducting lucrative business in the locality' whilst Englishmen fought on the battlefield. The rioting took place in Lambeth Walk where the shops attacked belonged not to Germans but to Italians and Russians. On the following day large crowds, composed mainly of women and children, paraded Oakley Street in Chelsea but they caused little damage.

Many people appeared in Police Courts throughout London facing various charges as a result of the weekend disturbances. At the North London Police Court, for example, Mr Hedderwick heard twenty cases on Monday. In some of these the Magistrate remanded the accused while in others he simply bound them over. Frank Wright, however, received 1 month's hard labour for striking a constable with a stone. Hedderwick remarked that although he could understand why people lost their tempers, they had to attempt to keep them under control. On the same day, Mr Knight, representing the Police Commissioner in a number of prosecutions at Old Street Police Court, declared that the Home Office took a 'very serious view' of individuals who attacked German property as they only aggravated the difficulties of the police. At the Westminster Police Court on Tuesday, meanwhile, Mr Harris imposed some firm sentences in cases arising out of the disturbances in Lambeth on the previous night. For instance, he imprisoned Charles Maskell for 21 days, with hard labour, for assaulting a special constable. People also appeared in other Police Courts on the same day (*South London Press*, 13 July 1917; *Islington Daily Gazette*, 10, 11 July 1917; *East End News*, 13 July 1917; *Hackney and Kingsland Gazette*, 11 July 1917).

With the exception of a disturbance in Newquay in September 1918 (*Newquay Express*, 13, 27 September 1918), no further anti-German riots occurred during the course of the war. Nevertheless, between 1914 and 1918 thousands of German shops and houses had come under attack in Britain at a cost of hundreds of thousands of pounds. While London and Liverpool may have experienced the worst violence, no area of the country seems to have totally escaped it. We can confidently assert that no immigrant community in twentieth-century Britain has endured violence on such a scale.

C.R. Hennings went so far as to describe the events of 1915 as a '*Pogrome in wahrsten Sinne des Wortes*' (Hennings, 1923, p. 151). Does this assertion contain any truth? If one of the aims of people who participate in a pogrom is to clear out the local alien community, then those who took part in the riots of May 1915 certainly achieved their aim; apart from destroying most German-owned businesses in Britain they also compelled the government to adopt a policy of wholesale internment or repatriation of alien enemies (Panayi, 1991, pp. 76–8). Another important characteristic of a pogrom is that 'The Establishment' should support or incite the violence. Certain sections of 'The Establishment' clearly did. The examples we can give are the press and various Opposition MPs such as Lord Charles Beresford, Ronald MacNeill and William Joynson-Hicks. However, other groups of those in authority clearly did not encourage the disturbances. The judiciary, for instance, acted fairly and firmly in its sentencing. At the same time the police, both regular and special constables, performed their tasks correctly.

Perhaps the most important factor contributing to a pogrom is the support of the government. In both Nazi Germany and tsarist Russia those in authority propagated anti-Semitism. In the same way the British government had to preach anti-Germanism during the First World War because the very survival of Britain as a state appeared to depend on the defeat of Germany. Although hardly any government propaganda was specifically aimed at Germans within Britain and although the official response to the question of enemy aliens was fair, in so far as it could be under the influence of the press and public opinion generally, we have to bear two things in mind. Firstly, would the people who rioted have distinguished between the Germans whom their relations were fighting at the Front and the Germans in their midst? Secondly, while the government did not make the connection between enemy aliens and German soldiers, the Unionist press and radical right-wing pressure groups and MPs certainly did. However, we still remain quite a long way from a Russian-style pogrom. In addition to the fact that both the judiciary and the police acted in an impartial manner, the scale of destruction, although great, does not compare with the thousand Jews killed during the 1905 pogroms in Russia. Nevertheless, within the history of British anti-alienism the anti-German riots of the Great War remain unique, both in terms of their severity and widespread nature.

References

Baines, Dudley, 1991, *Emigration from Europe 1815–1930*, London, Macmillan.
Castle, H.G. 1982, *Fire Over England*, London.
Crawford, W.M., 1962, 'A Cosmopolitan City', in N.J. Frangopulo (ed.).
Frangopulo, N.J. (ed.), 1962, *Rich Inheritance: A Guide to the History of Manchester*, Manchester, Manchester Education Committee.
Hansard, Commons, 5th series, vol. 71, 1915.
Haste, Cate, 1977, *Keep the Home Fires Burning*, London, Allen Lane.
Hennings, C.R. 1923, *Deutsche in England*, Stuttgart, Institut für Auslandsbeziehungen.
Liverpool Record Office, 352 POL 1/37, 'Orders of the Watch Committee to the Head Constable', May 1914–June 1915.
MacDonagh, Michael, 1935, *In London During the Great War*, London, Eyre and Spottiswoode.
Manchester Guardian History of the War, 1915, vol, 2, London.
Manchester Reference Library Archives, Manchester Watch Committee Minutes, vol. 47.
Marwick, Arthur, 1986, *The Deluge: British Society and the First World War*, London, Macmillan.
O'Mara, Pat, 1934, *The Autobiograhy of a Liverpool Irish Slummy*, London, Martin Hopkinson.
Panayi, Panikos, 1988, 'The Lancashire Anti-German Riots of May 1915', *Manchester Region History Review*, 2: 3–11.

Panayi, Panikos, 1991, *The Enemy in Our Midst: Germans in Britain during the First World War*, Oxford, Berg.

Pankhurst, E. Sylvia, 1932, *The Home Front*, London, Hutchinson.

Ponsonby, Arthur, 1928, *Falsehood in Wartime*, London, G. Allen and Unwin.

Price, Richard, 1972, *An Imperial War and the British Working Classes: Working Class Attitudes and Reactions Towards the Boer War 1899–1902*, London, Routledge.

P[ublic] R[ecord] O[ffice], H[ome] O[ffice] 45, 10944/257142.

Reay, W.T., 1920, *The Specials—How They Served London: The Story of the Metropolitan Police Special Constabulary*, London, W. Heinemann.

Roberts, Robert, 1971, *The Classic Slum: Salford Life in the First Quarter of the Century*, Manchester, Manchester University Press.

Taylor, A.J.P., 1985, *English History 1914–45*, Harmondsworth, Penguin.

Winter, J.M. 1986, *The Great War and the British People*, London, Macmillan.

5

The 1919 riots

Jacqueline Jenkinson

Introduction

The 'race' riots of 1919 occurred in nine British cities, all port towns, between January and August, and involved crowds of whites (often in their thousands) and dozens of black men. As a result of the clashes, five men (three white and two black) lost their lives, dozens were injured, and over two hundred arrests were made. Behind these stark figures lies a background of economic competition in the merchant shipping industry as it began to contract to suit peacetime conditions. That job competition should lead to riot, and riots between the black and white communities in particular, owed much to the effects of the post-war situation in Britain, as hundreds of thousands of men were unleashed upon the job market. Between November 1918 and March 1919 over 2,100,000 'other ranks' had been demobilised. The merchant marine became the focus of rioting due to a combination of factors, not the least of which was the weak level, and disorganised nature, of union representation in the industry, which meant that sailors were denied the traditional method of expressing their grievances through strike action. Similarly, the fact that the vast majority of black people employed in Britain were in the 'seafaring line' played an important part in the rioting, which was largely confined to the dock areas of the cities involved. This fact, however, should not lead to the conclusion that 'race' was the major factor in the rioting. Certainly, antagonism between black and white was an issue, but not an overriding one. White racialist thinking was too well established a social phenomenon in twentieth-century Britain for this to be anything more than a well-internalised mode of thought, called out into the open by a combination of economic and social pressures.

The low level of unionisation in the merchant service added to the problems of the general economic climate. Although this was an established feature of the merchant service, it took on an increased significance in the wake of the unprecedented sacrifices demanded of the service during the war. A general result of the post-war winding-down process was the increased level of aggression displayed by those who had served in the war. Trained to react violently in wartime situations, many men acted likewise in times of stress after their demobilisation. This phenomenon was no less evident among men who had served in the merchant navy, particularly when they had no recourse to traditional modes of industrial action when faced with the prospect of high levels of unemployment, exacerbated by the weakness of the unions in the industry.

Employers had used foreign sailors to undercut white British sailors' rates of pay for many years and this major long-standing grievance had resulted in violence, sometimes between black and white sailors, on numerous occasions before 1919. Added to this was the bad management of the largest seamen's union, the National Sailors' and Firemen's Union. Of the 194,500 merchant seamen in the service in 1914, petty officers, firemen and sailors made up 106,500, and of these 90 per cent allegedly belonged to the NSFU (Hopkins, 1920, p. 3). This appears to be rather a high figure, although perhaps the success of the 1911 National Strike, which finally won official recognition of the union and resulted in an increase in wages, bolstered the number of union members.

The merchant sailors' grievance against the employers was strengthened by the fear that the wide publicity given the shortage of seamen during the war was being exploited by the employers to increase the numbers of cheaper non-British workers in the industry. The sense among British sailors, white and black, that the employers and 'foreign' labour were conspiring to take advantage of the post-war decline in shipping tonnage to introduce wage cuts and usurp their position, unhampered by any noticeable union resistance, was strong, and it was in part from this feeling that rioting broke out.

The role of service- and recently demobilised men was a significant factor in the riots, one which was commented upon in many local press accounts of the violence, and it is clear that the specific grievances of the white British sailors, who viewed black British sailors from the colonies as foreigners, were not the only issues in the riots. The sense that the great sacrifices of the war years had been futile was being experienced at a national level, as post-war shortages in housing and increased competition in the job market were the first results of mass demobilisation. Wider frustrations were focused on the black community in Britain as a means of release. It is apparent from the light sentences often meted out to the white rioters in various centres around the country that the authorities in part recognised this frustration. However, there was also an element of racial antipathy revealed by the official response to the riots.

If support were needed for the theory that it was economic pressure and social dislocation which led to the outbreak of the 1919 riots in Britain, a consideration of the first incidence of rioting in Glasgow, towards the end of January, provides this (Jenkinson, 1985, pp. 43–6). Here, the riot broke out less than a week before a mass meeting of strikers at George Square was dispersed in a scene of chaos following a police baton charge. This was followed by the arrival of 10,000 troops and four tanks in the city, as the government sought to stamp out any threat to law and order, and remove any chance of a Bolshevist-type revolution on Clydeside. Such an official reaction is an indication of how seriously the government took the influence of the Russian Revolution upon the working classes in Great Britain. 'Red Clydeside' had a history of militancy, and there had been a number of industrial confrontations during the war period, but the seriousness with which this dispute (over the campaign for a forty-hour week) was viewed, owed much to the worldwide unrest of the post-war period.

The riot at Glasgow was the beginning of a spate of riots in Britain's major ports, as the frustrations of the white communities in these areas became focused on the black population as an easily recognisable target. In February, the pressure of employment again led to an anti-black riot, this time in South Shields. In April, there was a more minor disturbance in Salford and a full-scale riot in London. There were further riots in London in May, June and August of that year. June was the peak of the rioting, with outbreaks in Liverpool, Hull, Cardiff, Newport and Barry. Further riots occurred in 1920 and 1921 in Hull, and in the latter year in Newport and Salford. The riots, although owing much to the disrupting factor of the aftermath of war, were primarily rooted in economic grievances, breaking out again in the early 1920s when the fortunes of the merchant shipping industry fell even lower as the post-war recession set in. Further evidence for the role of economic tension creating a riotous situation is supplied by the fact that several of the riots broke out in and around the merchant shipping offices as men came face to face while attempting to sign on for work. Such evidence for the idea that economic competition directly provoked riots, reinforces the notion that racial antagonism rather than a basic 'cause' of the violence, was entrenched in the superstructure of Britain at this time.

Although black sailors were involved in the riots of 1919, not all black people in early twentieth-century Britain were employed in the merchant navy. A significant proportion were students, mainly in London, but also at Oxford, Liverpool, Edinburgh, Glasgow and elsewhere. There was also an element of a professional black community, which included lawyers and doctors in the main. There were also other working-class black people in Britain at this time, mainly involved in the service industries as servants and nurses, although a few worked in factories, and others as show people. Limited evidence for the size and condition of Britain's black population emerged during the 1910 Parliamentary Committee's survey into 'Distressed Colonial and Indian subjects', from which it appears that London had the largest concentration of black people at this time, followed by Liverpool and Cardiff. This report also found that discrimination in employment especially against black seamen, was a well-established phenomenon (Banton, 1955, pp. 31–2).

Economic factors in the riots

The paramount role of economic dislocation as a factor in the riots can be seen when attention is focused on the immediate background to the Glasgow disturbances. The dispute began in the yard of the mercantile marine on the dockside as black and white British sailors attempted to sign on for a ship then in port. A dispute arose over who was to be given employment and this led to the violence as a large crowd of white sailors armed with knives and sticks chased a group of black sailors out of the yard and into the street. The black sailors were pursued to their boarding house which was nearby, and this was then laid siege by the white crowd, which had been swelled by local people until the black sailors were taken into custody by a group of fifty police officers. The concerned black sailors offered no resistance to the police action. Three sailors, one black, and two white received serious injuries as a result of the violence. The trigger for the riot is clear: 'It is understood that the disturbance originated ... because of an alleged preference being given to British seamen over coloured seamen in signing on the crew of a ship at Glasgow harbour' (*Glasgow Herald*, 24 January 1919).

As in Glasgow the previous month, the rioting at South Shields in February 1919 arose from a dispute in the local shipping office, as a group of nine Adenese sailors who had been hired as a stokehold crew of a ship were refused permission to sail by two seamen's union officials. The violence which followed took place between a group of black sailors and a crowd of white seamen, British and foreign, and white locals. The sailors discriminated against at the shipping office were British subjects who came from Aden, yet they, like the British sailors from Sierra Leone in the Glasgow riot, were made the scapegoats for the social and economic pressures being felt by the white sailors and the wider white community. Subsequent incidents of violence between the two communities in the town suggests that tension was by no means eradicated by the full-scale riot on 4 February. Indeed, there are parallels between the pattern of sporadic outbreaks of unrest at South Shields and other riot centres where discontent habitually simmered under the surface, boiling over to violence from time to time; London and Salford are other examples of this.

The first rioting in London to receive widespread newspaper coverage (there are indications of lesser affrays as tension built up between the two communities in the preceding months), occurred on 16 April 1919. After this initial incident which was limited to the attack on a Muslim eating house, a month later there was a series of riots and disturbances in the Limehouse area of the city. These took place over the space of four days, beginning on Monday 16 May. On that day a number of black men were attacked by a crowd of whites. A further riot occurred in late August. Although rioting was confined to the East End of the city, within this area Limehouse, Poplar and Canning Town were all affected. There was also a riot at Limehouse the following year. A significant aspect of the London riots was the extent to which these disturbances were attributed to the sexual relations between black men and white women in these districts. The local public and press opinion being that the white violence these 'liaisons' occasioned was an 'understandable reaction'. This attitude is given far more press coverage than post-war social and economic issues, such as the limited job prospects in the shipping industry and on local housing shortages.

Even more so than in London, the black community in Liverpool had a long history of settlement in the area. The initial impetus to black settlement in Liverpool having receded with the ending of the slave trade, later in the nineteenth century a fresh source of settlers came by way of the Elder Dempster shipping line securing the main trade routes to West Africa for Britain, entailing the employment of a good number of native seamen. The company could even afford to keep a pool of unemployed black sailors stationed in Liverpool to fill any vacancies which arose. These, and other black sailors arriving at the port, augmented the growing number of locally born black people as a result of the inter-marriage of white local women and black settlers. The twentieth century in Liverpool saw a by now well-established and large black community, although unlike other settlements, e.g. Salford, this was not confined to a few streets wherein a 'colony' of black people resided.

Confined to slum dwellings in the city by reasons of economy and convenience, the large section of the black community involved in seafaring was also at a disadvantage with the introduction of different wage rates for black and white sailors introduced as a result of the national seamen's strike of 1911, which had the effect of doubling white ships' firemen's wages in relation to those of black firemen.

The number of black seamen affected by this racist differentiation in wages was increased as the heightened demands of wartime led many more black men to travel from the West Indies and West Africa to fill jobs vacated by whites enlisting in the forces. Many other blacks also served in HM Forces and made their way at the end of the war to Liverpool among other ports. By 1919 there were thousands of blacks looking for work at the docks in the city. So too were many demobilised whites, and given the increased tendency to violence established as a post-war phenomenon in Britain, coupled with the nature of black settlement on the margins of society (where they were considered as 'outsiders' by the white population), it is not surprising that the tension created by this dire unemployment situation resulted in rioting. Only the scale and sustained ferocity of the violence came as a shock as the rioting left one black man dead, dozens wounded on both sides, and led to the widescale destruction of black property in the city.

The riots which took place in Cardiff in June 1919 were the most serious of the racial disturbances which occurred in Britain throughout that year. Three people were killed, dozens hospitalised, and over £3,000 worth of damage inflicted on property in the city. Behind these dramatic figures lies a history of well-documented tension between the races over issues such as housing, jobs and 'mixed marriages'. The riots of 1919 were not the first examples of racial violence to occur in Cardiff. Disturbances took place as early as the 1870s. By mentioning earlier incidents an insight can be given into the nature and development of the black community in the city, owing its presence almost exclusively to the seafaring traditions of the town. Cardiff had become established as the leading British port for the tramp steamer trade by the last quarter of the nineteenth century, drawing on its traditions as a coaling centre. The mainstays of this type of vessel were the firemen, whose job was to ensure the vessel was coaled to a level sufficient to ensure enough steam pressure was created to power the engines. Both the nature of the work, and the type of ship involved (tramp steamers did not ply nominated trading routes, but went to whichever port offered a profitable cargo, thus making for an insecure and uncertain future for its crew) were hardly an attractive proposition, and as the least sought-after ships and jobs therein, they became established as the province of foreign and black British sailors.

The rioting in other parts of South Wales did not reach the same scale as the violence in Cardiff. The geographical proximity of Cardiff to the smaller Welsh ports (Barry is only ten miles from Cardiff and Newport twelve) was of course a major factor in the background to the lesser South Wales disturbances, and examples of the influence of events in Cardiff are not difficult to discover. Although the black communities of these towns were much smaller than the Cardiff settlement this did not prevent twenty-six blacks being arrested during the Newport incidents, nor the death, by violent means, of a white ex-soldier during a fierce fight in Barry. The murder charge levelled at black sailor, Charles Emanuel, will be discussed later in this chapter.

In common with many other British ports the black settlements in Newport and Barry had grown considerably during the war, although there is no suggestion that the war alone accounted for a considerable black presence in these two ports. It is likely that parallel (if more limited) communities became established in Newport and Barry at the time of black settlement in Cardiff, during the last quarter of the nineteenth century. There is evidence to support the conclusion that this growing black population was facing an increasingly insecure future in the shipping industry, a common fate shared with other blacks in Britain's ports in the period from the Armistice to the outbreak of the most severe racial violence in June 1919. A complaint was made to the Colonial Office by black sailors at Newport claiming that they were refused access to the local superintendent of the mercantile marine office to lay their unemployment grievances before him. A government memorandum compiled as a result of the complaint revealed the problem was not considered significant enough to merit any further enquiry. If the Colonial Office records provide evidence of black unemployment as an issue in the pre-riot period, in Newport at least, there is also evidence in the local press to suggest that violence between the black and white communities also was not a new phenomenon. During the riots it was reported:

> Trouble has been brewing in this quarter for some time. It will be remembered that a year or so ago, a number of American sailors and coloured men were concerned in a 'melee', and no secret has been made of the ill-feeling which many people feel towards the coloured men on account of their being seen so often in the company of white women. (*South Wales Argus*, 7 June 1919)

This extract, as well as raising the perennial black–white sex issue, also reveals that American sailors played a part in increasing the tension between the two communities in the port. Similar occurrences had been noted in Cardiff, although in Newport and Barry there was no evidence of white British colonial serviceman involvement in the riots, a point of divergence from the larger port. The active role of local service and ex-servicemen is clear however. It re-emerges in the Newport disturbances of 1920 and 1921, in one of which there is again evidence of American sailors fighting with blacks, suggesting that there was a sustained level of violent hostility between these two elements of the seafaring community.

Although this chapter is chiefly concerned with the 1919 riots it is worth concluding this section by commenting on the fact that the riots which broke out in 1920 and 1921 had similar economic roots. The issue of white opposition to black seamen shipping out in direct employment competition was in evidence in the anti-black riots in Hull in 1920 and Salford in 1921. Indeed it is clear that such a situation was in evidence throughout Britain's port areas in the inter-war period as merchant shipping worldwide continued to decline.

'Policing the riots'

To quell the Glasgow disturbance the police took the black sailors involved, thirty in all, into 'protective' custody. All of these men were subsequently charged with public order offences. One white man was also arrested for an incident involving a policeman arising from the disturbance. Other methods of policing were employed in the larger, more sustained, riots. In the London riots of May 1919 the police created a 'barrier zone' between the black community and white crowds in the East End of the city. The implication was that only by dividing the two communities physically could the authorities cope with the scale of violence.

Even before the Liverpool rioting began in June 1919, there was evidence of friction between the black community and the police, an undeclared state of war which was only overshadowed when the white crowd's aggressive stance against the black population became so severe that blacks were driven into police custody for their own protection, the alternative being to leave themselves open to attack. Despite the virulence of the white crowd's activities during the riots, the police view, when it came to the trials of those arrested in connection with the disturbances, remained the same: the blacks initiated the violence.

> Detective Inspector Burgess said that with one exception in every case the coloured men were the aggressors . . . in their defence several of the prisoners stated that they were actually in bed at the time of the disturbances and others said they were not in the neighbourhood when the fighting began. Others complained that they had been handled with unnecessary roughness by the police who made arrests indiscriminately. (*Liverpool Echo*, 10 November 1919)

On the contrary, it would appear the police were discriminating in their arrest procedure—on the grounds of colour. The suggestion of police bias here can be supported by the fact that out of twenty-nine blacks arrested as a result of the riots in June 1919, seventeen were found guilty and twelve not guilty, or freed without trial. On the other hand, of the thirty-six whites charged, all were found guilty as charged, many being imprisoned. The activities of the police in Liverpool are in keeping with those of other regional forces in Britain when faced with anti-black violence during 1919.

> The Head Constable begs to report to the Watch Committee that for some time there has existed a feeling of animosity between the white and coloured population in this city. This feeling has probably been engendered by the arrogant and overbearing conduct of the negro population towards the white, and by the white

women who live or cohabit with the Black men, boasting to the other women of the superior qualities of the negroes as compared with those of the white men. Since the Armistice the demobilisation of so many negroes into Liverpool has caused this feeling to develop more rapidly. (Liverpool Watch Committee Minute Book no. 57, 17 June 1919)

One of the most controversial aspects of the policing of the riots in Liverpool was the wholescale removal of black people into protective custody. The sources do not indicate whether the first impetus towards this situation came from the black population itself or from the local police authority. In fact this is less important than the implications of the mass evacuation of hundreds of black families from their homes. Whether the blacks themselves fled into police protection, or the police removed this section of the community into safe-keeping, one conclusion only can be reached; both sides recognised the fact that the forces of law and order could not provide adequate protection for black people not only in the streets where they lived, but in their very homes. The collection of so many black men and their families in one place, however shortlived (for many soon returned to their own homes), gave rise to the suggestion that this temporary arrangement should be regularised in the form of placing these people in a compound or camp pending the implementation of the repatriation scheme which was launched by the government around this time.

In Cardiff, the police strategy throughout the riots was to focus on the black community as the more serious threat to public order. Police advice to remain indoors was supplemented by the use of cordons thrown up at cross entrances to streets in which black people lived, not as one might suppose to protect this community, but for fear of the damages the blacks could inflict should the white mob enter the Bute Town area.

Attempts were frequently made by the crowd to reach Bute Town but they were thwarted by the police. If the crowd had overpowered the police and got through, the result would have been disastrous as the black population would have probably fought with desperation and inflicted great loss of life. (Williams, 1970, p.8)

The Chief Constable also deployed troops around the Bute Town area to support the police, and after the severe rioting of 11 and 12 June, only minor incidents occurred on 13 and 14 June. It appears, then, that the police tactics were successful in suppressing disorder as the level of violence diminished, and by 15 June had ceased. Peace, however, was achieved heavily at the expense of the black community in Cardiff, who were more or less barricaded into what became their own ghetto. The fact that white crowds had initiated the riots in Cardiff was apparently regarded as less important than the free rein the violence gave the black men to indulge their 'natural' aggressive tendencies. Moreover, the argument ran, the white crowds had valid reasons for their actions, namely, the unemployment situation in the merchant shipping trade and the association of black men with white women.

In the Newport disturbances, all the twenty-six blacks arrested were taken into custody after the same incident, namely a charge towards a white crowd which had gathered outside a group of black boarding houses. The nine white rioters on the other hand were taken over a period of several days: during the rioting on 6 and 7 June, one on 11 June, and the final two on 13 June. The implication of this is that the police were concentrating on the ringleaders of the whites, taking their time to identify the eight men and one woman who were finally arrested. The press reports at the time highlighted one man in particular as being prominent in the rioting, Gordon Maskell. 'Maskell continually incited the crowd and took a leading part in attacking three and four George Street and three Commercial Road and then urged "Now for the Chinese" and the laundry was wrecked' (*Monmouthshire Evening Post*, 21 June 1919). When charged at the police station with rioting offences Maskell, aged thirty, explained his actions: 'I did it for the benefit of the seamen of whom I am one, and cannot get a job because of these niggers being here, and we intend to take the law into our own hands' (*Cardiff Western Mail*, 3 July 1919). Maskell's viewpoint was evidently shared by many others in the town, and it is significant that this avowed ringleader was a sailor. Maskell was given the joint heaviest sentence meted out to a white for his part in the riot: three months' hard labour.

Police bias was also apparently in evidence in Hull in June 1920, for, while four blacks were arrested due to the rioting, two being charged with very serious offences, no whites were arrested, despite clear indications that the white mob were the aggressors, particularly on the second night of violence. The indication is that the authorities regarded the black people as the trouble-makers; the police moved blacks on, while allowing whites to loiter in the streets, and publicans refused to serve them on the second night of rioting. The examples of police and local prejudice against blacks in Hull in 1920 are common themes in the 1919 violence too, and it is unlikely that such a level of antipathy would soon diminish.

The reaction of the courts

The question of the courts' treatment of black people involved in the riots is complex and sometimes contradictory. In Glasgow, far more blacks were arrested than whites, and there was a similar story in the other riot centres in Britain. Yet, for example, in South Shields, of the sixteen black men arrested, seven were found not guilty by the courts. Other writers on the subject of the riots reveal the contradictory court attitudes to black rioters.

> Both in arrest and detention the Negroes, who were the victims of the violence, were subjected to scandalously biased treatment ... gross injustices inflicted on the various black communities in 1919 came, not solely from the mobs, but also at the hands of the police and the courts, although in London legal discrimination seems to have been absent. (Walvin, 1973, pp. 207–8)

The issue of black detention is not as clear-cut as Walvin's quotation suggests. Certainly there were far more blacks arrested than whites, which is suggestive of a degree of police bias, but this is not the whole picture. Neil Evans's study on the rioting in Wales states:

> The policy of police in arrests in Newport and Barry shows discrimination with a great imbalance in the numbers arrested. The courts were more equitable. At Cardiff the legal processes started with flagrantly unequal sentences imposed on black and white men for similar offences but eventually the decisions of the courts seem to have reflected the nature of the offences. (Evans, 1980, p. 18)

A review of the Cardiff riot trials based on the figures of people arrested suggests that although the black community were almost always the victims in a series of white attacks, more of the former were arrested; twenty-one blacks to eighteen whites. This was largely a result of the differing attitudes the police held towards the two groups—even when black rioters were literally fighting for their lives. This was the case when eleven blacks were arrested and charged with shooting and murder offences for an incident at 52 Millicent Street on 12 June. They were subsequently found not guilty by the courts. All the charges concerning black people in Liverpool were serious, most involving shooting and arms offences and police assault. The whites on the other hand were slow to be arrested, the police attitude being one of tolerance, arrest being only used as a last resort on persistent offenders in the riots.

The court cases involving those who took part in the Cardiff rioting were more equitable than the police methods which had resulted in the arrests (with a few glaring exceptions). All eighteen white offenders were found guilty, but in comparison with the charges against the blacks their offences were generally of a more minor nature. The exceptions to this were six of the whites who were initially charged with the murder of a black sailor named Mahomed Abdullah—but this charge was soon dropped for lack of evidence. Ten whites were found guilty of riotous assembly and some of these were additionally convicted of assault, two receiving twenty-month sentences, four eighteen months, the others' terms ranging from nine to two months. Apart from this major trial, the eight other whites received relatively lenient sentences from the courts, some for apparently serious offences. The most glaring example of this in comparison with the sentences meted out to black offenders, is the case of John Flynn Marden, aged fifty-four, who was charged with kicking a policeman and threatening him with a knife. Despite his sixty-one previous convictions he received only one month's imprisonment. This was in stark contrast to the six-month sentence imposed on Mohamed Abouki the same day for striking a policeman with a stick. Abouki himself walked with a limp, which he said was the result of a blow from a police truncheon. This instance of apparent racist bias on the part of the courts should not be taken as typical. It is possible that the magistrate on this, the first day of hearings as a result of the riots, was acting according to an in-built bias, which, as the court proceedings progressed, became less notable. It is a fact that judges began to take into account mitigating circumstances in terms of violence as a means of self-defence in the cases of some of the black defendants, and this will be discussed below. Five whites were merely given fines for their roles in the rioting, offences ranging from police assault to window-breaking and using bad language. The remaining two were found guilty and then discharged.

Given the apparent reluctance on the part of the Newport police to arrest all but persistent or serious white offenders, it appears that the courts, in convicting only five out of nine alleged offenders, and imprisoning but three of these, acted with similar restraint given the seriousness of the disturbances which had occurred. Perhaps the courts were influenced by the fact that rioting had abated of its own accord, and the threat to public order was no longer acute. A further reason for the relatively light sentences given is the degree of sympathy felt by the court towards the white crowd's feelings—if not in their manner of expressing it.

> The black men who were concerned in the affair were subjects of his majesty the king, as the persons then before them were, and were equally entitled to the protection of the law. He could understand and sympathise with the feeling of the white men when they saw white women associating with black men, but the white men had no right to take the law into their own hands. (*Monmouthshire Evening Post*, 4 July 1919)

The twenty-three blacks who were charged with rioting appeared the same day as the whites, and it is clear that an element of continuity was demonstrated in the court attitudes to both sets of rioters. Seven of the black men could not be positively identified and were released. The remaining sixteen were found guilty of riotous assembly and were each bound over for a year. The court attitude apparently was to play down the potential seriousness of the whole episode, and it is true that there were, for example, no serious injuries arising from the disturbance, but again, the basic injustice of the violence directed against Newport's black community is nowhere commented on, if in fact it was recognised as such by the general public, which is open to doubt.

A final court case worthy of consideration is that of Charles Emanuel, a black sailor charged with murdering a white ex-serviceman in Barry. Emanuel was taken into police custody by a policeman about 9.30 p.m. on 11 June, as he ran away from the scene of the disturbance, pursued by a crowd of whites. The policeman who arrested him noted that he seemed pleased to be taken out of the hands of the pursuing crowd, which was hardly surprising given the circumstances. When cautioned, Emanuel had stated:

> I defend myself with a pocket knife. I was coming down the street for a little walk, after signing on and this man (deceased) said 'Why don't you go in your own street?', I say 'Behave yourself'. By the time I turn around to him, I speak to one coloured woman, and he came behind me, and hit me one clout in the eye. Three more men hit me, one with a poker, and I defend myself with knife. I run away shouting murder. (*Barry Dock News*, 20 June 1919)

Emanuel was apparently well able to take care of himself in a fight, but he had been both verbally and physically abused by the white victim, Frederick Henry Longman who, evidently, was hostile to the black community. Longman too, was a tough customer, having twenty convictions behind him for offences including police assault and disorderly conduct. He had joined up in 1914 however, and had only recently been discharged after four and a half years' service with the Royal Field Artillery. In fact, his funeral was paid for by the Discharged Sailor's and Soldier's Associations. It may be concluded that Longman was an archetype for the white mobs during the riots. Emanuel's history too, was a common one: known to the Barry authorities for at least seven years, he had presumably served in the merchant service throughout the war. Even the white jury which tried Emanuel did not believe his attack upon Longman was unprovoked, hence his conviction was for manslaughter and not murder. The jury took 25 minutes to decide that Emanuel was guilty of manslaughter. He was sentenced to five years' imprisonment—the most severe sentence handed out to anyone as a direct result of the anti-black rioting in 1919.

The aftermath of the riots: repatriation

The subsequent fate of the black sailors in the wake of the violence directed against them for much of 1919 was equally bleak. The position of black sailors in Glasgow remained dismal according to a report of March 1919.

> We make no apology for returning to the subject of coloured seamen, British-born subjects, in Glasgow. The apology is due from the National Sailors' and Firemen's Union which took the disgraceful step of refusing them—although members—to serve on British ships. The only shadow of an excuse is the shallow pretence that the places the coloured men would take are to be reserved for discharged soldiers. That is sheer bunkum. One poor fellow has died as the result of privations, and of 'sleeping out' for he had no money and no bed. Yet he was a Briton who had defied the Hun and his devilries for the sake of Britain. There are 132 of these ill-treated fellows in Glasgow most of these without a square meal any and every day. Their appeal to the Lord Provost has been calmly ignored. They are modest enough to say—'first place for white Britishers; after that coloured Britishers'. Yet they are ordered to 'clear out' from ships at Glasgow, while they see Norwegians, Swedes and Spaniards taken on. (*John Bull*, 29 March 1919)

By the middle of the year, when the violence reached its peak, the government decided to act to remove the 'threat' to public order posed by the presence of black sailors in ports across the country. Repatriation was not simply an issue for black Britons; white colonial munition workers were also sent home at the end of the war, but in practice a 'colour' distinction prevailed. White colonials were given a £5 resettlement allowance from the outset—black British subjects had to wait until they had been the victims of violent attack before this gratuity was offered them. Similarly, it is unlikely that lists of white munition workers who refused repatriation (which of course, was a voluntary scheme) would be drawn up and circulated around the relevant authorities (in the case of black seamen this was the local mercantile marine offices) to prevent them moving on and receiving maintenance allowance elsewhere. From April to June 1919 over

200 such black seamen were listed as having refused repatriation from Manchester, South Shields, Hull, London, Barry, Swansea, Liverpool and Cardiff (over 100 alone from the last-named place). The reasons for so many refusals to the scheme, before the main outbreak of rioting, probably owed much to disinclination to return to colonies whose authorities did not want them and had little to offer. Post riot, many black seamen continued to decline the offer of repatriation, owing to the feeling of grievance against the British authorities for allowing the riots to go largely unchecked, and for their disregard for the rights of black people in this country, particularly after the part they had played in the war effort. The speed with which the sailings were organised and the consequent lack of consideration for the feelings of the black community were also reasons for the failure in the bid to rid the ports of their presence.

As the riots were in full swing, the government set up an inter-departmental committee to consider the best method of implementing the repatriation scheme. The first meeting on 19 June at the Colonial Office was attended by representatives of that body, of the Board of Trade, Home Office, Local Government Board, India Office, Ministry of Labour, and the Ministry of Shipping. At this meeting it was recognised that there were great difficulties in persuading seamen to accept repatriation and a number of means for overcoming this reluctance were discussed. It was decided that local Repatriation Committees be set up at a number of ports, to aid the working of the scheme. A resettlement allowance of £5 was also to be introduced, with a further £1 voyage allowance. Another issue raised was that of the possibility of interning black people prior to their repatriation, an issue which was also being discussed at ground level, in Liverpool at least. Although a reading of relevant government department papers suggests that this was for reasons of public order, the fact that it was considered reveals how far black people were regarded as the trouble-makers behind the riots. Their very presence among the white population was apparently considered as reason enough for violence:

> (Mr. Grindle, Colonial Office) . . . asked whether anything could be done in the way of interning these people. Mr. Scott (Home Office) replied that if they were willing to be interned, it could be done; but although the War Office had placed a camp at Liverpool at the disposal of the local authorities for the purpose, when it came to be made available it was found that the men had gone back to their homes. (PRO CO323/814)

As a consequence of this initial meeting the Colonial Secretary, Viscount Milner, issued a 'Memorandum on the Repatriation of Coloured Men' on 23 June 1919, which gave the 'official' response to the riots and the reasons behind the introduction of resettlement allowances.

> I am seriously concerned at the continued disturbances due to racial ill-feeling against coloured men in our large sea ports. These riots are serious enough from the point of view of the maintenance of order in this country, but they are even more serious in regard to their possible effect in the colonies . . . I have every reason to fear that when these men get back to their own colonies they might be tempted to revenge themselves on the white minorities there, unless we can do something to show that

His Majesty's Government is not insensible to their complaints . . . I am convinced
that if we wish to get rid of the coloured population whose presence here is causing
so much trouble we must pay the expense of doing so ourselves. It will not be great.
(Ibid.)

Milner's chief concern was the effect on the white minority in the colonies
when these men were returned home. Such fear of a black backlash is a
continuous feature of Colonial Office discussion throughout the history of the
repatriation scheme, and the arrival of returned seamen from Britain to the
West Indian colonies in particular, was closely monitored, and with reason in
some cases.

The establishment of repatriation committees indicates the seriousness with
which the government sought to implement the scheme. Committees were set
up in Hull, South Shields, Glasgow, Cardiff, Liverpol, London and Salford; all
areas where there had been riots, and where there were of course, sizeable black
communities. The composition of the repatriation committees, totally exclud-
ing the representation of the black community, would inevitably be biased in
favour of encouraging the repatriation of all these British subjects, especially in
the case of the seamen's union representative, bearing in mind the activities of
numerous union officials who time and again during the riots interfered with
the hiring of black sailors in favour of their white members.

Given the background to the launch of paid repatriation it is not surprising
that black people were not keen to take part in the scheme. In Salford there was
limited response to the offer:

—Way back to Dixie. Only 15 Salford negroes accept free passage—
Fifteen members of Salford's negro colony are now on their way to their own sunny
clime. They sailed from Cardiff at noon yesterday by the SS *Batanga* on which they
were given free passages. The offer of free passages was only communicated to the
Salford police on Wednesday night. When the negroes were informed the response
was not great, partly owing to the short notice. There were difficulties to be
overcome, the only solution of which was time, and that was not available. One
problem was that of English wives. At last the party of fifteen left the Board of Trade
office, Trafford Road, on Thursday night in time to catch the midnight train from
London Road station for Cardiff. Two detectives accompanied them. (*Salford
Reporter*, 21 June 1919)

This description of the practical working of the repatriation scheme gives a
clear picture of the speed and regimentation exercised by the authorities. The
information that the blacks were accompanied by two detectives indicates the
level of tension between the black and white communities at this time, when
any group movement of blacks had the potential to provoke a white reaction.

In Hull, like Salford, a local repatriation committee was established at the
Marine Office, and indeed even before the June 1919 riots which prompted the
introduction of paid repatriation, a close watch was being kept on black seamen
in Hull, as elsewhere, who refused a berth on ships to their home countries, the
Hull Mercantile Marine Officer reporting in May 1919 that nine black and
Asian sailors had refused repatriation from Hull, eight West Indians and one

man from Singapore. The continued existence of a fairly sizeable black population in Hull in 1920 perhaps owed something to the failings of the repatriation scheme, as perceived by the black sailors themselves.

The government's response to appeals to alter the scheme was to propose a further InterDepartmental Conference on this issue, but an amendment was not considered necessary and the basic two-part £6 gratuity remained. A later key concession by the government, namely allowing the white wives and families of black men to be repatriated with them, did however, benefit blacks in Hull, as elsewhere, with at least two families leaving the town under the scheme. In October 1919, R. Joseph and G. Steede left for Canada and Barbados respectively, with their white wives and their children. Despite the repatriation of such men, Hull as elsewhere, maintained a black community, partly owing to the arrival of black sailors who were signed on for a one-way trip only, and who were now stranded in Britain, unable to get a ship out due to the colour bar in operation at the ports.

The repatriation scheme's limited success in terms of the end to the rioting was short-lived, as further riots broke out in 1920 and 1921 in Salford, Hull and Newport, although these were less severe than the nationwide rioting of 1919. Between 1919 and 1921, the government's response to the plight of the black British community was negative; if they complained of conditions in this country they could be helped to return home. Nothing was to be done for blacks wishing to remain in the United Kingdom, for although British in name, this meant little in practice. The implication was that black Britons were all very well in their place, but that place was not in Britain (except in wartime emergencies). Such neglect of a growing section of the community amounted to a lack of vision on the part of the authorities which added up to an admission of the almost unavoidable conclusion that they were not wanted.

One of the most revealing aspects of the repatriation scheme was the question of the position of white wives. For the government's various stances on this issue suggest that feelings of the black seamen and their families came a very poor third to government concern for public order, and the expulsion of blacks as the cause of the unrest. The decision not to pay the repatriation costs of white wives and families encouraged many men to refuse the offer. Some men were actually pressed to return home leaving their families behind. By September 1919, however, the government position had changed back to that of the wider pre-riot scheme, namely repatriation for white wives and families was to be considered and granted on receipt of proof that a marriage had taken place, and that the sailor was in fact, from the colony to which he wished to return. By mid-September, the Marine Department of the Board of Trade were forwarding names of West Indian seamen with families to the Colonial Office to ascertain the veracity of the claims to West Indian birth pending their repatriation. During October and November 1919 the Colonial Office received numerous applications from local maritime marine offices for the repatriation of black seamen and their families. In all cases the authorities issued a 'warning' regarding the probable position of a white wife of a black man in the colonies. It is true that economically conditions were worse than those in Britain at this time, but it is equally clear that the main focus of such a warning would dwell on the hostile reception a 'mixed marriage' could receive, and it is a fact that many black people (notably Marcus Garvey) opposed marriage between black and white people.

The repatriation scheme left unsolved the problem of destitute coloured seamen in Britain. It was a voluntary process which did nothing for those who could not, or would not, return to the colonies. Even among those who took part in the schemes, many returned to the West Indies, in particular, with a sense of grievance against Britain, its government, and its residents, which spilled over into violence at a very sensitive time in the history of British rule in the West Indies.

The background to the unrest which took place in Jamaica, Trinidad, Tobago and Belize during 1919 was a combination of severe economic depression and the awakening of a sense of black solidarity—both of which owed much to the aftermath of the First World War, and the social dislocation which accompanied it. The introduction into this situation of hundreds of repatriated seamen in the wake of the violence in Britain, could only add to the growing sense of disquiet which spread throughout the region, including areas where no violence actually broke out.

Viewed from the angle of the consequences of the repatriation scheme, the unrest which occurred en route to the West Indies on the SS *Santille* and SS *Ocra* suggest that anger and confusion lay behind the violence. On the *Santille*, which departed from Cardiff on 27 June with 147 men on board, the seamen wrecked the ship's fittings and destroyed food rations. On their arrival in Barbados they besieged the treasury for their £5 gratuity, and for maintenance payments pending their dispersement around various West Indian Islands. On the *Ocra*, some imprisoned black soldiers initiated the violence, but it seemed that the returning seamen incited the mutiny. On arrival in Jamaica a number of men petitioned the Acting Governor in the hopes of gaining redress for property lost in the riots, and objecting to deductions being made from their £5 gratuity for the redeeming of goods they had in pawn in Britain. There was a disturbance at Kingston, Jamaica on 10 October involving a number of the repatriated seamen off the *Ocra*, as a result of which fifteen arrests were made. The victims of the violence were white residents, and particularly white seamen in the town. The fears, then, expressed by various quarters about the possibility of violence on the return of the repatriated seamen had been justified. The similarities of this disturbance to the riots in Britain is clear, only the positions regarding black and white were reversed: again the economic issue was paramount. The riot began after the sailors assembled at the immigration office as they did daily. As the police began to disperse the crowd some black sailors left and started trouble further up the town, attacking and beating a number of white sailors, looting a shop and attacking the shop owner and his two sons. Of the men arrested, eleven were found guilty, all receiving prison sentences; four being given twelve months' hard labour each. The Colonial Office view on this incident is revealing:

The repatriated seamen have been troublesome in Jamaica. It was however, impossible to retain them in this country, where they had been more troublesome still and had given rise to serious riots at Cardiff, Newport and Liverpool. (PRO CO 323/848)

The repatriation scheme enacted in 1919, although born out of the riots that summer can also be viewed in the wider context of the history of black political awakening in the West Indies. Although voluntary, the scheme by its very existence offered little hope to those who refused it. Emanating from central government, the attitudes behind it were shared by the colonial governments. Only with the direct action of dissatisfied repatriated seamen and soldiers did anything positive arise from the whole episode, with the tardy realisation that the cost of living was far outstripping wage rates in the West Indies. The political position of the black population, however, remained weak, despite the mobilising effect of radical black activists in the Islands, since the British authorities, while willing to act to improve the economic situation were not at this stage prepared to offer the native population a real say in government.

In terms of the purely British situation repatriation was a successful short-term policy because it signalled an end to the rioting. The subsequent plight of distressed black seamen was viewed in the context of a numbers game. Destitution could be allowed to prevail among these men, since they no longer existed in such numbers as to constitute a 'problem' requiring a central government scheme to help them out of the country. Instead, they were to be regimented along with 'aliens' while they remained in this country, a state of affairs which was to prevail for many years to come.

Racist public and press reaction to the 1919 riots

The main sources for the public reaction to the riots are contemporary press reports, readers' letters and police reports of the incidents, none of which can be deemed objective sources. Indeed, some press reporting on the black community in Britain at the time of the riots was of the most racist nature. In Glasgow, 'Hal O' the Wynd', who was the 'voice' of the *Glasgow Evening Times* in 1919, stated: 'In this country Sambo has been usually regarded with general tolerance. We have looked upon him as an "amoosin' cuss"', who would never create anything approaching a problem' (*Glasgow Evening Times*, 18 June 1919). A further example of this style of reporting may be taken from the *Manchester Guardian* (a report which was reproduced in the *Glasgow Evening News*), whose assessment of the black man was given as follows: 'The quiet, apparently inoffensive, nigger becomes a demon when armed with a revolver or razor, caring for nothing except the safety of his own skin and the speediest method of overcoming his opponent' (*Glasgow Evening News*, 18 June 1919).

There was also a widely held press belief that blacks had somehow done well out of the war, avoiding the sacrifices of the whites and taking advantage of the situation—a direct continuation in fact of the theme of black fecklessness so often the target of white abuse in popular novels of Empire and in contemporary press reports:

> There is . . . an unemployment grievance—the fact that large numbers of demobi-
> lised soldiers are unable to find work while the West Indian negroes, brought over to

supply a labour shortage during the war, are able to 'swank' about in smart clothes on the proceeds of their industry ... [to the annoyance of] the white man who regards him as part child, part animal and part savage. (*Liverpool Courier*, 11 June 1919)

The racist view that blacks had not taken the same risks as whites in the war was also voiced by the Liverpool police's Chief Constable in a report to the Ministry of Labour in November 1920, two years after the war, suggesting that this had become a sort of 'common knowledge', however ill-founded:

> The plight of the coloured men is no worse, in fact it is better than that of the ordinary white seamen of whom there are a large number out of work. These latter men have a higher standard of living and more family ties than the coloured men. Besides they took greater risks during the war than most of the coloured men, many of whom ... stopped ashore to avoid the submarine menace. (PRO CO 323/848)

An indication of how blacks reacted to this unfounded claim can be measured by the fact that many took to wearing their military service ribbons in a bid to prove that they had 'done their bit' for the British Empire. Another reason for sporting military insignia was the hope that somehow this would protect them from white crowds, to no great effect. The white claim that blacks had shirked their duty in the face of the German submarine threat cannot be substantiated by figures however, since the extent of black losses, for example, from the port of Liverpool, is nowhere quantified. What can be said is that the Elder Dempster shipping company suffered a very high casualty rate during the war in both ships, and, more importantly, men, and as has been mentioned, the Elder Dempster line employed many West Africans on their ships, principally as stokehold crews, a position particularly vulnerable to submarine attack. It is difficult to say how many of these sailors were black, since the Elder Dempster roll of honour did not list the place of birth of their seamen, and although some of their surnames are identifiably African, in other cases it is impossible to tell. However, the fact that the Elder Dempster line maintained a hostel for African seamen in Liverpool throughout the war period implies that these men were a constant feature on their ships at this time.

Readers' letters to newspapers on the 'colour question' often displayed an ingrained racism, particularly when dealing with relationships between black men and white women: 'Undoubtedly, these associationships—romantic enough in the case of Othello and Desdemona—are undesirable and harmful to the dignity of the white—that is to say, the dominant race' (*Liverpool Evening Express*, 6 June 1919). Such a view was echoed in numerous press reports, although not many expressed their opinion in such racist terms as the editor of the *Liverpool Courier* on 11 June:

> A very natural public anger against some results of negro immigration is doubtless behind these racial outbreaks. A casual row between white and coloured fires the combustible material and mob law is invoked ... One of the chief reasons of popular anger behind the present disturbances lies in the fact that the average negro is nearer the animal than is the average white man, and that there are women in Liverpool who have no self-respect. (*Liverpool Courier*, 11 June 1919)

The sex issue was simply the leading manifestation of a more general white dissatisfaction based on wider problems touching the very fabric of society, and it is clear that contemporary sources did appear rather to latch on to the sex issue as a ready explanation for the ferocity of the white violence. Other factors mentioned at the time were grievances, such as job competition, but what really made the white man's blood boil was the question of black–white sexual relationships.

Even those newspapers that demonstrated a degree of sympathy for the black population's plight in Cardiff could not totally vindicate that community:

> The riots that have taken place are a disgrace to the whole community: and every symptom of disorder of this character must be suppressed, however drastic and energetic the means employed necessarily have to be. There is no reason at all which justifies a crowd interfering with the blacks, who—whatever may be the doings of individuals—are as a body, peaceable and altogether well-behaved, and have been throughout the years ... Whatever be alleged in the way of wrongdoing on the part of the black men, that is for the authorities to deal with. Public order does not depend upon disorder. (*South Wales News*, 14 June 1919)

The viewpoint of the black community who were almost always the victims of the rioting is rarely considered in press and official reactions to the violence, a few journals, notably *John Bull* and the *African Telegraph* defended the black community, but the overwhelming press reaction was to apportion blame to the black community as the instigators of the violence.

Conclusion

Britain's 'race riots' of 1919 were much more than simply racially inspired. They were also more than 'riots' in the negative sense of mindless 'mob' violence. What the massive anti-black unrest during 1919 displayed was the deep sense of disquiet in British society in this immediate post-war period. Social and economic pressures came together in a way which made violence a not unexpected reaction. The dislocative effects of four and a half years of total warfare was a factor in the outbreak of the riots, and this element was present in many other instances of riot and social protest in Britain during 1919. Feelings of disappointment, unequal sacrifice, and pent-up aggression came into play, not simply during the race riots, but in the Luton peace riot and in various military riots, principally instigated by Canadian troops marooned in this country due to the lack of shipping to take them home. The shortage in shipping was, of course, a factor in the outbreak of the black–white riots, since most blacks in Britain were employed in this field. The growing unemployment in this industry in the post-war period caused not only increased hardship for black and white alike, but an increase in tension between these two sections of the community.

The position of the seamen's union organisation at this time had a crucial role to play in the outbreak of the riots. The weakness of the NSFU at this time meant that little could be done to negotiate a better position for men who were being thrown out of work after years of dedicated war service. It also meant that when decisions had to be made the union representatives came down heavily on the side of their majority white membership at the expense of black British members. This is clear from the imposition of a 'colour bar' at Britain's seaports, most forcefully in the events leading up to the South Shields riot, when the Adenese stokehold crew of a ship was replaced by an all-white crew by an NSFU official.

The position of the black community during the riots was not simply that of unwilling victims. They, too, shared the wider feelings of social dislocation and alienation which characterised the immediate post-war period. Although well used to the inherently racist attitudes which had permeated much of British society for decades, the virulence of the attacks upon them came as something of a shock, and one to which they reacted, on occasion, with equal violence. War service had created a body of trained men ready to use aggression when put under threat, not simply in the white community, but also among the black. The feeling among thousands of white ex-servicemen that their war service had not been truly appreciated was shared by the black population in Britain—with even more justification bearing in mind the violent white attacks upon them during 1919. Made the scapegoats for wider frustrations, blacks defended their position within British society against the twin threats of white crowds and the British authorities.

References

Banton, Michael, 1955, *The Coloured Quarter*, London, Jonathan Cape.
Evans, Neil, 1980, 'The South Wales Race Riots of 1919', *Llafur*, 3.
Hopkins, C.P., 1927, *National Service of British Seamen*, London, Routledge.
Jenkinson, Jacqueline, 1985, 'The Glasgow Race Disturbances of 1919', *Immigrants and Minorities*, 4: 43–67.
Liverpool Record Office, Liverpool Watch Committee Minute Book no. 57.
P[ublic] R[ecord] O[ffice] C[olonial] O[ffice], 323/814, 323/848.
Walvin, J. 1973, *Black and White*, London, Allen Lane.
Williams, D., 1970, 'Report to Cardiff Watch Committee on Colour Riots, July 9, 1919', *South Wales Police Magazine*, Winter volume.

6

Blaming the Blackshirts: the authorities and the anti-Jewish disturbances in the 1930s

Richard Thurlow

The passions aroused by the anti-Jewish disturbances of the 1930s were significant because they provided the trigger mechanism which led to the passing of the Public Order Act of 1936 and the amendment of the Public Meetings Act in 1938. It should be stressed at the outset that the impact of fascist anti-Semitism was mainly confined to three boroughs in the East End of London—Bethnal Green, Shoreditch and Stepney—and that part of the strategy of the authorities was to contain the problem to that area. Although there were significant Jewish minorities elsewhere, particularly in Leeds and Manchester, political anti-Semitism proved to be counter-productive in drumming up support for the British Union of Fascists (BUF). The state, mindful of the geographical proximity of the East End to Westminster, nevertheless decided that it needed new powers to control public order and defuse the threat of ethnic conflict. The issue proved to be the straw that broke the camel's back—and the Blackshirts were forever to receive the blame for both fomenting public disorder in the East End of London and for the introduction of new legislation that increased police powers which in practice were used more against left-wing than right-wing militancy.

Since its inception in October 1932 the BUF had distanced itself from anti-Semitism. Although there had been some evidence of anti-Jewish behaviour by some of his supporters as far back as the New Party in 1931, Mosley had wisely concluded that anti-Semitism was a political tactic that was perceived, in the title of Nicholas Mosley's two autobiographical books about his relations with his father, as being *Beyond the Pale* and against the *Rules of the Game* (N. Mosley, 1982, 1983).

Mosley's fascism was originally derived from the model of Mussolini rather than Hitler. This was disguised because the attempt to recruit establishment and entrepreneurial support meant policies must not be seen to offend the fundamental values of respectability of British political culture. The peak of this period was the support of Lord Rothermere's 'Hurrah for the Blackshirts' campaign in the *Daily Mail* between January and July 1934. However the violence associated with the Olympia meeting on 7 June, the negative impact of 'The Night of the Long Knives' in Germany for the reputation of fascism, and alleged pressure of Jewish advertisers on Rothermere ended the association.

Mosley, genuinely perplexed by Jewish hostility, asked A.K. Chesterton to conduct 'research' into Jewish influence in British life. Although never published this appears to be the trigger for Chesterton's obsession with anti-Semitism, for despite his family connections there was no previous evidence of this trait. The collapse of membership led to the search for new policies and tactics which would revive the fortunes of the movement. This meant the development of low politics, of street-corner meetings to tap local resentments in populist causes. With the loss of respectable backing Mosley decided he had nothing to lose by adopting Nazi tactics. In October 1934 at the Albert Hall Mosley attacked Jewish finance and Jewish communism. However, it took another year before the BUF discovered its most fertile ground for recovery. This arose when Jock Houston, a man with a criminal record, and a populist anti-Semite, E.G. Clarke, began to attract large audiences to BUF meetings in Shoreditch from August 1935, and other parts of the East End of London (T. Linehan, 1992, pp. 59–65). Virulent anti-Semitic speeches led to protests from local residents, the objections of the Labour Movement and more vigorous forms of self defence organised by militant Jews and communists. Political violence proved to be the consequence of the fascist campaign in the East End of London (Thurlow, 1987, pp. 92–118).

Revisionist accounts of these events have met with a mixed response. Sir Oswald Mosley's version was countered with the jibe that he was an 'expert forgetter' (Mosley, 1968). Robert Skidelsky's biography was criticised for whitewashing Mosley's 'gutter politics' (Skidelsky, 1975; Thurlow, 1975, pp. 15–19). On the other hand Colin Holmes's convergence theory approach, which emphasised the necessity of examining the political, economic and social development of the Jewish community, as well as the anti-Semitism of the fascists (Holmes, 1979), has now replaced the older scapegoating view of Mandle (1965), as the best interpretation of ethnic conflict in the 1930s. The method, if not the conclusions, would support Skidelsky's view of how the issue should be examined.

In particular it needs to be emphasised that the Jews of the East End of London felt themselves to be in a vulnerable position as a result of the introduction of fascist anti-Semitism and racial abuse after 1935. They were concerned that the authorities appeared to be unable to control the increase in political violence and adopted an attitude of benign neglect to the whole issue. Both the state and the conservative Board of Deputies of British Jews (BDBJ) thought the appropriate response was to deny the fascists the oxygen of publicity by ignoring the rise of political anti-Semitism. Into the political vacuum marched the British Communist Party (CPGB). Whilst the leadership appeared to view the National Government as the main fascist threat in Britain (Morgan, 1989; Branson, 1985) local cells in the East End put United Front policies into practice and in an early version of community politics organised the Jewish community and local labour movement in an anti-fascist campaign (Piratin, 1978; Jacobs, 1978, pp. 169–296; Skidelsky, 1979, pp. 78–99). Groups such as the Workers Circle provided a grass-roots political protest against the fascist abuse directed at ethnic Jews living in the East End. Local Labour parties were also critical of official attempts to ignore the issue (Smith, 1989, pp. 53–71). The BUF benefited from the collapse of the Liberal vote in Bethnal Green and the passivity, and accusations of Labour party mismanagement in Stepney (Linehan, 1992, pp. 129–30, 184). The Jewish People's Council against anti-Semitism and Fascism (JPC) emerged to challenge the BDBJ as the political voice of British Jews (Lebzelter, 1978, pp. 136–154). The secret meeting between Neville Laski, Herbert Morrison MP and Harry Pollitt, designed to put pressure on the CPGB to follow establishment policy towards the BUF, failed to halt the road to Cable Street (Holmes, 1976).

If the subject of anti-Semitism in the East End of London remains controversial, then the same is true with regard to the problem of public order. Whilst there have been numerous critical accounts of the authorities' actions only a few revisionist voices can be heard expressing neutral interpretations of National Government policy (Stevenson and Cook, 1977; Stevenson, 1975, pp. 146–165). Even the more detached accounts tend to be critical of the government's civil liberties record (Anderson, 1983). D.S. Lewis, who appears to be heavily influenced by the United Front perspective of the 1930s, went further and attacked the 'reactionary' and 'regressive' measures passed by the National Government with regard to public order and internal security issues (Lewis, 1987, pp. 149, 159). He used the evidence accumulated by the National Council for Civil Liberties (NCCL) to criticise state management of law and order. The security authorities, the Metropolitan Police and the Home Office dismissed such views as an attempt by a communist front organisation to undermine public order (Thurlow, 1994, pp. 169–172, 195–196).

Historians of public order have tended to argue that the state's main concern was not with racial violence but controlling left-wing militancy. Changes in the law and the police methods used to manage strikes, processions and demonstrations were primarily a response to communist or trade union activity (Morgan, 1987; Weinberger, 1990). There is indeed much truth in this argument. A survey of the Cabinet records and the Metropolitan Police Commissioner's papers show that the issue came on the political agenda in the 1930s as a result of the disturbances associated with the National Unemployed Workers Movement (NUWM), particularly the hunger march in 1932 (Stevenson, 1975, pp. 146–175; Morgan, 1987, pp. 229–75). The Attorney-General, Sir Thomas Inskip, finally persuaded the Cabinet that it would be better to experiment with binding over public order offenders to keep the peace as a means of social control. The issue was also discussed several times in Cabinet during 1934 and several draft bills were produced in the Home Office.

The release of most of the Home Office papers pertaining to British fascism has provided much new evidence on the background and evolution of public order policy. They supply additional information to that already available in the Mepol 2 and Cabinet papers. There are important files on British fascism and disturbances, anti-Semitism and the background to the Public Order Act in both the HO 45 and HO 144 series. These normally have a seventy-five or one-hundred-year closure period, but as a result of the thirty-year rule being applied to them following political pressure from a most unlikely alliance of

Lady Mosley and left-wing Labour MPs, they enable us to see the forces operating which led to the Public Order Act and the assumptions behind government management and control of political violence. They show quite clearly that most of the contemporary criticism was exaggerated and the United Front concern for civil liberties was unjustified. Although there were voices in the state calling for restrictions there were stronger political and administrative pressures which advised caution and stressed the importance of the freedom of expression within the law. The Home Office officials did not wish to increase the powers of the Home Secretary nor to undermine local autonomy.

It was the failure of the authorities to control the situation with existing powers which reluctantly led the state to change the law. Political anti-Semitism was a powerful argument used by the hawks to bring pressure to bear to produce this change. The doves in the Home Office ensured that the Public Order Act addressed more general concerns. The 1936 legislation represented a response to a number of unresolved issues apart from those posed by fascism and left-wing militancy. These included clarification of how the authorities should judge a meeting or procession within existing case law; whether they were designed to convert (*Beatty* v. *Gilbanks* 1882) or intimidate (*Wise* v. *Dunning* 1902) (Skidelsky, 1975, pp. 418–19). It also attempted to increase protection for those subject to abuse or physical violence but stopped short of defending specific minorities or outlawing named organisations. Matters pertaining to conflict situations which had arisen as far back as the 'Skeleton Army' and Trafalgar Square riots of the 1880s, the Kensitite demonstrations of 1903–9 and the Suffragette disturbances of 1906–14, were all dealt with under the bill. The concern of the authorities had been shown in 1931 when a circular was issued which said the police had to notify the Home Office of every disturbance no matter how trivial the incident.

The Public Order Act represented a compromise between the different pressures operating at the various levels of the state apparatus. Politicians, the Home Office, the Security Service and the police all had very different views on how political extremism and public order should be managed. Whilst the change of law was fundamentally a political decision its nature and operation was heavily influenced by both civil servants and the Metropolitan Police Commissioner. It was the fear of ethnic conflict that provided the clinching argument for the addition to state powers.

What is particularly significant was the large degree of political consensus about the introduction of the new law. The National Government itself represented a coalition of the Conservatives and sections of both the Labour and Liberal parties. However, what was revealing about the debate was the extent to which the Opposition influenced the introduction of the legislation. The three attempts to bring forward a bill in 1934 were finally dropped when it became clear that the Opposition was lukewarm about the idea (PRO HO 144/20158/304–09). Sensitivity to the criticisms of the Labour and Liberal parties developed from the campaign which tended to merge their opposition with the low politics demonstrations of the CPGB and the recently formed National Council for Civil Liberties (NCCL) against the Incitement to Disaffection Act of 1934, and which forced the government to amend its proposals somewhat (Thurlow, 1994, p. 141). The National Government was particularly keen that the possibility of such informal alliances should be avoided wherever possible in future.

Although they were critical of certain sections of the Act, particularly clause 3, nevertheless the Labour Party supported most of the legislation in 1936. Similarly when clause 3(3) was invoked in the East End of London in 1937, the Labour Party suggested the time limit for the outlawing of all political processions, and were consulted and agreed to the extension of the ban until the Second World War (PRO HO 144/21086/17). The Home Secretary's memorandum, discussed in Cabinet on 14 October 1936, argued the main reason for action was that the BUF campaign was stimulating the Communist Party and influencing the Jewish community to support the Labour Party. The only redeeming feature as far as government was concerned was that a deputation of leading Jews recognised that allegations of bias against the police were quite unfounded (PRO HO 144/20158/296).

The Labour Party was as equally concerned as the government at the propaganda potential for the growth of extremism in the East End. It was particularly worried by the activities of the CPGB. Communists had been expelled from the Labour Party and their organisations were proscribed. There had been a negative reaction to the CPGB call for a United Front against fascism by the Labour Party. Indeed, leaders like Herbert Morrison had attacked the 'hysterical utterances' of local Labour leaders like the Mayor of Stepney, Mrs Roberts, and had praised the actions of the police in controlling public order (PRO MEPOL 2/3043).

There was thus a certain degree of unanimity between politicians about the iniquities of Mosley and the BUF. Most supporters of the National Government agreed with Baldwin that 'Tom Mosley was a cad and a wrong 'un' (T. Jones, 1969, p. 195). Conservative opinion at the Olympia meeting in June 1934 blamed Mosley for the violence, and thought he had been deliberately provocative in ejecting interrupters, rather than trying to answer them (290 HC Deb 5s, 11 June 1934, 1935–37, 1952–53).

Both the Labour and Liberal parties were hostile to what they perceived as the authoritarian and élitist structure of the BUF. They objected to the paramilitary aspects and the increasing anti-Semitism of Mosley's Blackshirts. Labour politicians considered Mosley a traitor; Dalton called fascists a 'political bad smell' (317 HC Deb 5s, 5 Nov. 1936, 294–97), and Attlee thought Mosley was a megalomaniac who was not entirely stable (309 HC Deb 5s, 27 Feb 1936, 1932). The Labour Party argued that unless the government took action against the BUF the Labour Movement would be unable to control the justified anger of extremists, who were already forming anti-fascist organisations such as the Greyshirts (PRO HO 144/20141/51).

Such public hostility to British fascism by the representatives of the 'old gangs' of British politics was not surprising given that Mosley's aim was to replace parliamentary government with the Corporate State, and to outlaw all political opposition parties to the BUF. However, such negative tactics expressed from all sides of the House of Commons did not make the administrative problems of regulating fascist activity any easier.

The preferred method for dealing with British fascism was through informal techniques of political management. Tinkering with the Common Law was viewed as a measure of last resort by the politicians and the Home Office as it let out a pandora's box of problems, encompassing resistance to the restrictions on civil liberties, a dread of special legislation discriminating against or protecting specific groups, and limiting the administrative freedom of manoeuvre of the authorities. Hence the pressure applied to the media either in the form of polite requests from the government or more subtle ways of ensuring Sir John Reith's co-operation at the BBC. After the ending of Rothermere's 'Hurrah for the Blackshirts' campaign in the *Daily Mail* in July 1934 it appears that the National Government approached newspaper editors to avoid unnecessary publicity for the BUF. The BBC avoided presentation of extremist views through an unofficial ban which denied both fascists and communists, as well as maverick opinions critical of government policy, including Winston Churchill, in the 1930s. Indeed Mosley and the communists were not allowed to broadcast until 1968. Finally newsreel companies were asked not to film mass demonstrations in the 1930s. (West, 1987, p. 91; PRO HO 144/20710/3; MEPOL 2/5507). Only when such measures were shown to be insufficient in 1936 was the nettle finally grasped and the politicians strengthened the powers necessary to maintain public order.

Within Whitehall there were also important administrative forces which acted as a counterweight to the restrictionist attitude of the security authorities in the 1930s. The permanent officials of the Home Office interpreted the law in a liberal manner and acted as a conservative brake on over-enthusiastic or impatient police and security officers. The Home Office officials were suspicious of the Colonial Office influence and military background of many in the police and security administrations. Always emphasising the necessity for caution they stressed the need to have sufficient powers to control fascist–communist and anti-Semitic political violence, whilst at the same time preserving the maximum degree of civil liberty. What then is most interesting is the conflict which arose in Whitehall as a result of the competing views, and pressure from within the administration, which helped to explain the hesitant views of the state to the problems posed by fascism (Cohen, 1986, pp. 416–34; Thurlow, 1988, pp. 77–99).

It was the Home Office which was responsible for formulating policy towards the fascists. In the 1930s four very different Home Secretaries, Sir John Gilmour (1932–35), Sir John Simon (1935–37), Sir Samuel Hoare (1937–39) and Sir John Anderson (1939–40), reacted according to the conflicting information and advice they received from Home Office mandarins, the Cabinet, Parliament, the law officers, the Metropolitan Police Commissioner, the Chief Constables, MI5 and public opinion in general. Of these Gilmour and Hoare tended to follow the advice of Lord Trenchard and Sir Philip Game, their respective Metropolitan Police Commissioners, whilst Simon was more inclined to accept the views of his officials, and Anderson, the personification of the liberal traditions of the Home Office, was prepared to challenge the increased authority of MI5 once war had broken out.

Of the politicians both Sir John Simon and Sir Samuel Hoare outlined succinctly their defence of civil liberties and their opposition to anti-Semitism. Simon argued in a speech at Spen Valley on 7 October 1936 that the essence of British social life was tolerance and that fascism and communism were both

intolerant creeds and were un-British in sentiment and purpose (PRO HO
144/20159/171–78). At a conference at the Home Office on fascist Jew-baiting
on 4 March 1936, he argued that the better discipline of the fascists meant they
obeyed police orders whilst the communists challenged the authority of law
enforcement officers to stop the justified protest of those who felt threatened by
the Blackshirts. He also pointed to the anomaly whereby police broke up
meetings outside Labour Exchanges whilst allowing Jew-baiters to operate in
Jewish areas (PRO HO 144/21378/3–7). The difficulty of the situation was
however that he could not ban all anti-Jewish or fascist meetings in a particular
place because although it would afford relief to the police, there were no powers
under existing legislation for the authorities to ban meetings of a particular type
or by a specific organisation (PRO HO 144/21378/138). In July 1936 following
a debate in parliament Simon sent an *aide memoire* to the Metropolitan Police
Commissioner outlining the measures he now thought necessary to counter
growing anti-Semitic violence. He argued strongly that the right of free speech
should not be made a cloak for insult and abuse. He considered the issue to be
of such significance that police should be temporarily taken away from other
duties. Police should take shorthand notes of speeches. Careful attention
should be given to all fascist publications and the attention of the Director of
Public Prosecutions and Home Office called to statements that were defama-
tory or constituted a seditious libel or public mischief. Monthly reports should
be submitted to the Home Office about the general situation in Jewish districts
(MEPOL 2/3043). Such reports were continued until 1944.

The serious principles behind the concern of the Home Secretary were
shown in the response of his successor, Sir Samuel Hoare, to a demand that a
fascist march in St Pancras should be banned. He argued that political
opposition to a meeting was no reason to ban it. Britain with its tradition of free
speech, allowed every political creed to voice its opinion provided that the law
was not being subverted. Only in the exceptional circumstances of the East End
of London could that principle be modified. For Hoare the maintenance of civil
and political liberties depended on the extent we were to tolerate our political
opponents. Street brawls between fascists and anti-fascists only served as
advertisements to alien political creeds which would otherwise gain no footing
in this country. The authorities would maintain public order and could not
tolerate attempts to intimidate by the threat of force. Hoare considered his
response to this private letter to be such a significant general principle that he
released its contents to the press (PRO HO 144/21086/85–87).

The permanent Home Office officials under Sir Russell Scott (1932–38) and
Sir Alexander Maxwell (1938–48) as Under-Secretaries of State, played an
increasingly important role in upholding the liberal traditions of the Home
office. The influence of Sir John Anderson was to dominate official responses
until the 1960s. The continuity of policy and personnel is perhaps best
illustrated by the part played by Frank Newsam, deputy to Arthur Dixon in the
Police Department and the Home Office mandarin most concerned with law
and order and security issues in the 1930s. Newsam had acted as personal
secretary to Anderson in the 1920s, was later knighted and was Permanent
Under-Secretary between 1948 and 1958. The critical reaction of Home Office
civil servants, and of Section F, in charge of police administration under Arthur

(later Sir Arthur) Dixon, to police reforms shows that tighter co-ordination of police organisation was only partly achieved in the inter-war period (Morgan, 1987, p. 276). They had more influence over Game and were later to moderate the impact of Trenchard's radical reforms (Boyle, 1962, pp. 665–68). The Home Office officials did not wish to increase the powers of the Home Secretary nor to undermine local autonomy. They basically reacted to events and only suggested changes in the law as a result of political initiative.

The Home Office view was developed in response to the pressure applied by the police, particularly the Metropolitan Police Commissioners. Apart from voicing general worries that Chief Constables and Watch Committees were exceeding their powers in prohibiting or threatening to ban BUF marches and meetings, the Home Office had little control outside the Metropolis. It was extremely concerned that over-vigilant policing would be challenged success-fully in the courts. This was shown in the administrative response to over-zealous policing in Leicester and Manchester prior to the passing of the Public Order Acts, which had banned fascist meetings despite the lack of powers to do so (PRO HO 144/20158/272; HO 144/20143/107).

The problem for the Home Office was further complicated by the person-ality of the Metropolitan Police Commissioner between 1931 and 1935, Lord Trenchard. Brought in to reform the Metropolitan Police, he had ridden roughshod over some of the objections presented by Home Office officials, and had appealed successfully to Sir John Gilmour over their heads. Although he co-operated fairly amicably with Section F, the sometimes fraught relations between Home Office officials and the Commissioner found expression in differences over public order policy as well. Trenchard considered several leading Home Office officials to be administrative lightweights.

These problems were shown quite clearly in 1934 in response to Trenchard's call for the banning of the BUF. The Home Office replied that the same consideration still applied as when General Horwood wished to ban the communists in the 1920s. There was no argument for outlawing extremist beliefs provided the expression of such policies did not break the law. Only if the authorities' management of the situation under existing powers appeared to be threatened, could changes in the law be contemplated. So long as public opinion believed we had a fair and efficient government which upheld the law, the state should not attempt to restrict the holding of political beliefs no matter how obnoxious they appeared to those who held democratic values. Political surveillance of such movements was necessary, but attempts to restrict liberty would drive political expression underground, and create worse problems in the long run (PRO HO 144/20158/162–63).

Trenchard's trenchant views on fascists were somewhat ironic given the communists accused him of being a closet fascist himself, because of his autocratic style of management, and the alleged close connections Mosley had with the RAF, of which the Metropolitan Police Commissioner had been the founder. Trenchard wished to ban the fascists because of the public order problems they presented, and the waste of police resources associated with controlling processions and meetings. He particularly wanted to outlaw the wearing of uniforms and paramilitary organisations. He did not want uniformed stewarding of meetings outside police control, neither did he want them to be seen as protecting fascists. He was also concerned that 'respectable' people would appear on Communist Party platforms in support of their anti-fascist activity. Police should also be given powers to enter fascist meetings to prevent disturbances. Just before his retirement he began to advocate the view that fascist processions should be banned. In spite of his autocratic views, even Trenchard recognised that fascist–communist violence was amongst the most difficult problems he ever had to deal with, and this recognition was behind his successful request to expand Special Branch from 136 to 200 officers in 1934 in an era of drastic financial retrenchment.

Trenchard's case developed in response to practical problems, after it was made clear to him that restricting the rights of fascists outside the use of emergency powers was not a feasible political or legal option. Trenchard was succeeded by Sir Philip Game, who as his leading administrator in the RAF had been personally selected to succeed him. However although the Home Office officials found him more reasonable to deal with, he was even more anti-fascist than his predecessor. His experience as Governor-General of New South Wales in the early 1930s, when he had sacked the Prime Minister and had had problems with fascist demonstrations, gave him the right background for dealing with violence in the East End (Foott, 1968; Moore, 1990, pp. 62–72). Game was to argue that political anti-Semitism added a new dimension to the public order problems posed by fascism and made it even more imperative that the movement should be banned. He was to argue strongly that the new powers granted under the Public Order Act should be used to maintain the ban on political processions in the East End of London until the Second World War. He wished to extend the ban to the whole of London but this was turned down by the Cabinet, after objections by Home Office officials and consultation with the Opposition (PRO HO 144/21087/208–10, 215–19, 225–31). Although willing to listen to Home Office advice, Game also used his personal connections to good effect. Hoare had been Trenchard's closest political supporter in the inter-service battles of the 1920s, and the Home Office and Commissioner's files have several congratulatory notes from the Home Secretary relating to Game's efficient and hard line management of fascist disturbances in the 1930s. The problems associated with the alleged partiality of the police in favour of the fascists in the 1930s most certainly did not originate in official policy.

However, if official attitudes were not pro-fascist, there were problems of interpretation of the law in developing conflict situations amongst junior ranks, and local magistrates treated anti-fascists more harshly than fascists (PRO MEPOL 2/3109, MEPOL 2/3115). The attitudes of individual policemen meant that an even-handed approach to fascists and anti-fascists was difficult to implement. H division in Bethnal Green and the Shoreditch constabulary were particularly notorious for policemen allegedly treating anti-fascist protestors less fairly than the fascists. Constables were often confronted, however, with the dilemma that police intervention could provoke more disorder than the inflamed language of the anti-Semitic diatribes, and as a result the discretion of the authorities led to no action being taken.

Game was worried by this problem and tried to address it in an internal memorandum to police stations about the measures necessary to curb political anti-Semitism. He argued that the right of free speech should not be made a cloak for insult and abuse. This was always liable to provoke a breach of the peace and if allowed would increase the danger and lower the prestige of the Metropolitan Police. Officers should act firmly and immediately when the occasion demanded. Notes of what speakers said were to be taken at all meetings attended by police and there was to be no question of good-humoured toleration of language. The police were also prepared to initiate common assault proceedings to prevent violence. They would do everything in their power to suppress the growing mischief of Jew-baiting and to prevent any tendency for it to develop into serious trouble (PRO MEPOL 2/3043).

The hostile perception of British fascism by the State was reinforced by reports from Special Branch and MI5. The former were mainly concerned with the overt behaviour of fascists, particularly monitoring demonstrations and anti-Semitism in the East End of London between 1936 and 1939. The Commissioner's monthly report to the Home Office was based on the information he received from Special Branch. They took an interactionist perspective on the violence between fascists and communists in the 1930s. However, although such disorder was portrayed as the work of a criminal and hooligan element, official fascist reactions were presented in a more neutral manner. Fascists for the most part obeyed all police requests without question and kept the authorities informed of their plans for processions and meetings. Communists were less accommodating and complained vigorously about police harrassment and infringement of civil rights.

Special Branch tended to assume that all left-wing and radical anti-fascist organisations which were not explicitly aligned to the Labour Party were communist front organisations that were directly or indirectly controlled by the Comintern in Moscow. They were even suspicious of populist independent non-political anti-fascist groups which opposed anti-Semitism and were not aligned to respectable law-abiding organisations, such as the Democratic Union and Legion of Democrats. These were not regarded as genuine movements by Special Branch, but groups run by confidence tricksters, who were mainly concerned with pocketing financial contributions from the public.

Since 1931 Special Branch had become the police arm of the Security Service which was directed by MI5. The declassified MI5 reports on the BUF are informative with regard to official attitudes towards public order. They particularly stress the constitutional implications for Mosley's adherents of supporting the BUF. For MI5, public order disturbances, such as those following the Olympia meeting of 7 June 1934 and the Battle of Cable Street on 4 October 1936 led to publicity and the growth of extremism in general. Many of the middle and working classes, who were worried about unemployment, were also attracted to fascism by the argument that Mosley was upholding the right of free speech, he was making a stand against 'red violence' and the disruptive tactics of Communists and other radicals at political meetings since the war. MI5 argued that many of those recruited to fascism were unaware of the central contradiction of the BUF. A party which ostensibly stood for the principle of free speech would, according to its platform, capture power at a general election, which would then be followed by the suppression of all opinion opposed to the fascists.

Like the communists the fascists were patently insincere in using civil rights and democratic arguments to harness support. For Newsam at the Home Office fascism and political anti-Semitism strengthened communism, as it encouraged the growth of a united anti-fascist front (under communist influence) which included individuals who in no other circumstances would appear on the same platform as communists. Newsam also disliked the fact that the police could be portrayed as protecting fascists when they prevented violence at meetings. This was being misrepresented by communist and others who were arguing that the authorities were pro-fascist and that the law was not being administered impartially (PRO HO 144/20142/211–12). There was absolutely no truth in these allegations. MI5 saw the failure of Mosley to make more capital from the East End campaign either as a result of his incapacity, an unwillingness to challenge the law, or the threat of new legislation (PRO HO 144/20162/404).

The attitude of the authorities to public order was not a simple one. The state recognised that political anti-Semitism was as potent a source of conflict as fascist–communist disturbances. This was shown quite clearly in the response of Sir Philip Game to the Battle of Cable Street. When asked to submit a memorandum on the incident he argued that the anti-Jew cry of fascism was the one real danger and that moderate opinion would support drastic legislation to combat anti-Semitism rather than milder measures to deal with the effect of disorders. For Game anti-Semitism appealed to a subconscious racial instinct which was almost universal, and appealed to Colonel Blimps with a conspiracy mentality and with great force in the East End where economic jealousy of Jewish acumen caused prejudice and resentment (PRO HO 144/20159/155–62).

If the authorities were nervous, hesitant and often divided about further restricting civil liberties, the same was true about their attitude towards immigration and anti-Semitism. The authorities viewed political liberty as a precious flower which was constantly threatened by issues like unemployment and immigration, which could be whipped up by political extremists to influence the masses against the government. This nervousness about extremism also became manifest during the abdication crisis when despite political consensus across the political spectrum not to form a 'King's Party' in support of Edward VIII, MI5 became worried about BUF support for the King (PRO HO 144/20710/38–42).

Whilst the authorities trusted the ability of the democratic electorate to see through what they regarded as the false claims of extremists under normal conditions, they became far less confident if the political system was seen to be in crisis. This led to a schizophrenic attitude. In the 1930s the state's reaction to the anti-Semitic campaign highlighted the contradiction between political asylum for those fleeing persecution on the continent and increasing restrictionist pressures on immigration caused by establishment fears of working-class unrest, as a result of increased competition for employment and housing (Holmes, 1979, pp. 175–219; Holmes, 1988, pp. 124–60; Porter, 1979). One such alarmist view came from Sir Philip Game, who despite Home Office scepticism expressed the fear that any influx of refugees coming from the continent might bring the political extremes together: the fascists who had been attacking the Jews for three years, and the communists who might argue that Jewish refugees were taking away gentile employment (PRO HO 144/21381/186).

The state also feared any mass reaction to changes in the law which would specifically protect minorities, even against the most vicious forms of racist propaganda. This was made clear in the government response to the *Rex* v. *Leese* case in 1936. Unlike the summary jurisdiction of magistrates' courts used to regulate public order, Leese was indicted on charges of seditious libel and creating a public mischief in September 1936. Leese was 'Director-General' of the Imperial Fascist League, Mosley's most significant, if unsuccessful, rival in the 1930s. In February 1936 Leese's newspaper, *The Fascist*, had alleged that the Jews practised ritual murder against Christian children. Leese was found guilty of the lesser charge but was found not guilty of seditious libel by the jury (PRO HO 45/24967/52). Leese still went to prison for six months because he refused to pay a small fine.

The Attorney-General was astonished at the verdict and concluded that the jury viewed Leese as a stupid crank with honest convictions who should not be found guilty of the serious charge of seditious libel. The Home Office viewed this as a precedent and resisted all attempts to include specific clauses with respect to racial incitement in the Public Order Act. Unless it could be proved to have provoked disorder the authorities refused to prosecute even the worst cases of anti-Semitic or racist libel. This proved to be the case in three more blatant transgressions in the following years (Thurlow, 1987, pp. 75–7). Uncertainty over how possible acquittals would be interpreted by public opinion and fear of an imagined nativist reaction which could be used by both right and left extremists proved a more potent influence on policy than the need to protect minority groups from verbal abuse (Thurlow, 1988, p. 83).

What was most significant in the state's response to violence and anti-Semitism was the administrative concern of Whitehall to avoid the impression of reacting to pressure from street politics. Whilst proper attention at all times was made to secure the support of the Opposition, particularly the Labour Party, to proposed changes in legislation, care was taken to encourage a proper distance between labour and more left-wing opinions, and to avoid any connection between the Home Office and what were deemed Communist Party front organisations. With regard to political anti-Semitism the support of the moderate BDBJ, as the leaders of Jewish public opinion, was cultivated and government distanced itself from the militant JPC. Similarly, no deputation from the National Council of Civil Liberties (NCCL) to protest about aspects of the Public Order Bill was allowed, on the grounds that such opinions had been fully considered in Parliament in the debates on the Public Order Act.

However, other reasons were given in a Home Office minute. This argued that both the JPC and the NCCL were alleged to have 'close subterranean connections' with the CPGB particularly through the NCCL's secretary, Ronald Kidd. Although distinguished persons were vice-presidents, and it ostensibly had laudable aims, the CPGB vilified the police and alleged they displayed partiality to fascists in the East End of London. The BDBJ had also made clear that the JPC was not a body which commanded respect in responsible Jewish quarters. The Home Office pointed out that at the JPC delegate conference one of the speakers argued that fascist violence should be met with counter-violence in the streets. Both organisations appeared to oppose fascism as a political philosophy, and for the government to receive a deputation from organisations who wished to prevent the lawful propagation of a political creed, might be open to misrepresentation.

The denigration of extra-Parliamentary pressure does not change the fact that the authorities were as concerned with preserving civil liberties as their critics, and that they acted with hesitation and reluctance to alter the law. The point that Sir Thomas Inskip, the Attorney-General, advised finally against banning hunger marches in 1932, that the Opposition were not fully supportive of new public legislation and that the situation suddenly improved after July 1934, were the chief reasons why the law was not altered after the major public order disturbances of the early 1930s. It took the problems posed by Cable Street, and possible threats to public order by the abdication crisis and hunger marches in December 1936, to force the government to change the law and bring forward aspects of previously proposed legislation which was hastily cobbled together in a Cabinet inter-departmental Committee to form the Public Order Act of 1936.

The change in the law resulted from Sir Philip Game's perceived inability to ban Mosley's proposed march in the East End of London on 4 October 1936. This was because he realised in advance that he did not have sufficient police resources to control the proposed massive counter-demonstration. When informed by the Home Office that he had no powers to ban a perfectly legal march, and that it was inadvisable to make a martyr of Mosley, as this would give him unfavourable publicity from the authorities' standpoint, he used the only legal power at his disposal, to re-route Mosley's march to the West End of London (PRO HO 144/21061/93). This would avoid a confrontation between 1,900 fascists and 100,000 anti-fascists. The Home Office was unsure of police legal powers because although outside London the chief officers of police often interfered with meetings and processions, in law they had no power to do so and they only evaded a legal setback because nobody had challenged their powers. The Home Office was particularly conscious of the fact that Mosley had never lost a case in court and was therefore loath to overreach police powers in their dealings with him. They also felt that attempts to bind Mosley over to keep the peace, the favoured legal weapon to control mass demonstrations since 1932, would rebound against the authorities and lead to bad publicity, with Mosley claiming he was being unfairly discriminated against. The NCCL wanted Mosley to be bound over, a view the Home Office considered humbug given their opposition to its use against left-wing processions.

In retrospect the Home Office was far too cautious in its appreciation of the legal powers of the police. *Thomas* v. *Sawkins* (1935) and *Duncan* v. *Jones* (1936) both appeared to show that police powers were far more extensive than the law officers and the Home Office realised (Morgan, 1987, pp. 265–6; Lewis, 1987, pp. 163–5). The former showed that the courts would support the police if they entered a private meeting where they had reason to believe a breach of the peace was threatened, and the latter that the police had extensive powers to ban meetings in public places, even though it was law-abiding and orderly.

The significance of these two judgments illustrates the reluctance of the Home Office to strengthen the law. The Home Office until *Thomas* v. *Sawkins* argued that the police could attend meetings only if asked by the organisers under the terms of the Public Meetings Act of 1908, and as Mosley's policy was based on showing that fascists could keep order at their own events, this invitation was unlikely. The changed situation following the fracas at Olympia and *Thomas* v. *Sawkins* was implicitly recognised by the government when Gilmour's proposed public order legislation in 1934, which included police powers to enter meetings, did not become part of the Public Order Act in 1936, as the police were now seen to have sufficient powers already (PRO HO 144/20158/350).

The extensive control the police possessed over meetings also did not become part of the new legislation. Although police regulation of processions was to become one of the main issues of contention over the bill, police interference with meetings did not noticeably increase before the Second World War, except where disorder was threatened. This was shown in the East End of London where over 1,000 political meetings were held in each of the summer months between 1937 and the Second World War (PRO MEPOL 2/3043,2/3127; Kidd, 1940, pp. 24–9). Many of these were explicitly pro- or anti-fascist and were not interfered with by the authorities. Although there was some continuing political violence there were no fatalities resulting from fascist–communist disturbances or from anti-Semitic attacks. However *Duncan* v. *Jones* does suggest that if Game had had his wish and banned Mosley's march he would have been supported by the courts. The response of the Home Office was partly a liberal rearguard action and some bureaucratic inertia.

The Public Order Act was rushed through in December at the height of the abdication crisis and just after the 1936 hunger march. Although a large number of amendments were not allowed by the government, the most controversial elements of the Bill were debated thoroughly and in some cases altered. The attempt in clause 2(4) to enable the statements of any adherent of an organisation admissible in evidence for the prosecution of its leaders, was dropped at the Committee stage of the Bill, thus denying the evidence of *agents provocateurs* (Anderson, 1983, p. 186; Kidd, 1940, p. 141). Newsam argued in a Home Office minute that the Chief Officer of Police should not be allowed to prohibit processions by imposing stringent conditions on individuals groups. This was a point which was raised at several stages of the discussion in Parliament. The Public Order Act was not an anti-fascist bill and it was particularly emphasised that the impression should be given, in fact as well as in theory, that extremists of right and left should be dealt with in an even-handed fashion (PRO HO 144/21086/16).

The legislation had three main objectives. These were the prohibition of political uniforms, the outlawing of paramilitary groups and the regulation and control of public processions and assemblies. Section one made it an offence to wear a political uniform; section two made it illegal to manage or control a group designed to usurp the function of the police or armed forces; section three gave the police the power to impose conditions on marches, or the Chief Constable the power to approach a local council, or in London the Home Secretary, for an order to ban all political processions in a locality for three months; section four made it illegal to possess an offensive weapon at a public meeting; section five made it an offence for anybody to use threatening, abusive or insulting words or behaviour with intent to provoke a breach of the peace, and section six enabled chairmen of a meeting to ask a constable to take the name and address of an offender, who if he refused or provided false information, was liable to arrest (Lewis, 1987, pp. 145–80). The aim was to increase police powers to regulate public order and prevent disorder and not to discriminate against any particular creed or party. In practice sections one and two were specifically aimed at fascists, five and six at communists and other left-wingers, and three and four at other forms of low politics.

In general the Public Order Act has not been treated kindly by historians. Left-wing critics have complained that in the guise of neutral legislation, prompted by fascist-inspired disturbances, the government smuggled in a new law which restricted civil liberties significantly, and which was used specifically by the authorities to discriminate against left-wing groups (Lewis, 1987, p. 160; Kidd, 1940, p. 75). The police, too, have been criticised for partiality against left-wing militancy (Morgan, 1987, pp. 229–75; Croucher, 1987). Revisionists see the public order problems of the 1930s developing from a conflict between the two political extremes with the state authorities attempting fairly success-fully to regulate and control public order (Thurlow, 1987, p. 115; Stevenson, 1980, pp. 135–49).

The operation of the Public Order Act of 1936 proved somewhat con-troversial. With regard to the containment of political anti-Semitism the legislation was relatively successful. Whilst communists challenged attacks on their civil liberties, fascists obeyed all police instructions. The BUF stopped wearing uniforms and dropped their paramilitary organisation. Neither of these actions appear to have caused a decline in the organisation however. Large fascist meetings were regularly held in the East End until 1940. These were matched by even bigger anti-fascist protests. The point was that although there was continuing political violence the authorities contained hostilities. Whilst police had to be taken from normal duties and often were used to patrol the inflamed areas the framework of law and order did not break down. Indeed the evidence suggests that patriotic East Enders distinguished between political anti-Semitism and Mosley's pro-Nazi sympathies. Although populists like Jock Houston could still enthuse large audiences with anti-Semitic diatribes in 1939 many of Mosley's cockney supporters became disillusioned with his uncritical response to Hitler's expansionism after Munich. Support for Mosley declined and more importantly political anti-Semitism did not assume such a threat to public order outside the East End.

Section 3 of the Act proved more of a headache for the authorities. Here there was a continuing clash between the Home Office tradition of protecting civil liberties and the more security- and public-order-conscious police and MI5. Whilst the civil servants insisted on the public right to hold public meetings which reflected legal political opinion the police fretted about having to take so many officers off normal duties. Game used his own powers to limit the use of loudspeakers and banned torchlight processions in the East End. However, the Home Office stopped Game from banning specific marches under section 3(1) of the Act and insisted that if political demonstrations threatened public order then only a general ban lasting for up to three months could be used under 3(3) (PRO HO 144/21086/245). This could only be implemented after discussions with the Opposition. After difficulties in the 1937 council elections and Mosley's determination to march through the East End, Game was able to establish a ban on all political processions after July 1937 in the East End (PRO HO 144/21087/201). The time limit for this ban was initially for six weeks at the suggestion of the Labour Party, although it was to be extended until 1947. Interestingly enough the attempts to end the ban by the Home Office in 1938 were thwarted by the combined pressure of Sir Philip Game and the Labour Party. The Cabinet refused to sanction the extension of the ban to the rest of London and to other areas and allowed Mosley's marches to Kentish Town in July and Bermondsey in October 1937 (PRO HO 144/21087/268,350). It argued that a ban would be a gross infringement of civil rights and would not gain the support of the Opposition. Other areas like Liverpool also had well-entrenched public order problems and only in the most justified situations could curtailment of rights be contemplated.

The other area of particular controversy was provided by the problems posed by section 5 of the Act. The difficulties encountered by the outlawing of abusive language proved difficult to resolve. Although Sir Philip Game was especially firm on asking constables to err on the side of harshness with regard to the arrest of offenders, the police in a potential conflict situation found it difficult to implement. Fascist speakers developed the technique of criticising the Jews as an ethnic group rather than as individuals. Officers in practice found it difficult to distinguish between *badinage* and abuse. Although some speakers were successfully prosecuted, like E.G. Clarke and Raven Thomson, the cases often went to appeal and some were thrown out by magistrates. The authorities became increasingly cautious about using their powers given the delicacy of the issue and that they didn't want the wrong signals being sent to public opinion. Section 5 was in fact used more against the left. The Harworth Colliery dispute rather than anti-Semitism in the East End was to prove more typical of how the legislation was to be operated in practice (PRO HO 144/20729/8, 10).

Indeed, in the immediate period before the Second World War the authorities were more concerned with the activities of anti-fascists than they were with fascists. Although Special Branch had expanded by about one-third in the 1930s, mainly to monitor the activities of fascists, communism was still the main public order and internal security problem as far as the state was concerned. What was particularly interesting about the extensive monthly reports on Special Branch surveillance of anti-Semitism in the East End (PRO MEPOL 2/3043) between 1936 and 1944 was the discrepancy between the rather longer reports on the protests of anti-fascists than on the extensive criticisms and verbal abuse fascists aimed at Jews at their meetings. Many more anti-BUF demonstrations were closed down than anti-Jewish diatribes. Similarly, despite pressure from both the Home Secretary and the Metropolitan Police Commissioner, the authorities were more inclined to arrest disturbers of the peace who objected to the nasty insults aimed at the Jewish community by fascists than they were with those who inflamed opinion. The police closed down the anti-fascist meetings held adjacent to fascists meetings rather than address the cause of the protest in the first place.

Whilst blanket coverage of meetings stretched police resources to their limit the use of Special Constables on normal duties enabled the authorities to cope with the situation. It does appear that the appearance of uniformed note-takers at fascist meetings did lead to less insulting language being deployed against the Jews than otherwise would have been the case. The evidence suggests that the police decided that in most cases ending meetings prematurely would create more disorder and that less damage would be created by allowing the veiled abuse to continue if it was unlikely that political violence would be fomented. What is most interesting is that there were relatively few complaints of violence against Jews that appear in police records. Most anti-fascist memoirs suggest that there were regular fights between fascists and communists in the East End and that there was much unrecorded violence against the Jewish community. The lack of known fatalities and the failure of the fascists to capitalise on their impact in the East End suggests that the combination of official benign neglect in limiting publicity, popular indignation, often orchestrated by CPGB activists, and increased police presence controlled the situation.

Elsewhere the combination of anti-Semitism and fascist–communist violence was not such a problem as in the East End. Whilst the authorities were concerned that anti-fascism was a successful recruiting sergeant for the CPGB this proved to be in the context of recruitment for the forces of Republican Spain rather than as an opposition to Mosley or as a defender of the Jewish community. The United Front against fascism was more concerned about events on the continent than in Britain. The CPGB, outside the East End, saw Chamberlain's government as more likely to introduce fascism than Mosley (Morgan, 1989). If anti-fascism grew as a force then the BUF changed its character in the later 1930s. The 'Mosley and Peace' campaign appealed to a significantly different audience than that which had supported anti-Semitism for the most part. The available evidence suggests that it was a mainly middle-aged, lower-middle-class audience which cheered Mosley at the world's biggest indoor audience at Earl's Court in July 1939. Peace appealed to other groups than the youthful hoodlum element that were most attracted to the BUF by anti-Semitism.

Like the CPGB the BUF continued a less spectacular recovery in the immediate pre-war years. What was most important, however, was that Mosley's new supporters were better behaved than those in the East End campaign. Although still prone to anti-Semitic sentiments Mosley's followers now preferred being preached at in peaceful closed meetings than becoming victims of potential violence at street-corner slanging matches. Whilst such events still continued it is noticeable that both the reports on East End anti-Semitism and the Home Office files on the BUF are much thinner for the 1938–9 period than earlier in the 1930s. Whilst some files have not been released the total number held back would not detract from that conclusion.

This suggests that the period following the introduction of the Public Order Act showed that the new legislation achieved its objective. Although the issues which underlay social tension did not disappear, public opinion accepted the assumptions on which the restrictions on civil liberty had been based. Neither the fascists nor the communists were prepared to challenge the new law. Political extremism and anti-Semitism were contained and the authorities able to manage the situation. The conclusion, however, was that this was achieved by sweeping under the carpet the nasty ethnic abuse which had deepened the crisis in the first place. This problem was to return in many inner city areas when a new wave of immigrants was to bear the brunt of nativist hostility after the Second World War.

References

Anderson, G., 1983, *Fascists, Communists and the National Government*, London, University of Missouri Press.

Boyle, A., 1962, *Trenchard*, London, Collins.

Branson, N., 1985, *History of the Communist Party of Great Britain*, London, Lawrence & Wishart.

Cohen, P., 1986, 'The Police, the Home Office and Surveillance of the British Union of Fascists', *Intelligence and National Security*, 1, (3), 416–34.

Croucher, R., 1988, *We Refuse to Starve in Silence*, London, Lawrence & Wishart.

Foott, B., 1968, *Dismissal of a Premier: The Philip Game Papers*, Sydney, Morgan Publications.

Hansard Parliamentary Debates.

Holmes, C., 1976, 'East End Anti-Semitism, 1936', *Bulletin of the Society for the Study of Labour History*, 32.

Holmes, C., 1979, *Anti-Semitism in British Society, 1876–1939*, London, Edward Arnold.

Holmes, C., 1988, *John Bull's Island*, London, Macmillan.

Jacobs, J., 1978, *Out of the Ghetto*, London, Janet Simon.

Kidd, R., 1940, *British Liberty in Danger*, London, Lawrence & Wishart.

Kushner, T. and Lunn, K. (eds), 1989, *Traditions of Intolerance*, Manchester, Manchester University Press.

Lebzelter, G., 1978, *Political Anti-Semitism in England 1918–39*, London, Macmillan.

Lewis, D., 1987, *Illusions of Grandeur*, Manchester, Manchester University Press.

Linehan, T., 1992, 'The British Union of Fascists in East London and South West Essex, 1933–40: A Study of the District Branches, their Memberships, and the local context of Branch Recruitment', University of London, Ph.D. thesis.

Lunn, K. and Thurlow, R., eds, 1980, *British Fascism*, London, Croom Helm.

Mandle, W., 1968, *Anti-Semitism and the British Union of Fascists*, London, Longman.

Middlemas, K., (ed.), 1968, *Tom Jones Diaries*, Vol. 2, London, Oxford University Press.

Moore, A., 1990, 'Sir Philip Game's Other Life: The Making of the 1936 Public Order Act in Britain', *Australian Journal of Politics and History*, 36, (1).

Morgan, J., 1987, *Conflict and Order*, Oxford, Oxford University Press.

Morgan, K., 1989, *Against Fascism and War*, Manchester, Manchester University Press.

Mosley, N., 1982, *Rules of the Game*, London, Secker & Warburg.

Mosley, N., 1983, *Beyond the Pale*, London, Secker & Warburg.

Mosley, O., 1968, *My Life*, London, Nelson.

Peele, G. and Cook, C., (eds), *The Politics of Reappraisal*, London, Macmillan.

Piratin, P., 1978, *Our Flag Stays Red*, London, Lawrence & Wishart.

Porter, B., 1979, *The Refugee Question in Mid-Victorian Politics*, Cambridge, Cambridge
    University Press.
P[ublic] R[ecord] O[ffice], HO 45, HO 144, Mepol 2 series, Kew.
Skidelsky, R., 1975, *Oswald Mosley*, London, Macmillan.
Skidelsky, R., 1980, 'Reflections on Mosley and British Facism', in Lunn and Thurlow
    (eds): 78–99.
Smith, E., 1989, 'Jewish Responses to Political Anti-Semitism and Fascism in the East
    End of London', in Kushner and Lunn, (eds): 53–71.
Stevenson, J., 1975, 'The Politics of Violence', in Peele and Cook, (eds).
Stevenson, J., 1980, 'The BUF, the Metropolitan Police and Public Order', in Lunn
    and Thurlow, (eds): 135–50.
Stevenson, J. and Cook, C., 1977, *The Slump*, London, Cape
Thurlow, R., 1975, 'The Black Knight', *Patterns of Prejudice*, 9(3), 15–19.
Thurlow, R., 1987, *Fascism in Britain 1918–85*, Oxford, Basil Blackwell.
Thurlow, R., 1988, 'British Fascism and State Surveillance', *Intelligence and National
    Security*, 3(1), 77–99.
Thurlow, R., 1994, *The Secret State*, Oxford, Blackwell.
Weinberger, B., 1990, *Keeping the Peace?*, Oxford, Berg.
West, W., 1987, *Truth Betrayed*, London, Duckworth.

7

The anti-Italian riots, June 1940

Lucio Sponza

On 10 June 1940, the progress of the German army in France prompted Mussolini into his fatal move of declaring war on Britain and France. His overacted announcement from the balcony of Palazzo Venezia was broadcast to the 'Italian Empire' and relayed to the rest of the world. Less than half an hour later Italians in Britain began to be rounded up for internment and deportation. Shortly afterwards, anti-Italian disturbances erupted in various parts of the United Kingdom, and were particularly vicious in Scotland.

Sometimes small groups of people gathered in front of Italian shops and restaurants to stage a more or less noisy boycott operation and to boo their unperturbed customers. Sometimes isolated missiles were aimed at the premises' windows, with some damage and to the curiosity of passers-by. Sometimes anything was thrown, from bottles to bicycles, and the crowd cheered at any successful hit. Sometimes angry mobs were led into a rampage and the shops were wrecked and looted.

I will begin with a survey of the major trouble spots and the different degrees of violence; I will then consider the Italians' reaction and the debate which the riots aroused. This will enable me to offer some general reflections on the attitudes to Italians. I will then return to the riots, set them in the context of those attitudes and draw the conclusion, bearing in mind the general conditions of British society.

Patterns of violence

London was punctuated with instances of smashed windows of Italian shops and restaurants on the evening of 10 June—but only on that evening (if the scanty sources of information we have—mainly newspapers—are correct). In most cases these were isolated actions, perhaps accomplished under the influence of alcohol. The main disturbance was in Soho, where many Italian cafes and restaurants were concentrated.

The national newspapers exaggerated the degree of damage and violence, as did the enterprising newsvendors who scribbled 'The Battle of Soho' on their blank advertising sheets. Only three premises actually had their windows smashed by bottle-throwing. 'Pitched-battles' were reported between Greeks and Italians. That was odd, since Greece was not attacked by Italy until a few months later. Perhaps personal and professional hostility had been the crucial ingredient. A journalist from the *Daily Express* pointed out that many anonymous informants were sending him names of Italian waiters who were said to have changed their views and become pro-British only too suddenly. The writer commented that such anonymous denunciations could have been sent 'in private spite' (12 June).

Several newspapers reported that the only person to be wounded in Soho was a policeman who was slightly cut by flying glass. However, in the same article of the *Express* it was also pointed out that in one case an Italian was pushed to the ground by 'half-a-dozen [hooligans] [who] kicked his face brutally'.

It appears that firearms were not used. Some bystanders did tell a reporter that they had heard shots being fired, but it was later admitted that it must have been the backfiring of a car. According to the *Daily Mail* (12 June), apart from the few crashes of breaking glass, it had been 'rather like the Cup Final crowds streaming away from Wembley, though more tense'.

The following day, the streets of Soho were full of curious people who were rather disappointed to see that business had resumed to near-normality, but for the disappearance of known Italian faces and the replacement of some of the most obvious Italian signs—although advertisements about restaurants under their Italian names continued to appear in the local papers.

Mass-Observation sent three observers to Soho. Their conclusion was that 'the police kept crowds under control, very little damage was done, and only a small number of people felt violently about it in this area. There was no mass movement or surging tides of racial feeling in Soho' (Mass-Observation, No. 184, 1940).

There was little disturbance in Birmingham and Manchester, despite a not insignificant presence of Italian shops. In Belfast and other places crowds expressed their feeling by demanding that customers leave the ostracised premises.

But an angry multitude of some 4,000—led by women and girls—demonstrated against Italians in Liverpool. In addition to the damage to shop windows, stones and bricks were thrown 'over the heads of the police at upper windows of the premises', where the Italians lived and had taken refuge in the back rooms. Great Homer Street was blocked in three places, cars were able to pass through only with enormous difficulty—and some were struck by the missiles (*Evening Express* (Liverpool), 11 June).

Women were also prominent in Middlesbrough, where several people were eventually charged with larceny, as well as with malicious damage to ice-cream shops. In court they stated that 'they found the articles concerned in the streets and some said that they took them home to look after them' (*Newcastle Journal and North Mail*, 13 June).

There were ugly scenes in Sunderland and Newcastle-upon-Tyne, too. In Sunderland hundreds of people demonstrated outside the houses of two Italians, but they dispersed before the intervention of the police. In Newcastle, shopwindows were wrecked, mainly as a result of the action by small groups of youths.

In Wales the situation was checkered. On the one hand, in the small towns and villages of the Rhondda, in each of which there were Italian 'refreshment houses', small crowds gathered outside the premises, but out of curiosity and even sympathy rather than bad feeling. On the other hand, substantial acrimony was shown in Newport, Cardiff and Swansea, where the police had to intervene with baton charges to limit the damage to the shops. Not only were windows smashed; some looting took place as well. The most coveted items were cigarettes, tobacco and sweets, and 'the crowd of about two hundred reacted violently when the police tried to arrest one of their number' (Hughes, 1991, p. 94).

A 'smash-and-loot' campaign characterised instead the anti-Italian demonstrations in Scotland, with two epicentres: Glasgow and the Clydebank, and Edinburgh.

A mob of a few hundred gathered in the Paisley district of Glasgow at about midnight (10 June), moved along various streets smashing 'the windows of every Italian shop they came to, and loot[ed] the contents' (*Daily Record and Mail* (Glasgow), 11 June). When the police arrived they had to face intense hostility from the crowds and twenty people were arrested. Many years later, a Scottish woman, married to an Italian, remembered witnessing how a large mob worked its way along Parliamentary Road 'systematically smashing, looting, and setting ablaze the Italian shops' (Colpi, 1991, p. 106). Similar disturbances occurred in other districts of Glasgow, but were not repeated the next night, possibly because of the effective deployment of police officers and special constables.

> Scenes unprecedented in Greenock and Port Glasgow took place late last night—it was reported in the Greenock paper—when gangs of infuriated persons gave vent to their feelings against local Italians . . . Almost all Italian premises, ice-cream shops and fish and chip restaurants, were wrecked, and looting was freely indulged in. (*Greenock Telegraph and Clyde Shipping Gazette*, 11 June)

It appears that young men and women were in the majority; children were also prominent.

Again, in Port Glasgow the crowds strongly resented the protective intervention of the police, but rather than attacking them they soon learned how to disperse and regroup in other parts of the town to resume their rampage. A specialisation along lines of gender and age characterised looting: women took away smaller pieces of furniture (like chairs, electric bulbs and other fittings); men—their pockets full of tobacco and cigarettes—made off with the heavier items (such as tables, mirrors and cash registers—the latter to be smashed outdoors, emptied and left in the middle of the road); children went for sweets—although chocolate appears to have crossed those gender and age boundaries. Many people were arrested in both Greenock and Port Glasgow.

It was even worse in Edinburgh, where an 'orgy of destruction' was said to have taken place, with angry crowds swelling to some three thousand. 'The police made a number of baton charges. Sections of crowd showed hostility, and in the course of the exciting skirmish policemen had their helmets knocked off' (*The Scotsman*, 11 June).

The *Edinburgh Evening News* (11 June) reported that 'the damage created by the demonstrators appeared to be confined to the main streets—Leith Street and Leith Walk, for example, looked as if a series of heavy bombs had fallen.' Sporadic attacks occurred in other parts of the city: in Stockbridge, Dalry, Portobello, the South Side and Abbeyville; shop windows were smashed also in the High Street, not many yards from the police headquarters.

The next day, after a second night of rioting, it was pointed out that 'in several instances . . . stones were thrown through windows of Italian-owned shops which had escaped the attention of angry crowds on Monday.' There was also arson in two cases and the Fire Brigade was called out. Six people, three of them women, were taken to the Royal Infirmary to be treated for head injuries caused by stones. There were many arrests. In *The Times* (11 June) there was only a laconic and vague mention of 'several persons' being injured. How many of them were Italians, policemen, bystanders or assailants, we do not know. This is not surprising, since the press was subject to heavy self-censorship and any kind of civil disorder was bound to have some demoralising effect at a very critical moment of the war.

Rumours circulated within the Italian–Scottish community that there had been fatal casualties among the Italians. They were bewildered and frightened. Remembering the events forty years later, Dominic Crolla said that 'it seemed as if the work of fifty or sixty years had vanished into thin air' (quoted in Rodgers, 1982, p. 18).

The Italians' attitude

The Italian community had been tense and apprehensive for some time, despite the attempts by the Italian authorities in Britain to maintain that the relationship between the two countries was normal. Only a few days before 10 June the Italians were told that free holidays to sea resorts in Italy for their children would be organised as usual in the summer, 'notwithstanding the present difficulties' (*L'Italia Nostra*, 7 June).[1]

But there had been disturbing signs; for instance, the accusation that the Italians represented a potential danger, at the onset of the 'fifth column' panic. 'The London Italian is an indigestible unit of population—John Boswell wrote in the *Daily Mirror*—. . . Now every Italian colony in Great Britain and America is a seething cauldron of smoking Italian politics . . . We are nicely honeycombed with little cells of potential betrayal' (quoted by Gillman and Gillman, 1980, pp. 149–50).

Some decided to leave Britain and to return to Italy weeks and even months before the declaration of war. They were the better off and less integrated component of the community, but also petty merchants and shopkeepers made hurried preparations to sell their businesses, 'often for a mere song', it was commented. For those who had been resident in Britain for a long time, had raised their families and worked hard for everything they had at last achieved, to go away was impossible.

There were therefore those who had thought of preparing themselves for the worst and in desperation. Three men were fined for illegal possession of firearms: one in the Rhondda (who was also fined for failing to obscure lights), the second in Sunderland (who said he did not know there was a revolver in his house, which was then said to have been left by his brother-in-law, who had died), and the third in Edinburgh (he was found in possession of an automatic pistol and ninety-seven rounds of ammunition).[2] In Manchester three British-born Italians were charged with behaviour 'likely to cause a breach of the peace' after they presented themselves with knuckledusters before the policeman who had knocked at their door during the night. One of them explained that he thought 'it was the English who had come to break the house up'. They were cautioned (*Manchester Evening News*, 11 June).

Sometimes cafés and shops were closed and shutters put up as soon as the news of the declaration of war was heard. But in many other cases the terrified Italians were trapped in their shops when they came under attack by the mob. They tried to escape the violence by barricading themselves into back rooms or, if they lived with their families above the shop, they moved into the upper rooms, crouching behind furniture while listening to the fearful cries and the crash of glass breaking. In one instance, in Walworth (London), the owner of an ice-cream shop took refuge on the roof of his house (*Daily Express*, 11 June).

In Glasgow, it was reported that in a number of cases Italians who lived at some safe distance from their looted shops were so frightened that they refused to leave their homes when summoned by the police to inspect the damage at their premises (*Daily Record and Mail* (Glasgow), 11 June). In Soho, it was written that: 'Panic had entered, suddenly, the homes of peaceful, likeable Italians. I saw a girl crying in one doorway. "Mother's terribly frightened", she said. Her father hadn't been to work that day' (*Daily Herald*, 12 June).

A few cases of verbal defiance by Italians were reported. In Old Compton Street (Soho), the occupant of a black saloon car shouted through the open window: 'Long live the Duce!' He was lucky that the police were there to take him away through the enraged crowd (*Daily Herald*, 11 June). In a similar (perhaps the same) instance, the crowd was said to have shouted 'Lynch him!', but nothing was said about the way the story ended (*Daily Mail* and *Daily Mirror*, 11 June). In Middlesbrough a young Italian woman shouted 'Heil Hitler!', when the police arrived to arrest the men for internment. She was eventually also charged with doing damage to an electric light in the police cell and taken into custody under the Defence Regulation 18 B (which provided the Home Secretary with powers to detain people without trial). Her action was said to have set the spark to the anti-Italian riots in Middlesbrough (*Newcastle Journal and North Mail*, 13 June).

Much more common was another reaction: painting out or taking down the Italian signs, while posters and inscriptions were put up disowning any connection with Italy and claiming instead to be under Swiss, Belgian or French management. In many cases the Britishness of the businesses was pointed out: 'One Hundred Per Cent English' was how it was once rendered. 'Mussolini has changed the face of Soho [it was written with some exaggeration] and his countrymen move guiltily in these brimming streets, which have heard Italian spoken for well over two centuries' (*The Observer*, 16 June). At Bertorelli's, in Charlotte Street (near Soho), it was pointed out that: 'The proprietors of this restaurant are British subjects, and have sons serving with the British Army.'

Sometimes announcements were published in the local papers to dispel any suspicion as to the family position. In Swansea, the following appeared:

> VIRGIE CRESCI—51/a, High Street—wishes to inform the public that he and his Family are British subjects. His Brother Nesto is at present serving in the Royal Welsh Fusiliers, and his Brother Orlando is serving in the British Mercantile Marine. HIS WIFE AND HER FAMILY ARE NATIVE-BORN BRITISH SUBJECTS—Cresci's Café is Carrying On as Usual. (*South Wales Evening Post* [Swansea], 11 June)

Nationality (original or acquired) and family connections were not always as clear-cut as that. In fact, that was an exception. In most instances all sorts of complications applied, which constituted an additional bewildering and distressing factor. Such was the case of a London–Italian, a British citizen due to be soon called up, who confided in near-desperation that he had two sisters, also British, who were at the moment in Italy with their mother—who was Italian. He also had two first cousins, 'one British by nationality, one Italian: the British one is in Italy, the Italian in Britain' (*Daily Express*, 12 June).

It was therefore with some combination of sincerity and opportunism that the Union Jack was displayed outside shops and restaurants, or tied up to ice-cream barrows. In at least one instance it was regarded as a perfidious hypocrisy—and it was forced down (at Largs: *Evening Citizen* (Glasgow), 11 June). But apparently nobody complained to the ice-cream seller who was trundling his barrow up Fleet Street, in London, with 'gaudy pictures' of the King and Queen of Britain on one side of the barrow, and with 'equally gaudy pictures' of the Italian Royals on the other side (*Yorkshire Evening News* (Leeds), 12 June). However, the most widely publicised anecdote was the disclaimer displayed by a witty organ grinder in Leeds, who chalked on his musical instrument the notice: 'I AM BRITTISH—AND THE MONKEY—IS FROM INDIA' (picture in the *Yorkshire Evening News* (Leeds), 13 June).

The issue of double loyalty was at the centre of Albert Mackie's sensitive play, *Gentle like a Dove*, which deals with the disturbance in Edinburgh. The protagonist, to whom the title refers, is an old ice-cream man, a widower, who expresses himself in broken Scots. When he was asked whether his claiming to be 'a Breeteesh . . . a Breeteesh nationalize', meant that he was ashamed to be Italian, he emphatically replied:

> Me? No shame. I'm-a proud to be Italian. But I'm-a glad to be Breeteesh . . . because-a Breeteesh is geev-a me work, and stop-a da hungry. Breeteesh is take-a my boy and make-a heem learn at a school . . . Breeteesh is what I like, but I dinna want Italia to go doon. Is my country. Is where-a da sun shine when I run aboot on-a bare feet, I tink away back when I'm a leetle-a boy, when my madre . . . keesa me on da cheek and say 'Luigi, never forget your madre, never forget Italia, your madre country'. And my wife, Elisabeta, she say da same-a t'ing. (Mackie, 1952, p. 19)[3]

Sometimes there were different loyalties within the same family. An interesting case was noted by Naomi Mitchison in the diary she kept on behalf of Mass-Observation.

> I had a talk to Ian MacLaren, the plumber [she wrote on 11 June] who said there had been anti-Italian riots in Campbeltown [Kintyre]; the three Italian shops had been broken up. The [Italian] old man had been rather rash, saying that England needed a totalitarian government and so on, but the younger ones were all decent, good citizens who gave money in charity and paid their taxes; one had contributed £50 to the Provost's fund; one of the youngest generation was in a mine sweeper. (Mitchison, 1986, p. 65)

Views on the riots

Naomi Mitchison then added further particulars as had been told her by the plumber:

> If the tide had been in they would have put the old man into the harbour; the worst were the Polish sailors. But mostly they were like 'grown-up boys', out for a bit of fun . . . Half of them were no good, on public assistance and so on. Someone had said it was a shame, and had promptly been knocked down. He, Ian, had stood by; you couldn't help thinking it was funny. But he would be as friendly as he could to the Italians next time he saw them. (ibid.)[4]

Who were the rioters (apart from the Greek shopkeepers in Soho and the Polish sailors in Kintyre)?

In his own War Diaries, on 12 June 1940, George Orwell wrote: 'Disgusting though these attacks on harmless Italian shopkeepers are, they are an interesting phenomenon, because English people, i.e. people of a kind who would be likely to loot shops, don't as a rule take a spontaneous interest in foreign politics.' His explanation, therefore, was that 'the low-down, cold-blooded meanness of Mussolini's declaration of war at that moment must have made an impression even on people who as a rule barely read the newspapers' (Orwell and Angus, 1968, p. 347).

Different though the degree and nature of the anti-Italian disturbances were in various parts of the country, there were at least two common features: violence was mainly against property, rather than against persons; the protagonists were mostly young men, although in some instances the participation of young women and children was also marked. The details given by some newspapers when offenders appeared in court suggest that the level of violence was related to young age (early to mid-20s). In about forty cases, mostly in Scotland, the occupation was also given: eight were labourers, five apprentices to various manual trades, five soldiers on leave, three unemployed, and then there were miners and other low-skilled workers. Among the latter, incidentally, was a coal carrier from Port Glasgow, who took advantage of his training: he was charged 'with the theft of a tin of water biscuits, tins of beans, tomatoes,

condensed milk, dripping, jam, candles, a pull-over, a lady's umbrella, etc.'
(*Port Glasgow Express*, 21 June).

The intensity of violence was less related to the number of Italian shops, and
Italian presence generally, than it was to the economic and socially depressed
conditions. Could it be a coincidence that the 'smash-and-grab' riots were
preceded by many years of diminishing consumers' expenditure, as a consequence of the depression; that the severest drop (–11 per cent) occurred in
1940 (Deane and Cole, 1969, p. 333); that in the spring of 1940 there were still
over one million people out of work, and that unemployment was particularly
high in Wales, North-East England and Scotland—exactly the areas where
looting followed the smashing of windows? It does seem that Orwell's explanation needs some refining.

Furthermore, as far as the concentration of Italians is concerned, out of some
18,000 of them in the United Kingdom at the time (not including their
British-born children) well over 4,000 lived in four neighbouring London
districts around Clerkenwell (Holborn, Finsbury, Islington and St Pancras). In
Soho, with a high number of cafés and restaurants run by Italians, and the
nearby streets, some 1,000 of them lived. Big London hotels had many Italians
in their staff, mostly cooks and waiters, but also in various other occupations. In
all these cases Italians offered easy targets, yet violence was very limited. So was
harassment. There were, instead, frequent manifestations of sympathy and
support, as was reported for well-known Italians in the West End circles.

> The Quaglino brothers . . . who have been never naturalized despite reports to the
> contrary, were carrying on . . . with sick smiles as many of their clients sympathised
> with them. Both of them were detained later . . . At the May Fair, Ferraro, the
> restaurant manager, was also invited to drinks by clients who knew he had spent
> almost all his life in England but, like so many other Italian restaurateurs, had never
> bothered to become naturalized. Sartori at the Coq d'Or, was particularly shaken.
> (*Daily Mail*, 12 June)

At the opposite end in terms of violence, only some 500 Italians lived in
Edinburgh. In Glasgow, incidentally, there were three times as many, but the
degree of destruction was much inferior. It may be even more puzzling to
realise that overall living conditions in Edinburgh were much better than in the
Clyde district; within the Scottish capital, however, there were patches of severe
unemployment—and the worst was Leith (Fogarty, 1945, p. 143), where Italian
shopkeepers bore the brunt of the violence.

Yet more specific local factors, other than the number of Italian shops and
the socio-economic conditions, must have influenced the nature of the agitations. One element which was considered instrumental to the viciousness of
the Edinburgh mob was the fierce anti-Roman Catholic sentiment which had
been bellowed for some time by the Protestant Action Society. This was led by
councillor John Cormack, who was a fanatic Baptist lay preacher, in whose
jurisdiction the worst disorders took place (Gallagher, 1987, pp. 150–3). He
thought it was necessary to disclaim such rumours by writing to the *Evening
Dispatch* ((Edinburgh), 14 June) and pointing out that 'the people who actually
in the main caused the demonstrations were the very people who 24 hours

previously were giving the Italians money for ice-cream and fish and chips' (thus implying, perhaps, that his followers were on a different diet).

John Cormack was not the only person who expressed his views of the Italians by writing to a newspaper. Perhaps because of the more violent nature of the anti-Italian disturbances north of the border, readers there were induced to write to the newspapers' editors (unless, of course, only the Scottish editors decided to print letters on that subject).

One particular paper, the *Edinburgh Evening News*, gave significant space to this correspondence, if only for three days. It is worth giving an account of the contents.

Three letters appeared on Wednesday 12 June. All of them manifested the writers' disgust at the actions of 'a set of rough and uncouth hooligans', and stressed the cowardice of attacking harmless people—a most un-British action, it was pointed out.

Five letters were published on the following day: four indicated the same sentiments of strong disapproval, with two of them emphasising the law-abiding and non-fascist character of the Italian shopkeepers. Only one correspondent begged to differ. He noted that anti-British demonstrations had taken place in Italy and that the Italians in Britain had sent money and gold to support the aggressive policies of their government towards Abyssinia and Albania. He then concluded with a rhetorical question: 'Why squeal now when retaliation takes place?'

By Friday 14 June, the tide had turned. Six letters were published, only two reiterating their unreserved condemnation of violence; the other four, instead, dismissed the distinction between the Italians in Britain and the Italian government policies. In one case the anti-Italian resentment took a peculiarly patriotic form, when readers were told not to forget 'that thousands of pounds of good British money had left these shores for sunny Italy'.

The next day, no letters appeared, and the editor explained why:

> We have received numerous letters about anti-Italian disorders in Edinburgh [he wrote] but great pressure on space prevents publication, while we consider that the incident is closed. Most of the letters are critical of Italians and their policy, and point to the insults to British citizens in Italy and the outrages committed by Nazis and Fascists. All aliens must be interned, urges one correspondent.

(They presumably meant all *enemy* aliens.)

To be fair to the editor of the *Edinburgh Evening News*, he had enabled both sides of the debate to express their views, even if the dominant tone of the newspaper was indicated in a main article where it was stated that 'for a number of years back the Italian population [in Scotland, had] been very much under the influence of fascist propaganda' (12 June). This opinion was not shared by other newspapers. Most of them, whether national or local, showed a more measured attitude. They either restricted the reports to the concise text received from the news agencies (so did *The Times*, for example), or they had no hesitation in attributing the disturbances to 'hooligans' and 'thugs', which in no way could be justified by the action of the Italian government. In many other cases, sympathy was expressed for the Italians in Britain, and examples of solidarity by their British neighbours and acquaintances were reported. We have already sampled a few of them, and here is another interesting instance (*News Chronicle*, 11 June):

> It was a sad, a disastrous day for the whole Italian community in London. In the Old Compton Street and Frith Street area of Soho . . . the tragedy of Mussolini's act was clearly evident. Hard-working restaurateurs faced calamity. Crowds of them gathered in the streets and looked their despair . . . Passing strangers showed no sympathy. But there was at least one touch of human kindness. A shopkeeper, an Englishman, went into the restaurant of a neighbour—an Italian he has known for years—to speak a word of sympathy. The Italian, moved almost to tears, gratefully accepted the gesture.

Among the national papers only the *Daily Mirror* (12 June) qualified its condemnation of the violence by adding that, unfortunately, it was an 'all too human' manifestation of people's 'natural indignation and anger', since 'for months past we have allowed the Italian monkey to play with us'. In another article of the *Mirror* (13 June), it was stated that public opinion had been enraged and shocked by the sight of Italy 'callously flung into the furnace of war by a bunch of cynical Wop gangsters'.

This gives us the opportunity to explore briefly the context of how the Italians were generally perceived.

General attitudes to Italians

Now that Italy was officially an enemy, the plugs on any restraint in belittling the Italians were pulled. In a rather cheerful manner, most popular papers resorted to the 'monkey' and 'Wop' labels with reference to Italians, partly because ridiculing the enemy is morale-boosting, and partly because those were conventional expressions to connote the Italians. A battery of old mocking stereotypes was there to be used. The Sunday newspapers, in particular, gloated over it.

The *Sunday Dispatch* (16 June) presented Italy's war declaration with the jolly-sounding sequence: 'First a Sitz-Krieg, then a Blitz-Krieg, and now a Wops-Krieg.' The *Sunday Express* (16 June) offered a presumably amusing gossipy 'party dialogue' which contained, for instance, the following utterances: ' "Marjorie always thought that all Italians were either waiters or hokey-pokey men, except for a few counts and opera singers"—"Thousands emigrate to America and become marvellous criminals"—"Of course, what they hate most is being called Wops." ' The *Sunday Graphic* (30 June) printed a satirical little poem entitled 'Wopships', in which the protagonists were 'Captain B. Spaghetti' and 'Admiral Vermicelli'.

Jokes and cartoons were also produced by all kinds of newspapers. For example, on 11 June, the 'Hanner Swaffer's Headline' (a regular column of the *Daily Herald*), entitled 'The Day comes—to Soho', was transformed into 'The Day comes—and the dagoes . . .', with the additional comment: 'I have been waiting to use that joke for years!' An equally fanciful epigram on the Italian press was quoted in the *Daily Express* (12 June):

These organs grind out German scores
Fortissimo and very *obbligato*;
The world remarks, with limited applause,
'Se non è vero, e RibBen trovato'[5]

A cartoon in the *Star* (14 June) was less imaginative and more sober. It showed a squatty, moustached middle-aged ice-cream man crouched on one bar of his barrow—eyes wide open—while he disconsolately said: 'Me—I tink I scuttle da barrow.' In the *Daily Mail* (12 June), a monkey was depicted while turning the handle of a barrel-organ; a placard hanging on it read: 'Owner away for health.'

Such common stereotyping of the Italians was mainly based on the partial and prejudiced knowledge of them as immigrants to Britain. For most of the nineteenth century their chief occupations had been as street musicians (notably organ-grinders with their little monkeys), plaster-figure pedlars and petty artisans. By the end of the century, however, most of them had become ice-cream vendors, café and restaurant waiters, cooks, etc. (see Sponza, 1988, ch. 3). If itinerant music and street selling were regarded as a disguised form of begging, equally inferior and servile was considered the nature of the subsequent occupations in food dealing and catering. That was not the stuff of an imperial race.

On the other hand, a different kind of prejudice shaded the perception that educated people had of the Italians: it had more to do with the literary and romanticised appreciation of Italy than with the real life of her inhabitants.

> I am sure that most of us experienced love at first sight when . . . we set eyes for the first time on Italy . . . The hill-towns perched on the rocks, the olive groves, the vines, the white oxen in the ploughs, the lizards in the sun, the swallow-tail butterflies, the smiling people, the lovely language—how beautiful the numbers 'cinque' and 'dieci' sound when heard for the first time from the lips of a waiter. (*New Statesman and Nation*, 15 June, p. 744)

Paradoxically the two views stemming from a different origin (one was contempt, the other benevolent condescension) converged into one ambivalent and unstable image. It so happens that Mass-Observation carried out an investigation on the attitudes to the Italians just before Italy entered into the war. At a time when they were regarded as potential military enemies, some expressions were straightforward: the Italians were 'Wops', 'lousy scum—not fit even for the dustbin', 'yellow'; in war they were 'rotten fighters—[look at] the last war'. But there were also comments such as: 'I like all Italians, except Mussolini and his generals and the students', 'the people are all right, it's the leadership that's wrong' (Mass-Observation, No. 194, 1940, p. 1).

Six months later—and the first resounding military failures for Italy in the Mediterranean, Albania and North Africa in between—Mass-Observation carried out a survey on attitudes to some foreign nationalities. With reference to Italians, 20 per cent of the people interviewed thought they were 'Cowards', but a close 19 per cent regarded them as 'Peace-loving'. Lower ratings applied to the following attributes: 'Lazy or easy-going', 12 per cent; 'Weak or easily led',

11 per cent; 'Attractive or likeable', 9 per cent; 'Cultured or artistic', 7 per cent. A young man from West Wickham was quoted, in particular, as saying that 'The Italians only want to lie asleep amidst their vines. I think that they really don't like fighting as much as any race' (Mass-Observation, No. 541, 1941, p. 11).

The equivocal argument, therefore, went like this. The Italians are quiet, peace-loving, hence likeable, even charming, individually; but that quality is also the result of their innate laziness, which at time of war means cowardice, hence they deserve contempt.

Drumming on about the poor fighting qualities of Italians was naturally the commonest reaction to Italy's entrance into the war. On the same evening of Italy's declaration of war, Duff Cooper, the new Minister of Information, broadcast a vehement assault on Mussolini's shameful decision, but did not draw a clear line between fascism and the dictator's gang, on the one hand, and Italian common people, on the other. Not an easy distinction, to be sure, especially under the dramatic circumstances requiring the tonic of the clarion call, rather than speculative fine points. (But Attlee did manage to draw that line in his terse speech at the Commons on the following day.)

Duff Cooper's blast—which was said to have incited the mob into the window-smashing and looting spree, by the way (Cavalli, 1973, p. 76)— underlined the Italian defeat at Caporetto during the Great War as the final word on their military ineptitude. Both the tone and the contents of the speech raised some criticism, as well as applause, in Parliament (where the riots were never mentioned) and with the public at large. In a letter to the *New Statesman and Nation*, for instance, the historian John Lawrence Hammond lamented that 'this hasty speech, and not Mr Attlee's speech in the House of Commons, was the first British comment to the world on Mussolini's crime . . . To taunt with cowardice [the Italians] because an army of ill-fed peasants broke at Caporetto is the very way to help [Mussolini] to whip up passion' (15 June, p. 748). On the other hand, it was also written that the Minister's brisk reply to his critics, in which he indicated that if they wanted 'someone to be kind and sympathetic to the Italians, they could go elsewhere', expressed 'sentiments with which the majority of the public heartily agreed' (Panter-Downes, 1971, p. 68).

Anyhow, Duff Cooper's remarks were eagerly taken up by the media, which offered variations on the theme ranging in style from the playful to the grandiloquent. In the *Sunday Express* of 16 June, for example, the following questions were put to the readers, as part of the quiz 'Are you sure?':

1) Caporetto, whence the Italians were driven in flight in the battle of 1917, is a (a) river, (b) town, (c) small mountain, (d) province?
2) Did the Italians then lose more or fewer guns than the Allies recently lost in Belgium?

There was little jollity in what the London evening paper The *Star* (11 June) had to say on the subject: 'A good many English people, when they think of Italy, think instinctively in the same instant of Caporetto, that shameful rout which we had to retrieve . . . [The Italians] fought like tired men, men with little stomach for fighting. They distinguished themselves only in their speed of retreat.'[6] As for the pontifical style, here is an example from *John Bull* (15 June):

> [The Italians] may have modern equipment . . . but it would take more than one man to alter the fundamental characteristics of a nation that has been wretchedly craven for centuries . . . Mussolini [has] done much for a country that was tragically decadent. He has swept away the Italy of organ-grinders, ice-cream sellers, disease-ridden slums, lackadaisical officials, meandering railways and impossible plumbers . . . [Yet, the Italians'] fondness for knives, sub-machine-guns and back-alley ambushes is significant of their courage . . . Mussolini knows that his artillery officers and men still take time off for lunch, still keep to their dug-outs when rain falls, and still spend more time creating bawdy songs than in drilling.

It is interesting to note, incidentally, that *John Bull*'s disdain for Italians mirrored praise for what fascism stood for: prowess and martial spirit.

Mass-Observation thought that the scorn poured on the Italians by various opinion-makers had not created a contempt for them. It had rather 'put a stamp of official approval upon already existing prejudice and contempt' (Mass-Observation, No. 194, 1940, p. 5).

This is the general backdrop to the anti-Italian riots. We now need to take a step further.

The riots and the attitudes to Italians

How did the outlined general attitude of scorn materialise in the day-to-day life of the immigrants? How did it affect the actual context in which the riots sparked off and developed? Harassment motivated by deep-seated racial and religious prejudices had been a traditional feature in the life of the Italian community in Britain. Assaults on individual street organ-grinders and ice-cream sellers had been frequent in the past. Wild accusations of immorality, violent behaviour and dangerously insanitary customs had been made continually throughout the nineteenth century (Sponza, 1988, chs 4–8). When they entered into catering and food dealing, contempt was actually mixed with laughter because, as the *New Statesman and Nation* put it (15 June, p. 742), 'owing to a silly British convention Italy suggests macaroni and ice-creams and is funny in itself like beer and Wigan.' Not so funny, though, when seen from the Italians' point of view. In particular, they had soon to live with the higher propensity to violence of the Scottish mob. An Italian wrote in his autobiographical notes:

> The first English word [the Italians] learned soon after their arrival in Scotland was 'fight'. The Saturday night 'fight' was inevitable. It usually started as an argument among the Scots themselves which quickly degenerated into a free-for-all. When that happened no one was safe from insults of the most vulgar kind, foul language, cursing and swearing, flying fists and butting heads, vinegar bottles and salt-cellars sailing through the air . . . The damage was seldom serious—one or two broken tables or chairs, some smashed crockery and of course the vinegar bottles . . . A good sweep

up and in no time at all it was business as usual again. (Sereni, 1974, pp. 10–11; see also Mack, 1954, pp. 227–40)

Being foreigners and making this a characteristic of their shops left the Italians particularly exposed to the mob rage, whatever the causes. Some Italian shops in Liverpool were damaged during the anti-German riots there in May 1915. During the bitter dispute between miners and coal-owners in Wales, in November 1910, when fierce street battles broke out between demonstrators and the police, several shops suffered damage and were ransacked, but none as seriously as a well-known Italian confectionery. It was wrecked and looted 'of everything inside, including pans of ice-cream, sweets, cigarettes, etc.' (*Rhondda Leader*, 12 November 1910). Curiously enough, as has already been mentioned, no anti-Italian demonstration took place in the Rhondda thirty years later, despite the notably increased number of shops there and a more ostensible motivation, which suggests that there are degrees of volatility in people's reactions to disturbing events.

It is also necessary to reflect on the nature of the targets. Why was it that virtually only shops were attacked? To be sure, Italians were verbally abused in those June days. Some were mishandled, but there were probably as many signs of sympathy and compassion. In a few cases hostile crowds did gather in front of houses where Italians lived, but only if they were close to, or even above their shops, which had been the source of the demonstration. In the urban districts where most Italians lived with their families, no mass protest materialised.

No demonstration took place in front of Italian institutions either. Not even the notorious official fascist places such as the 'Casa d'Italia' in Charing Cross Road (London), where the Italian weekly *L'Italia Nostra* sponsored by the fascist government was published. And similar organisations existed in Glasgow and Edinburgh as well. These buildings were immediately seized by the police and MI5 officers on 10 June, but it was not a move to prevent them from being attacked by angry crowds. In the end not one window-pane of these institutions was damaged.

Even more significant was the complete absence of any gathering in the vicinity of the Italian Embassy in London and the Italian Consulates, either in England, Wales or Scotland. The Embassy, incidentally, could not try to keep a low profile because of the continuous arrival there of prominent Italians looking for temporary refuge and hoping to be repatriated. These were business and professional people, doctors and leading restaurant and hotel managers—in many cases people who had manifested in the past their pro-fascist views. This coming and not going lasted for a few days. Not all the fugitives were allowed by the British government to join the diplomatic corps which boarded a train at Euston, heading for Glasgow, where the evacuation was to be organised by ship.[7] It is also worth noting that—again—no demonstration was held in Glasgow during the week before the ship (*The Monarch of Bermuda*) left the port, bound for Lisbon. The only recorded discourtesy was the prolonged tea-break by the porters which was judged to be intentional and induced the nervous passengers to carry on with the loading of the luggage themselves.

Back to the Embassy in London. Sylvia Pankhurst thought that a protest was to be held outside the imposing premises in Grosvenor Square, but when she arrived there nobody was around. She then 'threw on to the steps of the Embassy a copy of *The New Times and Ethiopia News* . . . A policeman then intervened. The two spoke for a couple of minutes and Miss Pankhurst went quietly away' (*Star*, 12 June).

That seems to have been the only truly anti-fascist action taken as a consequence of Italy's entry into the war. If anything, there was regret that the Embassy had to be closed and deserted:

> When Signor Bastianini [the Ambassador], with his wife and two toy-laden children, left the Embassy, watched by a crowd of about a hundred, there was nothing in the nature of a hostile demonstration. Indeed, such remarks as 'Good-bye and good luck', with the rejoinder 'The same to you', was exchanged between some of the Embassy staff and the members of the crowd with whom they had made friends while in London. (*Birmingham Gazette*, 14 June)

Yet to juxtapose as potential targets official Italian institutions and private shops is misleading. In the eyes of the people who indulged in violence and looting, the Italian shops were the quintessence of the Italian presence in Britain, and had therefore acquired a quasi-institutional status (even apart from the sheer material gains in ransacking them).

As far as individuals were concerned, the Italians had lived as part of the local communities for many decades, either spread in towns and villages or concentrated in some areas of the main cities. In most cases, their children were born in Britain, and if males of majority they were—or would be—serving in the British forces (unless they chose—as a small number did—to abandon their British citizenship and acquire Italian nationality as a political gesture). Prejudices were there, of course, but they were not such as to consolidate into a coherent hostile attitude to the Italians as individuals.

I have already mentioned the British perception of the Italians investigated by Mass-Observation in June 1940 and January 1941. I shall now add the third instalment of the story, when a similar survey was made in April 1943 (the time when the Italian–German armies in North Africa finally collapsed). The majority of the persons approached had taken part in the 1941 exercise, so that a comparison does provide a fairly accurate assessment of the ways in which opinion had changed.

Forty-one per cent of the people interviewed expressed a 'favourable' opinion of the Italians (19 per cent said they were 'unfavourable'), doubling the favourable score recorded two years earlier. It showed that these strange enemies were, as people, preferred to such allies as the Poles (27 per cent 'favourable'; 17 per cent 'unfavourable') and the Americans (33 per cent 'favourable'; 21 per cent 'unfavourable') (Mass-Observation, No. 1669 Q, 1943, *passim*). It is also significant that the inquiry was addressed to the attituded towards the allies ('Fighting French', Poles, Czechs, Dutch, Greeks and Americans) *and* the Italians.

Mass-Observation analysts commented:

> In 1943 people no longer look upon [the Italians] as dangerous enemies, sympathy comes to the fore and those who made generalisations about them two years ago can

now consider them as individuals without feelings of disloyalty. Many regard them
with great sympathy and liking, feeling sorry for them and their fate in Libya and
Tripolitania. (ibid., p. 10)

Conclusion

The anti-Italian demonstrations and riots were a highly differentiated and
complex affair which must be seen in the context of the attitudes to Italians in
general and the Italian immigrants to Britain in particular. At its worst, in
Scotland, the widespread and organised looting, together with systematic
assaults on the police, suggest that the escalation developed into a deliberate —
if unplanned — attack upon social order. It was triggered by anti-Italian feelings
motivated by Mussolini's decision, and based ambivalently on xenophobic
attitudes and the depressed socio-economic conditions of the Scottish youth.
Yet the peculiarity of the situation in Scotland should not obscure the rarely
acknowledged fact that British society experienced serious social difficulties
throughout the war. These were:

> widespread racketeering in the 'black market'; episodic fears of violent crimes by
> deserters from the armed forces who numbered in tens of thousands; and outbreaks
> of hooliganism that were laid at the door of street-lighting restrictions during the
> black-out . . . Epidemics of looting in London, Sheffield, Manchester, Coventry and
> elsewhere in the aftermath of air-raids also excited considerable alarm. Children and
> youths . . . were brought before the courts for looting and vandalising household
> belongings in bomb-damaged dwellings. (Pearson, 1983, p. 241)

When viewed as a whole and in perspective, therefore, the anti-Italian
disturbances were not an exceptional phenomenon, and its xenophobic conno-
tations appear to have been rather restrained. After all, in our 'peaceful' times
the recurrence of racial hatred and violence against immigrants of darker
complexion is cold-blooded, lethal and unmotivated.

There were four main reasons for the relatively restrained reaction against
the Italians in June 1940: two had to do with the nature of the Italians' presence
in Britain; the other two were related to the prompt actions taken by the
authorities.

Firstly, and most importantly, the quiet, hard-working and family-centred
Italians had enjoyed the sympathy and friendship of the communities they lived
in, although in a peculiar mix with soft but entrenched prejudice. Thus, a small
excited minority could not reverse this perception, nor find support in the
organised working class. In fact, it seems that the Clydebank shop stewards set
up 'protective patrols for the local Italian ice-cream shopkeepers', as an old
Glaswegian recently put it (*Weekend Guardian*, 19–20 August 1989, Letters, p.
35).

Secondly, the dispersion of Italians throughout the kingdom contributed to
their closeness to, if not integration into the local communities and prevented
them from appearing as a threat even during the 'fifth column' hysteria of

spring 1940, when some voices did point the accusing finger at them. This also applies to the main cities, where they were much more numerous: the old 'Italian Quarter' around Clerkenwell was more a myth than a reality by the 1930s. Soho was already a multi-national commercial centre, rather than an Italian enclave.

Thirdly, large numbers of policemen were immediately drafted in the areas where disturbances were thought to be likely to occur; so the narrow streets around Clerkenwell were patrolled by many Metropolitan constables on the evening of 10 June and the following days. In Edinburgh the police were certainly taken by surprise by the scale of the troubles, but in most cases of violent behaviour by the crowd the police acted swiftly and with determination, and the ring-leaders were apprehended.

Fourthly, many Italian men themselves were quickly removed to be interned, thus defusing potential tensions and confrontation. How the concurrence of the rounding up for internment and the intervention against rioters presented the police with a dilemma is best illustrated by a bizarre episode which happened in Greenock:

> A police van which had been rounding-up Italians for internment encountered a crowd smashing up a shop. Batons were drawn and the police charged the mob. Several arrests were made, the Italian internees, who were inside the van, were taken out, and the van drove off with the newly-arrested prisoners. (*Daily Record and Mail* (Glasgow), 11 June)

Significantly, the nasty experience some shopkeepers had on 10 and 11 June 1940 left only few traces on the collective memory of the Italians in Britain, and virtually all — understandably — in Scotland. This is partly because that memory was overshadowed by the more widespread and dislocating trauma of internment, and the connected tragedy of the sinking of the *Arandora Star*, with the loss of nearly 500 Italian lives and the shattering of almost as many families.[8] It is partly also because self-pity was outweighed in the Italian community by the pride in what was achieved in terms of respect and well-being when the storm was over.

Post Scriptum

Since the publication of this essay early in 1993, I have been informed by the Assistant Archivist of the Edinburgh City Archives (City Chambers) that documents relating to the anti-Italian riots have emerged, having 'languished among unsorted papers'. They reveal that many Italians took legal action against the City Corporation to claim damages. Their cases were heard throughout 1941 and the total sum claimed amounted to nearly £10,000. In most instances the Italians were compensated under the Riotous Assemblies Act 1714 and the Riotous Assemblies (Scotland) Act 1822. The documentation is held at the Scottish Record Office, The Sheriff Court Interlocutor Book, Reference D136.

I am very grateful to the City Chambers' officer, Mr Alan Murdock, for drawing my attention to these files which surfaced — again in his own words — 'from apparently unpromising bundles'.

Notes

1. *L'Italia Nostra* was the newspaper published in London and the mouthpiece of the Partito Fascista. Issue No. 593 of 7 June was the last to appear.
2. The cases of guns were reported, respectively in *Confectionery Journal*, 12 June; *Evening Chronicle* (Newcastle), 11 June; *The Scotsman*, 12 June.
3. The author was a young journalist in Edinburgh in 1940, and the fate of the Italians there made much impression on him. A recent play which touches upon the anti-Italian disturbances in Edinburgh is Ann Marie Di Mambro's *Tally's Blood*. It deals with Italians in Scotland during the 1940s and 1950s and was presented at the 1990 Edinburgh Festival.
4. In other diaries kept during the war years as part of the Mass-Observation exercise, similar sentiments of sympathy towards the Italians were expressed. See in particular, among men diarists: R.J. Nichols, 10 June. Among women diarists: A.A. Crouch, 11 June; M. Kornitzer, 14 June; E.M.E. Oakley, 11 June. Unlike Mitchinson's, these diaries can only be seen, either in their manuscript version or on microfilm, at the Library of Sussex University, where all Mass-Observation documents are kept.
5. The author of the verses was Douglas Woodfuff. The translation of the Italian line was added below: ' "Se non è vero, è ben trovato" is an Italian tag meaning 'If it isn't true it's well invented." ' 'RibBen', of course, referred to the German foreign minister Ribbentrop.
6. Here are the views of two authoritative British historians of modern Italy. Denis Mack Smith wrote: 'Considered dispassionately, [Caporetto] was a straightforward military defeat . . . Lloyd George and Foch both agreed that poor organisation and staff work were chiefly responsible . . . Only by a herculean effort was [the Austro-German] penetration into the plain of Lombardy halted at Monte Grappa beyond the River Piave' (1969, pp. 311–12). After the completion of the Italian retreat to Mount Grappa and the River Piave, Christopher Seton-Watson wrote: 'six French and five British divisions were sent to Italy . . . Their arrival greatly boosted Italian morale, but at first . . . they were kept back in reserve in case there should be another breakthrough. The credit for holding the enemy on the [Grappa and the] Piave was therefore entirely Italian' (1967, pp. 481–2).
7. An eye-witness account of those hectic days at the Embassy has been recently written by a then young official; see Egidio Ortona, 1990, especially pp. 178–80.
8. On the internment of Italians and the sinking of the *Arandora Star*, see Colpi (1991, ch. 4); on the general policy towards 'enemy aliens', see Holmes (1990). Both references contain useful bibliographies.

References

Cairncross, A.K. (ed.), 1954, *The Scottish Economy*, Cambridge University Press.
Cavalli, C., 1973, *Ricordi di un emigrato*, London, Edizione 'La Voce degli Italiani'.
Colpi, T., 1991, *The Italian Factor: The Italian Community in Great Britain*, Edinburgh, Mainstream.

THE ANTI-ITALIAN RIOTS, JUNE 1940

Deane, P. and Cole, W.A., 1969, *British Economic Growth, 1688–1959*, Cambridge, Cambridge University Press.

Fogarty, M.P., 1945, *Prospects of the Industrial Areas of Great Britain*, London, Methuen.

Gallagher, T., 1987, *Edinburgh Divided: John Cormack and No Popery in the 1930s*, Edinburgh, Polygon.

Gillman, P. and Gillman, L., 1980, *'Collar the Lot!' How Britain Interned and Expelled Its Wartime Refugees*, London, Quartet Books.

Holmes, C., 1990, 'Enemy Aliens?', *History Today*, 40, September: 25–31.

Hughes, C., 1991, *Lime, Lemon and Sarsaparilla: The Italian Community in South Wales, 1881–1945*, Bridgend, Seren Books.

Kay, B. (ed.), 1982, *Odyssey: The Second Collection: Voices from Scotland's Recent Past*, Edinburgh, Polygon.

Mack, J., 1954, 'Crime', in A.K. Cairncross (ed.).

Mackie, A., 1952, *Gentle Like a Dove*, Edinburgh, Oliver & Boyd.

Mack Smith, D., 1969, *Italy: A Modern History*, Ann Arbor, University of Michigan Press.

Mass-Observation, 1940, File Report No. 184, 'Anti-Italian Riots in Soho' (11 June).

Mass-Observation, 1940, File Report No. 194, 'Attitudes on Italy' (12 June).

Mass-Observation, 1941, File Report No. 541, 'A Particular Study of Subjective Feeling about Various Racial Groups' (9 January).

Mass-Observation, 1943, File Report No. 1669 Q (April).

Mitchison, N., 1986, *Among You Taking Notes . . .: The Wartime Diary of Naomi Mitchison, 1939–1945*, edited by D. Sheridan, Oxford, Oxford University Press.

Ortona, E., 1990, 'L'esodo da Londra dell'Ambasciata italiana nel 1940', *Storia Contemporanea*, a.XXI, (1), February: 173–82.

Orwell, S. and Angul, I. (eds), 1968, *The Collected Essays, Journalism and letters of George Orwell*, II, London, Secker & Warburg.

Panter-Downes, M., 1971, *London War Notes, 1939–45*, edited by W. Shann, New York, Farrar, Straus & Giroux.

Pearson, G., 1983, *Hooligan: A History of Respectable Fears*, London, Macmillan.

Rodgers, M., 1982, 'Italiani in Scoz[z]ia', in B. Kay (ed.).

Sereni, B., 1974, *They Took the Low Road*, Barga, Edizione 'Il Giornale di Barga'.

Seton-Watson, C., 1967, *Italy from Liberalism to Fascism*, London, Methuen.

Sponza, L., 1988, *Italian Immigrants in Nineteenth-Century Britain: Reality and Images*, Leicester, Leicester University Press.

8

Anti-Semitism and austerity: the August 1947 riots in Britain[1]

Tony Kushner

In the first week of August 1947 a series of anti-Semitic disturbances ranging from the breaking of a few windows to mob violence, including assaults on individuals, occurred in many British towns.[2] These were not the first such disturbances in Britain since the readmission of the Jews in the modern era, nor were they the most intensive (those in Limerick in 1904, South Wales in 1911 and Leeds in 1917 were marked by greater violence towards Jews and their property). The riots and disturbances of August 1947 were, however, the most geographically extensive with major incidents in three British towns and minor disturbances in at least ten other locations. Nevertheless, the violence of August 1947 has largely been forgotten both in terms of British and Anglo-Jewish historiography.[3] It is only within the context of the history of Britain and the last years of the Palestine Mandate that the riots have received any attention. Even here they are often literally treated as footnotes to the issue of Zionist terrorism in the post-war period (Kirk, 1954, p. 245; Louis, 1984, p. 465). This article will attempt to place the riots in a wider framework and particularly that of the domestic context of 1947, the most 'crisis'-ridden of all the austerity years immediately following the war. It will also examine the issue of memory and history. How and why have the anti-Semitic riots of 1947 been collectively forgotten by British society and its Jewish minority?

The riots require to be placed in context and the most obvious but, I will argue, the least satisfactory is that of the Palestinian connection. The link is clear—on 30 July 1947 the brutal murder by hanging of two kidnapped British sergeants and the booby-trapping of the area around their bodies in Palestine by members of the *Irgun*, the military wing of the extreme Revisionist movement, took place. The following day the news received its first publicity in Britain and on Friday 1 August, the *Daily Express* published a massive front-page photograph of the hanging sergeants in a picture 'that will shock the world'.[4] The first violence occurred later that day. A week after the events the riots were mentioned in Parliament, but, setting a pattern that has yet to be seriously challenged, it was as a minor aspect of a general debate in both chambers on the question of Palestine. Containing the riots in Britain within a

Palestine-linked framework is appealing because of its neatness. Viscount Hall in the House of Lords put the case succinctly:

> Following these murders [of the sergeants], there has been a vicious circle of terror and retaliation, with resultant loss of life in Palestine, and the outbreak of anti-Jewish feeling in this country, which in turn has resulted in rioting and much anti-Semitism.[5]

There are, however, problems with this approach. If the riots were simply a response to the terrorist activities in Palestine, one-off occurrences with no greater significance other than a curious anomaly, why did they not happen earlier? The activities of extremists within the Zionist movement against the British presence and policies in Palestine had occurred in the war, most notably with the assassination of Lord Moyne in 1944. They escalated in the post-war period as frustration mounted and anger increased with the new Labour government refusing survivors of the Holocaust permission to settle in Palestine (and apparently backtracking on its earlier support for a Jewish homeland). In July 1946 the most devastating act of terrorism occurred with the bombing of the King David Hotel in Jerusalem, leading to the loss of ninety-one lives, many of them British. There was, however, no violence in the United Kingdom after this event. The King David Hotel explosion led to a spiral of British retaliation against even moderate Zionists in Palestine and further acts of terrorism against the British forces and administration. Indeed, the kidnapping of the sergeants and their subsequent killing was in response to the execution of several *Irgun* members.[6] Why was it this event rather than, say, the explosion at the King David Hotel (which, after all, led to much greater loss of life) that provoked the riots of August 1947?

Two linked and largely complementary explanations have been offered by historians. David Leitch writing in 1963 (in what is still, at one and a half paragraphs, the longest academic treatment of the riots) suggested that the King David Hotel explosion:

> had thrust events in a remote country the size of Wales into the forefront of the public imagination, and sown a seed of hostility against the Jewish community in Britain, the Jew next door, which took twelve months almost to the day to bring forth its fruit. In the interim it required nourishment—and this was provided by a year's press reports of violence against British troops who had the misfortune to be doing a job no one should be required to do. (Leitch, 1986, p. 57)

Christopher Sykes, writing two years later, suggested that;

> A very remarkable thing about the persistence of terrorism [in 1946 and the first half of 1947] . . . is that this did not lead to any considerable outbreak of anti-Semitism in England. It almost certainly would have done but for a very unusual circumstance, namely that the abnormal cold in England during January, February and the first part of March had led to a fuel crisis which occupied the minds of most people to the exclusion of most else.

Sykes concludes that widespread revulsion at the hanging of the sergeants later in the year almost inevitably led to the 'anti-Jewish disorders, some of serious proportions, in several British cities' (Sykes, 1965, pp. 368, 383).

Sykes at least allowed for a domestic angle to the riots—even if it was confined to considerations of the British climate. Others concerned with the Palestine situation after the war have also at least hinted at a wider context other than simple revulsion at the terrorist activities. Michael Cohen, for example, has referred to 'a wave of anti-Semitic outbursts in some of the large towns, particularly in Manchester and Liverpool, where an economic depression presented fertile soil for such manifestations.' The total lack of attention given to the riots by British historians of the post-war period has made it hard for scholars such as Cohen to go much further (Cohen, 1988, p. 231).

One context for the riots, perhaps as obvious as the Palestinian one, is that from within a tradition of British anti-Semitism or more broadly, as Colin Holmes has suggested, as 'part of the post-war picture of collective violence' against immigrant and minority groups in Britain (Holmes, 1991a, p. 213). The historical study of racial violence on an individual and collective basis in British society, as the need for this volume makes clear, is still in its infancy. It is therefore all the more remarkable that just ten days after the riots in August 1947 an article was written by a young refugee historian, Caesar Aronsfeld, entitled 'Not For the First Time . . .'. In unrestrained language Aronsfeld suggested that 'The hideous extravagances of pogromist banditry last week . . . were not the first of their kind in Anglo-Jewish history.' Aronsfeld referred not to the Middle Ages, but to an 'immaculate progress, in fact in the life of this present generation, 36 years ago, almost to the day'—the anti-Jewish riots in South Wales, 1911, and those in Leeds, 1917. The *Jewish Standard*, organ of the Zionist Revisionist movement in the United Kingdom, was also anxious to stress that 'the incidents in Britain cannot be attributed solely to the hanging of the two British sergeants by the *Irgun* in Palestine.' Instead it stressed 'anti-alienism, and anti-foreignism that always raises its head in periods of a shrinking economy.'[7]

As will be shown, one of the dominant responses to the August 1947 riots was to label them as 'un-British'. Such an approach made the process of forgetting much easier. Recognition that the events were actually part of a longer tradition of intolerance in British history enables a domestic perspective that few contemporaries were willing to consider. Nevertheless, if the riots are seen as part of a history of anti-Semitism in Britain, questions still remain. First, why were they directed towards the Jews at that particular time? Secondly, why did they take place in certain British cities and not in others? It is, for example, ironic that the three major towns witnessing violence—Glasgow, Liverpool and Manchester—had not experienced anti-Semitic riots before. South Wales, Leeds and East London, places of earlier collective violence, were actually quiet in the first week of August.[8]

Thirdly, reference to an anti-Semitic or xenophobic tradition is too imprecise. Before and after the riots there had been renewed fascist activities, particularly in East and North East London. The riots of August 1947 could be seen as part of those activities and therefore as fitting in to a broader pattern of organised anti-Semitism in twentieth-century British history. Thus Israel Finestein, when referring in a brief history of Anglo-Jewry to the issue of anti-semitism, moves from an account of Mosley's activities in the 1930s to 'The post-war re-emergence of Fascism [which] was encouraged but not caused by anti-British acts of violence in Palestine.'[9] Contemporary Jewish intelligence reports, however, backed up by police and government sources make it clear that the riots were *not* organised and although fascist groups were willing to capitalise on the violence, they were not generally the instigators of the disturbances. In a direct sense, therefore, the riots cannot be placed in a tradition of organised racist extremism. Furthermore, the *Jewish Standard*, in suggesting that the riots were part of an inherent British anti-alienism, failed to recognise that those Jews and their property attacked were actually British-born — the refugee Jews were not singled out for particular attention.[10] What, indeed, is of a greater significance is how the Jews of Britain, despite their contributions to the country and massive efforts at anglicisation were *seen to be foreigners* at this point in time. It is here that one of the keys to understanding the nature of the riots is revealed — the rioters were attacked widely as un-British but the disturbances themselves can only be understood properly in the context of contemporary definitions, however informal, of notions of Britishness. The riots were an indication of who did and did not belong to British society. They defined the status of minority groups and under what conditions they would be tolerated. The riots of 1947 are thus important for what they reveal about the limitations of both intolerance and toleration in modern Britain.

The riots of 1947, whilst part of the story relating to the final years of Britain and Palestine, are also integral to our understanding of British national identity in the immediate post-war years. Before the socio-economic and cultural factors relevant to this question can be raised, however, a description of the chronology of the riots is required.

On Wednesday 30 July 1947 unconfirmed news was received about the death of the two British sergeants. The same day the Board of Deputies of British Jews issued a statement voicing 'Anglo-Jewry's detestation and horror at the appalling crime committed against innocent British soldiers' (BDA, JDC minutes, 11 August 1947). That the Board was expecting trouble is made clear by the summoning of an emergency Defence Committee meeting on the Wednesday with emergency plans in place by Thursday, 31 July. The Association of Jewish Ex-Servicemen (AJEX) was contacted on a national and local level and in turn AJEX organised an emergency meeting for Friday 1 August where, 'in the event of dire emergency . . . they were to call upon their members to place themselves at the disposal of the Police authorities on the side of law and order' (ibid.).

It is clear that for the forty-eight hours preceding the *Daily Express* photograph on Friday 1 August, the 'official' leaders of Jewish defence organisations in Britain were expecting trouble. The first incidents occurred in the Liverpool area on the Friday evening, the start of the Bank Holiday weekend. First, the Birkenhead slaughtermen announced that they would refuse to process meat for Jewish consumption until the atrocities in Palestine ceased. Shortly afterwards the initial violence began with attacks on Jewish individuals and property in and around Liverpool, including Birkenhead itself. Throughout the Saturday rumours of increased violence against individuals and property circulated and precautions were taken to protect obvious Jewish targets. Liverpool remained

the focus of the disturbances with sixty-eight incidents on the Saturday night—
mainly attacks on property—and a further 101 such attacks on Sunday 3
August.[11]

Elsewhere early on the Saturday Jewish shops were attacked in the Gorbals
area of Glasgow with further incidents there in the the evening (BDA C6/4/2/
16; *Glasgow Evening News*, 2 August 1947). Also on the Saturday evening the
first violence in Manchester occurred with damage inflicted on Jewish shops
and factories (BDA JDC minutes, 11 August 1947). By Sunday 3 August, the
scope and spread of the disturbances had increased. The first major demonstrations occurred in Manchester on Sunday afternoon where a crowd (of up to
four hundred according to the *Jewish Chronicle*, and a thousand according to a
Jewish intelligence report) gathered in the Cheetham Hill area causing some
damage and intimidating a Jewish wedding reception. There was also violence
in Hull, Brighton and Leicester with less serious and more isolated incidents
across London and in Plymouth, Birmingham, Bristol, Cardiff, Swansea,
Devonport and Newcastle (BDA JDC minutes, 11 August 1947; *Jewish
Chronicle*, 8 August 1947; MCL, Manchester Watch Committee minutes, vol.
80, 26 August 1947). The violence continued on Bank Holiday Monday with a
further seventy-three incidents in Liverpool, the beating-up of a Jewish shopkeeper in Glasgow and more gatherings in Manchester and areas around it. In
Eccles a crowd of up to 700 people gathered in an anti-Jewish demonstration
causing over £1,000 of damage. Looting and violence against Jews and Jewish
property continued in Eccles and Liverpool on the Tuesday and Wednesday.
Indeed, it was only by the end of the week that the disturbances can be said to
have ended. What then was their extent (BDA JDC minutes, 11 August 1947;
Jewish Chronicle, 8 August 1947; *Daily Graphic*, 4 August 1947; *News Chronicle*,
7 August 1947; *Manchester Guardian*, 12 August 1947)?

The fact that the riots took place over a week period and were located across
most of Britain makes generalisations difficult. Some towns, such as
Birmingham, suffered nothing more than anti-Jewish graffiti whereas
Manchester, Liverpool and Glasgow witnessed more serious violence and
gathering of crowds of up to two thousand. The *Jewish Chronicle* was quick to
point out that 'A notable feature of the riots is that there were comparatively few
cases of personal violence' and, in contrast to the attacks on property, the
absence of serious injuries is remarkable—certainly in comparison with other
examples of collective racist violence in twentieth-century British history (*Birmingham Evening Dispatch*, 2 August 1947; *Jewish Chronicle*, 8 August 1947;
Holmes, 1991). Nevertheless, violence against individuals did occur in
Liverpool, Manchester and Glasgow and the suggestion that 'only one case of
assault was recorded' is inaccurate. Attacks on a solicitor in Liverpool and on
the shopkeeper in Glasgow were serious although in neither case life-
threatening. Some restraint does appear to have been exercised on a general
level on those attacking the Jews (in an isolated incident in Northampton it was
alleged that a cinema doorman pointed a pistol at a Jew and threatened to kill
him but actually only struck the individual), but the existence of some violence
against persons had an important psychological impact on British Jewry, as will
be discussed below.[12]

The attacks on property were more widespread and give an indication of the impetus behind the violence. Synagogues and cemeteries did not escape attack and there were half-hearted attempts at arson or threats of arson against Jewish religious buildings.[13] The most important targets were, however, secular buildings—houses, business premises and particularly shops. It is significant that looting became more prominent as the disturbances progressed. Not only Jewish property was attacked—in Ardwick in Manchester at least half the shops damaged belonged to non-Jews. As a result of the riots, thousands of pounds worth of damage was caused to shops and other buildings and over a hundred arrests were made on charges of public order, damage to property and looting.[14]

What was the motivation of those rioting? In Parliament and the press there was great emphasis put on the 'hooligan' element in the violence. The Home Secretary, James Chuter Ede, stated that 'it would be a mistake to regard these regrettable incidents, which were the work of a few disorderly persons seeking an excuse for hooliganism, as any indication of public feeling' (*Hansard*, vol. 441, cols 256–7, 13 August 1947). At a meeting between representatives of the Board of Deputies and the Home Office, Sir Alexander Maxwell for the latter suggested that 'In Liverpool and Manchester where most of the disturbances occurred, it was generally pure hooliganism and the desire for looting' that was responsible for the violence and disorder (BDA JDC minutes, 11 August 1947). The official explanation begs more questions than it answers. What, for example, was meant by 'pure hooliganism'? One suspects that the police and others who suggested that the Palestine situation was used as a 'pretext for rowdyism' were suggesting that the riots were in essence non-ideological and in fact only inspired by Bank Holiday exuberance, drink and an excuse for violence for violence's sake. The evidence, especially from the court cases, suggests that all these factors existed, but it does not follow that such 'hooliganism' was non-ideological. However crude and inappropriate, it would be misleading to say that the violence had no direction or purpose or wider significance (although this was the dominant public response of contemporary public figures to the disturbances). The Jewish MP, Maurice Edelman, stated in the Commons that he believed the riots were 'the work of hooligans and looters, and when the Lord Mayor of Liverpool described them as un-British he said all that needed to be said about it (*Hansard*, vol. 410, cols 2330–1, 12 August 1947). Edelman's curt attempt to dismiss the importance of the riots reveals more about the desire to deny a domestic popular anti-Semitism than it does about the motivations of those involved in the violence. Moreover, the frequent connection made between looting and hooliganism is not straight forward—violence and economics were linked but separate motivations.

In an editorial in the middle of the riots, the *Manchester Guardian* asked how much of the disturbances was due to hooliganism and how much due to anti-Semitism and concluded that it was 'hard to say'. Its difficulty, I would suggest, came from employing a false dichotomy. A quote from a crowd in Manchester illustrates this point neatly: 'Get the Jews, get the stuff, and get into the shops.' In the middle and later sections of the riots, an element of sheer economic opportunism became a more notable feature. It was reported from Liverpool that 'children were sent by adults to grab clothes and kitchen utensils' from a smashed large suburban store. It would be wrong, however, to see all the looting that took place as purely mercenary in inspiration without any ideological foundations (*Manchester Guardian*, 6 August 1947; *Daily Worker*, 6 August 1947; *Daily Chronicle*, 4 August 1947).

For the first two days of the riots nearly all the business premises attacked were Jewish. The percentage certainly declined, particularly after Bank Holiday Monday, but this in itself is not conclusive evidence of a random element in the riots. Myth and reality became interwoven, and the widespread belief that Jews controlled the retail trade in Britain and especially the chain stores was translated into attacks on shops which were falsely assumed to have been under Jewish ownership. The signs 'We are not Jews' outside a range of stores in Liverpool, the major centre of looting, illustrated the exaggerated sense of Jewish economic power at this point in British history. Jewish-owned shops and businesses or those that were perceived to be Jewish accounted for the vast majority of those attacked. Even allowing for a random element, the *Jewishness* of the properties subject to violence and looting is important. How far, then, was this a question of anti-Semitism?[15]

The immediate concern of the official Jewish community, the police and the government was that the riots had been organised. As has been mentioned, such fears were soon quashed. Police in Manchester and Liverpool believed that the sporadic and dispersed nature of the riots meant that they could not have been orchestrated. It appears that the disturbances were a series of spontaneous incidents which developed their own limited momentum. The Chairman of the Defence Committee of the Council of Manchester and Salford Jews suggested for his area that 'The crowds were not organised Fascists, but the fascist element was naturally involved (to about 5%). The main disturbances were hooliganism and not organised fascist attacks.'[16] None of the post-war fascist leaders was involved in the riots directly, and there is some evidence that they distanced themselves from the actual disturbances whilst welcoming the anti-Semitism which they believed would provide an impetus to their attempted revival. With a few minor exceptions due to the activities of individuals (particularly in Derby and Bristol), fascist activities were limited to London and more specifically to East and North East London. Here, battles between fascists and anti-fascists and attacks on Jews were becoming a growing problem every weekend. The relative absence of riots in London could be explained by this factor—there was an outlet for those of a violent anti-semitic outlook. Moreover, as one editorial pointed out, paradoxically the greater presence of fascist anti-Semitism in the capital may in this case have protected the Jews—all fascist activities were seen as being beyond the pale.[17]

The riots were not directly fascist-inspired although it should be acknowledged that the existence of over ten years of fascist propaganda against the Jews helped to prepare the atmosphere for the riots to occur. There were, moreover, individuals with no apparent fascist connections who attempted to lead the riots as anti-Semitic crusades. In Eccles ex-Sergeant Major John Regan was arrested for public disorder offences. Whilst the riots were in progress he urged on a crowd of 600 by marching up and down shouting 'Hitler was right, exterminate every Jew—every man, woman and child.' Similarly in Liverpool William Lloyd told a crowd of 300: 'Let them have it. We don't want the swines here.' Such individuals, it should be remembered, had not gathered the crowds together in the first place and they operated independently—although their activities could hardly have calmed the situation (*Daily Worker*, 9 August 1947; *Liverpool Echo*, 4 August 1947). What, however, of the hundreds who came out to demonstrate? The Manchester Watch Committee in its report on the riots suggested that many who had gathered in Cheetham Hill were 'people attracted by curiosity'. The *Manchester Guardian* also commented that 'great crowds have watched acts of savagery' but added that they had done so 'without any evidence of disapproval, still less any attempt to intervene'. The Watch Committee itself had to acknowledge that such crowds 'although kept on the move and dispersed . . . assembl[ed] again at another point.' Watching and sometimes participating in anti-Jewish disturbances was hardly the sign of engaging in neutral Bank Holiday entertainment. Those that gathered in their hundreds after the initial disturbances must also have been aware of their anti-Semitic nature—especially as the local and national press were not slow to report and comment on the violence.[18]

The riots certainly need to be contextualised as part of a tradition of what one synagogue official generously described as 'holiday boisterousness'. The August Bank Holiday was a notorious time for disorder and drink undoubtedly played its part in the riots as did the opportunities offered by the limited street lighting still imposed in the immediate post-war years. Such factors only helped to facilitate the violence and they do not explain the direction the disturbances took. An examination of one specific feature of the episode—the refusal in some towns of slaughtermen to process meat for Jewish consumption—will illustrate that there was more to the riots than a reaction to Jewish terrorism and Bank Holiday exuberance.[19]

On the surface the decision of the Birkenhead slaughtermen to boycott meat for the Jews appears to be totally bound up with the murder of the British sergeants. A meeting was called on Friday 1 August after some of the men had seen the photograph in the *Daily Express*. Explaining the decision to boycott, a spokesman stated it was 'a reprisal for what they are doing in Palestine' (BDA, C6/4/2/26, report, 21 August 1947). A more detailed investigation of their decision and the continuation of the boycott throughout August 1947 reveals that the domestic agenda was of greater importance. Indeed, the same spokesman was candid enough to admit that 'Apart from the hangings in Jerusalem [*sic*] the men have a personal grievance. Two years ago they applied for an increase in pay, but the Jews turned it down, and they have heard nothing since.' The Liverpool Shechita Board, responsible for the supervision of Kosher meat in the area, was faced with a particularly difficult situation as they had to deal with both the Birkenhead and Liverpool slaughtermen. This was exploited by the two abattoirs and agreement over rates of pay were not finally agreed with the Shechita Board until early 1948. One member of the Board believed this was no accident as the men in August were approaching their busy period which would last until February. Until then the Jewish trade was 'not remunerative to them, and so they had intended—at least the vocal members—to put the ban on for six months.' This, however, was more than a local trade dispute with the Palestine issue used as an opportune bargaining weapon. The men's altruism on the Palestine question was suspect, as the Defence Committee of the Board of Deputies later concluded. Nevertheless, issues of anti-semitism were not irrelevant and in this specific case study provide great insights into the whole episode. (ibid.; Liverpool City Archives, Liverpool Shechita Board, acc. 2997; BDA JDC minutes, August–October).

In 1941 the Economic League carried out a survey into anti-Semitism in Merseyside. It was a crude report that suggested widespread hostility. One of the major figures of Liverpool Jewry, Bertam Benas, rejected most of its findings, acknowledging that there was occasional anti-Semitism but 'nothing like an effective or persistent conscious anti-Semitic movement here'. It is significant, however, that Benas was willing to concede that one area of open conflict was in the area of meat where allegations were made that difficulties in supply were due to the Jews (BDA, C6/10/16). It is clear that such tensions had not disappeared by the time of the riots. At a meeting with the Liverpool slaughtermen a Jewish representative was greeted with 'a number of crude anti-Semitic interruptions' and it emerged that the men, whilst resenting most strongly allegations that they were fascist-inspired, had written a pamphlet for publication making anti-Semitic allegations and particularly that the 'Jews get the best meat'. That this was not just a local issue is evident from the last meeting before the riots of the Board of Deputies' Defence Committee, when the agitation 'against what was alleged to be favoured treatment of the Anglo-Jewish community in the matter of home-killed meat' was considered (BDA, C6/4/2/26, report, 21 August 1947; BDA JDC minutes, 30 July 1947).

During the Second World War the image of Jews in Britain as black marketeers gaining from the war but not contributing to the military effort was a powerful one. The end of the war did not stop such negative images and the continuation of rationing and shortages of goods created a sense of strain and gloom. The harsh winter of 1946–7 had intensified such domestic problems and the escalating economic problems added to the overall sense of depression. In that sense the Bank Holiday disturbances were linked to a short-lived period of release of tensions and frustrations.[20] It was no accident, however, that they were directed towards the Jews. Despite the disproportionate efforts of the Jews in the British forces, civil defence units and general war effort, Jews were still seen as separate, as different. Not only were the Jews outsiders, but the persistence of their Shylock stereotype made it hard for some to see that they, too, were affected by the economic crisis of 1947. The looting, in particular of Jewish pawnbrokers in the disturbances as well as the firing of Jewish factories, indicates that behind some of the attacks was the idea of Jews as economic exploiters. The depriving of meat to the Jewish communities of Liverpool (which had a knock-on effect in Manchester, Bradford and Leicester) was an indication of the belief that the sacrifices the British people were being urged to make through austerity measures—ones for the good of the country as a whole—were not being shared equally.[21]

The economic aspects to the riots were also revealed in their geographical location. Searching for clues of why the disturbances should be centred in Liverpool, Manchester and Glasgow, some contemporary observers—Jewish and non-Jewish—pointed to the existence of prior clashes between Roman Catholics and Orangemen in Liverpool and Glasgow. Publicly the communist *Daily Worker* and privately Maurice Edelman were more explicit. The former suggested that the riots occurred 'particularly in quarters where Roman

Catholic influence is most strongly exercised over the most ignorant people (*Daily Worker*, 11 August 1947; BDA JDC minutes, 11 August 1947). Investigations were made, especially in Liverpool, to examine whether the Irish were overrepresented in the disturbances. In fact, no substantial evidence of this could be found. The focus of these observers was too narrow— for example, *The Economist* in an editorial at the end of the riots pointed out that they had 'taken place in towns which have a bad record for racial intolerance' but saw this only in terms of Protestant–Catholic clashes.[22] Such friction, often with violent repercussions, was a feature of inter-war life in Glasgow and Liverpool but both these towns, and to a lesser extent Manchester, had seen other forms of racial intolerance, particularly in the form of riots against their small black communities after the First World War. Street attacks with a racist motive and a mass base were thus not uncommon to all these towns (although Manchester, of the three, had the least intensive tradition). It is not irrelevant therefore that riots against Liverpool's 8,000 black community occurred exactly a year later in 1948, also in the August Bank Holiday. It is important, however, to recognise that the 1948 riots were concerned, as Peter Fryer suggests, with 'a determined effort by the National Union of Seamen, since the end of the war, to keep black seamen off British ships.' The attempt to impose a colour bar in turn reflected not just the blatant racism of the National Union of Seamen but the real crisis of unemployment in post-war Liverpool (Neal, 1988; Bruce, 1985; Fryer, 1987, ch. 10, pp. 367–71; Jenkinson, 1988).

The link between unemployment and the 1947 riots is less direct but is nevertheless an important factor in understanding their occurrence and location. Rather than the Irish Catholics, it was actually the unemployed who appear to have been overrepresented amongst those involved in the disturbances. This is evident from the subsequent court cases and contemporary police observations.[23] The link to unemployment is made more generally if local rates of unemployment are considered. The economic crises of 1947 had put unemployment on the political agenda again. Unemployment had peaked by the spring of 1947 (at 1.9 million, all but half a million having been temporarily laid off because of the weather and the fuel crisis) and by the time of the riots stood at roughly 250,000 insured persons or 1.5 per cent. By the standards of the inter-war period or the last decades of the twentieth century the figures and percentages for late summer 1947 were relatively low, yet such comparisons hide both the regional impact and the sudden increase in unemployment in 1947 itself. From the local figures produced by the Ministry of Labour the domination of unemployment in absolute terms in both Liverpool and Glasgow is blatant. With 18,700 and 20,700 unemployed respectively, these cities had double the number out of work of any town or city outside the capital (which had only 14,300 unemployed in what was a massive area). Manchester at just 5,000 had the next highest total below Glasgow and Liverpool on the mainland. Such absolute figures cannot, of course, be used mechanically, but they could well provide some of the explanation of why a town such as Leeds, with a reputation for a stronger anti-Semitic reputation than say Manchester and Liverpool, escaped disturbances. Leeds, with just 2,000 unemployed, had a total and percentage unemployed which was much lower than even Manchester

(Robertson, 1987, ch. 1; Morgan, 1984, pp. 330–4; *Ministry of Labour Gazette*, September 1947).

So far I have endeavoured to show how it is mistaken and perhaps patronising to view the 'hooliganism' of the riots as 'mindless'. The economic aspects of the disturbances highlight this point but there is also a real danger that in exposing the economic roots of the riots a rationalisation is provided for those involved in the violence which somehow excuses the participants. This danger is avoided if one analyses the more encompassing question of national identity that underpins the whole question of the riots' origins, including issues of economics, the Palestine question and racial intolerance.[24]

The period of the Labour governments from 1945 to 1951 was marked by the retreat from Empire (of which the Palestinian episode was one of the messiest and least satisfactory) and the start of a general move towards a more inward-looking nationalism. The change is graphically illustrated by the swan-song of the Labour government, the Festival of Britain, which contrasted dramatically with the series of exhibitions and fairs held in Britain since the Great Exhibition, one hundred years earlier. In the previous exhibitions, international participation was welcomed and stress was placed on Britain's Empire and international role. The Festival of Britain, it has been suggested, 'was exclusively for and about the British . . . a thematic celebration of historic Britain and traditional Britishness.'[25]

The retreat inwards did not just occur on a cultural level. Historians have now shown the racist and ethnocentric basis of post-war immigration policies. As David Cesarani has illustrated, it was not only those of colour from the New Commonwealth who were effectively excluded by the British government, but also Jewish displaced persons, the survivors of the Holocaust. A clear strategy was developed in the acceptance of immigrants based essentially on their ability to assimilate. The immigration policies of the post-war years were concerned with the question of which outsiders could and could not become 'British' or why, as Cesarani puts it, 'East Europeans were deemed worth this exertion [to integrate], but Jews, Blacks and Asians were not' (Dean, 1987; Cesarani, 1992, p. 81). The 'British–Jewish' conflict over Palestine and, in particular, the riots of 1947 provided a domestic counterpart to the immigration debates. The whole episode represented the much more informal but still important internal process of forming a new British (or more accurately, English) national identity in a world in a total state of flux.

The growth of Jewish terrorism after the war revived one of the greatest fears of British Jewry—the charge of dual loyalty. That such fears were not unfounded was illustrated starkly at the start of 1947. In its leader addressed 'To British Jews' the *Sunday Times* made the accusation that British Jews had failed to denounce properly the Palestinian outrages and thus were failing to perform their 'civic duty and moral obligations'. Not since the 'loyalty letters' of the First World War, involving those of German origin, had so much direct pressure to behave and conform been placed on a minority in Britain. Despite their contributions to the war effort and the constant public denunciations of terrorism, the loyalty of British Jewry was being questioned. Only a tiny and totally uninfluential fascist fringe was demanding the removal of Jews from Britain, but throughout 1947 pressure, however informal, was placed on the

Jewish minority to be 'British'. The riots in August 1947 exposed the vulner-ability of British Jewry and in many ways the reaction to the disturbances, whilst almost uniformally hostile, further illustrated their marginality.[26]

Signs outside four shop windows at the time of the riots emphasise the importance of national identity and the question of who belonged to British society. The first was outside the smashed-up hardware shop near Manchester: 'Every member of this family volunteered for service and took part in the North Africa fighting.' It listed the injuries received during the conflict and the military achievements of the family before concluding: 'We denounce the horror and the thugs in Palestine. We are all Collyhurst born.' The second was outside an untouched major store in Wavertree, Liverpool, an area where damage was quite severe. Here those in charge traced the shop's ancestry to an Essex Methodist local preacher. The third and fourth were from Manchester and reveal starkly the issue of belonging; 'Hold your fire. These premises are British'; 'Don't make another mistake, chums. This shop is 100 per cent British owned, managed and staffed (*Daily Herald*, 4 August 1947; *Manchester Guardian*, 6 August 1947).

The riots were met with widespread condemnation and a sense of shock. In this process the notion of Englishness was used extensively. The riots, in the words of Viscount Hall, were 'not the British way of dealing with these problems'. Magistrates dealing with those responsible for the disturbances described them as 'un-English and unfair' and as 'both un-British and unpa-triotic'. The Earl of Perth and the Bishop of Derby used similar arguments but exposed in the House of Lords, in a manner similar to that in the same chamber forty years later in the War Crimes debate, how they could be employed further to marginalise the Jews. Perth stated that 'these outbreaks are contrary to the whole traditions of the country, and above all to the tenets of Christianity.' Further emphasising the roots of British society and the otherness of the Jews, the Bishop of Derby suggested that the riots represented 'a spirit and a temper and an attitude towards the *Jewish race* [my emphasis] which is in itself utterly out of keeping with our traditions and with what we like to hold to be true of our national character. Alike in the name of the religion which the majority of people in this country still claim to profess.' The position of Jews as outsiders in British society was also emphasised in a *Daily Express* editorial towards the end of the riots. It warned 'No More of This!' as the disturbances, by attacking innocent shopkeepers, were disgracing the whole nation. Nevertheless, the *Express*, which had triggered the riots, covered itself by stating that the events in Palestine had rightly stirred public indignation. After four days of rioting the paper was willing, for the reputation of Britain, to say 'no more'.[27]

As David Leitch has suggested, 'The Palestine affair produced a widespread sense of national *pique*.' It coincided in 1947 with a series of economic crises, a 'year when optimism disappeared'. Jews, like all other British citizens, suffered the hardships and disappointments of the austerity years and to them the Palestine crisis created in 1947 'the agony of Anglo-Jewry' (Leitch, 1986, p. 66; Hewison, 1988, p. 14; Nathan, 1977). This, however, was far from the view of popular conceptions where Britain and Jewry were at war and 'our boys' were being killed by Jewish terrorists. The riots are therefore important when considering the issue of national identity in this period of loss of esteem. As a

remarkable lead article in the *Jewish Standard* of 8 August 1947 put it in trying
to explain the *British* background to the riots: 'As Britain begins to shed
dominion over the races of the East, and falls back into its island and partner-
ship with the white dominions, so there must begin to pass the old broad
interest in things outside its immediate concern.' If Britain was turning in on
itself, what impact did the riots have on British Jewry?

The riots had a dual impact on British Jews. The first was on an immediate
level which was localised and generally short-lived. The second was on a
national level which is harder to measure but, if taken together with other post-
war issues, had a deep and lasting effect. The most obvious influence was in the
areas most affected by the disturbances and it is not surprising that for many
Jews the riots created much fear and anxiety. A non-Jewish chef in Liverpool,
four years after the riots remembered vividly the 'ugly scenes here . . . there was
a good few beatings up . . . a gang went around smashing windows in the Jewish
shops—there was a lot of fear among Jews who were quite innocent.' Mamie
Freedman remembers the impact on her sister's wedding which took place in
Liverpool on Sunday 3 August 1947:

> when it came to the wedding, at Greenbank Drive Synagogue, there were crowds of
> non-Jews outside, and no one was allowed to leave the building. In the evening my
> husband took me and my five year old son and niece out, and we had to walk through
> the back streets to our house in the same neighbourhood. Tension was very high for a
> few weeks.

In Liverpool, Manchester and Glasgow all the Jews were affected, but there was
an age factor involved. In Liverpool it was reported that 'some elderly people
have expressed a desire to leave the City for a while' and accommodation was
being sought for them. In Manchester an informal curfew for the older
generation was in operation. Amongst some of the younger Jews and especially
ex-servicemen there was a more militant response and some informal retaliation against the demonstrators. Such militancy created tension with the 'official'
representatives of the local Jewish communities who preferred behind the
scenes diplomacy to be employed. There was disquiet even amongst the more
militant who believed the communal bodies were allowing the situation to get
out of hand by being too reliant on the police authorities.[28]

The general strategy adopted by British Jewry was to adopt a low profile—
most immediately at the time of the riots by closing shops and avoiding public
contact. A reporter for the *Manchester Guardian* in a street in Liverpool with
glass still underfoot found voices muted and even the children playing 'a little
too quietly'. In the same street a Jew called Mendelsohn was removing his name
plate. During and after the riots attempts were made to limit the size of Jewish
functions in what became an 'austerity campaign'—again emphasising the
intimate connection of the riots to the troubled economic circumstances of the
time (*Manchester Guardian*, 6 August 1947; BDA JDC minutes, August 1947
onwards).

The less specific impact was on the psychology of British Jewry. As a member
of the Leicester Hebrew congregation, suffering from the meat boycott, put it:
'what can I do? Why should I, in Leicester, be connected with terrorism in

Palestine?' British Jewry appeared both marginal and powerless (*Leicester Mercury*, 9 August 1947). It is important to consider that its sense of insecurity had increased drastically when the scope and scale of the Holocaust became clear in the immediate post-war period. The riots of 1947 and other manifestations of anti-Semitism in Britain cast doubts on the possibility of a British–Jewish symbiosis. The Holocaust, so close then to the Jews of Britain, highlighted the potential of racial intolerance. A Jewish member of the RAF wrote to the *Liverpool Echo*: 'As a Jewish soldier returning to my unit it is a sad reflection to look upon the disturbances and remember our fight to end Nazi methods and make the world a decent place to live in' (*Liverpool Echo*, 8 August 1947). The great supporter of Anglo-Jewish patriotism and anti-Zionism, Basil Henriques, was forced to acknowledge in the middle of the riots that 'The growth of anti-Semitism has led many to fear that what happened in Europe may happen here.' The anti-Zionists and non-Zionists in Anglo-Jewry represented in the Jewish Fellowship and Anglo-Jewish Association desperately tried to downplay the importance of the riots. Henriques referred to the 'occasional acts of violence by a few hooligans' and suggested that those 'feeling a slight sense of insecurity should bear this in mind. None of us go to bed in terror of burglars because there is an occasional burglary.' Harold Soref, writing in the Anglo-Jewish Association's journal, stressed how weak the riots were and crudely blamed drunken Irish or as he put it 'a serious "Poor White" problem' for the disturbances in Liverpool and Glasgow. Both institutions emphasised the role of Jewish terrorism in provoking the riots. Not surprisingly, British Zionists and particularly the Revisionists rejected this explanation and focused attention on the domestic roots of antipathy and the constant dangers facing diaspora Jewry even in Britain. An editorial in the *Gates of Zion* went further, stating it would be 'a fatal mistake to underestimate the significance of the latest anti-Jewish riots in Great Britain', even saying that the country was 'becoming the centre of world anti-Semitism' (*Jewish Outlook*, September/October 1947; *Jewish Monthly*, September 1947; *Jewish Standard*, 8 August 1947; *Gates of Zion*, October 1947 USA AJ 195/11/6, Henriques reminiscences, 5 August 1947).

The solution of the extreme Zionists, to abandon the false and fading security of the diaspora, was rejected by British Jewry and has continued to be a solution only sought by a small minority. The Zionists' loss of faith and confidence in Britain was, however, shared by much of British Jewry in the tense post-war years. By 1948–9 even the Anglo-Jewish Association had accepted this state of affairs. In a special report on the future of British Jewry compiled in 1950 it was acknowledged that insecurity was a major feature of the British Jewish psyche increased by the destruction of apparently well-integrated Jewish communities in Europe, whilst the world 'was not prepared really to put itself out to save those who were threatened. Insecurity arises from the fear that the same thing might be repeated and the fear was stimulated by the backwash in this country of the conflict between the Jews of Palestine and the British Government.' The report acknowledged that 'All these fears have a basis in reality and cannot be dismissed as the invention of Zionist propaganda' (USA AJ 37/13/7).

The riots, as we have seen, created tremendous concern in Britain—the range of editorial comment during and for the few days after the violence was impressive. What is also very notable is how quickly debate about them stopped. One Jewish resident of Manchester who witnessed the riots recalls how after the riots 'it was all passed over as [if] nothing had happened'. The social survey organisation, Mass-Observation, found just a fortnight after the riots that there was little discussion of the hanging sergeants, opinions on the Jews had changed little and that generally the riots were not an issue. Indeed, at the time of the incidents they only found one in five (or what Mass-Observation saw as the out-and-out anti-Semitic group) in favour of such demonstrations against the Jews.[29]

Whether discussion was actively repressed by the British state is unclear as relevant material has not been released. Nevertheless, the memoirs of the actress Joan Littlewood give an indication that there was an unease in government circles about the riots receiving too much public attention. Touring Britain as part of the radical Theatre Workshop, a Jewish member of Littlewood's troupe stumbled across acts of anti-Jewish violence in Cheetham Hill. The theatre company immediately decided to adjust the anti-Nazi play *Professor Mamlock* to include references to the riots in Manchester. The script was sent to the Lord Chamberlain for official approval but it 'came fleeing back ... All scenes representing the street events of the 4th August [1947] TO BE CUT'. It would seem that the state and the media believed that keeping quiet about the anti-Semitic violence would help it go away.[30]

British Jewry was not so assured. There was relief and praise at the promptness of police attempts to stop the riots and protect the Jews, some reassurance at the national press's strong opposition to the rioting (although less happiness with the provincial press which gave space to anti-Semitic correspondents), and mixed reactions at the inconsistent sentencing given by the courts to offenders involved in the disturbances. The state on a local and national level had shown general concern for the well-being of British Jewry.[31] Nevertheless, the refusal to take action against the fascist revival and the acquittal of James Caunt, editor of the *Morecambe and Heysham Visitor*, after he had written editorials threatening public violence against the Jews of Britain, kept a sense of lingering doubt. There was also much evidence of grass-roots opposition to the riots, including petitions signed by workers, letters from church figures, protests from groups such as the National Council for Civil Liberties and individual acts of kindness, including offering protection, in the riots themselves. One Jewish Liverpudlian recalls that his wife's parents' shop was attacked and attempts were made to set it on fire: 'fortunately their neighbours ... had come to their aid and had put a ladder by a rear wall so that they were able to leave their own premises safely.' He adds that he 'found local non-Jews very sympathetic towards us and particularly towards my in-laws ... My own "daily" offered to take care of my very young son in case of any repercussions against our family.' Despite this genuine goodwill, there was a continuing fear of popular hostility amongst British Jewry — it was reported as late as 1951 in Liverpool with regard to the riots that there were 'Jews who are frightened to open their doors at night'.[32]

The stabilisation of relations between Britain and the new Jewish state and the increased economic prosperity of the 1950s brought this most difficult period for British Jewry, which perhaps reached its nadir in August 1947, to a close. How, however, have the riots been remembered?

There is an increasing literature on social and individual memory and its relationship to history. There has been less work on the process of collective forgetting, but, as Yosef Yerushalmi suggests, this is an equally important area. British Jewry has been a paradoxical community, proud on one level of a largely mythical history that it has invented for itself, yet indifferent on another to the preservation and writing of its real past. British Jewry is more than a little suited to collective forgetting. At the time of the riots this process was in operation, the *Jewish Chronicle* on its front page declaring that these riots in Britain were the first 'within memory'. It is revealing that it took a young refugee, Caesar Aronsfeld, to point out their error. Aronsfeld referred to them again briefly in a series of articles on anti-Semitic riots in Britain published in 1952 but there were few references in this or following decades in either memoirs or histories of British Jewry. The process of forgetting was revealed in the Anglo-Jewish Exhibition which was a part of the Festival of Britain. Brief reference was made to the 'unhappy period during the withdrawal of the Mandatory Power' but it concluded, 'These memories have become dim' — just a few years after the riots.[33]

In a case study of the Italian fishermen of Marseilles it has been suggested that 'like many ethnic minorities, the members of the community have removed from their minds any reference to anti-immigrant agitations.' This is not always the case for minorities but it has been a notable feature of British Jewry and certainly those in its establishment, including its historians who have wished to emphasise the rootedness of Jews in the host society. It is not surprising therefore that British Jewry has collectively forgotten the anti-Semitic riots of August 1947. It is revealing, for example, that the two testimonies in the oral history collection at the Manchester Jewish Museum recalling the riots both place them in the war years — the riots, half forgotten, have lost their context (Fentress and Wickham, 1992, p. 118; MJM tapes, J20S and J244).

The forgetting of the episode surrounding the riots of August 1947 is unfortunate for it is an important part of British history and the crucial formation of British national identity in the post-war period. This article has, in contrast to the existing literature, concentrated on the domestic background of the riots. Yet it is worth stressing that an understanding of the Palestine connection requires knowledge of British attitudes towards Jews. Ernest Bevin's quips in the fuel crisis about 'IsraeLITES' and his earlier comments about Jews of Europe pushing to the front of the queue were all conditioned by the image of the Jew at home as the economic 'other' — the root basis of so much of the riots themselves.[34] The riots are also an important part of the post-war British Jewish experience. It has been suggested that the reconstruction of memory and the squeezing of it for facts — the turning of it into history — does not mean that we are through with memory. The same is true of collective forgetfulness. The historisation of the riots of August 1947 is unlikely to make much impact on a community that does not want to remember. But British Jewry as well as society as a whole could learn much from the disturbances: their ironies, inconsistencies and hypocrisies which reveal so much about the nature of British racism — its strengths and limitations. These riots, part of a whole series in Britain during the twentieth century, were condemned as un-English and against the traditions of British tolerance and decency. These un-English riots further emphasised to that most British of minorities, Anglo-Jewry, how uneasy they were at 'home'. The final irony was that the riots were triggered off by the brutal and 'un-English' murder of two of 'our boys' by Jewish terrorists in Palestine. One, Clifford Martin, it later emerged, was actually Jewish. In August 1947 the Jews of Britain were punished for the loss of one of their own sons (*Jewish Chronicle*, 22 July 1987).

To conclude, it is the myth of Englishness rather than the survival of fascism that has been at the heart of racism in post-war Britain, including the disturbances of August 1947. Notions of Englishness have not only been at the basis of 'polite' discrimination but also of more brutal violence against minorities. The riots of 1947 were unfortunately (despite their real and lasting impact on British Jewry) one of the most restrained forms of collective racist violence in twentieth-century British history. This fact reflects the strength, and not the weakness, of racism in Britain.[35]

Notes

1. I should like to thank David Massel, Executive Director of the Board of Deputies of British Jews for permission to use his organisation's records and also for his interest in this project. Joe Wolfman, Jewish communal archivist at Liverpool, was also a great help with local sources.
2. Apart from the extensive press reporting of the riots, the most extensive materials on the riots are in the Board of Deputies archive (hereafter BDA). No government papers on the riots have yet been released.
3. For the earlier riots, see Holmes, 1979. For a list of the towns affected, see *Jewish Chronicle*, 8 August 1947, and BDA, Jewish Defence Committee (JDC) minutes, 11 August 1947.
4. The Revisionists were right-wing nationalist Zionists opposed to any compromise with the British and determined to battle for a maximalist territorial solution in Palestine. *Daily Express*, 1 August 1947.
5. See the debates in the House of Commons, 12 August 1947, and the House of Lords, 13 August 1947; Viscount Hall in *Hansard*, House of Lords, vol. 151, cols 1386–7, 13 August 1947.
6. For a general survey of Britain and the Palestinian mandate, see Sykes, 1965. A Mass-Observation survey on British attitudes towards the Jews was carried out shortly after the King David attack. It revealed a great deal of anti-Semitism but there was no indication that this was likely to manifest itself in violence at home. See the Mass-Observation Archive (M-OA), Directive July 1946, Box 103.
7. Aronsfeld in *Zionist Review*, 15 August 1947; A. Abrahams, 'To the Jews of Britain: A Nation of Hostages', *Jewish Standard*, 8 August 1947.
8. *Jewish Chronicle*, 8 August 1947, and BDA JDC minutes, 11 August 1947. Harold Soref in a review of the Jewish year 1946–7 pointed to the strange absence of riots in Leeds, 'the largest Jewish centre in Britain in proportion to its population'. Here he only considered anti-Semitism in relation to the size of the Jewish community, not the possibility of local circumstances and traditions existing totally independent of the Jews themselves. See *Jewish Monthly*, September 1947, p. 22.
9. Extensive material on fascist activities from 1945 to 1950 is available in the

National Council for Civil Liberties archive at the University of Hull. Finestein, 1957, p. 180. David Nathan in *Jewish Chronicle*, 26 August 1977, confuses the riots with contemporary fascist activities.

10. BDA JDC minutes, 11 August 1947. On the first night of the riots a refugee doctor was attacked but it was the only incident when refugees were subject to specific attack. *Glasgow Evening News*, 2 August 1947, and report of E. Felton to Roston of the JDC, 4 August 1947 in BDA, C6/4/2/26 of the attack.

11. For details of the events in Liverpool, see BDA C6/4/2/26 and the minutes of the Liverpool Association of Jewish Ex-Servicemen in Liverpool City archives, acc. 4407; *Jewish Chronicle*, 8 August 1947, and the local press, particularly *Liverpool Daily Post and Liverpool Echo*.

12. David Nathan minimises the level of personal violence in *Jewish Chronicle*, 26 August 1977 but does hint that unreported incidents may have been a feature. For the Northampton incident see *News Chronicle*, 7 August 1947.

13. See *Liverpool Daily Post*, 5 August 1947 for a report of an attempt to set fire to the Crown Street Synagogue.

14. Details of the damage caused in Manchester was produced in the Report to the Watch Committee, 26 August 1947. See *Jewish Chronicle*, August 1947 for fines and prison sentences.

15. *Jewish Chronicle*, 8 August 1947 suggested that the attacks on non-Jewish shops were totally unrelated to those against the Jews. It must be suggested that the paper was trying to minimise the significance of the anti-Jewish riots. See *Jewish Standard*, 8 August 1947 for the use of disclaimer signs outside shops.

16. See BDA C6/4/2/26 for Liverpool and letter, I. Sadler of Council of Manchester and Salford Jews to Roston, JDC, 13 August 1947 in BDA C6/4/2/29.

17. BDA JDC minutes, 11 August 1947; *Mosley Newsletter* no. 10, September 1947; *Unity* no. 7, August–September 1947 stated that whilst it did 'not condone acts of violence and destruction of Jewish property in this country, it was understandable that, in the heat of their rage, many British people were driven to demonstrate against those Jews here'; *Eastern Daily Press*, 4 August 1947 on lack of violence in London because of the fascist presence.

18. Manchester Watch Committee minutes, 26 August 1947; *Manchester Guardian*, 6 August 1947. At one stage in Liverpool it was reported that up to 2,000 people swarmed into a Jewish area in Liverpool. See *Liverpool Daily Post*, 5 August 1947.

19. An official of the Catford Synagogue quoted by *Lewisham Journal*, 8 August 1947. Some of those arrested had been drinking — see *Birkenhead News*, 20 August 1947; *South Wales Evening Post*, 11 September 1947. The August Bank Holiday became the key period for later disturbances in Britain involving 'Mods' and 'Rockers' — see Cohen, 1980.

20. For the Jew–black marketeer link, see Kushner, 1989. On the impact of the weather and the fuel crisis, see Robertson, 1987. Mass-Observation diaries for 1947 confirm the picture of general frustration.

21. For the war effort of British Jewry, see Kushner, forthcoming. See *Daily Graphic*, 4 August 1947; *South London Observer*, 8 August 1947; *Daily Dispatch*, 5 August 1947; *Evening Argus*, 11 August 1947, for incidents of looting of Jewish shops and attacks on property which suggest a large element of economic jealousy in the riots; *Leicester Mercury*, 9 August 1947, and *Bradford Telegraph and Argus*, 7 August 1947, for the impact of the meat ban outside the Liverpool area.

22. Mr E. Felton, secretary of the Council of Liverpool and District Jews, wrote to the JDC, 7 August 1947, that after enquiries it was found 'that there was no preponderance of Irishman'. In BDA C6/4/2/26; *The Economist*, 9 August

1947.

23. Thus in the Liverpool report of 7 August 1947 referred to in note 22 it was concluded that with regard to those who participated in the riots 'the only definite information is that they were for the most part unemployed people.' John Regan, the individual who attempted to orchestrate the riots in Eccles, was also unemployed — an ex-sergeant major. See *Daily Worker*, 9 August 1947.

24. See Pearson, 1976, for a 'defence' of hooliganism, and Cohen, 1980, pp. viii–xviii, for a critique of the possible dangers of going too far with this approach.

25. See Ovendale, 1984. The comments on the Festival of Britain are from the introduction to the exhibition staged at the Manchester City Art Gallery, October 1990–January 1992, 'The New Look: Design in the Fifties'. For earlier British exhibitions, see Greenhalgh, 1988.

26. *Sunday Times*, 5 January 1947. See Holmes, 1988, pp. 97–9, for the 'loyalty letters' and contemporary violence against Germans in Britain during the First World War. See *Jewish Chronicle* throughout 1947 for the constant attacks on Jewish terrorism from this paper and a wide range of Jewish organisations in Britain.

27. Viscount Hall in *Hansard*, House of Lords, vol. 151, cols 936–7, 5 August 1947; magistrates in Liverpool and Eccles quoted by *Daily Mail*, 6 August 1947, and *News Chronicle*, 7 August 1947; Perth in *Hansard*, House of Lords, vol. 151, vol. 936, 5 August 1947, and Derby in *Hansard*, House of Lords, vol. 151, col. 1379, 13 August 1947; *Daily Express*, 5 August 1947.

28. See (for the chef) M-OA: TC Anti-semitism Box 4 File D, 1951; Mrs M. Freedman, letter to the author, 15 April 1992. See Felton to Roston, 7 August 1947, for Liverpool in BDA C6/4/2/26 and *News Chronicle*, 6 August 1947, for the curfew and divisions in the community. See also the debate in BDA C6/4/2/29 within the Council of Manchester and Salford Jews and the papers of the Manchester Anti-Fascist Committee in the National Council for Civil Liberty papers, 42/4. Similar internal battles and concern amongst the more militant younger and ex-servicemen community was evident in Glasgow. See the correspondence in BDA C6/4/2/16 and the correspondence between Glasgow Workers Circle and Lazar Zaidman in the Zaidman papers, University of Sheffield.

29. Mr L. Scholes, letter to the author, 26 April 1992. The Wiener Library, London, now possesses the *Jewish Chronicle* press cuttings on the riots which consists of a large file including many editorial comments from local and national papers, some from areas with no Jews at all; Manchester Jewish Museum (MJM), tape J244; M-OA; FR 2515, September 1947, 'Attitudes to Palestine and the Jews'.

30. Littlewood, J., 1994, *Joan's Book: Joan Littlewood's Peculiar History As She Tells It*, London, Methuen, pp. 283–9.

31. See JDC minutes, 11 August 1947, in BDA archives. A local Manchester Jew recalls that the police were sympathetic to local Jews who tried to stop trouble — see MJM tape J244 and also the praise of the police in the Manchester Watch Committee, 26 August 1947. For concern over sentencing see Felton to Roston, 7 August 1947, in BDA C6/4/2/26.

32. Shortly after the riots the Board of Deputies went to see the Home Secretary about the re-emergence of British fascism. See JDC minutes, August–September 1947, in BDA archive. See *Morecamble and Heysham Visitor*, 6 August 1947, and for the Caunt decision see Leitch, 1986, p. 59, and (no author), 1947, *An Editor on Trial*, Morecambe, Morecambe Press. Evidence of local and national opposition to the riots can be found in *Civil Liberty*, August and September 1947; *Daily Mirror*, 6 August 1947, *Manchester Evening Chronicle*, 12 August 1947; M-OA: TC Anti-semitism, Box 4, File D, 1951.

33. Yerushalmi, 1989, pp. 105–17; see Kushner, 1992, for British Jewry and its own history; *Jewish Chronicle*, 8 August 1947; Aronsfeld in *Zionist Review*, 15 August 1947, and in *Gates of Zion*, July 1952. For the lack of attention in memoir material, see, for example, Brodetsky, 1960, pp. 273–4. Brodetsky, President of the Board of Deputies, referred to the murdered soldiers but not to the subsequent riots in Britain; (no author), 1951, *Festival of Britain 1951: a Survey of Some of the Aspects of Anglo-Jewish Life Illustrated in the Anglo-Jewish Exhibition*, no publisher, London, p. 17.

34. Sykes, 1965, p. 339, suggests that Bevin's quips about Jews and queues would not have been understood in Britain. This was far from the case. See *Zionist Review*, 21 June 1946. See Louis, 1984, p. 13, for the later 'joke'.

34. For further analysis of the impact of 'Englishness' on minorities, see Gilroy, 1987.

References

B[oard of] D[eputies of British Jews] A[rchives], selected documents.

Brodetsky, S., 1960, *Memoirs*, London, Weidenfeld and Nicolson.

Bruce, S., 1985, *No Pope of Rome: Anti-Catholicism in Modern Scotland*, Edinburgh, Mainstream.

Cesarini, D., 1992, *Justice Delayed: How Britain became a Refuge for Nazi War Criminals*, London, Heinemann.

Cohen, M., 1988, *Palestine to Israel: From Mandate to Independence*, London, Cass.

Cohen, S., 1980, *Folk Devils and Moral Panics*, Oxford, Martin Robertson.

Dean, D., 1987, 'Coping with Colonial Immigration, the Cold War and Colonial Policy; The Labour Government and Black Communities in Great Britain 1945–51', *Immigrants and Minorities*, 6: 305–33.

Fentress, J. and Wickham C., 1992, *Social Memory*, Oxford, Blackwell.

Finestein, I., 1957, *A Short History of Anglo-Jewry*, London, Lincolns-Prager, *Hansard, Parliamentary Debates*.

Fryer, P., 1987, *Staying Power: The History of Black People in Britain*, London, Pluto.

Gilroy, P., 1987, *There Ain't No Black in the Union Jack*, London, Hutchinson.

Gourvish, T. and O'Day, A. (eds), 1991, *Britain Since 1945*, London, Macmillan.

Greenhalgh, P., 1988, *Ephemeral Vistas*, Manchester, Manchester University Press.

Hewison, R., 1988, *In Anger: Culture in the Cold War 1945–60*, London, Methuen.

Holmes, C., 1979, *Anti-Semitism in British Society 1876–1939*, London, Edward Arnold.

Holmes, C., 1988, *John Bull's Island: Immigration and British Society, 1871–1971*, London, Macmillan.

Holmes, C., 1991a, 'Immigration', in T. Gourvish and A. O'Day (eds): 209–31.

Holmes, C., 1991b, *A Tolerant Country: Immigrants, Refugees and Minorities in Britain*, London, Faber.

Jenkinson, J., 1988, 'The Black Community of Salford and Hull', *Immigrants and Minorities*, 7: 166–83.

Kirk, G., 1954, *The Middle East 1945–1950*, London, Oxford University Press.

Kushner, T., 1989, *The Persistence of Prejudice: Anti-semitism in British Society During the Second World War*, Manchester, Manchester University Press.

Kushner, T. (ed.), 1992, *Jewish Heritage in British History: Englishness and Jewishness*, London, Frank Cass.

Kushner, T., forthcoming, *The Heimische Front: Jews in War-Time Britain*, London.

Leitch, D., 1986, 'Explosion at the King David Hotel', in M. Sissons and P. French (eds): 43–68.

Liverpool City Archives, Liverpool Shechita Board records.

Louis, W.M. 1984, *The British Empire in the Middle East 1945–1951*, Oxford, Clarendon.

M[anchester] C[entral Reference] L[ibrary], Watch Committee Minutes.

M[anchester] J[ewish] M[useum], selected tapes.

Morgan, K.O. 1984, *Labour in Power: 1945–1951*, Oxford, Oxford University Press.

Nathan, D., 1977, 'The Agony of Anglo Jewry', *Jewish Chronicle*, 26 August.

Neal, F., 1988, *Sectarian Violence: The Liverpool Experience 1819–1914*, Manchester, Manchester University Press.

Ovendale, R., 1984, *The Foreign Policy of the British Labour Governments 1945–1951*, Leicester, Leicester University Press.

Pearson, G., 1979, 'In Defence of Hooliganism', in N. Tutt (ed.): 192–220.

Robertson, A., 1987, *The Bleak Midwinter 1947*, Manchester, Manchester University Press.

Sissons, M. and French, P. (eds), 1986 (orig. 1963), *Age of Austerity*, Oxford, Oxford University Press.

Sykes, C., 1965, *Crossroads to Israel*, 1965, London, Collins.

Tutt, N. (ed.), 1976, *Violence*, London, HMSO.

U[niversity of] S[outhampton] A[rchive], selected documents.

Yerushalmi, Y., 1989, *Zakhor: Jewish History and Jewish Memory*, New York, Schocken.

9

The West Indian community and the Notting Hill riots of 1958[1]

Edward Pilkington

I

The year 1958 was one of those freak years when England actually enjoyed a summer. From June to late September the country was bathed in hot sunshine, which drew people out of their houses to go sunbathing in the parks or just to bask on their front doorsteps. In the long evenings people would stroll in the streets of Notting Hill, an area of north Kensington in west London populated by a cosmopolitan mix of working-class whites and West Indians. They would drink on the pavements outside pubs, or sit at opened windows taking in the atmosphere. It was a peculiarly happy setting for the unhappy events that were to follow.

Attacks against the West Indian contingent in Notting Hill began to occur on an isolated basis from July 1958. At first the incidents could be classified as skirmishes rather than serious assaults, and West Indians on the receiving end would comfort themselves with the thought that they amounted to nothing more than a couple of lads letting off steam. One common form of harassment was to stop a black man in the street and ask him for a cigarette. The man could either offer one and be humiliated by losing the entire packet, or refuse and suffer a beating.

Gradually, the violence became more frequent and more brutal. White residents of the area set up a vigilante squad supposedly to clear the streets of vice and prostitution. They called for powers to deport back to the West Indies black people convicted of sexual offences (*Kensington Post*, 14 February 1958).

In the first week of August, a West Indian, Charles Appio, was attacked and punched in the face by a group of white youths outside Ladbroke Grove tube station. When three of the whites appeared in court the magistrate, E.R. Guest, commented that 'whether or not people walk safely in the streets distinguishes civilisation from the lack of it. Nobody looks upon this as a matter of the slightest importance' (*Kensington News*, 8 August 1958).

As August progressed there were further isolated incidents: two West Indian houses were pelted with bricks; a shop was smashed up and a local petition was organised calling for urgent action to stem the escalating violence. At the end of the month Mr Guest issued one more appeal for help to stem the mounting tide of racial violence: 'It is a matter of considerable public importance that something should be done seriously to stop street disorders in North Kensington. They are not only a disgrace to the neighbourhood but also extremely dangerous for ordinary decent citizens' (*Kensington Post*, 29 August 1958).

But one magistrate cannot hold back a storm. Even if his cry for help had not fallen on deaf ears it came, in any case, far too late: the first major incidents of race rioting erupted in Notting Hill the very next day.

II

To understand how a prominent area of London was brought to the brink of racial conflagration you have to step ten years back in time to when West Indians first began arriving in Britain in large numbers. The decade between 1948 and 1958 was formative in the development of Britain's modern race relations, and the seeds of many of today's conflicts and challenges were sown then.

The period opened on 22 June 1948 with the arrival of the *Empire Windrush*, an old troop-carrier, at Tilbury Docks. Five hundred Jamaicans, mostly men, had landed on what they had been taught to regard as their second home, the 'Mother Country'. Some of the newcomers had lived in England before, serving in the British Army during the war; others were leaving their birthplace for the unknown, partly in the hope that it would provide an escape from economic hardship in the West Indies and partly as an exploration of strong cultural ties.

'England was home in the mind of every small boy in the West Indies when I was growing up', wrote Michael de Freitas, who lived in Notting Hill at the time of the race riots and who, as Michael X, went on to become an influential figure in the 1960s British Black Power movement (Malik, 1968, p.31). Horace Ove, who came to Britain shortly before the riots, recalls that when he left the Caribbean he felt like he was 'coming to a paradise, like Alice in Wonderland'. The reality was a little less magical. London looked grey and drab compared with the vision of the imperial capital he had expected, the weather was cold and damp and there was the shock of being thrown among a white population. 'Nobody spoke to me when I said "good morning" and then a sea of white faces hit me.'

From a dispassionate perspective, the newcomers could not have been a more desirable body of workers. They helped to meet the post-war demand for labour, they paid their own passage here, and found their own accommodation and jobs without providing a drain on the nascent welfare state. By the mid 1950s, when machinery was lying idle because labour was in such short supply, employers began actively recruiting workers from the West Indies. In 1956 London Transport sent officials to Barbados to set up a scheme in which black people had their transport costs to Britain paid for them. As a result, by 1958 there were more than 8,000 West Indians working on the capital's buses and tubes.

But the reality of the welcome they experienced in Britain was more complicated. A belief prevalent in England in the 1950s was that most West Indians were poorly educated peasant people: a theory widely propounded in the press and even Parliament. A London newspaper complained shortly after the riots that England was becoming 'the dumping ground for the world's riff-raff' (*North London Press*, 8 May 1959), while in the House of Lords the Earl of Swinton declared that the great majority of West Indians coming to Britain were unskilled (*Parliamentary Debates*, Lords, 19 November 1958, col. 646).

The statistics tell a different story. It was estimated that 24 per cent of the newcomers had professional or managerial experience and a further 46 per cent were skilled workers. Indeed, the West Indies were losing the cream of their labour force to the Mother Country.

However, on arrival the newcomers were in for a rude awakening. They discovered that accountants could not hope to work in London as accountants, they would have to settle for a post as office clerk. Similarly, skilled technicians had to be content with a manual labouring job on the factory floor. When Horace Ove went for a job in an architects' office he was promptly told: 'We don't employ people like you.'

Throughout the 1950s, no black people were permitted to work in private companies in positions where they came into contact with the public because it was feared that customers would withdraw their trade. As one employer admitted: 'I know it is a terrible thing to say, but colour prejudice does exist and it is a risk we dare not take' (*The Times British Colonies Review*, 1st Quarter, 1957).

The West Indians were said, in prejudices commonly held at that time, to fight among themselves and to have a 'persecution complex' which made them react to any criticism as though it were racially motivated. They were accused by employers of being dirty, lazy, greedy for the highest rates of pay, threatening and abusive.

The trade unions' attitude to the black newcomers was hardly more welcoming. In towns such as Wolverhampoton and West Bromwich there were fully fledged strikes by the white workforce refusing to accept black colleagues, often with local trade union backing. Local branch officials adopted traditional union terminology to rationalise what was in effect a colour bar: black people, they said, were a threat to the English working class because they 'diluted' skills, even at a time of full employment.

Nationally, most national unions opposed the racial strikes and colour bars which brought them on occasion into direct conflict with their own local branches. In 1958 the National Musicians Union directed its Wolverhampton branch to boycott the Scala ballroom in protest against the dance hall's policy of refusing access to black people. Band members in Wolverhampton refused and were expelled from the union.

Overt colour bars operated in many entertainments such as public houses and dance halls. Pubs were regarded as liberal if they agreed to serve black people in the public bar—the lounge suites were universally considered above their station. George Powe, a Jamaican who fought in the British Army during the war and returned in 1950, remembers battling against colour bars. When he entered one pub alone he was told that single black men were not allowed in, so he returned with a group of white friends; this time he was told they didn't serve black men in the company of white women.

In August 1958, a few weeks before the riots erupted, the Mecca chain of dance halls was exposed in the press for operating its own peculiar form of colour bar in Birmingham, Nottingham and Sheffield. Only black men who brought their own partners would be let in and they were not allowed to 'pick up' another woman after entering. The chain's manager said it was not a colour bar, merely a question of mixing oil with water: 'Man from the beginning of time has always been suspicious of strangers,' he said (*The Times*, 28 August 1958).

These colour bars were allowed to flourish during the 1950s with remarkably little public comment or opposition. The law made no reference to racial discrimination. The established legal view was that the law must be 'colour blind' and should not distinguish between racial groups. As a result, it left no legal grounds for prosecuting those who practised discrimination, and black people had no positive redress: if they protested they were more likely to be arrested for causing a disturbance than the owner of the all-white premises.

III

After arriving at British ports the West Indians dispersed to those parts of the country where labour was most scarce and jobs easiest to find. Small communities began to form in England's manufacturing and industrial heartlands: in Birmingham, Manchester and Nottingham. London had the largest congregation, with 40,000 people of West Indian descent in 1958 (Wickenden, 1958, pp. 3–4).

One of the first hurdles they had to cross was the search for a roof over their heads. But the lack of official action against colour bars meant that discrimination that was experienced in employment and leisure was even more virulently expressed by landlords. When Baron Baker first went looking for accommodation, decked out in a smart suit and trilby, he first tried the Paddington area in west London, a run-down area in the 1950s full of seedy hotels and tawdry bedsits. Even so, whenever he applied for a room he received the same reply— 'No rooms to rent.'

Often landlords were more direct. They would place notices in the front windows saying, 'No rooms for coloureds to rent' or 'No coloureds, no dogs, Irish not required.' As Baron Baker put it: 'They didn't mind us fighting for them but when it came to living with them under one roof the iron gates slammed shut.' Some landlords banged the front door in Baker's face, others would make polite excuses about their husband or wife having just rented out the flat.

Discrimination in housing was widespread and entirely unabashed. One in eight 'To let' advertisements in a local paper in Notting Hill in 1958 stipulated that black people were not welcome. One landlady fainted on her doorstep when she saw her new black lodgers (Richmond, 1954, p. 73). Others took to throwing buckets of cold water over the heads of unsuspecting West Indian house-hunters. Not just the poorest black people suffered discrimination: even those who could afford to buy their own homes had to cope with it. Freeholders often wrote colour bars into the leases on their property. Fearing that if the building was sold to black people it would lose value they would insert clauses prohibiting sale to 'non-whites'.

With nowhere to go, the first West Indians to arrive in London after the war were literally forced on to the streets. Baron Baker ended up sleeping in charitable hostels for the homeless. More than once he spent the night in the Lyons Corner House, Piccadilly—a large entertainment centre with numerous restaurants and a dance floor that stayed open until the early hours.

Shunned in almost every quarter, the West Indians had no alternative but to live wherever landlords would take them. In London, as in most cities where the newcomers congregated, openings were very limited. They could rule out expensive and exclusive areas where even well-off black people would not be entertained. Staunch working-class districts were equally hard to penetrate.

Excluded from whole areas of London, they were trapped in the worst neighbourhoods, one of which was Notting Hill. Baron Baker was one of the first West Indian residents of the area, moving soon after the war into a house in Tavistock Road. 'My landlady's neighbours used to call her white-trash-nigger-lover for associating with me. But she was liberal-minded and didn't care.'

The West Indians made up for the shortage of accommodation open to them by looking out for each other. Fresh arrivals would be offered a floor to sleep on by friends until they found somewhere of their own. The handful of Notting Hill's black inhabitants grew into an entire community.

Notting Hill in 1958 was a varied and disparate area encompassing a cosmopolitan population and the extremes of wealth and poverty. Millionaires lived a street away from the destitute. The area was also centre of the empire of the notorious racketeering landlord, Peter Rachman. He came to England from Poland during the war without a penny to his name and died in 1962 a rich man. The fortune he made came from the cunning exploitation of his tenants, many of whom were West Indian. They were given tenancies on a weekly basis, with only a few hours' notice of eviction. Tenants would be crammed in six to a room, sometimes with beds occupied on a shift basis—day and night (*Observer*, 21 July 1963; *Sunday Times*, 6, 7, 21 July 1963; *Guardian*, 10 August 1963).

Hired henchmen accompanied by Alsatians made regular visits to his tenants to collect exorbitant rents and, as they knew that few other landlords would take them, they had no choice but to pay. 'They would beat you up as quick as look at you. If you didn't pay your rent on time there was no hope: you would be in hospital the same day,' a veteran of the area recalled.

Those who didn't would find all their belongings strewn across the street, rubbish emptied in the middle of the living room, itching powder sprinkled in their bedding or dead rats left under the sheets. Rachman once employed builders to lift off the roof of one of his houses to winkle out a particularly stubborn tenant (Crawford, 1963, p. 127).

Relations between the incoming black population of Notting Hill and the largely white population of neighbouring Notting Dale to the west were fraught from the start. Anti-black prejudices spread rapidly among people who were ignorant about the West Indies and the men and women who lived there were widely castigated as uneducated, lazy and corrupt. Of all the prejudices there was one burning passion that overshadowed the rest: the hatred expressed by white men in the area about sexual relations between white women and black men. Disapproval of miscegenation was rife. A woman interviewed after the riots whose daughter was living with a black man said: 'He's given her two little brown-skinned babies. Sweet they are, but I can't bear to look at them' (*Manchester Guardian*, 3 September 1958).

There was a common assumption that a white woman involved with a black man was bound to be a prostitute, as no 'respectable' woman would so demean herself. Needless to say, West Indians found the suggestion that only prostitutes were attracted to them highly offensive. 'If I was seen walking down the street with the Queen of England and nobody recognised who she was, it would be assumed she was a street girl,' said Baron Baker.

Virulent sentiments such as the fear of mixed relationships were exploited by extreme right groups to maximum effect in Notting Hill. Indeed, Notting Dale became one of the focal points of early post-war fascism. A number of splinter parties actively agitated among the white community, calling for repatriation of their West Indian neighbours.

The biggest and most influential was Oswald Mosley's Union Movement, the post-war version of his British Union of Fascists that had spearheaded attacks on Jewish people in London's East End in the 1930s. After the war he transferred his ire from Jews to blacks. Mosley wanted all black people to be repatriated, their boat fares to be paid for by the government (*Action*, 1958 *passim*).

Notting Hill held pride of place in the Union Movement's campaign to stir up racial unrest as its mix of a large West Indian population sitting next door to a stable and deeply prejudiced white community was a breeding ground for trouble. Throughout 1958 the party held regular meetings on street corners which were well attended, particularly by young white men, many of whom were Teddy Boys.

As the year progressed the fascists clearly felt that they were making headway among poor white communities such as Notting Dale. On 8 August, less than a month before the riots broke out, the Union Movement's paper, *Action*, made an accurate prediction: 'Times have changed. The people are waking up. Stick close, boys, hang on tight. There's a lot more coming' (*Action*, 8 August 1958).

IV

It all started one Saturday night, 23 August 1958, when a group of nine white youths crammed themselves into a car and set out on a pleasure tour of west London which was to end with three black men in hospital for several weeks and the nine youths locked up in prison for four years. Having been drinking in a pub called 'General Smuts' they cruised around Shepherd's Bush and Notting Hill 'nigger hunting'.

All the men were teenagers from west London. One lived in Hunt Street in the heart of the white working-class neighbourhood of Notting Dale. Why they embarked on a frenzy of race violence that night remains obscure. The leader of the Rugby Club in Notting Dale, where they were members, surmised it was because the centre was closed and being at a loose end the idea came to them to attack black people instead. 'Those sorts of boys take up any activity to break the boredom,' he said (Fyvel, 1963, p. 63).

They set out in the early hours, the boot of the car full of home-made weapons: a starting handle, air pistols, table legs, chains, iron-railings and four blocks of wood. Spotting the first solitary West Indian in a deserted street they pulled over, chased after the man and smashed him over the head with an iron bar. Then the teenagers calmly stepped back into the car and drove off. Between three and five o'clock in the morning they made three further attacks—the third in Notting Hill—seriously injuring five West Indians. Later, when the nine youths were hauled in front of the magistrates one of their victims had to be brought into court in a wheelchair. The magistrate, E.R. Guest, said he had 'never seen a man brought into court in such a state' (*Kensington News*, 29 August 1958; *Kensington Post*, 29 August 1958).

The following weekend, on Friday, 29 August, an incident occurred outside Latimer Road tube station in Notting Dale. A Swedish woman, Majbritt Morrison, was arguing with her Jamaican husband Raymond on the pavement. Noticing the row, curious white people began to gather round. Men started shouting at Mr Morrison, thinking it was their duty to protect a white woman from a black man. This display of chivalry failed to impress Mrs Morrison, however, who added fuel to the fire by protecting her husband against the growing crowd. In the eyes of white racists she had committed the ultimate sin by turning her back on her own race (Author's conversation with King Dick).

Just as the argument began to turn ugly, a group of the Morrison's West Indian friends stepped into the dispute. A fight broke out which was resolved without serious injury. But that was just the beginning. Word began to spread around the Dale that it was time to teach the 'niggers' and their 'white trash' a lesson. The following night the pubs were packed and bristling with anti-black sentiment. Instead of dispersing at closing time, men stood around in groups outside the pubs looking restive and aggressive.

As luck would have it, Majbritt Morrison was spotted walking towards them and a cacophany of jeers broke out. 'Nigger lover! Kill her!', they cried. She carried on walking straight ahead and was bruised by flying milk bottles before she reached home, where she found the police already waiting for her. They told her to go inside and when she refused she was arrested, charged with obstruction and held in Notting Hill police station until 5 a.m. the following morning (Morrison, 1964, pp. 28–30).

After she was led away, the crowd went on the rampage. Windows in side streets in Noting Dale were smashed and the police arrived just in time to prevent the crowd attacking a West Indian party. Opting for what they saw as the easiest means of defusing the crisis, constables carved a passage through the crowd and escorted the party-goers out of the area. This certainly averted a potentially disastrous confrontation by removing the object of the crowd's aggression, but it set an unfortunate precedent by seemingly confirming to the white rioters that through violence they could drive black people out of their neighbourhood.

Early in the evening of the following day, Sunday 31 August, a gang of about 100 white teenagers armed with sticks, iron bars and knives gathered under the railway arches outside Latimer Road station in Notting Dale. The crowd began to swell until by 8 p.m., 400 people were reported milling around the streets shouting, 'We'll kill the black bastards!' A group of West Indians were set upon, a woman stabbed in the shoulder and a boy, aged 10, hit in the mouth with a broken bottle (*Manchester Guardian*, 1 September 1958).

Black residents living in the area were startled by the fighting. 'It was totally unexpected. White people in hysterics, screaming "Let's lynch the niggers! Let's burn their homes!" ' said Baron Baker. Until the weekend of the riots, the West Indians had been accustomed to walking at night in groups for protection but now even that safeguard failed against the hordes of hostile whites. So they stayed indoors, in the hope that the crowds would fade away. Robbed of their prey, the white teenagers turned against the police accusing them of being 'nigger lovers'. Four officers were attacked and injured in one street, three in another. The fighting ran on sporadically for four hours until midnight (*Daily Mail*, 1 September 1958).

The following night Notting Hill experienced some of the worst rioting that Britain has seen this century. Already by the afternoon the area was gripped by an unhealthy mood and a tense atmosphere hung over it. Only a handful of black faces were seen outdoors. In an attempt to pacify the white crowds that began to gather again in the late afternoon, the local Labour MP, George Rogers, toured the area in a loud-speaker van appealing for calm, but to little avail (*Manchester Guardian*, 2 September 1958).

That afternoon a young African student, Seymour Manning, came down from Derby to visit a friend in Notting Dale, oblivious of the trouble. He walked out of Latimer Road station and was greeted by a wall of jeers coming from a large group of whites blocking the road. Manning froze, then spun on his heels and sprinted back towards the Underground. The gang caught up with him and he was thrown to the ground, kicked and his leg twisted. Somehow he managed to wriggle loose and again he ran for his life, finding safe haven in a greengrocer's shop. By good fortune, the owner of the shop was sympathetic and bolted the door against the crowd, now over 200 strong, baying 'Lynch him!' It took police on horseback and in radio squad cars, backed up by 20 constables on foot, half an hour to disperse the crowd before they could rescue Manning and escort him to safety (*Manchester Guardian*, 2 September 1958).

Although there is no evidence on which to base an accurate estimate, it appears that the rioters were acting with the blessing of the majority of Notting Dale's white community. The few white people from the neighbourhood who tried to stop the carnage were treated with disdain. Jean Maggs, who still lives in the area, remembers that one of her friends helped a black man who had been badly cut and was lying bleeding on the pavement. She called an ambulance and dressed his wounds with pieces of material torn from her clothing. When her brother found out that she had helped one of 'the enemy' he refused to talk to her for six months (Author's conversation with Jean Maggs).

There were a few examples of white people coming to the assistance of their black neighbours. Members of the local Communist Party, for example, ferried vulnerable individuals out of the worst trouble spots. But this was the exception to the rule. The author Colin MacInnes who lived in Notting Hill and described the riots in his novel *Absolute Beginners* expressed shock that apart from the woman in the greengrocer's there was such a passive response to the violence:

> What I'd seen made me feel weak and hopeless: most of all because except for that old vegetable woman no one, absolutely no one, had reacted against this thing. You looked around to find members of the other team—even just a few of us—and there weren't any. (MacInnes, 1980, p. 178)

Later that Monday night the fascists made their greatest impact. From the start of the riots the fascist groups were quick to make their presence felt. Broadsheets were distributed in the trouble spots. A far-right group, the National Labour Party, put out a tract called 'Look Out', which said:

> A square deal for the negro in his own country. Has a foreigner taken your job yet? Is a foreigner your employer? Does a foreigner represent you in Parliament? If not, then you are fortunate, for your country is steadily being taken over by the triumphant alien (*Kensington Post*, 12 September 1958).

Mosley's Union Movement also circulated a pamphlet in Notting Hill which advised the white population to 'Take action now. Protect your jobs. Stop coloured immigration. Houses for white people—not coloured immigrants.' On front of the pamphlet was a cartoon of a black man wearing a grass skirt and carrying a spear, above the caption: 'People of Kensington act now. Your country is worth fighting for. Fight with the Union Movement' (*Manchester Guardian*, 25 September 1958).

Local pubs provided the fascists with a vital platform. During the riots Notting Dale's pubs were crammed with white people of all ages and both sexes singing 'Old Man River' and 'Bye Bye Blackbird', punctuating the songs with vicious anti-black slogans and chants of 'Keep Britain white' (*The Times*, 3 September 1958).

At 8 p.m. that night Jeffrey Hamm, Mosley's number two in the Union Movement, gave a rousing speech to a crowd of about 700 people in front of Latimer Road station. Hamm was an able orator who knew how to manipulate his audience. He began in measured tones: black people should not be held responsible for the 'colour problem' and violence should be deplored, he said.

But gradually, as he warmed to his subject, his invective grew more extreme. Governments—both Labour and Tory—were the ones to blame, for allowing black people into Britain in the first place. Reaching the climax, he shouted: 'Get rid of them!' and threw hundreds of leaflets over the excited crowd. A cry exploded as the mob rushed off shouting 'Kill the niggers'. Women grabbed their small children and followed. Dogs ran in among the crowds, barking. Confusion reigned everywhere. Within half an hour the crowd, now over a thousand strong, had broken scores of windows. Women from the top floors laughed as they called down 'Go on boys, get yourselves some blacks' (*Kensington News*, 5 September 1958).

As news of the fighting spread through the media and by word of mouth, people were drawn into Notting Hill from other parts of London and as far away as Reading (*Kensington News*, 5 September 1958). Trouble began to spread like a bush fire and West Indians were attacked across London. A crowd of 150 white people blocked the tow-path along the canal which forms the northern boundary of Notting Hill and black people were chased and attacked.

In Paddington, a house was set ablaze by a gang of youths who smashed the front window with stones and threw lighted cloth soaked in paraffin into the living room. The Blue Parrot, a West Indian café in the Harrow Road, was wrecked by 800 bottle-throwing, club-wielding whites. It took over thirty policemen with a dozen squad cars and half-a-dozen Black Marias to clear the street. The terrified blacks inside had been bombarded with more than 300 milk bottles; everything in sight was smashed (*Kensington News*, 5 September 1958; *Daily Mail*, 2 September 1958).

Hundreds of outsiders descended on the riot area. The number 28 and 31 buses were full of 'English people coming to see the nigger run', as Chris Lemaitre, a Trinidadian then living in Notting Hill, recalls. The Underground trains were packed full of sightseers pouring in as though they were going to the funfair, many carrying weapons. Some came to ogle and gape, others to participate actively in the rioting. 'Notting Hill does not know what has hit it,' reported the *Manchester Guardian*.

> Among the faces, some of them distorted, some merely curious, that congregate along the pavements there lies an appalling pleasure with self. They are waiting for something to happen, and too many of them will be stirred to gratification when it does. (*Manchester Guardian*, 3 September 1958)

And it did. West Indians had to run the gauntlet between rows of whites lining the roads leading from Notting Hill tube station. Gangs of youths patrolled the streets armed with broken bottles, knives, sticks, chair and table legs, petrol bombs, iron bars and whips. Whites on motor-bikes toured the area looking for blacks to beat up. A Jamaican, King Dick, who bears a scar across his forehead where he was struck with a chain in the riots, remembers seeing a group of whites attacking a black woman. They casually kicked over the pram she was pushing, throwing her baby on to the pavement (Author's conversation). In another incident, a West Indian was slashed across the face with a knife. When the attacker was arrested he told the police: 'So a darkie gets chivved. Why all the fuss?' (*Manchester Guardian*, 4 September 1958).

One of the most extraordinary aspects of the riots was that while they raged in Notting Hill, outside this small patch of west London most people carried on their lives as though nothing was happening. Colin MacInnes wrote:

Believe me inside Napoli [Notting Hill] there was blood and thunder but just outside it—only across one single road like some national frontier—you were back in the world of Mrs Dale and What's My Line? and England's Green and Pleasant Land. Napoli was like a prison or concentration camp: inside, blue murder, outside, buses and evening papers and hurrying home to sausages and mash and tea. (MacInnes, 1980, p. 190)

The year before the riots, a distinguished Trinidadian journalist, Sir Charles Archibald, predicted racial violence and warned the black community in Britain that it would be incapable of defending itself. There was some truth in that, for the West Indian community in Notting Hill was indeed unprepared for the mass hostility against them.

For the first two nights of rioting they were dazed and shocked and stayed indoors in the hope that the violence would pass. But by the third day, the Monday, it began to dawn on them that a more active form of defence was required. 'We had to put our foot down. Our homes were being attacked and we had to fight back, which we did.'

On the Monday night West Indians in Notting Hill began to discuss what form that action could take. They congregated in a club called the Calypso where Michael de Freitas put the issue very bluntly: 'We don't want committees and representatives. We need as few pieces of iron and a bit of organisation so that tonight when they come in here we can defend ourselves' (Malik, 1968, pp. 76–9).

His words struck a chord. They gathered an armoury of makeshift weapons. 'Well, it was war, wasn't it?' says King Dick. As night fell they assembled in Blenheim Crescent—the men in number 9 which was a café frequented by West Indians and aptly nicknamed the Fortress, and the women in number 6. Three hundred West Indians crammed themselves into the two houses. The plan was to stay indoors, hidden, until the white crowd struck, when they were to use any and every means to repel the attack. King Dick had spent the afternoon collecting cans of petrol which he added with sand to milk bottles to make Molotov cocktails (Author's conversation).

As darkness fell the curtains of the two houses were tightly drawn and all the lights were out. Not a sound issued from either. White crowds, for the third day running, began milling around looking for blacks to attack and, knowing that number 9 was a café popular with West Indians, they gathered outside. 'We were all absolutely terrified,' remembers Baker. 'But we had decided to go down fighting. The crowds started to get worked up but they couldn't see us. When they started shouting "let's burn the niggers out", that's when we hit.'

Up shot the third-floor windows and out flew the Molotovs. Pandemonium ensued as the crowds scattered, dodging pieces of flying glass, with the West Indians in hot pursuit. Baron Baker shouted: 'Get back to where you come from'—enjoying the irony of the occasion (Author's conversation; Daily Mail, 2 September 1958).

By fighting back the West Indians added a new dimension to the riots, which now threatened to escalate into full-blooded racial war. For the police this was an alarming turn of events, caught as they were between a mass of violent white youths intent on killing 'nigs' and black people determined to defend themselves by any means necessary.

By Monday night the police finally brought reinforcements into Notting Hill from all over London and from other metropolitan forces in one of the largest crowd control operations of the decade. When the battle of Blenheim Crescent broke out they reacted swiftly. A Black Maria screeched into the road and rammed the front door of the Fortress. Eight West Indians, Baron Baker and Michael de Freitas included, and three whites were arrested and charged with affray (*Daily Mail*, 2 September 1958; *Kensington News*, 12 September 1958).

The next day, Tuesday 2 September, Notting Hill looked like a film set in the American South. People stood around in the heat outside their doors, leaned on balconies, or sat sweating behind the blistered window-sills of Rachman's properties. As it began to grow dark gangs of several hundred white youths began to assemble again. But it was on this fourth night of rioting that the police, who had until then been virtually overpowered by the crowds, at last gained the upper hand. It was described as a 'relatively quiet' night (*Manchester Guardian*, 3 September).

By the following day the crowds had noticeably thinned and only a few frightened faces were to be seen among the debris of bricks and broken glass that littered west London. Notting Hill was deathly quiet and unnaturally deserted. Pubs which had been packed during the riot weekend were now almost empty. The area had lost its concentration camp atmosphere; its enclosed claustrophobic feeling had gone as peace swept through the area. At 9.30 p.m. heavy thundering rain began to fall which would have dampened any violence had it not fallen on empty streets.

V

The riots hit black people like a bomb. The belief that they would be fully accepted as British citizens was badly, for some irrevocably, damaged. 'If I had money I'd tear out of this country fast,' a Jamaican living in Notting Hill said (*Daily Mail*, 3 September 1958). The image of Britain as the 'Mother Country' now looked like a cruel joke; all that remained was the daily drudgery of working to make ends meet. Elderly West Indians were the most severely affected. Sapped of strength and determination, they were left scared to go out of doors, humiliated and defeated.

Three weeks after the riots black people began leaving England by the trainload. Platform two at Victoria station was seething with homeward-bound West Indians. Their subdued mood was the antithesis of the effervescent high spirits of the passengers arriving on board the *Empire Windrush* exactly ten years previously. In a normal year, around 150 West Indians could be expected to go back to the Caribbean but in 1959 4,500 returned (Patterson, 1963, p. 44).

On a happier and more positive note, the riots helped to galvanise the nascent black community in Britain and led to the formation of their first organisations and publications. In Notting Hill a plethora of black groups sprang up, including Baron Baker's United Africa–Asia League which held open-air meetings in the area, the Association for the Advancement of Coloured People, run by Marcus Garvey's widow Amy, and the Coloured People's Progressive Association which adopted the motto: 'United we stand, divided we fall.'

. The rioting gave rise to some tough sentences that are still remembered by veteran white residents of Notting Hill. The nine white youths who had cruised around the area the week before the riots 'nigger hunting' were tried at the Old Bailey. Under cross-examination only one of the nine expressed any regret. The others offered comments such as 'Anyway, I hate niggers' or 'I whacked that nigger only a couple of times.' Summing up, Justice Salmon told them: 'It was you who started the whole of this violence in Notting Hill. You are a minute and insignificant section of the population and have filled the nation with horror, indignation and disgust.' He gave them each four years in prison (*The Times*, 16 September 1958).

In the weeks and months following the riots the Conservative government made no direct attempt to tackle the issues thrown up by the riots. There was no official investigation of the sort that Lord Scarman conducted into the 1981 Brixton riots. No more money was pumped into Notting Hill to improve its housing and Rachman's racket continued unhindered until his death in 1963.

In fact, one of the few government initiatives to flow from the riots was the Commonwealth Immigrants Act of 1962, which was heavily informed by the view that the only way to prevent further outbreaks of racial violence was to appease the racists by reducing the number of black people entering Britain. The riots of Notting Hill had claimed their prize.

Note

1. This is an edited version of Edward Pilkington, *Beyond the Mother Country: West Indians and the Notting Hill White Riots*, London, I.B. Tauris, 1988. Much of the material for this chapter was gained interviewing people who lived and worked in Notting Hill in 1958, both black and white.

References

Action, Journal of the Union Movement, 1958.

Crawford, Iain, 1963, *The Profumo Affair—A Crisis in Contemporary Society*, London, White Lodge Books.

Fyvel, Tosco, 1963, *The Insecure Offenders: Rebellious Youth in the Welfare State*, Harmondsworth, Penguin.

MacInnes, C., 1980 edn, *Absolute Beginners*, London, Allison & Busby.

Malik, M.A., 1968, *From Michael de Freitas to Michael X*, London, André Deutsch.

Morrison, M., 1964, *Jungle West 11*, London, Tandem Books.

Patterson, Sheila, 1963, *Dark Strangers: A Sociological Study of the Absorption of a Recent West Indian Migrant Group in Brixton, South London*, London, Tavistock Publications.

Richmond, Anthony, 1954, *Colour Prejudice in Britain: A Study of West Indian Workers in Liverpool*, London, Routledge and Kegan Paul.
Wickenden, J., 1958, *Colour in Britain*, Oxford, Oxford University Press.

10

The emergence of violent racism as a public issue in Britain, 1945–81

Benjamin Bowling

Conventional wisdom concerning the social problem of 'racial violence' may be summarised thus: after a period of relatively successful integration of large numbers of black and brown people arriving in Britain from the former Empire, racism suddenly flared into violence in the late 1970s or early 1980s. As the present collection of essays amply illustrates, however, racism has taken a violent form—fire-bombing, assault, harassment, intimidation, expulsion—throughout the history of ethnic minorities in Britain. This chapter reviews the academic literature and other documents on the subject from the post-war period until 1981, charting documented instances of violent racism and its emergence as a public issue.

This development is a complex one and any attempt at explanation must balance numerous important components. It is necessary to consider such factors as the specificity of English discourses of race and nation; the process of migration to Britain from the New Commonwealth and Pakistan; the development of explicitly racist and anti-racist political movements and the influence of racism on the political centre; and the extent of violent racism itself.

I

The period following the end of the Second World War marks an important juncture in the history of Britain's black population, of debates about 'race' and immigration, and, therefore, of the context within which violent racism takes place. Probably the most important development over this period is the onset of mass migration to Britain from the countries of its former empire.[1] This migration occurred for numerous reasons which can only be touched on here. Firstly, there was no legal restriction on the rights of British subjects to travel to or from the United Kingdom and elsewhere in the Empire. Under colonial rule, there was no distinction between British subjects born in the UK and those born elsewhere in the Empire; all had the right to enter the UK, find work and settle permanently. The 1948 British Nationality Act, which drew a distinction between citizens of the Commonwealth and those of the United Kingdom and Colonies, upheld the right of people born in such newly independent countries as India and Pakistan to come to Britain and had no impact on those countries which remained British. That colonial subjects enjoyed an inclusive British citizenship had implications that went beyond the possession of a legal right. For many, especially those who had contributed to the war effort, travelling to Britain was 'coming home' to the 'mother country'. This is not to deny the importance of colonial struggles for independence and oppositional politics. But none the less, the colonial education system had inculcated an inclusive notion of Britishness which was taken seriously. Many of the settlers from the colonies 'regarded themselves not as strangers, but as kinds of Englishmen. Everything taught in school ... encouraged this belief' (Deakin *et al.*, 1970).

Secondly, Britain was experiencing a shortage of labour in the effort to rebuild Britain's infrastructure and economy. The most important source of migrants to Britain from 1945 to 1951 was Europe from whence came as many as 300,000 people. During that period between 70,000 and 100,000 Irish people, some 128,000 Polish ex-servicemen and around 85,000 people from other east European countries settled in the UK (Solomos, 1989, p. 44; Rees, 1982, p. 83). The arrival in 1948 of the *Empire Windrush* at Tilbury docks in London carrying 492 Jamaicans has come to symbolise the onset of migration from the Caribbean (Solomos, 1989, p. 45; 21 25; Fryer, 1984, p. 372). However, although this migration from the Caribbean represented an unprecedented growth in Britain's black population, by 1958, migrants from the Caribbean still only totalled about 125,000. Between the mid-1950s and mid-1960s, migration from the Caribbean, and later from the Indian sub-continent, increased in volume. Over the next decades people who were facing economic uncertainty in the colonies and encouraged by British industry began to come to Britain in large numbers.[2]

It is during this period that the 'problem' of black immigration was constructed (Miles and Phizacklea, 1984, p. 24; Layton-Henry, 1984, pp. 16–30; Solomos, 1989, pp. 40-9). The political debate about immigration which had begun in the late 1940s began to focus increasingly throughout the 1950s on the need to control 'coloured' immigration. This debate, Solomos suggests, turned on two themes: firstly, revision of the 1948 Nationality Act so as to limit the number of black workers who could come and settle in the UK; and secondly, a parallel debate about 'the problems caused by too many coloured immigrants in relation to housing, employment and crime' (Solomos, 1989, p. 46).

The hostility of white Britons to the arrival of black migrants over this period does not seem to have been particularly extreme at first. Surveys cited by Banton (1983, 1985) suggest that during the early 1950s British people did not identify black people as a threat. Although racial prejudice was widespread, this tended to be based on beliefs about black people in the colonies, rather than in Britain itself. One survey found that two-thirds of Britain's white population held a low opinion of black people or disapproved of them. Those who were prejudiced saw black people as:

heathens who practised head-hunting, cannibalism, infanticide, polygamy and 'black magic'. They saw them as uncivilised, backward people, inherently inferior to Europeans, living in primitive mud huts 'in the bush', wearing few clothes, eating strange foods, and suffering from unpleasant diseases. They saw them as ignorant and illiterate, speaking strange languages, and lacking proper education. They believed that black men had stronger sexual urges than white men, were less inhibited, and could give greater satisfaction to their sexual partners. (Richmond, 1955, cited by Fryer, 1984, p. 374)

Half of this prejudiced two-thirds were 'extremely prejudiced'. These people:

strongly resisted the idea of having any contact or communication with black people; objected vehemently to mixed marriages; would not have black people in their homes as guests or lodgers; would not work with them in factory or office; and generally felt that black people should not be allowed into Britain at all. (ibid.)

These attitudes are reflected in the practices of employers, trade unions, landlords and local authorities over this period. On arrival in Britain, Caribbean and Asian people faced active discrimination in their search for jobs and homes, were ostracised socially and unrepresented politically. Colonial racism was transformed into indigenous racism.

II

By the end of the 1940s and into the 1950s there is evidence that violence was increasingly inflicted on black individuals and communities. Clearly, with attitudes such as those expressed above widespread, together with the enforced maintenance of the colour-bar, violence inflicted upon individual black people may well have been more prevalent than that which is recorded. Undoubtedly, there is scope for research to explore the oral history of violence among the first generation of black British and English people. What published documents there are focus on the several occasions in the late 1940s and throughout the 1950s when violence flared into visible public disorder.

In Birmingham in May 1948 a mob of between 100 and 250 white men besieged and stoned a hostel where Indian workers were living (Layton-Henry, 1984, p. 35). In August of the same year violence directed against unemployed black sailors broke out in Liverpool (Fryer, 1984, pp. 367–71). In July 1949, Deptford in south-east London was the scene of a serious disturbance which culminated in a siege of a black men's hostel by a white mob (Hiro, 1991, p. 38). In 1954 there were two days of violence in Camden Town, north London during which the home of a black family was petrol-bombed (Glass, 1960, cited in Layton-Henry, 1988, p. 35; Hiro, 1991).

By far the most serious outbreaks of violent racism during this period were the riots in Nottingham and west London in 1958 (Fryer, 1984; Miles, 1984; Pilkington, 1988). In both places sporadic attacks had occurred throughout the summer many of which were attributed to gangs of 'Teddy Boys' cruising the streets looking for West Indians, Africans or Asians (Fryer, 1984, p. 378; Hiro, 1991, p. 39). In Nottingham, where about 2,500 West Indians and 600 Asians were living, violence broke out at the end of August after an incident in which white people were said to have been stabbed (Miles and Phizacklea, 1984, p. 33). Then, on the evening of Saturday 30 August a crowd of white people— estimated to be as large as between 1,500 and 4,000 people (Layton-Henry, 1984, p. 35; Hiro, 1991, p. 39)—were on the streets shouting: 'Let's get the blacks' (Fryer, 1984, p. 377). However, the entire black community stayed indoors under a self-imposed curfew from Friday evening to Monday morning (Hiro, 1991, p. 39).

The outbreaks of disorder in Notting Hill and other parts of north Kensington in west London, which occurred between 23 August and 2 September, were, if anything, even more violent than those in Nottingham and involved extreme right-wing organisations including the Mosleyites (Hall *et al.*, 1978, pp. 333–4) who had been active for some time distributing leaflets, scrawling slogans, holding indoor meetings, and 'inciting the white people to "Act Now" to "Keep Britain White"' (Hiro, 1991, p. 39). In Shepherd's Bush a black-owned café was wrecked in July, and on 17 August a white crowd smashed the windows of a house occupied by black people. On 23 August gangs of Teddy Boys—probably influenced by the national radio and newspaper coverage of the Nottingham 'riots'—went 'nigger hunting' with iron bars, table legs and knives, leaving 'at least five blacks unconscious on the pavement' (Hiro, 1991, p. 39). As the *Manchester Guardian* put it, 'they chose streets where only an occasional black person was seen and then attacked in the ratio of six to one'. On 30 August widespread and vicious violence against black people and property occurred, including setting houses on fire (Hiro, 1991, p. 40). By the end of August racist attacks were a daily and nightly feature of life in north Kensington including shootings, petrol bombs, threatening letters and crowds hundreds strong shouting abuse at black people (Fryer, 1984, p. 379). The climax came on the night of 1 September and early hours of 2 September. After an open-air fascist meeting on Sunday 1st, a crowd of between 500 and 700 surged through north Kensington shouting 'Let's get the niggers', 'Lynch the blacks' and 'Give 'em to us and we'll string 'em up'. Attacks were also reported in other nearby parts of London, including Latimer Road, Harrow Road, Kensal Green and north Paddington; they were also reported further afield in Southall, Hornsey, Islington, Hackney and Stepney. In all, 177 people were arrested (Fryer, 1984; Hiro, 1991). By mid-September 1958 things had subsided to a ' "normal" incidence of racist violence' (Fryer, 1984, p. 380), though further tragedy occurred the following year in north Kensington when in May 1959 a West Indian carpenter, Kelso Cochrane, was stabbed to death by a gang of white youths (Layton-Henry, 1984, p. 112).

The 1958 riots are cited by many authors as a watershed in the politics of 'race' (Solomos, 1989, p. 48; Layton-Henry, 1984, p. 35; Hiro, 1991, pp. 38–49; Miles and Phizacklea, 1983, pp. 33–8). The riots and the media coverage which surrounded them brought the presence of black people and the problems associated with them to the centre of the political stage. The riots also served to politicise the black settlers. Four main constructions of the problem of the riots and solutions to them have been identified and should be mentioned here. The problem was identified, firstly, as a lack of respect for law and order by an unrepresentative section of British society, and, in particular, by the Teddy Boys. Although the Teds had been around since 1953 and had already become something of the 'folk devil' by 1956, it was this violence that fuelled one of the first 'moral panics' defining youth as a problem (Cohen, 1972: Cashmore, 1984). There was widespread condemnation of the riots by politicians, church leaders and leader writers in the press. Gaitskell, the Labour leader, wrote in *The Times* (4 September 1958): 'Whatever local difficulties there may be, nothing can justify the riots and hooliganism of the past few days'. The response to this 'hooliganism' was to be found in strict enforcement of the law. Nine youths were convicted of assault during the disturbances and were given 'deterrent' sentences which gained widespread public satisfaction.[3]

A second reaction to the riots 'was to assume that they were a response by host populations who felt under pressure from the new immigrant population and that the answer was immigration control' (Layton-Henry, 1984, p. 36). For some observers, the large number of people involved in the riots suggested, firstly, that it was not only young thugs who were involved in the violence and, secondly, that they represented only the most extreme manifestation of more widespread racial resentment of, and hostility towards, coloured immigration. Several commentators, most notably Cyril Osborne, Conservative MP for Louth, had been campaigning for immigration control since the mid-1950s. Osborne had been active in Parliament, within the Conservative Party and in the media on the issues of disease and crime among black immigrants and advocated immigration controls as the solution. On 27 August, *The Times* printed a story under the headline 'Nottingham MPs Urge Curb on Entry of Immigrants' in which two Nottingham MPs criticised the 'open door policy'. The following day, *The Times* followed this up with a story headlined 'Renewed Call for Changes in Immigration Law', which reported the views of Norman Pannell and Cyril Osborne calling for restrictions in coloured immigration. Lord Salisbury stated that he was: 'extremely apprehensive of the economic and social results, for Europeans and Africans alike, that were likely to flow from unrestricted immigration of men and women of the African race into Britain' (*Manchester Guardian*, 3 September 1958). It was not only those on the right of the Conservative Party who favoured controls, however. Mr George Rogers, Labour MP for North Kensington, told the *Daily Sketch*:

> The government must introduce legislation quickly to end the tremendous influx of coloured people from the Commonwealth ... Overcrowding has fostered vice, drugs, prostitution and the use of knives. For years the white people have been tolerant. Now their tempers are up. (*Daily Sketch*, 2 September 1958)

Most of those on the left condemned the riots as hooliganism, while others offered a third—'rarely heard, yet most accurate'—explanation for the riots—racial prejudice (Miles and Phizacklea, 1984, p. 34). Its proponents called for action to eliminate discrimination from British society (ibid.). For example, the Labour Party chairman Tom Driberg told the Trades Union Congress:

People talk about a colour problem arising in Britain. How can there be a colour problem here? Even after all the immigration of the past few years, there are only 190,000 coloured people in our population of over 50 million—that is, only four out of every 1,000. The real problem is not black skins, but white prejudice. (*Report of Proceedings at the 90th Trades Union Congress . . . 1958*, p. 326)

Fourth, the riots spurred the formation of black self-defence organisations and the development of community-support networks. Once black people had overcome their initial shock, alarm and despondency about the assault that they had experienced, they began to organise to help themselves. They provided escorts for those black employees of London Transport who had to work late-night or early-morning shifts and formed vigilante groups who patrolled the area in cars (Hiro, 1991, p. 40). Black community organisations had begun to emerge in the years prior to 1958, but the riots served to forge a new-found black community identity. In the immediate aftermath of the riots, Norman Manley, Prime Minister of Jamaica, and Carl Lacorbiniere, Deputy Chief Minister of the West Indian Federation flew to London for a tour of the riot areas, with the specific objective of reassuring the West Indian migrants and for consultations with the British government (Hiro, 1991, p. 41). Later, in December 1958, officials of the West Indian Federation helped to organise the West Indian Standing Conference to act as an umbrella for British West Indian organisations which was inaugurated in Birmingham a year later (ibid.).

III

The period between 1958 and 1968 is that in which British political debates became 'racialised' and in which 'race' became politicised (e.g. Miles, 1984; Solomos, 1989). Immigration control was not an issue in the 1959 General Election and neither was there provision for a debate about immigration at the 1960 Conservative Party annual conference (Layton-Henry, 1984, p. 38). At this time the majority of the Conservative government and the Labour opposition considered the Commonwealth an asset and were reluctant to take any action which might undermine the principle of the Commonwealth or Britain's moral authority at its centre. During 1960, however, the campaign for the control of black immigration within the Conservative Party, Parliament and the media gathered strength. This debate, which focused on the dangers of unrestricted migration and the problems associated with the presence in Britain of black people, led to the introduction of the Commonwealth Immigrants Bill in 1961 (Solomos, 1989, p.51). The Act was fiercely opposed by Gaitskell and the Labour Shadow Cabinet, who accused the government of betraying the Empire and the Commonwealth.

The Act which came into effect on 1 July 1962 was only a mild measure of control, introducing a system of employment vouchers for Commonwealth immigrants (Layton-Henry, 1984, p. 42). Although immigration from the New Commonwealth fell after the Act was passed, public concern over immigration was not allayed for long. Rather, 'the salience of immigration as an issue was greatly raised by [the Act's] controversial passage' (ibid.). Between 1962 and 1964 'the mood of the Conservative Party swung strongly in support of tougher controls', while the Labour Party abandoned its principled opposition to the Bill. In 1963, the new leader of the Labour Party, Harold Wilson, said that Labour did not contest the need for immigration control, but that it should be negotiated with Commonwealth countries. The position, together with a promise to 'legislate against racial discrimination and incitement in public places and give special help to local authorities in areas where immigrants have settled' formed the basis for their 1964 election manifesto (Labour Party, *Manifesto*, 1964).

The 1964 General Election, and in particular the nature of the campaign fought by Peter Griffiths in the West Midlands town of Smethwick, had 'a deep impact on both the local and national political scene' (Solomos, 1989, p. 53). Although immigration control was not an important issue in the national campaigns of the parties, the issue of black immigration was frequently raised. But it was when Peter Griffiths dramatically unseated Patrick Gordon-Walker, the Labour Shadow Foreign Secretary, that the electoral impact of the issue became clear. Griffiths had fought the election largely on a platform of defending the local white majority against the 'influx of immigrants'. When commentating on the slogan 'If you want a nigger neighbour, Vote Labour' which had been used during the campaign, Griffiths is reported to have said, 'I think that it is a manifestation of popular feeling. I should not condemn anyone who said that' (*The Times*, 9 March 1964). The result, which showed clearly that racial prejudice could be exploited for electoral advantage, was a 'shattering result and a disaster for race relations' (Layton-Henry, 1984, p. 57).

The Labour government, which was returned to power in 1964 with only a small majority, seemed vulnerable on the issue of immigration. In response, the government worked hard to establish a 'bipartisan consensus' on the issues of 'race' and immigration. This consensus consisted of a dual policy of strict immigration controls, on one hand, and positive measures to assist the integration of those immigrants already settled in Britain, on the other (Layton-Henry, 1984, p. 62). In an effort to consolidate this consensus and to offset the anti-immigration feeling which was growing in certain parts of the country, the White Paper *Immigration from the Commonwealth* was published. The Race Relations Bill, which outlawed racial discrimination in places of public resort and created the offence of incitement to racial hatred, was also passed in 1965.

In 1967 a renewed campaign for control was instigated by Enoch Powell, among others, which focused around the growing influx of British Asians from Kenya. This campaign reached a climax in February 1968, when, amid a media-generated moral panic, the second Commonwealth Immigrants Act was introduced. This Act, which was designed specifically to control the flow of East African Asians holding British passports, restricted immigration to those with close ties to the UK by birth, naturalisation or descent. During this period, Labour was forced further on to the defensive by Powell's 'rivers of blood' speech in Birmingham in April 1968. In highly emotive language Powell warned of what he saw as the dangers of immigration leading to a 'total transformation to which there is no parallel in a thousand years of British history' and of the increasing racial tensions that would result. According to Powell, the long-term solution to this problem went beyond immigration control to include the repatriation of immigrants already settled in the UK. Although he was sacked from the Shadow Cabinet as a result of this speech, Powell and his campaign became very popular with the electorate, inspiring demonstrations all over the country such as the strike by dockers and porters from London's Smithfield market who marched to Westminster in his support.

Although violent racism was not a particularly salient political issue between 1958 and 1968, attacks and disturbances were reported in key areas across the country. Anti-black riots occurred in the West Midlands towns of Dudley and Smethwick in 1962, in Wolverhampton in 1965 (Reeves, 1989, p. 44); and in Accrington and Leeds in 1964 (Hartley, 1973 cited in Pearson, 1976).

One of the more serious incidents in Dudley in 1962 was triggered by a fight outside a public house in which three black men were injured. Subsequently, 'a chanting mob of white people brandishing sticks, chair legs, coshes and bottles marched "like a pack of wolves to their prey" into a street where a number of black people lived' (Reeves, 1989). Over the following two nights crowds 300-strong gathered to hunt for, and beat up, black people. In Wolverhampton in 1965 a crowd of about 150 white people attacked a house occupied by Jamaicans (ibid.).

In 1964, there were around 250 Pakistani residents in Accrington, the population of which was around 37,000. Geoff Pearson winessed the 'trouble' which flared up after a white man died, allegedly stabbed by a Pakistani in a fight outside a coffee bar. Pearson describes seeing a gang of between 100 and 200 white youths and men aged between 15 and 30 moving down the main street of the town in search of 'Pakis'. Many of the gang carried chains, belts and sticks, and others had large, menacing dogs, 'most of which seemed to be Alsatians'. As the 'mob' moved down the street a few Pakistanis who were standing at bus queues were knocked down, beaten and trampled on.[4] A couple of police cars hovered about, but made no attempt to interfere. Over the next few days there were sporadic attacks on immigrants. The streets in which they lived were invaded, windows broken, the curtains of their houses set on fire, Muslim food-shops were wrecked and vandalised. Finally, several men were arrested when they appeared in the centre of the town with a double-barrelled shotgun shouting 'Black bastards. Stop or we will shoot you'.[5] Eight of 'the lads' were charged with, and four gaoled for, a range of offences including threatening behaviour, behaviour likely to cause a breach of the peace, possession of an offensive weapon, assaulting a police officer, damage to the door of a police cell. However, they were not charged with assaulting the Pakistanis. Indeed no one was charged with assault during the 'brief season of paki-bashing' in Accrington (Pearson, 1976, p. 52).

IV

The speeches made by Enoch Powell and others, and the tremendous publicity which they generated after 1968, changed the terms of political debate about black people and race relations, thereby destroying the 'bipartisan consensus' on race and immigration created by the Labour government. Firstly, the debate was shifted further towards the need for firm immigration controls; secondly, the debate focused on 'repatriation' of Commonwealth migrants already living in Britain; thirdly, the moral panic which was generated about immigration and the presence of black people provided the political space for the emergence of new and explicitly racist political forces.

Powell delivered his 'rivers of blood' speech three days before the parliamentary debate on the Race Relations Bill. The Bill, the purpose of which was to establish equality of treatment in housing and employment, was supported by the liberal wing of the Conservative Opposition as well as some members of the Shadow Cabinet, though the majority of back-bench and constituency opinion was opposed to the Bill. Powell attacked the Bill, playing on fears that it would place black immigrants in a privileged position. Using reported incidents and conversations he raised fears of immigrant invasion and take-over of streets and areas, and fears that old people would face harassment by 'grinning piccanninies' (Layton-Henry, 1984, p. 71). Despite the opposition which Powell had generated, the Act which outlawed discrimination, expanded the Race Relations Board and established the Community Relations Commisssion was passed in November 1968 (ibid., p. 72; Gay and Young, 1988).

The campaign waged by Enoch Powell and the public support which he generated during the summer of 1968 forced the Conservative Party Leadership to abandon the ideal of Commonwealth citizenship to which it had been firmly committed ten years previously. In response to Powell, Edward Heath, leader of the Opposition, gave several speeches calling for an end to immigration, demanding that a check should be kept on Commonwealth immigrants during their first four years and reaffirming the Party's policy of financial assistance to those migrants who wished to return to their country of origin. By now Powell was going further, arguing in November 1968 for a Ministry of Repatriation which would embark upon 'a programme of large scale voluntary but organised, financed and subsidised repatriation and re-emigration' of Commonwealth settlers. By June 1969 Powell had devised a scheme to repatriate 700,000 coloured immigrants which he costed at £300 million. In the run-up to the 1970 General Election the Conservatives were seen as the party most likely to 'keep immigrants out' (Butler and Stokes, 1974), reflecting the Conservative Manifesto which proposed still tighter control on Commonwealth immigrants along the lines proposed by Heath (Hiro, 1991, p. 251).

One of the early tasks of the newly-elected Conservative government was the passage of the 1971 Immigration Act. This Act, which replaced all the legislation of the 1960s, based immigration control around a single distinction between 'patrials' and 'non-patrials'. A patrial refers to persons born, adopted, naturalised or registered in the UK, or born of parents one of whom had UK citizenship, or one of whose grandparents had UK citizenship. Patrials had the right to live in Britain, while non-patrials holding British passports did not (though there was a system of vouchers which allowed a limited number of non-patrial British and Commonwealth passport holders to enter the country). The hope of the Conservative leadership that this legislation would finally end the immigration debate and defuse the 'race issue' was shattered, however, in August 1972 when General Idi Amin, President of Uganda, announced the expulsion of all Asians living in his country (Layton-Henry, 1984, p. 81). As most of these people were eligible for British passports, it was clear that Britain was primarily responsible for them. The announcement that 50,000 Asians might head for Britain was received with a large amount of hostile media coverage and racist rhetoric from some politicians, particularly Powell. Despite the Powellites lobbying MPs and the Home Office with reference to election promises, the Heath government decided that Britain would have to accept these British passport holders and 27,000 people from Uganda subsequently arrived in the UK. What became known as the 'Ugandan Asians crisis' received a great deal of media attention and acted as a major boost to anti-immigrant organisations both within the Conservative Party (such as the Monday Club) and further to the right (such as the National Front) (ibid.). This panic about immigration and the presence of black people, together with what many on the right saw as Heath's betrayal of the British nation, signalled a new development in British right-wing politics.

V

The National Front was a direct descendant of the far-right parties of earlier periods.[6] In late 1966 the leaders of the British National Party (BNP) and the League of Empire Loyalists (LEL) agreed the terms of a merger and in February 1967 the National Front was formed from these two organisations together with a section of the Racial Preservation Society. Later the Greater Britain Movement, led by John Tyndall, merged with the NF.[7] The aims of the party, led by A.K. Chesterton, were to provide a new arena for far-right activism outside the Conservative Party as an independent political organisation. It declared a commitment to parliamentary democracy, opposed entry to the European Economic Community, and advocated a strengthening of 'law and order' and a 'reconstruction' of the Empire (Miles and Phizacklea, 1984, p. 121). Most important for the current discussion, the National Front 'enthusiastically adopted the Powellite idea of repatriating black and Asian immigrants' (Hiro, 1991, p. 254).

Powell's campaign brought direct benefit to the National Front by giving tremendous publicity to the race issue which was their major *raison d'être* and by legitimating consideration and support for policies like repatriation (Layton-Henry, 1984, p. 92). The National Front began to field candidates in the 1969 local elections and put up ten candidates in the 1970 General Election where they averaged only 3.5 per cent of the vote. The 'Ugandan Asians crisis' of 1972 stimulated rapid growth for the National Front which, by 1973, claimed a membership of 14,000 organised into thirty-two branches and eighty groups (Nugent and King 1977, p. 175). In the May 1973 by-election in West Bromwich the NF candidate, Martin Webster, gained 4,789 votes, 16 per cent of the poll. In the General Election of February 1974 the National Front fielded fifty-four candidates, all of whom lost their deposit. In the second General Election of that year (in October) the National Front fielded ninety candidates, thus gaining television and radio broadcasting time. The election brought poor results, averaging only 3.1 per cent of the vote, with only their best results in London, Leicester, Wolverhampton and West Bromwich gaining more than 4.5 per cent of the vote.

In May 1976 a new immigration scare erupted when small numbers of Asians from Malawi began to arrive in Britain as a result of restrictive measures taken against them by the Malawi government. These Asians were UK passport holders entitled to come to Britain under the quotas established for non-patrials in 1968. The news that some of these migrants were being put up by West Sussex Council in a four-star hostel prompted a rash of headlines such as 'Scandal of £600 a week immigrants' (*Sun*, 4 May), 'New Flood of Asians in Britain' (*Daily Mirror*), '4 star Asians run up £4,000 bill' (*Sun*, 7 May). This panic led to further scare stories about the supposed extent of illegal immigration—'Immigration racket row' (*Daily Express*, 25 May), and about the scale of future immigration from the Indian sub-continent—'New Asian invaders' (*Sun*, 17 May, cited in Gordon and Rosenberg, 1989, p. 23). The National Front responded to this opportunity by organising symbolic acts of 'territorial reoccupation' in the form of demonstrations and meetings in areas populated by New Commonwealth migrants and their children (Miles and Phizacklea, 1984). In the local elections which followed this panic in 1976 and 1977, the NF obtained over 10 per cent of the vote in twenty-five districts and just over 20 per cent in two. In the 1977 Greater London Council election, the National Front contested 91 of the 92 seats. The East End provided nearly one-third of its total vote, the party gaining more than 20 per cent of the vote in some constituencies. After this success, however, the National Front began to decline in importance as a political force and in the 1979 General Election the party suffered electoral disaster and eventual fragmentation and collapse.

The National Front and the racism which it propagated did not go unchallenged during this period. During the mid-1970s, new movements began to develop from the self-defence and anti-racist movements of the 1950s and early 1960s, and from left-wing anti-fascist action. In June 1974 anti-fascists organised a march to Conway Hall in Red Lion Square, central London, to picket a National Front meeting. The resulting clash between the NF, anti-fascist demonstrators and the police led to the death of a demonstrator, Kevin Gately, who was on the International Marxist Group contingent on the march (Gilroy, 1987, p. 118). Between 1973 and 1976 a network of anti-fascist/anti-racist committees was formed, a development which gathered momentum after the 1976 elections in most towns and cities with large black populations (Gilroy, 1987, p. 119; Layton-Henry, 1984, p. 101). In February 1975 the anti-fascist magazine *Searchlight* was founded to challenge the electoral and popular support of the NF. Rock Against Racism was formed in August 1976 by a small group of activists associated with the Socialist Workers' Party, and in November 1977 the Anti-Nazi League was formed (Gilroy, 1987, pp. 120–30).

Opposition to the NF was also growing within the Labour Movement during this period. Following an internal report on the growing electoral success of the

National Front in September 1976, the National Executive Committee (NEC) of the Labour Party agreed to launch a campaign against racism jointly with the TUC. The 1976 TUC Annual Conference passed numerous resolutions against racism while the Labour Party conference which followed passed resolutions demanding the repeal of the 1968 and 1971 Immigration Acts. Both the TUC and the Labour Party conferences passed resolutions calling for a campaign against racialism, and advising all Labour councils to ban the use of council property by the far right and to lend their support to the formation of local anti-fascist committees (Layton-Henry, 1984, p. 100; Miles and Phizacklea, 1984, p. 103).

During the period following Powell's speeches at the end of the 1960s racial tension reached a peak and violent racism was reported in many locations across Britain. Although the term 'wog-bashing' has been used to describe violence such as that inflicted on black communities by the Teddy Boys in the late 1950s, the label 'Paki-bashing' is said by several authors to have emerged at some point in 1969 or 1970 (*Race Today*, 1969–71; Pearson, 1976; Layton-Henry, 1984, p. 112). It seems that at the turn of the decade there was a real upsurge in violent racism and also 'the emergence of a "moral panic" when the official and semi-official view of "public opinion", the mass media, the courts and the police found a new word to describe acts of "unprovoked assault" on people who are said to be racially inferior' (Pearson, 1976, p. 50). The violence itself can be associated with three inter-related developments: a wider moral panic about immigration and 'race' stimulated by the Powellites; the emergence of, and widespread public support for, the National Front; and the emergence of a new, violent and explicitly racist youth culture—the skinheads.

The skinheads emerged at the end of the 1960s, first in the East End of London and then elsewhere in Britain. The skins adopted a uniform with half-mast trousers, braces, 'bovver boots' and close-cropped hair which seemed to some authors to be 'at one and the same time, both a caricature and a re-assertion of solid, male, working-class toughness' (Mungham and Pearson, 1976, p. 7). The skinhead style with its 'severe and puritanical self-image [and] formalized and very "hard" masculinity' (Clark and Jefferson, 1976, p. 156) lent itself to an overtly violent stance towards 'Pakis' and 'queers'. The skins had a strong sense of class and geographical location: 'The importance of one's own patch, one's own football team, and the defence of working-class territory and neighbourhood loomed large in the skinhead's lifestyle' (Mungham and Pearson, 1976, p. 7). This territorial defensiveness is closely linked to Paki-bashing as a 'ritual and aggressive defence of the social and cultural homogeneity of the community against its most obviously scapegoated outsiders' (Clarke, 1975, p. 102, cited by Cashmore, 1984). Paradoxically, while Asians were the explicit focus of skinhead violence, the first skinheads listened and danced to West Indian musical forms of rock-steady, and later ska (Cashmore, 1984, pp. 32–3).

In 1970, in the East End of London, a 'wave' of Paki-bashing broke out. Over a three-month period, 150 people were seriously assaulted in the area and in April, Tosir Ali, a kitchen porter was stabbed to death only yards from his home in Bow (Gordon, 1990/1986, p.2). On one day in April 1971 arson attacks against West Indians were reported in Forest Gate and on an Asian family in

Manor Park (Newham Monitoring Project, 1991). Violent racism was also reported in schools in east London, two schools in particular gaining notoriety as those 'where "Paki-bashing" and "Nigger-bashing" were the norm' (Newham Monitoring Project, 1991, p. 26). In 1972, a young Sikh boy was stabbed at one of these schools by a white youth who told him, 'Unless you cut your hair and stop wearing your turban, we will kill you.' In another incident an 11-year-old boy, Sohail Yusaf, was beaten on his way home from school and left unconscious on a building site (ibid.).

In 1973 there were three apparently racist killings in Coventry, Leicester and Birmingham (Gordon, 1990, p. 8). In south London in 1975 a black bus conductor was fatally injured after a row over a fare for a dog. In Glasgow in the same year a West Indian man was shot dead by Brian Hosie, a National Front member who claimed to be pursuing his policy to 'boost emigration [and] start extermination'. At the time he told the police, 'Niggers mean nothing to me. It was like killing a dog' (*Searchlight*, 'The Murderers Are Amongst Us', p. 5; Gordon, 1990, p. 2). Violent racism hit a new peak in the wake of the anti-immigration reporting of the arrival of Asians from Malawi in May 1976. Following this media coverage black peoples' shops, homes and community organisations were stoned and set on fire in east London and Southall (Gordon and Rosenberg, 1989, p. 23). In the same month two Asians, Dinesh Choudhury and Ribhi Al Haddida, were killed in Essex; in June, Gurdhip Sing Chaggar was murdered in Southall and Emmanuel Alombah was murdered in west London; and in August, Mohan Gautam was murdered in Leamington Spa (Gordon, 1990, p. 8).

There is little doubt that while these killings were the result of the most extreme form of violent racism, less extreme variants of the same phenomenon were felt by minority individuals and communities across the country. Some of the violence inflicted on black and other ethnic minorities over this period can be directly attributed to members of far-right political parties and fascist sympathisers (*Searchlight*, 'The Murderers Are Amongst Us'). However, much of the violence seems more easily attributable to the mobilisation of white community hostility against black people. In some instances, this hostility was mobilised specifically by low-visibility activity of the far right. But it was mobilised and legitimated more generally through the rascist rhetoric of the news media and right-wing politicians.

Evidence of the direct involvement of far-right groups such as the National Front in violent racism was gathered during the mid-1970s by Paul Rose, MP. In February 1975 he founded an organisation to combat fascist and racist groups and in August that year he presented evidence of over 1,000 incidents of far-right political violence to the Home Secretary (Fielding, 1981, p. 177). This violence, Rose suggested, was not an organised campaign but rather, emerged from a culture in which violence was accepted or approved of. Nigel Fielding's detailed study of the National Front also provides evidence of 'covert action by the NF' (ibid.). Fielding notes that there is a difficulty in separating out covert attacks actually carried out by the NF against the 'coloured community' from 'those done by local residents in situations of racial harassment', though, given the level of local support for the NF over this period, perhaps the distinction is truly blurred. Fielding cites evidence linking the NF to a series of fire-bomb attacks, racist leafleting and attacks on a Community Relations Office in London during the mid-1970s (Fielding, 1981, p. 177–85). In 1974 an NF member who recruited outside West Ham football ground, speaking to *Skin*, a London Weekend Television programme, said, 'We used to buy the kids a few drinks, then wind them up and send them off to smash up a Paki's home. We just sat back. They did it all for us.'[8]

There is some evidence of direct links between racially inflammatory media reports and the incidence of violent racism. For example, the sensationalist reporting of the arrival in Britain of Asians expelled from Malawi was followed by an upsurge in racial attacks. Within twenty-four hours of the *Sun* reporting '3,000 Asians Flood Britain', an Asian-owned newsagent's shop in East London was daubed with the slogans '3,000 moor' (sic) and 'Packie Patel' and the following week the offices of the Joint Council for the Welfare of Immigrants narrowly escaped serious damage after an arson attempt (Gordon and Rosenberg, 1989, p. 10). At the time the journalist Paul Foot commented:

> Race hate and race violence does not rise and fall according to the numbers of immigrants coming into Britain. It rises and falls to the extent to which people's prejudices are inflamed and made respectable by politicians and newspapers. ('What the Papers Say', Granada TV; cited in Gordon and Rosenberg, 1989, p. 23)

VI

Several important political developments occurred between 1978 and 1981 which should be mentioned at this point. Firstly, between 1976 and the 1979 General Elections the rhetoric of the Conservative Party, and particularly of the Leader of the Opposition, Margaret Thatcher, took an increasingly anti-immigration stance. Secondly, in the late 1970s anti-racist organisations grew in strength and visibility, opposing the National Front wherever they marched. Thirdly, a new cross-party group, the Joint Committee Against Racialism, was formed, which was to play a crucial role in bringing official recognition to the problem of racial attacks. Fourthly, in the 1979 General Election the National Front suffered complete electoral disaster followed by political decline and fragmentation.

After narrowly losing the 1974 General Election, the Conservative Party became more aware of the electoral importance of white resistance to black immigration (Layton-Henry, 1984, p. 103). The success of the National Front during the mid-1970s gave a clear indication that 'race' and the fears of the white electorate could be exploited for political purposes. Anti-immigration feelings were clearly evident within the Conservative Party, which, for example, brought forward 140 resolutions on immigration at the annual party conference in October 1976, following the Malawi Asians panic earlier that year. Mrs Thatcher, the new leader of the Opposition, decided that the party should harden its attitude towards immigration, and the Home Secretary, William Whitelaw, said that the party would develop a policy which would end 'immigration as we have seen it in the post-war years' (Layton-Henry, 1980, p. 67; Layton-Henry, 1984, p. 104). On 30 January 1978, Margaret Thatcher stated in a television interview that 'People are really rather afraid that this country might be rather swamped by people with a different culture', and 'We do have to hold out the prospect of an end to immigration except, of course, for compassionate cases'. She said that while the Conservatives would not be highlighting immigration in the forthcoming election, it was important for major parties not to neglect people's fears about immigration, which otherwise would drive them to the National Front. When George Burns, the interviewer, asked, 'So, some of the support that the National Front has been attracting in recent by-elections you would hope to bring back behind the Tory party?' she replied, 'Oh, very much back, certainly, but I think that the National Front has, in fact, attracted more people from Labour voters than from us. But never be afraid to tackle something people are worried about. We are not in politics to ignore people's worries; we are in politics to deal with them' (Granada Television, 'World in Action', 30 January, 1978, cited in Layton-Henry, 1984, p. 104). Although Mrs Thatcher's comments were condemned as pandering to popular prejudice and even as 'giving aid and comfort to the National Front' (*The Sunday Times*, 26 February 1978), their effect was to boost support for the Conservatives and to undermine popular support for the NF (Hiro, 1991, p. 257). While Labour and Conservatives had been neck and neck in the opinion polls conducted in January 1978 prior to this speech, immediately afterwards the polls showed an increase in 9 percentage points in electoral support for the Tories over from Labour. Moreover, those who regarded immigration as one of the two most urgent problems facing the country leapt from 9 to 21 per cent (ibid.).

The Conservative Party entered the 1979 General Election campaign committed to tightening immigration controls. The manifesto promised: a new British Nationality Act to define entitlement to British citizenship; an end to allowing permanent settlement for those coming for a temporary stay; limits on the entry of the families of those already settled; restrictions on the issue of work permits; the introduction of a quota system to control all entry for settlement. Although there could be 'no question of compulsory repatriation' the Conservatives promised 'firm action against illegal immigrants and over-stayers and help to those immigrants who genuinely wish to leave this country' (Conservative Central Office, *Party Manifesto*, 1979). This tough line on immigration was accompanied by rhetoric which emphasised the dual approach to race relations, namely that racial harmony was only possible with effective immigration control (Layton-Henry, 1984, p. 151).

Although the Conservatives had become aware of the importance of the black electorate and made efforts to attract black voters during this period, these met with little success (Layton-Henry, 1984, p. 152). In opposition, the Conservative Party had begun to recognise that black people were an important potential source of political support and part of the future of British politics. The formation of Anglo-Asian and Anglo-West Indian Conservative societies were just part of the Conservatives attempt to become attractive to black voters. The decision not to oppose the 1976 Race Relations Act showed an awareness of the need to tackle racial discrimination and that the Conservatives were prepared to take some steps to avoid alienating British blacks. That William

Whitelaw gave personal endorsement to the Federation of Conservative Students' campaign against racialism in the autumn of 1977 also indicated that the party was opposed to incitement to racial hatred and the activities of the National Front (Layton-Henry, 1984, p. 149)

The 1974–9 Labour government suffered more acutely than did the Tories from 'facing in opposite directions'. It 'maintained the structure of immigration control which had been established to keep "coloured immigrants" out of Britain, and yet campaigned against racism' (Miles and Phizacklea, 1984, p. 94). Although it had opposed the 1971 Immigration Act, the government did not regard its repeal as a priority. The Labour government did make some concessions, however, allowing, for example, the entry of husbands and fiancés of women living in Britain, and increasing the number of vouchers for UK passport holders denied the right to enter Britain. The government also introduced the Race Relations Act (1976), which strengthened legislation against racial discrimination and set up the Commission for Racial Equality to replace both the Race Relations Board and the Community Relations Commission (Miles and Phizacklea, 1984, p. 95). Over this period, the Labour Party began to lose some of the political initiative, partly as a result of their small majority in the House of Commons and partly as a result of the onslaught from the Powellites (and eventually Mrs Thatcher), whose accusations that Labour were 'soft on immigration' were fuelled by media panics about 'race'. The proposals devoted to immigration and race relations by the Labour Party in its 1979 election manifesto concentrated on the need to strengthen anti-discrimination and race relations legislation. These were to promote equality of opportunity in employment in the public sector; to help those whose first language is not English; to introduce monitoring; to clarify the role of the Public Order Act and to widen the scope of the Race Relations Act; and to review the 1828 Vagrancy Act with a view to repealing section 4 (commonly known as 'sus') (Labour Party *Manifesto*, 1979, 29).

More direct opposition to racism and to the racist violence associated with the National Front was to be found in other spheres of left-wing politics. Paul Gilroy charts the development of such anti-racist movements as the Anti-Nazi League (ANL), Rock Against Racism (RAR) and the Campaign against Racism and Fascism. These movements grew from 1976 onwards, RAR in particular drawing on the emergence of and growth of the anti-authoritarianism and cultural style of Punk (1987, pp. 120–30). From 1978 onwards RAR co-operated with the ANL in organising several large demonstrations/rock concerts in various parts of the country. The first of these 'carnivals', as they were called, in London in May attracted 80,000 people.

At this time the Asian self-defence movements were also becoming better organised. For example, in the wake of the murder of Altab Ali, on 14 May 1978 7,000 people, mostly Bengalis, marched from Whitechapel, where he had been murdered, to a rally in Hyde Park and a protest to 10 Downing Street. This was one of the biggest demonstrations by Asians ever seen in Britain (Bethnal Green and Stepney Trades Council, 1978, p. 56). The ANL and RAR formed part of a loosely formed anti-racist alliance which was willing and able to take swift, direct action to prevent the National Front from marching (cf. Webster 1980). For example, the ANL organised, in conjunction with local Bengali community organisations, a protest demonstration for 18 June a week after an 'organised racist rampage' down Brick Lane in the East End of London. Over 4,000 people, black and white, joined the demonstration (Miles and Phizacklea, 1984, p. 104; Bethnal Green and Stepney Trades Council, 1978, p. 57). Further action was taken against the National Front demonstrations in Brick Lane on Sunday 9 and Sunday 16 July, and the next day 8,000 workers stayed away from work in response to the Hackney and Tower Hamlets Defence Committee call for a Black Solidarity Day (ibid.).

At the Old Bailey on 19 July 1978 four Sikh brothers from East Ham— Mohinder, Balvinder, Sukvinder and Joginder Singh Virk—were found guilty of causing grievous bodily harm and were sentenced to a total of twelve years and three months' imprisonment. The incident had occurred a year before when, on 23 April 1977 (the same day as a National Front march through Wood Green), five drunk white youths approached the brothers shouting racist abuse, provoking and then attacking them. During the ensuing fracas, one of the white youths was stabbed. The Virks phoned the police, who, when they arrived, arrested and charged the brothers. In court, the police chief prosecution witnesses were the white youths who had attacked them, and the Virks' lawyer's attempts to establish the racist nature of the attack (by questioning whether they were members of the NF or had been at the Wood Green demonstration) were ruled out of order. For the black community it seemed that the victims of an attack were the ones arrested and the 'offence' of self-defence was the one punished (Bethnal Green and Stepney Trades Council, 1978, p. 59; Newham Monitoring Project, 1991, p. 35–6). The Virk case and the subsequent result was an important catalyst in the development of black self-defence organisations such as the Steering Committee of Asian Organisations and the Newham Defence Committee.

Throughout the summer of 1978 anti-racists and black communities in East London and in Southall organised against the National Front and racist attacks. Union leaders visited Brick Lane to express their concern. David Lane, Chairman of the Commission for Racial Equality visited, promising a major investigation into the situation in the East End (published as Commission for Racial Equality, 1979). Other visitors included the High Commissioner of Bangladesh and Arthur Latham MP, Chairman of the Greater London Regional Council of the Labour Party, who called for a public inquiry into the events in Brick Lane (*Hansard* vol. 955, no. 166). The Labour Home Secretary, Merlyn Rees, declined repeated requests to visit the area and expressed his total confidence in the police (Bethnal Green and Stepney Trades Council, 1978, p. 60)

In the 1979 General Election the National Front fielded an unprecedented 303 candidates. Not only did this give the impression that the NF was able to contend as a national political party, but also entitled it to radio and television air time and free postal distribution of electoral material. In response to this the Anti-Nazi League and its supporters decided to oppose the National Front wherever it held election meetings. On 23 April the Anti-Nazi League and the local Asian community mobilised to prevent a National Front meeting in Southall. It was estimated that 10,000 anti-fascists demonstrated against a meeting of only fifty National Front supporters. Clashes occurred between demonstrators (who were determined that the NF should not be allowed to meet), and the police (who were determined to keep a path clear for the National Front supporters to attend the meeting). In the outbreak of serious disorder which ensued, Blair Peach was killed, allegedly by the Metropolitan Police Special Patrol Group (SPG) (Layton-Henry, 1984, p. 105).

The Conservative victory marks the decline of both the NF and the ANL. The National Front won only 0.6 per cent of the vote in October 1974, despite its massive increase in candidates from ninety to over three hundred in 1979. Even in its traditional strongholds in the East End, the National Front achieved little more than 5 per cent of the vote, against a swing to the Conservatives averaging 14.2 per cent. As Layton-Henry suggests, 'It seems clear that the major reason for the electoral reverse was the public identification of the Conservative Party with a tough line on immigration' (1984, p. 106). The defeat was a shattering blow to the NF. They had lost much prestige and resources fighting the election campaign, and the mobilisation of the ANL against them 'had shown the National Front that it was unlikely to ever achieve its goal of becoming a respectable political party' (ibid.). It has been suggested by some commentators that the demise of the National Front as a contending national political party led to an upsurge in street-level racist activity.

From the mid-1970s community-based organisations such as the Steering Committee of Asian Organisations, the Newham Defence Committee, the Southall Youth Movement, the Bangladesh Youth Movement and the Asian Youth Movement became increasingly well organised in response to violent racism and to the way in which it was being dealt with by the police. These organisations and their offshoots were galvanised into a new phase of action after the murder of Akhtar Ali Baig in Newham in July 1980. In the immediate aftermath of the murder 150 Asian and some Afro-Caribbean youths held an impromptu march to Forest Gate police station, and later to the spot where the murder had taken place (Newham Monitoring Project, 1991, pp. 40–4). During these demonstrations sixteen people were arrested, which further politicised the young people and led to the formation of the Newham Youth Movement (ibid.). On 19 July, 2,500 people marched through Newham in a protest which resulted in a further twenty-nine arrests after clashes with the police. A second march was organised by the Newham Youth Movement and the Steering Committee of Asian Organisations which was supported by over 5,000 people (ibid.). In 1980, representatives from these organisations came together around the issue of racial harassment to form the Newham Monitoring Project (Newham Monitoring Project, 1991, p. 44).

Although demonstrations against the National Front and against racist attacks served to raise the profile of the issues involved, it is the activities of interest groups with greater political influence which led to the government giving official recognition to the problem of 'racial attacks'. The Joint Committee Against Racialism (JCAR) was formed in the autumn of 1977 and formally launched in December 1978. This committee included the Conservative, Labour and Liberal Parties, the British Council of Churches, the Board of Deputies of British Jews, the National Union of Students, the British Youth Council and leading immigrant organisations. Nominees from the Labour and Conservative parties acted as joint chairmen. Although Mrs Thatcher vetoed the appointment of John Moore, MP to JCAR (which was seen as an anti-racist organisation involving not only the Labour Party but the far left as well), Mrs Shelagh Roberts, a prominent Conservative from outside Parliament was appointed (Layton-Henry, 1984, p. 150). During 1980 and early 1981 some of the organisations associated with JCAR, in particular the CRE, the Board of Deputies of British Jews and organisations representing ethnic communities lobbied the Home Secretary to act against racial attacks.

VII

In 1978 Bethnal Green and Stepney Trades Council published their report on racial violence in the East End of London. Drawing on the records of the Bangladesh Welfare Association, the Bangladesh Youth Movement and Tower Hamlets Law Centre, they looked in some detail at over 110 attacks on Asians and their property that had occurred between January 1976 and August 1978. Together with evidence from individuals, trade union branches, community and ethnic minority organisations, the community relations council, anti-racist bodies, the churches and councillors they produced the first in-depth report on the problem to be published in Britain.[9] The report uncovered an 'appalling catalogue of violent crime' which appeared to be targeted directly against the Bengali community and which had often led to the hospitalisation of the victims. This violence included hammer attacks, stabbings, slashed faces, punctured lungs, clubbings, gunshot wounds, people beaten with bricks, sticks and umbrellas and kicked unconscious in broad daylight.[10] In addition to attacks on individuals, the report also dealt with what it referred to as 'serious mass outrages' by racist groups in the area against the black community. The most serious of these 'outrages' occurred after a National Front meeting in Brick Lane on Sunday 11 June 1978.[11]

Elsewhere in the East End, in London and in the country as a whole between 1978 and 1980 there were a number of apparently racist killings,[12] and also growing evidence that violent racism was, as in Tower Hamlets, a persistent feature of the lives of members of the black communities. In April 1978, ten-year-old Kennith Singh was murdered near his home in Plaistow, east London. The murderer was never found. The same month, a nine-year-old Asian boy on his way home from school for lunch was stopped outside his front gate by five white boys armed with a knife. They pinned him to a wall and 'One of them shouted, "Stab him now." "No, let's just take his eye out", another replied. They cut open his face from his left eye across to his left ear' (Newham Monitoring Project, 1991, p. 38). Then, on 17 July 1980 Akhtar Ali Baig was murdered on East Ham High Street by a skinhead gang. Two boys and two girls aged fifteen to seventeen stopped him in the street, abused him and spat in his face before one of them, seventeen-year-old Paul Mullery, pulled out a sheath knife and stabbed him in the heart (Newham Monitoring Project, 1991, p. 40). Although the police described the incident as a 'mugging gone wrong', the evidence of racism was overwhelming. During the trial it emerged that some local youths who had witnessed the killing had followed the skinheads to a house, called the police who subsequently arrested those involved. Two of the skinheads were known by teachers at Plashet school who had heard racist remarks and seen them attacking Asians at school. The police told the judge that on searching the bedroom of one of the gang, they had found material with swastikas, the letters 'NF' and 'Pakistanis Out' written on it. The judge in the case ruled that the murder was 'plainly motivated by racial hatred'. The killer, Paul Mullery, was said to have boasted at the time of the murder, 'I've just gutted a Paki.' As he was led from the Court he gave the nazi salute and shouted "Sieg Heil" and "All for a fucking Paki" ' (Newham Monitoring Project, 1991, pp. 42–3).

On 18 January 1981 thirteen young Afro-Caribbean people died and thirty others were injured in a fire in Deptford/New Cross, south London (Smith and Gray, 1985, pp. 328–434; Layton-Henry, 1984, p. 114). Although the cause of the fire was never established beyond doubt (the inquest arrived at an open verdict), there was circumstantial evidence which led many people to believe that the fire was started by racists. In particular, during the period leading up to the fire, the black community of Deptford had been the focus of National Front activity and racist attacks and harassment (Layton-Henry, 1984, p. 114; Smith and Gray, 1985, pp. 328–434). In the immediate aftermath of the fire, Mrs Rudock (whose house was burnt down and who lost a son and daughter in the fire) received 'highly offensive and racialist [letters which] gloated over the deaths and saw the fire as a first step in ridding Britain of black people' (Smith and Gray, 1985, p. 430). At the inquest it was revealed that an unexploded incendiary device was found outside the house (Smith and Gray, 1985, p. 433). A mass demonstration organised by a 'Massacre Action Committee' was held on 2 March in which an estimated ten to fifteen thousand people took part (ibid.). During the march from Deptford to central London clashes occurred between the police and demonstrators and at least twenty-eight arrests were made (Smith and Gray, 1985, p. 428; Small, 1983).

Evidence of less publicly visible, but often persistent, racially motivated attacks and harassment which were affecting black individuals and communities across the country was also gathered during the early 1980s.[13] For example, in January 1981 (the day after the Deptford fire) the Joint Committee Against Racialism (JCAR) presented to the Home Secretary a dossier of over 1,000 racial attacks (JCAR, 1981). This provided evidence of attacks directed specifically against ethnic minorities in areas where there was strong evidence of far-right activity and recruiting.[14] The report found among the hundreds of cases across the country numerous attacks on synagogues, temples and places of burial. Another report published in 1981 by the Union of Pakistani Organisations suggested that racist attacks had grown from an average of twenty-five a week in 1980 between fifty and sixty a week in 1981 (Layton-Henry, 1984, p. 116).

During a spate of attacks on black people and their property in Walthamstow in March, a school was smeared with five-foot-high swastikas and National Front daubings (Hesse et al., 1992, 5). On 10 April a young black man, Malcolm Chambers, was murdered in Swindon in an anti-black riot (Layton-Henry, 1984, p. 115). On 18 April Satnam Singh Gill, a twenty-year-old student, was stabbed to death in Coventry City centre by skinheads (ibid.).[15] In the early hours of 2 July the home of the Khan family in Walthamstow was set ablaze after petrol was sprayed through the letter box (Hesse *et al.*, 1992, p. 10). Mrs Parveen Khan and her three children died in the fire and Mr Yunus Khan was seriously burned. The inquest verdict of unlawful killing confirmed that four murders had taken place but failed to address the concern that this had been a racist arson attack (ibid.).[16]

The London Borough of Newham was a particular focus of violent racism during the early 1980s. Attacks and harassment were directed, in particular, against the homes of Asian families and against Asian school children, though attacks were also reported on ethnic minority workplaces and places of worship (Gordon, 1986, pp. 8–16; Tompson, 1988; Newham Monitoring Project, 1991). Newham was also a site of community self-defence and vigorous organised opposition to violent racism over this period and in 1980 the Newham Monitoring Project (NMP) was formed to monitor racist attacks and presented a dossier of cases to local MPs.[17]

Violence occurred on Friday 3 July in Southall (the centre of one of west London's largest Asian communities) after 'a large group of white skinhead youths mainly from the East End of London, who were on their way to attend a concert[18] at a public house, began smashing shop windows in The Broadway' (Scarman, 1981, p. 30; Hiro, 1991, p. 174). This led to a confrontation between the skinheads and young Asians who saw the action of the former as clear racist provocation. When the police intervened to protect the skinheads a confronta-tion between the young Asians and the police rapidly ensued and disorder erupted.

VIII

In February 1981 JCAR met with the Home Secretary to discuss what they saw as an increasing degree of violence being inflicted on ethnic minority people and their property in Britain. The Home Secretary, William Whitelaw, was 'impressed by the detailed evidence' compiled by JCAR and was concerned with the contention that the 'frequency of racial attacks was increasing and that this was not entirely attributable to sporadic incidents of hooliganism but was the result of organised attempts at intimidation by extreme right-wing move-ments' (Layton-Henry, 1984, p. 114). In response to JCAR's approach the Home Secretary agreed to set up a Home Office inquiry into racial attacks and the activities of the racist organisations alleged to be responsible (*Hansard*, 5 February 1981, col. 393, Home Office 1981).[19]

The study consisted of two complementary research strategies—a survey of reported incidents in selected police areas across the country and interviews with the police, local community organisations and local officials in each area (see Bowling, 1993; McLauglin, 1991). The finding that has been most frequently cited by reports which followed (e.g. GLC, 1984; Brown, 1984) was that the rate of racially motivated victimisation was 'much higher for the ethnic minority population, particularly the Asians, than for white people. Indeed the rate for Asians was 50 times that for white people and the rate for blacks was 36 times that for white people.'[20] But the report also commented on the lived experience of racial harassment:

> In most places, it was said that the problem had deteriorated significantly within the space of the last year, and that the main perpetrators were of the skinhead fraternity. Assaults, jostling in the street, abusive remarks, broken windows, slogans daubed on walls—these were among the less serious kinds of racial harassment which many members of the ethnic minorities (particularly Asians) experience, sometimes on repeated occasions. The fact that they are interleaved with far more serious racially-motivated offences (murders, serious assaults, systematic attacks by gangs on people's homes at night) increases the feeling of fear experienced by the ethnic minorities. It was clear to us that the Asian community widely believes that it is the object of a campaign of unremitting racial harassment which it fears will grow worse in the future. In many places we were told that Asian families were too frightened to leave their homes at night or to visit the main shopping centre in town at weekends when gangs of young skinheads regularly congregate. (Home Office, 1981, p. 16)

The impact of the report, published in November 1981, was considerable. In the foreword to the report, the then Conservative Home Secretary William Whitelaw, declared that racial attacks were 'wicked crimes which can do our society great harm'. He stated that:

> the study has shown clearly that the anxieties expressed about racial attacks are justified. Racially motivated attacks, particularly on Asians, are more common than we supposed; and there are indications that they may be on the increase. (Home Office, 1981, p. iii)

The study was of particular importance because it demonstrated that although police forces in England and Wales had no means of recording crimes with racial motivation, such crimes could be found in their records. Additionally, by identifying these acts as 'wicked crimes'[21] the Home Secretary ensured that henceforth it was impossible to deny that racial violence was an object for policing or police policy. A direct result of the production of this report was the introduction of an 'operational definition' and recording and monitoring procedures within the Metropolitan Police[22] (see House of Commons, 1982).

While the Home Office study was under way, riots occurred in numerous locations across Britain, most notably in Brixton during April, and in Southall, Toxteth, Moss Side and the West Midlands in July.[23] In response to the Brixton riots, the government set up a committee of inquiry chaired by Lord Scarman (1986). Scarman commented that while the Afro-Caribbean community complained principally of police harassment, the Asian community complained that the police were 'not sufficient' to protect their community from racist attacks. The disorder in Southall, Scarman concluded, was an indication

> not only of racial tension but of relations between Asian youths and the police which were at best characterised by lack of communication and at worst by outright hostility. It seems clear that the Asian youths were prepared to take the law into their own hands rather than rely on the police to protect them and, when the police got in their way, to attack them. (Scarman, 1986, p. 31)

Here, Scarman reflects the findings of the Home Office study *Racial Attacks*, and the experiences of the Asian community, and indeed other black and ethnic minority communities. From the perspective of the latter, the police had consistently failed to protect communities from attack which had led to the need for community-based strategies of self-help and self-defence. As Scarman noted, alleged police inaction influenced the attitude of the Asian community towards the police. In the context of a long history of racist provocation and violence directed against Southall's Asian community, many thought that the role of the police should have been to protect and defend the minority community from attack and to express a firm stance against racism. The approach of the police, however, was to de-racialise the event, explaining it in terms of an attack by an Asian gang against a minority of white youths harmlessly attending a pop concert.[24]

Scarman concluded that a significant cause of the hostility felt towards the police in Brixton and elsewhere in the country was a loss of confidence in the police by significant sections of the population. This, he argued, was due to: a lack of communication between police and public in the areas affected; the use of 'hard' vigorous policing methods without consulting community representatives; a distrust in the official complaints procedure; and unlawful and racially prejudiced conduct by some police officers when stopping, searching and arresting young black people on the street. Local government also began to put pressure on the police and central government to act against racial violence. For example, in 1981 the Greater London Council began to campaign for an elected police authority for London and in June 1981, the Chair of the GLC Police Committee, Paul Boateng, wrote to Labour-controlled authorities in London urging them to establish their own police committees and police committee support units which many subsequently did (Keith and Murji, 1990).

McLaughlin (1991) argues that as a consequence of the high degree of autonomy of the police and of the powerlessness of black communities to voice their experiences of oppressive policing, political and (frequently) violent conflict intensified during the 1980s. Moreover, the lack of accountability of the police is reflected in the evidence which emerged over this period of the failure of the police to protect black individuals and communities against racial attacks and for police officers actually to engage in oppressive practices themselves (Hunte, 1965; Bethnal Green and Stepney Trades Council, 1978; Commission for Racial Equality, 1979; Institute of Race Relations, 1979/1987; Home Office, 1981; House of Commons, 1982; Smith and Gray, 1985; GLC, 1984).

The publication of the Home Office and Scarman reports, and a subsequent report of the House of Commons Home Affairs Committee (1982) put the police in a position where they, too, had to respond publicly to the issue of violent racism. The events of 1981 had brought into high relief questions surrounding the relationship between the police and black community, and a public response to violent racism was a political necessity. As the police put it, a new policy was necessary to 'engender confidence in minority communities that [they had] the willingness and ability to respond to the particular problems facing them'. Reiner (1985/1992) identifies 1981 as the year in which the legitimacy of the police organisation was at its lowest ebb in the post-war period. The promise of an improved response to racial incidents was an important part of a strategy aimed to restore some of that lost legitimacy.

IX

The published literature and other documents reviewed above indicate that violence seems to have been an enduring feature of the British reaction to the presence of ethnic minorities who have settled on this island. This is not to say that 'racialised' violence is an unchanging, trans-historical phenomenon, fixed either in the psyche of the British or in some characteristic of victimised individuals or communities. Rather, at various historical junctures racist ideas had identified black, brown, or simply 'foreign' people as a 'problem' on the basis of which white Britons have sought to attack, harass and terrorise them, often with the stated goal of expelling them from specific localities and, indeed, from the country as a whole. Exactly how violent racism becomes manifest in particular locations at particular times depends on such factors as local tradition, the health of local and national economies and prevailing ideologies of race and nation. The first explicitly 'anti-black' riots in 1919 illustrate that during periods of crisis, the presence of black people may be seen not only as a problem, but also as an explanation for other, broader, social problems. In this case, the crisis of the post-war slump and soaring unemployment in certain sectors of the economy (particularly shipping) was identified with the presence of black sailors in British ports. The most prominent interpretation of the events at the time was that these black people were themselves the cause of the violence inflicted against them. Correspondingly, the solution which was advocated by the authorities was their evacuation and eventual repatriation (see Jenkinson, this volume).

While it is clearly not the case that violent racism was a new phenomenon in the late 1970s, neither is it strictly true that such violence was not on political agendas until 1981. From the point of view of black and brown-skinned people, violent racism has formed an integral part of their politics, ever since a specifically 'black politics' existed in Britain. And even prior to the development of British black self-organisation in the 1950s, the experience of violent racism formed part of the political consciousness of individual black people and their communities of formation. The experiences of the pre- and post-war colonial settlers has, by and large, been neglected by history, and their oral histories have yet to be recorded. However, drawing on the evidence that we do have of British racism in the colonies and of the colour-bar at home, it seems likely that the early colonial migrants met considerable hostility and violence as they looked for work, homes and places to socialise. The riots of 1958 brought home to black people that, whatever their views about their relationship to Britishness, the fact that they were perceived as belonging to some 'other race' could be used as the basis for exclusion, attack and terrorisation. The 1958 racist riots, and the sense of threat which they engendered, were important catalysts in the development of black political organisation (Hiro, 1991, pp. 26–43).

The riots of 1958 also placed violent racism on national political agendas. They were covered by national newspapers and drew commentary from individuals from all the major political parties as well as from the judiciary, the church and other moral entrepreneurs. However, as was the case in the aftermath of the racist riots of 1919, the dominant explanation for their occurrence was the presence of black people. Indeed, the politics of 'race' which emerged after the 1958 riots led to an increasing focus on the problems associated with black people and on the dangers of unrestricted immigration. Rather than addressing the racism which had given rise to, and focused, the violence of large numbers of white people against the small black communities in Nottingham and London, commentators used the riots as an example of the problems that are caused by the presence of black people. After 1958 an inclusive notion of Britishness which encompassed the entire Empire was abandoned in favour of one defined in terms of British 'blood and bone', subsequently institutionalised in the immigration legislation of 1960s and 1970s.

Racist outbursts serious enough to merit news media attention occurred sporadically throughout the 1960s and early 1970s. Little is known about the daily experiences of African, Caribbean, Asian, Jewish, Arab and other dark-skinned minorities as they struggled to take their place in British society over this period. But the colour-bar did not crumble as soon as anti-discrimination legislation was passed. Rather, explicitly whites-only residential neighbour-hoods, places of entertainment and sections of the employment market persisted long after the Race Relations Acts of 1965, 1968 and 1976. The vestiges of the colour-bar are still evident to this day (Smith, 1989). As a consequence, individual black people have had to learn where they could or could not work, what pubs and clubs it was safe to attend and where it was safe and unsafe to live. The colour-bar, like any other ban, needed coercion, the threat of violence and actual violence to keep it in place. Throughout this period, racism was made respectable and institutional through the rhetoric of politicians such as Powell and through immigration controls that discriminated one British passport holder from another on the grounds of their 'race'. The dominant theme that runs through the racialised discourses of this time is that black people are a problem the solution to which is halting and then reversing migration from the Commonwealth.

During the mid- to late 1970s violent racism became more open and explicit than hitherto. Several murders of Afro-Caribbean and Asian people were carried out by people specifically identifying themselves as racist. Numerous other murders occurred in a context of racist antipathy and which black communities believed to be the work of racists but for whom no one was caught. In some localities, such as the West Midlands, parts of London and the North-West, racist harassment and attacks became a daily reality for black individuals and communities. Again, the racialised rhetoric of politicians and media panics about immigration and the problems associated with (black) immigrants served to justify the 'territorial defensiveness' of the host community. The rise of the National Front and the popular support which it gained over this period served to strengthen the resolve of those committed to resisting and repelling the settlement of black people. Moreover, there is good evidence that the NF were actively and directly organising racist attacks, and through their demonstrations and distribution of literature were inspiring sympathisers to take direct violent action against their black neighbours.

By the end of the 1970s, a fairly well articulated moral panic had emerged about the National Front and the violence with which they were associated. More problematic from the viewpoint of the media, the police and central government, however, was the resulting conflict between the NF, anti-fascists and the police. The most visible manifestation of the racial conflict which was occurring at this time was that such as which occurred in Southall in 1979. For many commentators, the anti-fascists were just as much to blame for the resulting public disorder as the National Front.

Racist violence seems to have been on the agenda of central government, albeit at the periphery, long before being acknowledged as such. Clearly, the racist riots of 1919 and 1958 and the activities of the National Front during the 1970s were government concerns and required much behind-the-scenes Ministerial and official activity. From the mid-1970s, concern about violent racism had begun to reach a critical mass, particularly on the left but also among those on the liberal wing of the Conservative Party. Both Conservative and Labour governments were forced to respond to lobbying on the issue of violent racism by MPs, black organisations and anti-racist groups. However, it was only when the all-party Joint Committee Against Racialism (JCAR) was formed and began to influence government thinking at the very end of the 1970s that a route was found to communicate the experiences and fears of Britain's black communities to central government politicians.

In 1981 there was a turning point in the history of the state response to violent racism. In November of that year, the Home Secretary, William Whitelaw, announced that 'racially motivated attacks' were 'wicked crimes' that were 'more common than we had supposed' (Home Office, 1981). Thus violence directed at people specifically because of their 'race' became, for the first time, recognised officially as a social problem by the British state. As the central government Inter-Departmental Racial Attacks Group commented in 1989, 'the 1981 Home Office study, with the advantage of its official status, put racial attacks on the political agenda for the first time' (Home Office, 1989, p. 1). Hitherto, as the problem did not officially exist, there had been no police, central or local government policies aimed at tackling the problem. There had been no government-funded research nor even an official definition of the problem; no information about its nature or prevalence was published.

As is clear from the present volume, however, violent racism was far from a new phenomenon. There is evidence that violence has been directed speci-fiacally against black people and others from ethnic minorities on numerous occasions throughout the history of their residence in Britain. It is clear that violent racism was widespread during the late 1950s and throughout the 1960s and 1970s, some instances of which were cause for national concern. The recognition of the problem in 1981 came about partly because it was believed by many that violent racism escalated to an unprecedented level of intensity and ferocity between 1979 and 1981. The view that violent racism was on the increase was expressed in every report on the subject published at the time.

Certainly, 1981 marks a peak in instances of black people dying in apparently racially motivated attacks (see Gordon 1986/1990).

The issues of racism, violence and policing were in newspaper headlines during 1981, not only because of the high incidence of racist attacks, but also because of the widespread outbreaks of violence between the police and young (and frequently) black people which occurred during the spring and summer of that year. The clashes between ant-racist demonstrators, organised racists and the police, evident throughout the latter part of the 1970s, continued into the 1980s. Violent clashes between Asian young people, far-right political groups and the police occurred in Southall, Bradford and Coventry during the spring and summer of 1981 (Hiro, 1991, pp. 175–6). A long-overdue public policy response to violent racism and policing became a political necessity in 1981.

In conclusion, it might be said that for the British ethnic minorities, violent racism has always been on the agenda. But until the 1980s, central and local government and the police saw such violence (at best) as a personal trouble, or (at worst) as a problem emanating from the presence of black people themselves. Having belatedly discovered the problem, activity directed at the problem of violent racism on the part of local and central state agencies increased dramatically.[25]

Notes

1. People of non-European origin (mainly from the diaspora of Africa and the Indian sub-continent) still comprise only a small minority of the British population. In 1951 'black' and other 'ethnic minorities' represented 0.4 per cent of Britain's population, 1 per cent in 1961, 2.3 per cent in 1971, 3.9 per cent in 1981 and 5.5 per cent in 1991 (OPCS, *Monitor*). As the present volume shows, racism has been expressed in a violent form even when black and other ethnic minorities have been present in only tiny numbers. However, an increase in the numbers of people of non-European origin from around 100,000 in the post-war years to around 2 million by 1981 significantly changes the context within which racial violence occurs. Most obviously, there are more potential targets and greater possibilities for resistance.

2. It is worth noting that during the period 1951–81 699,000 more people migrated out of Britain than migrated in. After net in-migration of 12,000 during 1951–61 more than 700,000 people left Britain between 1961 and 1981. See Tompson (1988), Appendix 2 for further information.

3. On conviction Lord Justice Salmon condemned the actions of those convicted saying: 'You are a minute and insignificant section of the population who have brought shame on the district in which you lived and have filled the whole nation with horror, indignation and disgust. Everyone, irrespective of the colour of their skin is entitled to walk through our streets erect and free from fear. This is a right which these courts will always unfailingly uphold' (cited in Rose *et al.*, 1969, p. 214).

4. Pearson (1976, p. 52) notes that '[o]n one occasion as the gang passed a bus-stop, a "paki" who had not been visible from within their ranks, emerged from under their feet—as if he had been "heeled" from a rugby pack. "The lads" were literally walking "on the pakis". Whites at the same bus queue stood by watching this. The "paki" lay on the floor, bleeding from the head and face, dazed and struggling to get off the floor.'

5. The gun was stuck into the ribs of one Pakistani, police intervened, there was a struggle and (in the words of the *Accrington Observer*) the police were told: 'You — nigger lover. They all want shooting' (Pearson, 1976, pp. 52–3).

6. Its origins may be found in the pre-war British Brothers League; Mosley's British Union of Fascists and the Imperial Fascist League of the inter-war years; and A.K. Chesterton's League of Empire Loyalists (LEL), the Racial Preservation Society, The National Labour Party and the White Defence League of the post-war years (Hiro, 1991, p. 254; Tomlinson, 1981; Taylor, 1982). In 1960, the White Defence League and National Labour Party merged to form the British National Party (BNP) from which splintered off, in 1962, the more openly fascist National Socialist Movement (from which John Tyndall later split to form the Greater Britain Movement).

7. See Walker, 1977; Fielding, 1981; Tomlinson, 1981; Taylor, 1982; Solomos, 1989, p. 130; Miles and Phizacklea, 1984, p. 120; Layton-Henry, 1984, pp. 87–107; Edgar, 1978; and Billig, 1978 for a discussion of the emergence of the National Front.

8. Fielding (1981) suggests that violence is functional for the extreme right by providing new recruits and publicity and by generating negative publicity for their opponents. During the period of National Front electoral success there remained an emphasis on street politics in the form of marches, demonstrations and inflammatory propaganda campaigns. While committed members are prepared to be involved in electoral activity with little chance of success, those on the periphery are more attracted to such direct action as provocative marches in areas of ethnic minority settlement (Fielding, 1981). In the period following the failure of the National Front in the 1979 General Election and its subsequent collapse and fragmentation, there is evidence of a shift towards more violently oriented groups (such as the British Movement) and towards direct action more generally (Hiro, 1991; *Searchlight*, June 1982; Layton-Henry, 1984, p. 118).

9. Hunte's (1965) earlier work catalogued racist violence perpetrated by the police.

10. The report concluded that: 'While the East End is traditionally a "high-crime" area, there is clear evidence that the local Bengalee community has suffered physical attacks and harassment over recent years on a totally different scale to that inflicted on the rest of the community. There is a danger in assuming that this violence is confined to the occasional isolated incident or outburst that finds its way into the headlines ... Behind the headlines is an almost continuous and unrelenting battery of Asian people and their property in the East End of London. The barrage of harassment, insult and intimidation, week in week out, fundamentally determines how

the immigrant community here lives and works, how the host community and the authorities are viewed, and how the Bengalee people in particular think and act' (Bethnal Green and Stepney Trades Council, 1978, pp. 3–4).

11. On this occasion: '150 white youths ran down Brick Lane shouting "Kill the Black Bastards" and smashing the windows of a dozen shops and the car windscreens of Bengalee shopkeepers. 55-year-old Abdul Monan was knocked unconscious by a hail of rocks and stones hurled through his shop window. He ended up in hospital where he needed five stitches in his face. He lost two of his teeth' (Bethnal Green and Stepney Trades Council, 1978, p. 41)

12. On 4 May, 1978 Altab Ali was murdered in Whitechapel; in June Ishaque Ali was murdered in Hackney; in July Benjamin Thompson and Michael Nathaniel were murdered in north-west London; Vernon Brown was murdered in Birmingham in September; and Michael Ferreira was murdered in east London in December. In January 1979 Abdul Aziz was murdered in Peterborough; in August Kaymarz Anklesaria was murdered in east London and Sawdegar Khan was murdered in Birmingham. In January 1980 Mohammed Arif was killed in Burnley and Sewa Singh Sunder was killed in Windsor; Famous Mgutshini was killed in London in March; Pala Majumbar was killed in Greenwich in June and Louston Parry in Manchester in September. While the murderers were never found in most of these cases, in each the murder was widely believed by local communities to have been carried out for racist motives. (See Gordon, 1986, p. 8; Newham Monitoring Project, 1991, p. 40).

13. Other reports published over this period included those compiled by Ealing Community Relations Council on *Racialist Activity in the London Borough of Ealing* (1981), the Commission for Racial Equality (1981), and the Runnymede Trust (Klug, 1982).

14. JCAR drew on information from Community Relations Councils, informants and publications from ethnic minority organisations, *Searchlight* magazine, local law centres and community organisations. They provided detailed case studies of attacks in High Wycombe, Oldham and Lambeth and noted that a similar story could be told of many other London boroughs (such as Greenwich, Hackney, Tower Hamlets, Lewisham, Camden, Barking or Hounslow) as well as London suburbs, towns in the North-West (such as Blackburn) and major cities (such as Bristol and Manchester). JCAR is an umbrella organisation representing the major political parties and the largest ethnic minority pressure groups including representatives of the Board of Deputies of British Jews. JCAR's representation was the event which precipitated action by the Home Office. However, pressure had been mounting for some time from a variety of sources. A number of organisations campaigned against racism and racial violence during the 1970s. Organisations such as the Anti-Nazi League and Rock Against Racism were concerned with issues such as police violence, immigration laws and the rise of the National Front and other neo-fascist organisations. Monitoring groups such as Lewisham Action on Policing in

South-East London and the Southall Monitoring Group were active specifically in organising and demonstrating against racial attacks.

15. Around the same time a Sikh temple was petrol-bombed and the Indian and Commonwealth Club in London suffered an arson attack (Layton-Henry, 1984, p. 115).

16. Other murders believed to have had racist motives during 1981 include Amil Dharry in Coventry in April; Fenton Ogbogbo in south London and Charan Kaur and Poran Singh in Leeds in June; Asif Ahmed Khan Shamsuddin in north London in July; and Mohammed Arif in Bradford in November (Gordon, 1990, p. 8).

17. In 1982 NMP set up an advice centre in Forest Gate and launched a 24-hour emergency help-line for black people experiencing violent racism or police harassment (Newham Monitoring Project, 1991, pp. 44–5). Violent racism, policing and the question of self-defence organisation were again issues of national concern in 1982 as a result of the 'Newham 8' case (see Newham Monitoring Project, 1991).

18. The band—the 4-Skins—were part of the explicitly racist Oi! movement.

19. From published official documents it appears that the immediate trigger for this was a meeting between the Home Secretary and JCAR at which the latter expressed their anxieties. Clearly, however, recent events, and the Deptford fire in particular will probably have made a public response more likely.

20. This may seem an obvious point, but some constituencies—notably the police and right-wing politicians—had argued consistently that racially motivated crime committed by black against white people was widespread. Moreover, there are clearly circumstances when white people may be the victims of violent racism—most obviously when they are non-British, Jewish or when they are targeted because of their association with black people.

21. Although this is the first official recognition of racial violence as crime, clearly some of these incidents have been defined as crimes previously. Indeed, the most serious of them (such as murder, arson and serious assault) would certainly have been recorded as crimes, even if they were not recorded as racial (Institute of Race Relations, 1987). For example, Gordon (1990) lists 74 racist murders in Britain between 1970 and 1990. Many of the more mundane events involved in racial harassment would also come within legal and police definitions of crime. The offences of assault, criminal damage, threatening behaviour are broad enough to cover all types of racial violence. Additionally, although a Private Member's Bill to make racial attacks a specific form of crime within the law was defeated in 1985, the Police and Criminal Evidence Act (PACE, 1984) has defined 'Incitement to Racial Hatred' as a criminal offence.

22. The Metropolitan Police were the only force to start routinely collecting 'racial incident' statistics at this time. It was not until 1985 when the Association of Chief Police Officers (ACPO) issued *Guiding Principles* for the responses to 'racial incidents' that other large urban forces began to follow suit (see Home Office, 1986).

23. A discussion of the conflict between the police and Afro-Caribbean (and other) young people over this period can be found in Kettle and Hodges (1982), Scarman (1986), Benyon and Solomos (1987), Solomos (1988), Hiro (1991).

24. Contrary to Scarman's evidence and other independent accounts, Metropolitan Police Deputy Assistant Commissioner Radley commented to the 1981–1982 Home Affairs Committee: 'As I understand that particular incident, it was in fact the supporters of a particular group who went to the particular licensed premises where the group was playing ... there is nothing we can do about a pop group appearing at a public house and nothing we can do about the followers of that pop group ... As far as I am aware there is no intention of anyone attacking anyone on that occasion ... I am not of the opinion that that was in any way a concerted, organised or planned form of attack on the inhabitants of Southall' (House of Commons, 1982, p. 29).

25. Since January 1981 racial violence has been the subject of four House of Commons select committee reports (1982, 1986, 1989, 1994) and five Home Office research reports (Home Office 1981; Ekblom and Simon, 1988; Seagrave, 1989; Saulsbury and Bowling, 1991 (see also Bowling and Saulsbury, 1993; Bowling 1993b); Sampson and Phillips, 1992. In addition, racially motivated attacks were surveyed in the 1988 and 1992 British Crime Surveys (see Mayhew *et al.*, 1989, 1993; Aye Maung and Mirrlees Black, 1994). In 1986 a central government inter-departmental group (RAG) was formed and produced two policy papers (Home Office 1989, 1991) both of which were accompanied by circulars sent to all central government departments, all local authorities (housing, social services, education departments), all police forces, the Crown Prosecution Service, and a range of voluntary organisations. The Metropolitan Police took the lead in developing policy in this area (Metropolitan Police, 1982, 1986, 1989, 1990) and the Association of Chief Police Officers (1985) has also offered guidance to police forces. Numerous reports on racial violence and the statutory response to it were produced in the 1980s and early 1990s by (usually Labour-led) local authorities (e.g. GLC, 1984; Hesse *et al.*, 1992), by Councils for Racial Equality (e.g. Commission for Racial Equality (CRE), 1979, 1981, 1987a, 1987b, 1988), anti-racist pressure groups (e.g. Institute for Race Relations (IRR), 1987; Newham Monitoring Project, 1991, see also Newham Monitoring Project, *Annual Reports* 1980–92). Recent academic reports have concentrated on police service delivery (Cutler and Murji, 1990), housing policy (Ginsburg, 1989) and services for victims (Kimber and Cooper, 1991). Recent reviews include Gordon (1990), FitzGerald (1989), Tompson (1988), FitzGerald and Ellis (1992), Francis and Matthews (1993), Bowling (1993a). For recent international perspectives see Bjorgo and Witte (1994), Hamm (1993).

References

Alderman, G., 1972, 'The Anti-Jewish Riots of August 1919 in South Wales,' *Welsh History Review*, No. 6.

Association of Chief Police Officers, 1985, *Guiding Principles Concerning Racial Attacks*, London, ACPO.

Aye Maung, N. and Mirrlees Black, C., 1994, 'Racially Motivated Crime: A British Crime Survey Analysis', Home Office Research and Planning Unit Paper No. 82, London, Home Office.

Banton, M., 1983, *Racial and Ethnic Competition*, Cambridge, Cambridge University Press.

Banton, M., 1985, *Promoting Racial Harmony*, Cambridge, Cambridge University Press.

Benyon, J. and Solomos, J., (eds), 1987, *The Roots of Urban Unrest*, Oxford, Pergamon.

Bethnal Green and Stepney Trades Council, 1978, *Blood on the Streets*, London, Bethnal Green and Stepney Trades Council.

Billig, M., 1978, *Fascists: A Social Psychological View of the National Front*, London, Academic Press.

Bjorgø T. and Witte, R. (eds), 1993, *Racist Violence in Europe*, London, Macmillan.

Bowling, B., 1993a, 'Racial Harassment and the Process of Victimization: Conceptual and Methodological Implications for the Local Crime Survey', *British Journal of Criminology*, vol. 33, no. 1, spring.

Bowling, B., 1993b, 'Racial Harassment in East London', in M.S. Hamm (ed.), *Hate Crime: International Perspectives on Causes and Control*, Academy of Criminal Justice Sciences/Anderson Publications.

Bowling, B. and Saulsbury, W.E., 1993, 'A Local Response to Racial Harassment', in T. Bjorgø and R. Witte (eds), *Racist Violence in Europe*, London, Macmillan.

Brown, C., 1984, *Black and White Britain*, The Third PSI Survey, London, Heinemann.

Butler, D., and Stokes, D., 1974, *Political Change in Britain*, London, Macmillan.

Cashmore, E., 1984, *No Future: Youth and Society*, London, Heineman.

Clarke, J., 1973, 'The Skinheads and the Study of Youth Culture', Paper presented to the 14th National Deviancy Conference, University of York.

Clarke, J., 1975, 'The Skinheads and the Magical Recovery of Working Class Community', *Cultural Studies*, vols 7 and 8, pp. 99–102; also in S. Hall and T. Jefferson (eds), *Resistance through Rituals*, London, Hutchinson.

Clarke, J., and Jefferson, T., 1976, 'Working Class Youth Cultures', in G. Mungham, and G. Pearson, *Working Class Youth Culture*, London, Routledge.

Cohen, S., 1972, *Folk Devils and Moral Panics: The Creation of the Mods and Rockers*, London, MacGibbon and Kee.

Commission for Racial Equality, 1979, *Brick Lane and Beyond: An Inquiry into Racial Strife and Violence in Tower Hamlets*, London, CRE.

Commission for Racial Equality, 1981, *Racial Harassment on Local Authority Housing Estates*, London, CRE.

Commission for Racial Equality, 1987a, *Living in Terror: A Report on Racial Violence and Harassment in Housing*, London, CRE.

Commission for Racial Equality, 1987b, *Racial Attacks: A Survey in Eight Areas of Britain*, London, Commission for Racial Equality.

Commission for Racial Equality, 1988, *Learning in Terror: A Survey of Racial Harassment in Schools and Colleges in England, Scotland and Wales, 1985–87*, London, Commission for Racial Equality.

Constantine, L., 1954, *Colour Bar*, London, Stanley Paul.

Cook, D., 1978, *A Knife at the Throat of Us All: Racism and the National Front*, London, Communist Party.

Cutler, D. and Murji, K., 1990, 'From a Force into a Service?: Racial Attacks, Policing and Service Delivery', *Critical Social Policy*, March/April.

Deakin, N. *et al.* 1970, *Colour, Citizenship and British Society*, Panther.

Edgar, D., 1977, 'Racism, Fascism and the Politics of the National Front', *Race and Class*, vol. 19(2), autumn.

Ekblom, P. and Simon, F. (with Birdi, S.), 1988, *Crime and Racial Harassment in Asian-run Small Shops: The Scope for Prevention*, Crime Prevention Unit Paper 15, London, Home Office.

Evans, N., 1980, 'The South Wales Race Riots of 1919', *Journal of the Society for the Study of Welsh Labour History*, III/1, spring.

Fielding, N., 1981, *The National Front*, London, Routledge.

FitzGerald, M., 1989, 'Legal Approaches to Racial Harassment in Council Housing: The Case for Reassessment', *New Community*, vol. 16 (1), pp. 93–106.

FitzGerald, M. and Ellis, T., 1990, 'Racial Harassment: The Evidence', in C. Kemp (ed.), *Current Issues in Criminological Research*, British Criminology Conference, vol. 2, Bristol, Bristol Centre for Criminal Justice.

Francis, P. and Matthews, R., 1993, *Tackling Racial Attacks*, Leicester: Centre for the Study of Public Order.

Fryer, P., 1984, *Staying Power: The History of Black People in Britain*, London, Pluto.

Gay, P. and Young, K., 1988, *Community Relations Councils: Roles and Objectives*, London Policy Studies Institute/Commission for Racial Equality.

Gilroy, P., 1987, *There Ain't no Black in the Union Jack: The Cultural Politics of Race and Nation*, London, Hutchinson.

Ginsburg, N., 1989, 'Racial Harassment Policy and Practice: The Denial of Citizenship', *Critical Social Policy*, no. 26, pp. 66–81.

Glass, R., 1960, *Newcomers: West Indians in London*, London, Allen & Unwin.

Gordon, P., 1986/1990, *Racial Violence and Harassment*, Runnymede Research Report (2nd edn), London, Runnymede Trust.

Gordon, P. and Rosenberg, D., 1989, *Daily Racism: The Press and Black People in Britain*, London, Runnymede Trust.

Greater London Council, 1984, *Racial Harassment in London*, Report of a panel of inquiry set up by the GLC Police Committee, London, GLC.

Hall, S., Critcher, C., Jefferson, T., Clarke, J. and Roberts, B., 1978, *Policing the Crisis: Mugging the State and Law and Order*, London, Macmillan.

Hamm, M.S. (ed.), 1993, *Hate Crime: International Perspective on Causes and Control*, Academy of Criminal Justice Sciences/Anderson Publications.

Hanna, M., 1974, 'The National Front and Other Right-Wing Organisations', *New Community*, vol. 3, no. 1–2, pp. 49–55.

Hartley, B., 1973, *Son of Alf Garnett: Riot in Leeds*, Paper given to conference on working-class culture, University College, Cardiff, November.

Hesse, B., Rai, D.K., Bennett, C. and McGilchrist, P., 1992, *Beneath the Surface: Racial Harassment*, Aldershot, Avebury.

Hiro, D., 1991, *Black British White British: A History of Race Relations in Britain*, London, Grafton.

Home Office, 1981, *Racial Attacks: Report of a Home Office Study*, London, Home Office.

Home Office, 1986, *Home Office Good Practice Guide for the Police: The Response to Racial Attacks*, London, Home Office.

Home Office, 1989, *The Response to Racial Attacks and Harassment: Guidance for the Statutory Agencies*, Report of the Inter-Departmental Racial Attacks Group, London, Home Office.

Home Office, 1991, *The Response to Racial Attacks and Harassment: Sustaining the Momentum*, Second Report of the Inter-Departmental Racial Attacks Group, London, Home Office.

House of Commons Home Affairs Committee, 1982, *Racial Attacks*. Second Report from the Home Affairs Committee, Session 1981–82, HC. 106, London, HMSO.

House of Commons Home Affairs Committee, 1986, *Racial Attacks and Harassment*. Third Report from the Home Affairs Committee, Session 1985–86, HC. 409, London, HMSO.

House of Commons Home Affairs Committee, 1989, First Report, *Racial Attacks and Harassment*, London, HMSO.

House of Commons Home Affairs Committee, 1994, Third Report, *Racial Attacks and Harassment*, London, HMSO.

Hunte, J., 1965, *Nigger Hunting in England?* London, West Indian Standing Conference.

Institute of Race Relations, 1979, *Police against Black People, Evidence Submitted to the Royal Commission on Criminal Procedure*, London, IRR.

Institute of Race Relations, 1987, *Policing against Black People*, London, IRR.

Jenkinson, J., 1985, 'The Glasgow Race Disturbances of 1919', *Immigrants and Minorities*, vol. 3, no. 3, November.

Joint Committee Against Racialism, 1981, *Racial Violence in Britain*, London, JCAR.

Keith, M. and Murji, K., 1990, 'Reifying Crime, Legitimising Racism: Policing, Local Authorities and Left Realism', in W. Ball and J. Solomos, *Race and Local Politics*, Basingstoke, Macmillan.

Kettle, M. and Hodges, L., 1982, *Uprising: The Police, the People and the Riots in Britain's Cities*, London, Pan Books.

Kimber, J. and Cooper, L., 1991, *Victim Support Racial Harassment Project London*, Community Research and Advisory Centre, The Polytechnic of North London.

Klug, F., 1982, *Racist Attacks*, London, Runnymede Trust.

Layton-Henry, Z., 1980, *Conservative Party Politics*, London, Macmillan.

Layton-Henry, Z., 1984, *The Politics of Race in Britain*, London, Allen and Unwin.

Little, K., 1943, 'Colour Prejudice in Britain', *Wasu* 10/1 May.

McLaughlin, E., 1991, 'Police Accountability and Black People: Into the 1990s', in E. Cashmore, and E. McLaughlin, *Out of Order?: Policing Black People*, London, Routledge.

May, R. and Cohen, R., 1974, 'The Interaction between Race and Colonialism: A Case Study of the Liverpool Race Riots of 1919', *Race and Class*, 16, 2, pp. 111–26.

Mayhew, P., Elliot, D. and Dowds, L., 1989, *The 1988 British Crime Survey*, Home Office Research Study No. 111, London, HMSO.

Mayhew, P., Aye Maung, N. and Mirrlees-Black, 1993, *The 1992 British Crime Survey*, Home Office Research Study No. 132, London, HMSO.

Metropolitan Police, 1982, *Racial Attacks*, Police Order 29, 30th April 1982, London, Metropolitan Police.

Metropolitan Police, 1986, *Recording and Monitoring Racial Incidents Guidelines*, A7 Branch, January 1986, London, Metropolitan Police.

Metropolitan Police, 1989, *London Racial Harassment Action Guide*, London, Metropolitan Police.

Metropolitan Police, 1990, *Working Together for Racial Harmony*, London, Metropolitan Police.

Miles, R., 1984, 'The Riots of 1958: Notes on the Ideological Construction of "Race Relations" as a Political Issue in Britain', *Immigrants and Minorities*, 33: pp. 252–75.

Miles, R., and Phizacklea, A., 1984, *White Man's Country: Racism in British Politics*, London, Pluto.

Mungham, G. and Pearson, G. (eds), 1976, *Working Class Youth Culture*, London, Routledge.

Newham Monitoring Project, 1991, *The Forging of a Black Community*, London, Newham Monitoring Project/Campaign against Racism and Fascism.

Nicholson 1974, 'Strangers to England: Immigration to England 1100–1945', Leyland.

Nugent, N. and King, R., 1977, *The British Right*, London, Saxon House.

Pearson, G., 1976, "Paki-bashing" in a North Eastern Lancashire Cotton Town: A Case Study and its History', in J. Mungham, and G. Pearson (eds), *Working Class Youth Culture*, London, Routledge.

Pilkington, E., 1988, *Beyond the Mother Country: West Indians and the Notting Hill White Riots*, London, I.B. Taurus.

Rees, T., 1982, 'Immigration Policies in the United Kingdom', in C. Husbands, *Race in Britain*, London, Hutchinson/Open University.

Reeves, F., 1989, *Race and Borough Politics*, Aldershot, Avebury.

Reiner, R., 1985/1992, *The Politics of the Police* (2nd edn), London, Harvester Wheatsheaf.

Richmond, A.H., 1954, *Colour Prejudice in Britain: A Study of West Indian Workers in Liverpool, 1941–51*, London, Routledge and Kegan Paul.

Richmond, A.H., 1955, *The Colour Problem: A Study of Racial Relations*, Harmondsworth, Penguin.

Rose, R. and Associates, 1969, *Colour and Citizenship: A Report on British Race Relations*, London, Oxford University Press.

Sampson, A. and Phillips, C., 1992, *Multiple Victimisation: Racial Attacks on an East London Estate*, Police Research Group Crime Prevention Unit Series Paper 36, London, Home Office Police Department.

Saulsbury, W.E. and Bowling, B., 1991, *The Multi-Agency Approach in Practice: The North Plaistow Racial Harassment Project*, Home Office Research and Planning Unit Paper No. 64, London, Home Office.

Scarman, Lord, 1986, *The Scarman Report, The Brixton Disorders, 10–12 April 1981. Presented to Parliament by the Secretary of State for the Home Department by Command of Her Majesty, November 1981*. Harmondsworth, Penguin.

Seagrave, J., 1989, *Racially Motivated Incidents Reported to the Police*, Home Office Research and Planning Unit Paper 54, London, Home Office.

Searchlight, undated, 'The Murderers Are Amongst Us: The Criminal Records of Britain's Racists', London, Searchlight.

Small, S., 1983, *A Group of Young Black People and Police in London*, vol. 2, London, PSI.

Smith, D.J. and Gray, J., 1985, *Police and People in London*, London, PSI.

Smith, S.J., 1989, *The Politics of 'Race' and Residence: Citizenship, Segregation and White Supremacy in Britain*, Cambridge, Polity.

Solomos, J., 1989, *Race and Racism in Contemporary Britain*, London, Macmillan.

Taylor, S., 1982, *The National Front in English Politics*, London, Macmillan.

Tomlinson, J., 1981, *Left, Right: The March of Political Extremism in Britain*, London, Platform.

Tompson, K., 1988, *Under Siege: Racial Violence in Britain Today*, Harmonsworth, Penguin.

Walker, M., 1977, *The National Front*, Glasgow, Collins.

Webster, M., 1980, Submission of evidence from the National Front to the House of Commons Select Committee on Home Affairs 1979–80: in respect of possible changes to the Public Order Act, the Representation of the People Act and the Race Relations Act.

Weeraperuma, S., 1979, *So You Want to Emigrate to England Mohandas: Letter to a Coloured Emigrant*, Lake House, Colombo, Sri Lanka.

Index

DATE DUE

DEMCO 38-297